M A S T E R I N G

PORTUGUESE

HEAR IT · SPEAK IT · WRITE IT · READ IT

Developed for the
**FOREIGN SERVICE INSTITUTE,
DEPARTMENT OF STATE**
by Jack Lee Ulsh
and Associates

BARRON'S

Cover design by Milton Glaser, Inc.

This course was developed for the Foreign Service Institute, Department of State, by Jack Lee Ulsh and Associates.

The title of the original course is Portuguese Basic Course

This edition published in 1988 by Barron's Educational Series, Inc.

All inquiries should be addressed to:
Barron's Educational Series, Inc.
250 Wireless Boulevard
Hauppauge, New York 11788

Paper Edition

International Standard Book No. 0-8120-3989-0

A large part of the text of this book is recorded on the accompanying tapes as follows:

Unit 1	Tape 1A	Unit 14	Tape 5B, 6A
Unit 2	Tape 1A	Unit 15	Tape 6B, 7A
Unit 3	Tape 1B	Unit 16	Tape 7A, 7B
Unit 4	Tape 1B	Unit 17	Tape 8A
Unit 5	Tape 1B, 2A	Unit 18	Tape 8B
Unit 6	Tape 2A	Unit 19	Tape 8B, 9A
Unit 7	Tape 2B	Unit 20	Tape 9B, 10A
Unit 8	Tape 2B, 3A	Unit 21	Tape 10A, 10B
Unit 9	Tape 3B	Unit 22	Tape 10B, 11A
Unit 10	Tape 3B, 4A	Unit 23	Tape 11A, 11B
Unit 11	Tape 4A, 4B	Unit 24	Tape 11B, 12A
Unit 12	Tape 4B, 5A	Unit 25	Tape 12A, 12B
Unit 13	Tape 5B		

PRINTED IN THE UNITED STATES OF AMERICA

456   800   987 ·

Preface

This course in <u>Mastering Portuguese</u> is part of a series being offered by Barron's Educational Series. If you are a serious language student, this course will provide you with the opportunity to become truly fluent in Portuguese.

This is one of the famous language courses developed by the Foreign Service Institute of the United States. These courses were designed to train United States Government representatives who need to be able to communicate clearly and accurately in a foreign language.

<u>Mastering Portuguese</u> provides an excellent opportunity for you to learn Portuguese on your own, studying at your own pace. In addition, these tapes are ideal for students who are studying Portuguese in a school and would like to supplement their classroom work with additional practice in the spoken language.

TO ÂNGELA

Foreword

This volume contains twenty-five units of work. Units one through twenty-four contain new material. Unit twenty-five is a review.

A portion of the materials is presented through programming. Indeed, the word programmatic in the title means just that: partially programmed.

In the typical programmed format, information is given to you by means of a carefully designed sequence of numbered 'frames.' What is a 'frame?' A frame is simply a step in a learning sequence, and it bears a number for identification. Let us illustrate.

1. Right now you are looking at a frame. It is frame number one, and we have given it that number. It is the first step in a very brief learning sequence that you are now undertaking.

2. This is frame number 2. Usually a frame will refer you to an item recorded on the tape. When this is the case, you will see one or more sets of parentheses appearing right after the frame and just below it, like this:

( )   ( )

3. The parentheses will always mean that something is recorded on the tape, and the number of sets of parentheses will always tell you the number of times that that particular 'something' is recorded on the tape. Thus, two sets of parentheses will indicate that the item appears twice. Likewise, you can expect to hear an item <u>three</u> times if you see this:

( )   ( )   ( )

4. So, when you see one or more sets of ( ), you should <u>turn on</u> the tape and listen. But, always be sure you read the frame first. You will probably find it necessary to <u>turn off</u> the tape after the last set of ( ) to keep the tape from getting ahead of you.

5. You will often see an 'x' after some or all of the parentheses, like this:

( )   ( )x   ( )x   ( )x

6. That 'x' means that you are to mimic aloud (at the very least, under you breath, softly) what you have just heard. In this case you would repeat aloud after <u>each</u> of the last three times you hear the item. You may let the tape run as you do this.

( )   ( )x   ( )x   ( )x

7. Beginning in Unit 10 you will be asked questions which will be
   based on information we have given you. You are to answer
   <u>aloud</u>. The correct answers will appear just below the frame,
   to the left of the page, partially in the margin, like this:
(Answer)

8. Always give you answer aloud first. Then check the answer
   in the left margin to see if you were right. To avoid
   temptation you should keep the answer covered with your hand
   or a suitably sized piece of paper.* Reveal the answer only
   after you have spoken it aloud. You should then further
   verify the correct response by listening to it on the tape,
   where we have pre-recorded it, and by repeating it aloud as
   shown. This procedure will usually be indicated as follows:

Verify: ( )x   ( )x

So much for our very brief introduction to programming. It
is unlikely that you will have any trouble following along.

<u>All</u> portions of these materials, whether they are programmed
or not, lend themselves well to self-instruction. It is
recommended, however, that you have a 'check-out' session with an

------

* The author once saw a student using a fat cigar. No objections,
  provided it's not lighted!

vii

instructor at regular intervals to assure yourself that you are progressing satisfactorily. During these sessions the instructor can verify what you have prepared, polishing it and practicing it with you. In an intensive course where you are studying Portuguese up to eight hours a day it is advisable to plan on two to three or more hours of 'check-out' per day, preferably not all at one sitting.

In the first six units the programming leads to brief conversational exchanges. These exchanges appear in the text and they are pre-recorded on tape. You should take the time to learn them well, because you will be asked to exhibit them and practice them with your instructor during the check-out sessions.

A series of longer exchanges called dialogs begins in Unit seven. These too you will want to prepare thoroughly so that you feel comfortable participating in them with your instructor.

In Units eight through twenty-four you will find a variety of practice exercises dealing with one or another grammatical point. Most of these exercises are recorded on tape. Follow the instructions for each one and work conscientiously. Your instructor will want to verify that you have mastered the point being drilled.

CONTENTS

Preface

Foreword

Unit 1

Unit 2

Unit 8

Unit 9

Unit 10

Unit 11

Unit 12

Unit 13

Unit 14

Unit 15

Unit 16

Unit 20

Unit 21

Unit 1

1. Listen to this vowel sound on the tape. Do not repeat it
    yet.

    ( )   ( )

2. The sound you just heard is a Portuguese nasal vowel.
    Listen to it again.

    ( )   ( )

3. This nasal vowel sound is seldom heard all by itself.
    Usually it is heard in combination with other sounds. To
    illustrate, we can put a b sound before it. The result is
    a one-syllable word. Just listen.

    ( )   ( )

4. Here is your chance to repeat that word. Mimic the voice
    on the tape as accurately as you can.

    ( )x   ( )x

5. Now we will put an s in front of this same nasal vowel.
    This gives us another Portuguese word. Just listen.

    ( )   ( )

6. Here is your chance to repeat that word. Mimic the voice
    on the tape as accurately as you can.

    ( )x   ( )x

7. Now we will put a d in front of the vowel. This gives us
    still another word. Just listen.

    ( )   ( )

1.1

8. Now say the word. Mimic the voice on the tape as accurately
    as you can.

                        ( )x   ( )x

9. In this frame we will review the three words just given,
    and we will show you what they look like. Mimic the voice
    on the tape as your eye follows along below.

            bom   ( )x   ( )x
            som   ( )x   ( )x
            dom   ( )x   ( )x

10. This visual stimulus may tempt you to say an _m_ sound
    when pronouncing these words. This would be wrong. There
    is no _m_ sound in these words. Be sure that you do not let
    yourself say one.

            bom   ( )x
            som   ( )x
            dom   ( )x

11. Here is another common word in which this same nasal vowel
    occurs. Just listen.

            com   ( )   ( )

12. Now repeat the word, making sure that you do not end it
    with an _m_ sound.

            com   ( )x   ( )x

13. Here are two common names that contain this nasal vowel.
    Just listen. Do not repeat yet.

            Afonso   ( )   ( )
            Alonso   ( )   ( )

14. Now repeat. Be careful that you say the nasal vowel and
that you do not say an <u>n</u> sound.

     Afonso   ( )x ( )x

     Alonso   ( )x ( )x

15. Let us now go on to another nasal vowel. Listen to the
voice on the tape. Do not repeat yet.

        ( )   ( )

16. As before, we will prefix several consonant sounds to this
nasal vowel in order to form words. First we will prefix
an <u>s</u> sound. Just listen.

        ( )   ( )

17. Now imitate the voice on the tape as well as you can.

        ( )x ( )x

18. Listen to this same nasal vowel preceded by an <u>m</u> sound.

        ( )   ( )

19. Now imitate.

        ( )x ( )x

20. Listen to this same nasal vowel preceded by a <u>v</u> sound.

        ( )   ( )

21. Now imitate.

        ( )x ( )x

22.   In this frame we will review the three words just given,
       and we will show you what they look like. Continue to
       mimic the voice on the tape as your eye follows along
       below.

                 sim   ( )x ( )x
                 mim   ( )x ( )x
                 vim   ( )x ( )x

23.   The <u>sight</u> of the <u>m</u> may tempt you to <u>say</u> an <u>m</u>. Do not let
       that happen. Pronounce a nasal vowel instead.

                 sim   ( )x
                 mim   ( )x
                 vim   ( )x

24.   Here is the same nasal vowel preceded by the <u>1</u> sound.
       Just listen.

                      ( )   ( )

25.   That was the first syllable of a two-syllable word. Now
       repeat the syllable.

                      ( )x ( )x

26.   The second syllable of the word does not have a nasal
       vowel. Just listen.

                      ( )   ( )

27.   Now repeat the second syllable.

                      ( )x ( )x

28.   By combining the two syllables we produce the word. Listen,
       then mimic.

                 ( )   ( )x ( )x ( )x

29.   Here is how the word appears in print. Mimic carefully as you look at it.

        lindo   ( )   ( )

30.   As you see, in this word an n appears, but you should try not to say an n. Instead, say the nasal vowel.

        lindo   ( )x   ( )x

31.   You will often find this same word said with a different ending. Just listen.

        linda   ( )   ( )

32.   Now repeat. Try not to say an n sound.

        linda   ( )x   ( )x

33.   The word you just said can also be a proper name. Repeat it again, being sure to make the vowel nasal.

        Linda   ( )x   ( )x

34.   In a brief conversational exchange that will soon be presented, you will offer the greeting 'Good day.' Here is the word 'good.' It is a word you have already practiced. As you say it again, remember to make the vowel nasal.

        bom   ( )x   ( )x

35.   And here is the word 'day.' It is a new word for you, and there is no nasal vowel.

        dia   ( )x   ( )x

36.   Many Portuguese speakers pronounce the d of dia as you just heard it, very similar to our English d. Other speakers pronounce the d much like the j of English jeep, as you

will hear at this point on the tape.

dia   ( )x ( )x

37.   Either pronounciation is correct. Both are common. For the moment we will ask you to copy the j of jeep.

dia   ( )x ( )x

38.   It may also be useful to represent this sound with the symbols dg, as in the English word 'fudge.' Say the word 'fudge,' then transfer the dg to the Portuguese word dia.

fudge   ( )x ( )x

dia   ( )x ( )x

39.   If we put bom and dia together we have the greeting 'Good day,' or 'Good morning.'

bom dia   ( )x ( )x

40.   The person responding to this greeting will likely use the same phrase in returning the greeting.

bom dia   ( )x ( )x

41.   In the third line of the conversational exchange to which we are leading you, the speaker says 'The day is beautiful.' You already know 'day.'

dia   ( )x ( )x

42.   Here is 'the day.'

o dia   ( )x ( )x

43.   Notice that the word 'the' in this phrase is simply the sound u.

o   ( )x ( )x

44.   Here again is 'the day.'

o dia   ( )x ( )x

45. The word 'beautiful' is also a word you have already
    practiced. As you say it again, remember to make its
    first vowel nasal.

    lindo   ( )x   ( )x

46. Listen to the way you say 'is.'

    está   ( )   ( )

47. Now repeat.

    está   ( )x   ( )x

48. Here, then, are the last two words of this sentence: 'is
    beautiful.'

    está lindo   ( )x   ( )x

49. And here is the complete sentence: 'The day is beautiful.'

    O dia está lindo   ( )x   ( )x

50. In the fourth line of this exchange the speaker agrees
    that it is a beautiful day. He says, 'Yes, it is.' You
    already know 'it is.'

    está   ( )x   ( )x

51. And you have already practiced the word 'yes.' As you
    say it again, remember to make the vowel nasal.

    sim   ( )x   ( )x

52. Here, then, is the fourth and final line of the exchange:
    'Yes, it is.'

    Está sim   ( )x   ( )x

53. The normal sequence in Portuguese is 'It is, yes' rather
    than 'Yes, it is.'

    Está sim   ( )x   ( )x

You are now ready for the first of a series of brief
conversational exchanges. The exchange appears on the next page
and it is pre-recorded at this point on the tape. As with all the
exchanges which are to follow, we have recorded it twice, once with
a pause after each sentence, to enable you to repeat while the tape
is still running, and once straight through, without pauses, so you
can hear the exchange as a bit of normal conversation. Work through
the recorded presentations several times, especially the one with
pauses, mimicking and practicing both roles until you feel you know
the material well enough to participate in it with your instructor
in the check-out session. Then go on to frame 54.

Exchange ≠ 1

_____ Bom dia.

_____ Bom dia.

_____ O dia está lindo.

_____ Está sim.

_____ Good morning.

_____ Good morning.

_____ The day is beautiful.

_____ Yes, it is.

54. As part of the next exchange one of the speakers asks if
'everything is well.' Here is the word for 'everything.'
Do not repeat it yet.

tudo ( ) ( )

55. The first syllable is <u>tu</u>-. Just listen.

<u>tu</u>- ( ) ( )

56. This syllable sounds a lot like our English word 'too.'
but the 't' is different. If you say English 'too' and
put your hand about an inch from your mouth you will feel
a puff of air. Try it.

too ( )x ( )x

57. This puff of air is a part of the English 't' sound when
it comes at the beginning of a word. Say these English
words and feel the air hitting your hand.

tall ( )x ( )x

tan ( )x ( )x

tin ( )x ( )x

ten ( )x ( )x

toe ( )x ( )x

too ( )x ( )x

58. The Portuguese 't' does not have this puff of air. Try
to say the following Portuguese syllables without it.

ta ( )x ( )x

to ( )x ( )x

tu ( )x ( )x

1.10

59. A degree of control is required to keep the air flow in
    check. Practice the syllables again.

    ta   ( )x   ( )x
    to   ( )x   ( )x
    tu   ( )x   ( )x

60. Here again is the word 'everything.' Say it without the
    puff of air on the 't.'

    tudo   ( )x   ( )x

61. The second syllable is much like our English word 'do.'

    tudo   ( )x   ( )x

62. Now listen to the word 'well.' Do not repeat it yet.

    ( )   ( )

63. We can approach the pronunciation of the word 'well' via
    the English word 'bay.' First, say the English word 'bay.'

    bay   ( )x   ( )x

64. Second, pronounce just the '-ay' portion of 'bay.'

    -ay   ( )x   ( )x

65. Third, say the '-ay' with nasalization. Mimic carefully.

    nasalized -ay   ( )x   ( )x

66. Finally, put a b sound in front of the nasalized '-ay.'
    This should give you the Portuguese word 'well.'

    b plus nasalized -ay   ( )x   ( )x

67. Continue to mimic the word as you now see it for the first
    time.

    bem   ( )x   ( )x

1.11

68.   Seeing the way the word is written might tempt you to
       pronounce it with an m̲ sound. There is no m̲ sound.
       Continue to mimic.

                  bem   ( )x   ( )x

69.   Now let us put tudo̲ and bem̲ together so that we can ask
       'Is everything well?' or 'Is everything okay?'

                  Tudo bem?   ( )x   ( )x

70.   No verb is needed in this expression. Observe that in
       English too we can do without the verb: 'Everything okay?'

                  Tudo bem?   ( )x   ( )x

71.   The response to this question is likely to consist of the
       very same words delivered as a statement: 'Everything (is)
       fine.'

                  Tudo bem   ( )x   ( )x

Exchange ≠ 2

____ Bom dia.

____ Bom dia.

____ Tudo bem?

____ Tudo bem.

        ____ Good morning.

        ____ Good morning.

        ____ Is everything okay?

        ____ Everything is okay.

72. A useful variation in the above exchange is to have the
    second speaker respond with 'So-so' rather than 'Everything
    is fine.' In Portuguese 'so-so' is said literally as 'more
    or less.' First, just listen to the phrase 'more or less.'

           ( )   ( )

73. Here is the word 'more.' Listen and repeat.

           ( )   ( )x ( )x

74. Here is the word 'or.'

           ( )   ( )x ( )x

75. Now we put them together: 'More or ....' Notice the z
    sound between the two words.

           ( )   ( )x ( )x

76. And finally here is the word 'less.'

           ( )   ( )x ( )x

77. Now we have the complete phrase: 'More or less.'

           ( )x ( )x

78. This is what the phrase looks like.

    a. mais....   ( )x

        Be sure you pronounce a z sound here.

    b. mais ou.... ( )x

    c. mais ou menos ( )x ( )x

Exchange ≠ 3

_____ Bom dia.

_____ Bom dia.

_____ Tudo bem?

_____ Mais ou menos.

_____ Good morning.

_____ Good morning.

_____ Everything okay?

_____ So-so (more or less).

79.   So far our exchanges have concentrated on greetings in the
       morning. In the next exchange we will direct ourselves to
       the afternoon. Here is the word 'afternoon.' Listen, but
       do not mimic yet.

                    tarde   ( )   ( )

80.   The first syllable of the word is <u>tar</u>-. Just listen.

                    tar-   ( )   ( )

81.   The pronunciation of an <u>r</u> at the end of a syllable varies
       a bit from region to region. Many speakers pronounce it in
       a way that suggests a strong English <u>h</u> sound, that is, an
       <u>h</u> sound with a bit of friction or rasping added to it.
       Try to mimic that pronunciation here.

                    tar-   ( )x   ( )x

82.   That is the pronunciation we will use in these frames.
       Mimic it again.

                    tar-   ( )x   ( )x

83.   The second syllable is -<u>de</u>. Just listen.

                    -de   ( )   ( )

84.   The consonant sound here is the <u>j</u> sound of 'jeep,' or the
       <u>dg</u> of 'fudge.'

                    -de   ( )x   ( )x

85.   Many speakers will have a <u>d</u> sound here, much like our
       English <u>d</u>, but for the moment we will ask you to use the
       <u>j</u> of 'jeep' or the <u>dg</u> or 'fudge.' Mimic again.

                    -de   ( )x   ( )x

86.   Here are both syllables, forming the word for 'afternoon.'

                    tarde   ( )x   ( )x

87. The word <u>tarde</u> requires a different form of the word for 'good.' We can not use the form <u>bom</u>. Instead we use the form <u>boa</u>. Just listen.

        boa   ( )   ( )

88. There is no nasal vowel in <u>boa</u>. Mimic what you hear.

        boa   ( )x   ( )x

89. Here is the complete phrase 'Good afternoon.'

        boa tarde   ( )   ( )x   ( )x

90. The person addressed is likely to respond with the same greeting.

        boa tarde   ( )   ( )x   ( )x

91. In a previous exchange we said that the day was beautiful. Here we will say that the afternoon is beautiful. Here is '<u>the</u> afternoon.'

        a tarde   ( )x   ( )x

92. As you say the word 'beautiful' remember to make the first vowel nasal.

        linda   ( )x   ( )x

93. Notice that the word in this instance is <u>linda</u> and not <u>lindo</u>.

        linda   ( )x   ( )x

94. Here is the sentence: 'The afternoon is beautiful.'

        A tarde .... ( )x
        A tarde está ..... ( )x
        A tarde está linda ( )x   ( )x

95. The response to that sentence is translatable as 'It certainly is,' or 'It is, indeed.' Here is the word which serves as the equivalent of 'certainly' or 'indeed.'

  mesmo ( ) ( )x ( )x

96. Notice the <u>z</u> sound in <u>mesmo</u>.

  mesmo ( )x ( )x

97. And here is the response: 'It certainly is.'

  Está mesmo ( ) ( )x ( )x

Exchange # 4

____ Boa tarde.
____ Boa tarde.
____ A tarde está linda.
____ Está mesmo.

              ____ Good afternoon.
              ____ Good afternoon.
              ____ The afternoon is beautiful.
              ____ It certainly is.

98.   Now we will go on to an appropriate greeting for evening
       or night. Here is the first syllable of the word for
       'night.'

                    ( )   ( )x   ( )x

99.   Here is the whole word.

                    ( )   ( )x   ( )x

100.   Here is what the word for 'night' looks like.

                    noite   ( )x   ( )x

101.   The word can be pronounced with a t sound, as above, or it
       can be pronounced with a sound resembling the ch of 'cheese'.

                    noite   ( )x   ( )x

102.   Either way is correct, but for the moment we will ask you
       to use the ch of 'cheese.'

                    noite   ( )x   ( )x

103   You already know the proper form for 'good.'

                    boa   ( )x   ( )x

104   So here is the greeting 'Good evening.'

                    boa noite   ( )x   ( )x

105.   The person responding to this greeting is likely to use the
       same greeting in return.

                    boa noite   ( )x   ( )x

106.   In the next exchange the first speaker wants to know if it
       is raining. Listen to the word for 'raining.'

                    ( )   ( )

107.   Mimic the first syllable of the word.

                    ( )x   ( )x

108. Mimic the second syllable. The vowel here is nasal.

( )x   ( )x

109. Here is the third syllable.

( )x   ( )x

110. Now mimic the whole word.

( )x   ( )x

111. Here is what the word 'raining' looks like.

chovendo   ( )x   ( )x

112. Notice that the ch spelling calls for an sh pronunciation.

chovendo   ( )x   ( )x

113. Try to make the second vowel nasal and try not to pronounce
an n.

ven... ( )x   ( )x

chovendo   ( )x   ( )x

114. We already know the word 'is.'

está \ ( )x   ( )x

115. So we can ask 'Is it raining?'

Está chovendo?   ( )x   ( )x

116. The answer is one that you have seen before: 'Yes, it is.'

Está sim   ( )x   ( )x

117. Or, as a variation, and depending on the weather, the answer
might well be 'No, it is not.' In this frame listen to
the Portuguese word that serves for both 'no' and 'not.'
Do not repeat it yet.

( )   ( )

118.   Now let's pronounce the word. First, say an n̲ sound
        followed by a nasalized u̲h̲ sound. Be sure you nasalize
        the u̲h̲. Mimic carefully.

                n̲ + nasalized u̲h̲   ( )x   ( )x

119.   Now, proceed to add a u̲ sound to the above, and continue
        the nasalization.

                n̲ plus nasalized u̲h̲ plus nasalized u̲ (·)x   ( )x

120.   The above maneuvers should give you the Portuguese word
        that serves for both 'no' and 'not.' Mimic the word
        again.

                        ( )x   ( )x

121.   Here is what the word looks like.

                    não   ( )x   ( )x

122.   And here is the alternate answer, 'No, it is not.'

            Não, não está   ( )x   ( )x

123.   The first não corresponds to English 'no,' the second to
        English 'not.'

            Não, não está   ( )x   ( )x

Exchange ≠ 5

____ Boa noite.

____ Boa noite.

____ Está chovendo?

____ Está sim.

                ____ Good evening.

                ____ Good evening.

                ____ Is it raining?

                ____ Yes, it is.

Exchange # 6

____ Boa noite.

____ Boa noite.

____ Está chovendo?

____ Não, não está.

    ____ Good evening.

    ____ Good evening.

    ____ Is it raining?

    ____ No, it's not.

Unit 2

Part 1

1. Here is an easy phrase which often serves as a greeting.
    It means 'How are you?', or 'How goes it?'. Just listen.

    ( )   ( )

2. The first word means 'how.' Mimic the word.

    ( )x   ( )x

3. The second word literally means 'goes.' Mimic the word.

    ( )x   ( )x

4. The two words together mean 'How are you (going)?', or
    'How goes it?'. This is a greeting.

    ( )x   ( )x

5. Here is what the words look like.

    Como vai?   ( )x   ( )x

6. A common response to this greeting is 'Well, thanks.' You
    already have the word for 'well.'

    bem   ( )x   ( )x

7. Listen to the word for 'thanks.'

    ( )   ( )

8. Here it is syllable by syllable. Just listen.

    1. ( )
    2. ( )
    3. ( )
    4. ( )
    Together: ( )   ( )

2.1

9.   Now mimic the word.

                                1.   ( )x
                                2.   ( )x
                                3.   ( )x
                                4.   ( )x
                        Together: ( )x   ( )x

10.   This is what it looks like.

                obrigado   ( )x   ( )x

11.   If you are male, you will say the word as it was just given.

        If you are female, you will say it like this.

                obrigada   ( )x   ( )x

12.   Here, then, is 'Well, thanks,' said by a male.

        Bem obrigado   ( )x   ( )x

13.   And said by a female.

        Bem obrigada   ( )x   ( )x

Exchange ≠ 1

____ Bom dia.

____ Bom dia.

____ Como vai?

____ Bem obrigada.

           ____ Good morning.

           ____ Good morning.

           ____ How are you?

           ____ Fine, thanks.

Exchange ≠ 2

____ Boa tarde.

____ Boa tarde.

____ Como vai?

____ Bem obrigado.

           ____ Good afternoon.

           ____ Good afternoon.

           ____ How's it going?

           ____ Fine, thanks.

2.3

14. 'You' is said several ways in Portuguese. Here is one way.
     Just listen.

                         ( )   ( )

15. There are three syllables in that expression. Observe and
     listen, but do not repeat yet.

          1. o   ( )   ( )
          2. se-   ( )   ( )
          3. -nhor   ( )   ( )

          Together: o senhor ( )   ( )

16. Mimic the first syllable. It is simply a <u>u</u> sound.

                    o   ( )x   ( )x

17. Now mimic the second syllable.

               se-   ( )x   ( )x

18. And the third syllable.

             -nhor   ( )x   ( )x

19. The <u>nh</u> of the third syllable resembles the <u>gn</u> of the English
     or French word co<u>gn</u>ac.

             -nhor   ( )x   ( )x

20. The <u>r</u> varies a bit. For many Portuguese speakers it is a
     sound which is similar to a strong English <u>h</u> sound. That
     is the pronunciation we are using in these frames.

             -nhor   ( )x   ( )x

21. Now let us put the three syllables together.

          o senhor   ( )x   ( )x

22. What you have been practicing is the way to say 'you' when you are addressing a man.

    o senhor   ( )x ( )x

23. When addressing a woman the corresponding expression is a bit different. Just listen in this frame.

        ( )   ( )

24. Here is the expression syllable by syllable. Observe and listen, but do not mimic yet.

    1. a   ( )   ( )
    2. se-   ( )   ( )
    3. -nho-   ( )   ( )
    4. -ra   ( )   ( )

    Together: a senhora ( )   ( )

25. The third syllable begins with the 'gn' sound of 'cognac.' Just listen.

    3. -nho-   ( )   ( )

26. The vowel sound in -nho- is like the vowel sound in the English word 'paws.' Now, mimic this sequence, maintaining the same vowel sound throughout.

    1. paws   ( )x ( )x
    2. aw   ( )x ( )x
    3. -nho-   ( )x ( )x
    4. senho-   ( )x ( )x
    5. a senho- ( )x ( )x
    6. a senhora ( )x ( )x

27.   The r of the last syllable is a quick flap of the tongue
       against the front of the roof of the mouth. It is the same
       sound we are likely to hear in English words such as
       'gotta', 'buddy', and 'caddy'. Mimic the following English
       words as they are said on the tape and notice what happens
       to your tongue as you run over the t and the d.

       buddy   ( )x   ghetto ( )x   nitty-gritty ( )x
       baddy   ( )x   batty   ( )x   should'a   ( )x
       caddy   ( )x   catty   ( )x   would'a   ( )x
       woody   ( )x   auto   ( )x   ought'a   ( )x

28.   This flap of the tongue is the r of Portuguese senhora.
       Maintain that flap as you mimic this sequence.

       (English) ought'a   ( )x   ( )x
                     -ora   ( )x   ( )x
                    -nhora   ( )x   ( )x
                   senhora   ( )x   ( )x
               a   senhora   ( )x   ( )x

29.   Now repeat the two forms for 'you.'

                o senhor   ( )x   ( )x
                a senhora   ( )x   ( )x

30.   We can use the forms for 'you' in the greetings we have been
       practicing. We can add them to como vai?

       Como vai o senhor?   ( )x   ( )x
       Como vai a senhora?   ( )x   ( )x

Exchange $\neq$ 3

____ Como vai o senhor?

____ Bem obrigado.

                    ____ How are you?

                    ____ Fine, thanks.

Exchange $\neq$ 4

____ Como vai a senhora?

____ Bem obrigada.

                    ____ How are you?

                    ____ Fine, thanks.

2.7

31.   We can also phrase the greeting like this:

        O senhor vai bem?   ( )x   ( )x

        A senhora vai bem?   ( )x   ( )x

32.   This greeting literally asks 'Are you (going) well?' The
response to it may include the form for 'I go' or 'I am
going,' which is vou. Mimic carefully.

           vou   ( )x   ( )x

33.   The response could thus be 'Yes, I am (going well).'

         Vou sim   ( )x   ( )x

Exchange ≠ 5

_____ O senhor vai bem?

_____ Vou sim.

        _____ Are you well?

        _____ Yes, I am.

Exchange ≠ 6

_____ A senhora vai bem?

_____ Vou sim.

        _____ Are you well?

        _____ Yes, I am.

34.   The expression 'very well' often finds its way into these
       greetings. The word 'very' requires some special attention.
       First, mimic this item.

                       moo-i   ( )x   ( )x

35.   Now, nasalize the vowels.

                       mõõ-ĩ   ( )x   ( )x

36.   Don't let it drag out too much.

                       mõõĩ   ( )x   ( )x

37.   Now add the syllable -to.

                       mõõĩ-to   ( )x   ( )x

38.   That was the word 'very.' Here is what it <u>really</u> looks
       like.

                       muito   ( )x   ( )x

39.   Now you can say 'very well.'

                       muito bem   ( )x   ( )x

40.   You will need the word for 'and' in the next several
       exchanges. Here is 'and.'

                                 ( )x   ( )x

41.   This is what 'and' looks like.

                       e   ( )x   ( )x

42.   Now you can ask 'And you?' as part of your greeting.

                  e a senhora?   ( )x   ( )x

                  e o senhor?   ( )x   ( )x

Exchange # 7

____ O senhor vai bem?

____ Vou sim, e a senhora?

____ Muito bem, obrigada.

        ____ Are you going well?

        ____ Yes, I am, and you?

        ____ Very well, thanks.

Exchange # 8

____ Como vai a senhora?

____ Muito bem, obrigada. E o senhor?

____ Muito bem, obrigado.

        ____ How are you?

        ____ Very well, thanks, and you?

        ____ Very well, thanks.

Exchange ≠ 9

____ Como vai o senhor?

____ Vou muito bem, obrigado.

E o senhor?

____ Muito bem.

          ____ How are you doing?

          ____ I'm doing very well, thanks, and you?

          ____ Very well.

43. Listen to this item, which is the word for 'until.'

     atế   ( )   ( )

44. Repeat the first syllable.

     a-   ( )x   ( )x

45. Repeat the second syllable. Try to avoid a puff of air on the 't.'

     -tế   ( )x   ( )x

46. The vowel of the second syllable is similar to the _e_ of English 'set.'

     -ế   ( )x   ( )x

     atế   ( )x   ( )x

47. We are leading you to say 'Until later.' In Portuguese, 'later' is literally the equivalent of 'more late.' You already know the word for 'more.'

     mais   ( )x   ( )x

48. And you know the word for 'late,' which is also the word for 'afternoon.'

     tarde   ( )x   ( )x

49. Therefore, 'later' is mais tarde.

     mais tarde   ( )x   ( )x

50. Now let's precede the above with atế, 'until,' in order to say 'until later.'

     atế mais tarde   ( )x   ( )x

2.13

51. Até mais tarde is one of several phrases that are
     appropriate when departing someone's company. In such
     circumstances it expresses the idea 'See you later.'

            até mais tarde   ( )x   ( )x

52. Listen to this item.

            logo   ( )   ( )

53. Repeat the first syllable. The o is similar to the a of
     English 'paws' or 'laws.' Mimic carefully.

            lo-   ( )x   ( )x

54. Repeat the second syllable.

            -go   ( )x   ( )x

55. Repeat the word.

            logo   ( )x   ( )x

56. Now precede it with até.

            até logo   ( )x   ( )x

57. The above phrase is another way to express the idea 'See
     you later.'

            até logo   ( )x   ( )x

58. Now listen to the word for 'tomorrow.'

            amanhã   ( )   ( )

59. Mimic the first syllable.

            a-   ( )x   ( )x

60. Mimic the second syllable.

            -ma-   ( )x   ( )x

61. The nh of the third syllable is similar to the gn sound of 'cognac.' The vowel is nasal. Mimic carefully.

     -nhã   ( )x   ( )x

62. Try the third syllable again. The nasal vowel might be described as a nasalized 'uh.'

     -nhã   ( )x   ( )x

63. Now mimic the whole word.

     amanhã   ( )x   ( )x

64. Precede it with até and you will say 'Until tomorrow.'

     até amanhã   ( )x   ( )x

65. Now when you leave somebody you can say 'I'll see you tomorrow.'

     até amanhã   ( )x   ( )x

Exchange ≠ 10

____ Até logo Linda.

____ Até logo Afonso.

                    ____ See you later, Linda.

                    ____ See you later, Afonso.

Exchange ≠ 11

____ Até amanhã Linda.

____ Até amanhã Afonso.

                    ____ See you tomorrow, Linda.

                    ____ See you tomorrow, Afonso.

Exchange ≠ 12

____ Até mais tarde.

____ Até mais tarde?! Não, até amanhã.

                    ____ See you later.

                    ____ See you later?! No, see you tomorrow.

2.16

Unit 2

Part 2

66. In the next few exchanges you will be using the word
'married.' First, listen to the word.

( )   ( )

67. Now repeat it syllable by syllable.

1.   ( )x

2.   ( )x

3.   ( )x

Together: ( )x   ( )x

68. This is what the word 'married' looks like. Mimic.

ca-   ( )x

-sa-   ( )x

do-   ( )x

Together: casado   ( )x   ( )x

69. The above form is the appropriate form when referring to
males. When referring to females the form has a different
ending.

1.   ca-   ( )x

2.   -sa-   ( )x

3.   -da   ( )x

Together: casada   ( )x   ( )x

70. Here is how you say '<u>is</u> married.'

é casado   ( )x   ( )x   referring to a male

é casada   ( )x   ( )x   referring to a female

71.   In this instance the verb 'is' is é.

                    é   ( )x   ( )x

72.   The verb form é is a single vowel sound, the vowel sound
        which is similar to the e of 'bed.' Again, mimic carefully.

                    é   ( )x   ( )x

73.   Here again is the phrase 'is married.'

                é casado   ( )x   ( )x   a male

                é casada   ( )x   ( )x   a female

74.   Now you can say, for example, 'Afonso is married.'

                Afonso é casado   ( )x   ( )x

75.   And you can say 'Linda is married.'

                Linda é casada   ( )x   ( )x

76.   The verb é is also the form that accompanies o senhor
        and a senhora, in which case it translates as 'are.' So
        you can also say 'You are married.'

                O senhor é casado   ( )x   ( )x

                A senhora é casada   ( )x   ( )x

77.   By changing the intonation on the two previous items you
        can make questions out of them.

                O senhor é casado?   ( )x   ( )x

                A senhora é casada?   ( )x   ( )x

78.   The answer to these questions will more than likely
        involve the verb form for 'I am.' Here it is.

                        sou   ( )x   ( )x

79. The form <u>sou</u> rhymes with the form <u>vou</u>. Do not confuse them.

   'I go' vou   ( )x   ( )x

   'I am' sou   ( )x   ( )x

80. So you can answer the question by saying 'Yes, I am.'

      Sou sim ( )x   ( )x

81 Notice the word order: 'I am, yes.'

      Sou sim ( )x   ( )x

82 Or the answer might be 'No, I am not.'

    Não, não sou ( )x   ( )x

83. The first <u>não</u>, is 'no,' the second is 'not.'

    Não, não sou   ( )x   ( )x

Exchange ≠ 13

____ O senhor é casado?

____ Sou sim.

    (or)

____ Não, não sou.

                   ____ Are you married?

                   ____ Yes, I am.

                       (or)

                   ____ No, I'm not.

Exchange ≠ 14

____ A senhora é casada?

____ Sou sim.

    (or)

____ Não, não sou.

                   ____ Are you married?

                   ____ Yes, I am.

                       (or)

                   ____ No, I'm not.

Exchange ≠ 15

____ A Linda é casada? *

____ Não, não é.

         ____ Is Linda married?

         ____ No, she's not.

Exchange ≠ 16

____ O Alonso é casado? *

____ É sim.

         ____ Is Alonso married?

         ____ Yes, he is.

*The definite articles frequently accompany names. The Portuguese speaker literally says 'the Alonso' and 'the Linda,' etc.

2.21

84. The response might also include the word for 'single.'
Listen to the word 'single' syllable by syllable. Do not
mimic yet.

1. ( )
2. ( )
3. ( )

Together: ( ) ( )

85. This is what the word 'single' looks like. Mimic.

sol- ( )x
-tei- ( )x
ro- ( )x

Together: ( )x ( )x

86. Be sure the r̲ is a flapped r̲, the same kind of r̲ that is
in senho̲ra. Compare.

senho̲ra ( )x ( )x
soltei̲ro ( )x ( )x

87. The word solteiro is the appropriate form when referring
to a male.

solteiro ( )x ( )x

88. When referring to a female, the word has a different ending.

solteira ( )x ( )x

89. Your answer, then, might be 'No, I'm single.'

Não, sou solteiro ( )x ( )x

(or)

Não, sou solteira ( )x ( )x

Exchange ≠ 17

____ O senhor é casado?

____ Não, sou solteiro.

                 ____ Are you married?

                   ____ No, I'm single.

Exchange ≠ 18

____ A senhora é casada?

____ Não, sou solteira.

                 ____ Are you married?

                 ____ No, I'm single.

Exchange ≠ 19

____ O senhor é casado?

____ Não, não sou. Sou solteiro.

                 ____ Are you married?

                 ____ No, I'm not. I'm single.

2.23

Exchange ≠ 20

____ O senhor é solteiro?

____ Não, não sou. Sou casado.

               ____ Are you single?

               ____ No, I'm not, I'm married.

Exchange ≠ 21

____ A senhora é solteira?

____ Sou sim.

               ____ Are you single?

               ____ Yes, I am.

Exchange ≠ 22

____ A Linda é casada?

____ É sim.

               ____ Is Linda married?

               ____ Yes, she is.

Exchange ≠ 23

_____ O Afonso é solteiro?

_____ Não, não é.

           _____ Is Afonso single?

           _____ No, he's not.

90.   If you receive the response 'I'm married,' your next question
        is likely to be 'Do you have any children?' Listen to the
        word 'children.'

                        ( )   ( )

91.   Here is the first syllable of the word. Mimic.

                fi-   ( )x   ( )x

92.   The second syllable begins with a consonant that resembles
        the lli of 'William.' Listen carefully and mimic the
        second syllable.

                ( )   ( )x   ( )x

93.   Here is what the second syllable looks like.

                -lhos   ( )x   ( )x

94.   And here is the whole word.

                filhos   ( )x   ( )x

95.   You also need to know how to say 'have.' Here is the
        proper form of the verb 'have.'

                tem   ( )   ( )

96.   The word rhymes with bem. Mimic.

                bem   ( )x   ( )x

                tem   ( )x   ( )x

97.   Try to pronounce the t with little or no puff of air.

                tem   ( )x   ( )x

98.   Now you can ask 'Do you have (any) children?'

              O senhor tem filhos?   ( )x   ( )x

                            (or)

              A senhora tem filhos?   ( )x   ( )x

99. In order to answer, you need the verb form for 'I have.'
Listen to it.

( )   ( )

100. Listen to it syllable by syllable.

1.   ( )

2.   ( )

Together: ( )   ( )

101. Here is the first syllable. Try to mimic it without a puff
of air on the t sound.

te-   ( )x   ( )x

102. Here is the second syllable. Mimic it. The nh resembles
the gn of 'cognac.'

-nho   ( )x   ( )x

103. Now mimic the whole word. Remember, it means 'I have.'

tenho   ( )x   ( )x

104. The response, then, might be 'Yes, I do (have).'

Tenho sim   ( )x   ( )x

105. Notice the word order: 'I have, yes.'

Tenho sim   ( )x   ( )x

106. Or it might be 'No, I do not (have).'

Não, não tenho   ( )x   ( )x

107. The first não is 'no,' the second is 'not.'

Não, não tenho   ( )x   ( )x

108. The form tem also goes with Alonso, Linda, etc. So you
can ask, 'Does Linda have children?'

Linda tem filhos?   ( )x   ( )x

109.   And you can answer, 'Yes, she does.'

Tem sim   ( )x   ( )x

Exchange ≠ 24

____ A senhora tem filhos?

____ Não, não tenho.

____ Do you have children?

____ No, I don't.

Exchange # 25

____ O senhor tem filhos?

____ Tenho sim.

> ____ Do you have any children?
>
> ____ Yes, I do.

Exchange # 26

____ O Afonso tem filhos?

____ Não, não tem. Afonso é solteiro.

> ____ Does Afonso have children?
>
> ____ No, he doesn't. Afonso is
>
> single.

Exchange # 27

____ A Linda tem filhos?

____ Tem sim.

> ____ Does Linda have children?
>
> ____ Yes, she does.

110.   In the next exchange the response will continue with 'I
        have two daughters.' Here is the word for 'daughter.'

                filha   ( )x   ( )x

111.   Notice that the word is closely related to the word for
        'children.'

                filhos   ( )x   ( )x
                filha   ( )x   ( )x

112.   And here is 'two daughters.'

            duas filhas   ( )x   ( )x

113.   Mimic 'two' again.

                duas   ( )x   ( )x

114.   Mimic 'two daughters' again.

            duas filhas   ( )x   ( )x

115.   Now you can complete the response with 'I have two
        daughters.'

            Tenho duas filhas   ( )x   ( )x

Exchange ≠ 28*

____ O senhor tem filhos?

____ Tenho sim. Tenho duas filhas.

> ____ Do you have any children?
>
> ____ Yes, I do. I have two
> daughters.

Exchange ≠ 29

____ A Linda tem filhos?

____ Não, não tem.

> ____ Does Linda have any children?
>
> ____ No, she doesn't.

* You will learn more about adopting this response to your own
particular situation in a later unit.

2.31

116.   In the next set of exchanges you will be asking 'Which is
        the older (one)?' and 'Which is the younger (one)?' Here
        is the word for 'which.' Do not mimic yet.

                Qual   ( )   ( )

117.   As you mimic the word, notice that the l sound is very
        close to a w sound. This happens when Qual stands alone.

                Qual   ( )x   ( )x

118.   However, the w sound is lost and the l sounds like an l
        when Qual is followed by a vowel sound. This is the case
        in the phrase Qual é. The phrase means 'Which is?'

                Qual é?   ( )x   ( )x

119.   Be sure to make the verb é sound like the e of 'bed.'

                Qual é?   ( )x   ( )x   'Which is?'

120.   Now listen to the word 'old' as it is used in reference
        to a female. Do not repeat it yet.

                          ( )   ( )

121.   Here it is syllable by syllable.

                    1.   ( )
                    2.   ( )
            Together: ( )   ( )

122.   Mimic the first syllable. The vowel is the e of 'bed.'

                ve-   ( )x   ( )x

123.   The second syllable begins with the sound which is
        reminiscent of the ll sound in the English word 'William.'
        Mimic the syllable.

                -lha   ( )x   ( )x

                        2.32

124. Now mimic the word 'old.'

      velha   ( )x ( )x

125. In order to say 'the older' you say 'the more old.' You already know the word 'more.'

      mais   ( )x ( )x

126. So you can now say 'the more old' or 'the older.'

      a mais velha   ( )x ( )x

127. And by starting with Qual é, you can ask 'Which is the older (one)?'

      Qual é ..... ( )x ( )x

      Qual é a mais velha? ( )x ( )x

128. From 'old' we go to 'young.' Here is the word 'young.'

      nova ( )x ( )x

129. The o of nova should sound like the a of English 'paws.'

      paws ( )x ( )x

      no- ( )x ( )x

130. Mimic the word again.

      nova ( )x ( )x

131. 'The younger' is said literally as 'the more young.'

      a mais nova ( )x ( )x

132. You can now ask 'Which is the younger (one)?'

      Qual é a mais nova? ( )x ( )x

133. In the upcoming exchanges 'Maria' is the younger one. Mimic the name 'Maria.'

      Maria ( )x ( )x

134.   If the flapped r gives you trouble, try the following
        sequence. First, say the English 'muddy.'
                muddy   ( )x   ( )x

135.   Now, put the stress (accent) on the second syllable, i.e.
        on the -dy, as the voice on the tape will now do. Mimic.
                muddȳ   ( )x   ( )x

136.   Finally, attach the vowel -a to the end.
                muddȳ-a   ( )x   ( )x

137.   That bit of trickery ought to give you something reasonably
        close to the pronunciation of Maria.
                Maria   ( )x   ( )x

138.   Now you are prepared to say 'Maria is the younger one.'
        Here is the first part.
                A Maria é ...   ( )x   ( )x

139.   And here is the whole sentence.
                A Maria é a mais nova   ( )x   ( )x

140.   Maria is the younger and Sandra is the older. Listen to
        the name 'Sandra.'
                Sandra   ( )   ( )

141.   The first syllable of Sandra has a nasal vowel in it, but
        it has no n sound. Mimic carefully. Make the vowel nasal.
                San-   ( )x   ( )x

142.   The second syllable has the flapped r coming right after
        a d. The r may be a bit more difficult to pronounce in
        this location.
                -dra   ( )x   ( )x

143.　　Now mimic the complete name.

　　　　　　Sandra　　( )x　　( )x

144.　　You are now able to say 'Sandra is the older (one).'

　　　　　　　A Sandra é ...　　( )x　　( )x

　　　　　A Sandra é a mais velha ( )x　　( )x

Exchange ≠ 30

_____ Qual é a mais nova?

_____ A Maria é a mais nova.

                             _____ Which is the younger one?

                             _____ Maria is the younger one.

Exchange ≠ 31

_____ E a mais nova?

_____ A Maria é a mais nova.

                             _____ And the younger one?

                             _____ Maria is the younger one.

Exchange ≠ 32

_____ Qual é a mais velha?

_____ A Sandra é a mais velha.

                             _____ Which is the older?

                             _____ Sandra is the older one.

2.36

145. Listen to the question 'What is her name?'

           ( )   ( )

146. The first part of that phrase is a word you already know, the word 'how.'

        como   ( )x   ( )x

147. The second part is new. Mimic carefully.

        se chama   ( )x   ( )x

148. Literally it means 'calls herself.'

        se chama   ( )x   ( )x

149. Be sure that you give an <u>sh</u>-type sound to the <u>ch</u> of <u>chama</u>, as you did earlier with <u>chovendo</u>. Compare.

        chovendo   ( )x   ( )x

        chama   ( )x   ( )x

150. In <u>Como se chama</u>? you are asking 'How does she call herself?' i.e., 'What is her name?'

        Como se chama? ( )x   ( )x

151. Now you are equipped to ask the longer question 'And the younger one, what is her name?'

        E a mais nova, como se chama? ( )x   ( )x

152. In the response the two elements 'se chama' are reversed.

        Chama-se   ( )x   ( )x

153. The hyphen is a writing convention that need not concern us at this point. Just mimic.

        Chama-se   ( )x   ( )x

154. Here is the complete response: 'Her name is Maria.'

        Chama-se Maria ( )x   ( )x

Exchange ≠ 33

____ E a mais nova, como se chama?

____ Chama-se Maria.

                           ____ And the younger one, what's her name?

                           ____ Her name is Maria.

Exchange ≠ 34

____ Como se chama a mais velha?

____ Chama-se Sandra.

                           ____ What's the name of the older one?

                           ____ Her name is Sandra.

End of Tape 1A

Unit 3

1. Several words thus far presented have a flapped 'r' between
    vowels. Practice those words again.

    senho<u>r</u>a   ( )x   ( )x

    soltei<u>r</u>o   ( )x   ( )x

    Ma<u>r</u>ia   ( )x   ( )x

2. Here is another commonly heard name that has the same flapped
    'r' between vowels.

    Yara   ( )x   ( )x

3. If you have trouble with the <u>r</u>, try saying English 'atta,'
    as in 'Atta boy!'

    Atta   ( )x   ( )x

4. Now if you prefix a <u>Y</u> and change the first vowel to the
    appropriate Portuguese vowel, you should come out with a
    good pronunciation of 'Yara.'

    Yara   ( )x   ( )x

5. In the next exchange we are going to ask 'Do you know Yara?'
    This requires a particular form of the verb 'know.' Here
    is the form.

    ( )   ( )

6. Here it is by syllables.

    1.   ( )

    2.   ( )

    3.   ( )

    Together: ( )   ( )

3.1

7.   Mimic the first syllable.

               co-   ( )x   ( )x

8.   The second syllable begins with the gn sound of 'cognac.'
      The vowel is similar to the e of 'bed.'

               -nhe-   ( )x   ( )x

9.   Here is the final syllable.

               -ce   ( )x   ( )x

10.   Now mimic the whole word.

               conhece   ( )x   ( )x

11.   Now you can ask 'Do you know Yara?'

               O senhor conhece a Yara?   ( )x   ( )x

               A senhora conhece a Yara?   ( )x   ( )x

12.   In order to answer that question you need to have the form
      of the verb that corresponds to 'I know.' Here is that
      form, syllable by syllable.

               1.   ( )

               2.   ( )

               3.   ( )

      Together: ( )   ( )

13.   Now mimic.

               1.   co-   ( )x   ( )x

               2.   -nhe-   ( )x   ( )x

               3.   -ço   ( )x   ( )x

14.   The printed symbol ç always represents an s sound.

               -ço   ( )x   ( )x

15. Here are the syllables together. This is the verb form
    that corresponds to 'I know.'

    conheço ( )x ( )x

16. Now you can answer 'Yes, I know (her).'

    Conheço sim ( )x ( )x

17. There is no need for the word 'her' in this response. Your
    answer is 'I know, yes.'

    Conheço sim ( )x ( )x

18. You can also answer 'No, I do not know (her).'

    Não, não conheço ( )x ( )x

Exchange $\neq$ 1

____ A senhora conhece a Yara?
____ Conheço sim.

            ____ Do you know Yara?
            ____ Yes, I do.

Exchange $\neq$ 2

____ O senhor conhece a Maria?
____ Não, não conheço.

            ____ Do you know Maria?
            ____ No, I don't.

19.   You can amplify your response with such phrases as 'She's a teacher, friend,' etc. We will introduce information of this sort in these frames. First, here is the word 'teacher.'

        professora   ( )x   ( )x

20.   Notice the flapped <u>r</u> in -<u>ora</u>.

          -ora   ( )x   ( )x

        professora   ( )x   ( )x

21.   The <u>r</u> in the first syllable, <u>pro</u>-, is also flapped. Coming just after the <u>p</u> as it does, and not between vowels, it may be a bit more difficult for you to say. Mimic as well as you can.

          pro-   ( )x   ( )x

        professora   ( )x   ( )x

22.   Here is the word for 'she.' First, just listen.

            ela   ( )   ( )

23.   Now mimic the first syllable, <u>e</u>-. The vowel sound is like the <u>e</u> of 'bed.'

            e-   ( )x   ( )x

24.   Mimic the second syllable.

           -la   ( )x   ( )x

25.   Now say the whole word.

            ela   ( )x   ( )x

26.   Repeat the phrase 'She is ....'

         ela é ...   ( )x   ( )x

27.   Now you can say 'She is a teacher.'

           Ela é professora   ( )x   ( )x

28.   Notice that Portuguese does not include an indefinite
       article here, a word corresponding to English 'a.'

           Ela é professora   ( )x   ( )x

29.   Be sure the vowel of é (the verb 'is') is similar to the
       e of 'bed.'

                   é   ( )x   ( )x

           Ela é professora   ( )x   ( )x

30.   Here is the word 'my.'

               minha   ( )x   ( )x

31.   Once again, the nh is reminiscent of the gn of 'cognac.'

               minha   ( )x   ( )x

32.   Now you can say 'my teacher.'

               minha professora ( )x   ( )x

33.   Many times the definite article will precede. Thus you may
       hear, and say:

               a minha professora ( )x   ( )x

34.   Here is the sentence 'She's my teacher.'

           Ela é a minha professora   ( )x   ( )x

Exchange ≠ 3

____ A senhora conhece a Yara?

____ Conheço sim. Ela é professora.

           ____ Do you know Yara?

           ____ Yes, I do. She's a teacher.

Exchange ≠ 4

____ O senhor conhece a Maria?

____ Conheço sim. Ela é a minha professora.

           ____ Do you know Maria?

           ____ Yes, I do. She's my teacher.

35.   You may want to say 'our teacher.' Here is the appropriate
      form of 'our.'

              nossa   ( )x   ( )x

36.   Notice the sound of o. It is like the a of English 'paws.'

              paws   ( )x   ( )x

              no-   ( )x   ( )x

              nossa   ( )x   ( )x

37.   Now mimic 'our teacher.'

              nossa professora   ( )x   ( )x

38.   Once again the definite article may precede.

              a nossa professora   ( )x   ( )x

39.   Here is the sentence 'She's our teacher.'

              Ela é a nossa professora   ( )x   ( )x

Exchange ≠ 5

____ A senhora conhece a Yara?

____ Conheço sim. Ela é a nossa professora.

              ____ Do you know Yara?

              ____ Yes, I do. She's our teacher.

40. Here is the word 'friend,' as applied to a female friend.

      amiga   ( )x ( )x

41. Now you can say 'She's my friend.'

      Ela é minha amiga ( )x ( )x

42. And 'She's our friend.'

      Ela é nossa amiga ( )x ( )x

Exchange ≠ 6

____ O senhor conhece a Yara?

____ Conheço sim. Ela é nossa amiga.

____ Do you know Yara?

____ Yes, I do. She's our friend.

Exchange ≠ 7

____ A senhora conhece a Maria?

____ Conheço sim. Ela é minha amiga.

____ Do you know Maria?

____ Yes, I do. She's my friend.

3.10

43. You might also answer with a word which translates as
     'certainly.' Here is the word 'certainly.'

               claro   ( )x   ( )x

44. Once again we have a flapped r between vowels.

               -aro   ( )x   ( )x

               claro   ( )x   ( )x

45. Now you can answer 'Certainly, she is my friend.'

          Claro, ela é minha amiga   ( )x   ( )x

46. Or, 'Certainly, she's our teacher.'

          Claro, ela é a nossa professora   ( )x   ( )x

Exchange ≠ 8

____ O senhor conhece a Yara?
____ Claro, ela é a minha professora.

                          ____ Do you know Yara?
                          ____ Certainly, she's my teacher.

Exchange ≠ 9

____ A senhora conhece a Yara?
____ Conheço claro, ela é a nossa professora.

                          ____ Do you know Yara?
                          ____ Certainly I know her, she's
                          our teacher.

47. In the next several exchanges we will make some substitutions
    for <u>Yara</u> and <u>Maria</u> in the question 'Do you know ....?' To
    begin with, here is a word meaning 'girl,' or 'young lady.'

    moça   ( )x   ( )x

48. If we want to say '<u>that</u> young lady,' we can say:

    essa moça   ( )x   ( )x

49. <u>Essa</u> translates as 'that.' The <u>e</u> of <u>essa</u> is like the <u>e</u> of
    'bed.'

    essa   ( )x   ( )x

    essa moça   ( )x   ( )x

50. Now we can ask, 'Do you know that young lady?' First, just
    listen.

    O senhor conhece essa moça?   ( )   ( )

51. Mimic the last three words.

    conhece essa moça?   ( )x   ( )x

52. Now mimic the entire sentence.

    O senhor conhece essa moça?   ( )x   ( )x

53. Here is a word for 'young man.' First, just listen.

    rapaz   ( )   ( )

54. This word gives us another opportunity to practice the <u>r</u>
    sound that resembles an English <u>h</u> sound. Here the <u>r</u> comes
    at the beginning of a syllable, rather than at the end.
    First, mimic the English word 'ha' said with a bit more
    rasping than usual.

    ha   ( )x   ( )x

3.13

55.   Hold on to that rasping sound as you say the Portuguese
       syllable <u>ra</u>.

                    ra   ( )x   ( )x

56.   Now continue, and say the word <u>rapaz</u> 'young man.'

                    rapaz   ( )x   ( )x

57.   Notice that the word ends in an <u>s</u> sound ... not a <u>z</u> sound.

                    rapaz   ( )x   ( )x

58.   Here is 'that young man.'

                    esse rapaz   ( )x   ( )x

59.   Notice, the form for 'that' is <u>esse</u>, not <u>essa</u>. Compare:

                    esse rapaz   ( )x   ( )x

                    essa moça   ( )x   ( )x

60.   Now you are ready for the question 'Do you know that young
       man?' First, just listen.

            A senhora conhece esse rapaz?   ( )   ( )

61.   Mimic the last three words.

                    conhece esse rapaz?   ( )x   ( )x

62.   Now mimic the entire question.

            A senhora conhece esse rapaz?   ( )x   ( )x

Exchange ≠ 10

_____ O senhor conhece essa moça?

_____ Conheço sim. É a Sandra.

                 _____ Do you know that young girl?

                 _____ Yes, I do. It's Sandra.

Exchange ≠ 11

_____ A senhora conhece esse rapaz?

_____ Não, não conheço.

                 _____ Do you know that young man?

                 _____ No, I don't.

3.15

63.   You know the word 'daughter.'

      filha   ( )x   ( )x

64.   Here is the word 'son.'

      filho   ( )x   ( )x

65.   Here is the word for 'friend' when the friend is a male
      friend.

      amigo   ( )x   ( )x

66.   And here is the word for 'teacher' when the teacher is a
      male teacher.

      professor   ( )x   ( )x

67.   The word for 'my' changes its form when used with these
      'male' persons. The appropriate form is <u>meu</u>, not <u>minha</u>.
      First, just listen.

      meu   ( )   ( )

68.   The <u>eu</u> portion of the word <u>meu</u> is easier than it may seem.
      Mimicking the first vowel is no problem.

      e   ( )x   ( )x

69.   Nor is mimicking the second vowel.

      u   ( )x   ( )x

70.   Now run them together.

      eu   ( )x   ( )x

71.   And prefix an <u>m</u> sound.

      meu   ( )x   ( )x

72.   Now you can say 'my son.'

      meu filho

      ( )x   ( )x

73. You can say 'my friend' when the friend is a male friend.

    meu amigo   ( )x   ( )x

74. And you can say 'my teacher' when the teacher is a male teacher.

    meu professor   ( )x   ( )x

75. The word for 'our' will have a different form too with these items. First, just listen.

    nosso   ( )   ( )

76. The vowel sound of <u>no</u>- is the vowel sound of English 'paws.' Listen to it, and mimic it.

    no-   ( )x   ( )x

77. Here is the whole word.

    nosso   ( )x   ( )x

78. Now you can say 'our teacher.'

    nosso professor   ( )x   ( )x

79. And 'our friend.'

    nosso amigo   ( )x   ( )x

80. All of the above items may be preceded by the definite article <u>o</u>.

    o meu filho   ( )x

    o meu amigo   ( )x

    o meu professor   ( )x

    o nosso amigo   ( )x

    o nosso professor   ( )x

    o   nosso filho   ( )x

3.17

81.   Here, now, is a common name.

               Paulo   ( )x   ( )x

82.   Take special care to pronounce the first syllable correctly.

               Pau-   ( )x   ( )x

83.   Here is the name again.

               Paulo   ( )x   ( )x

84.   Here is another common name.

               Luís   ( )x   ( )x

85.   Notice that the i receives a strong stress.

               -ís   ( )x   ( )x

86.   Here is the name again.

               Luís   ( )x   ( )x

87.   Here is another common name.

               Marcos   ( )x   ( )x

88.   Notice the h-type pronunciation of the r at the end of the
       first syllable.

               Mar-   ( )x   ( )x

89.   Here is the name again.

               Marcos   ( )x   ( )x

90.   You have had the pronoun 'she.' Here is the pronoun 'he.'

               ele   ( )x   ( )x

91.   Notice the contrast between 'she' and 'he.'

               ela   ( )x   ( )x

               ele   ( )x   ( )x

92.   The final vowels of the two pronouns are different. In
        addition, the initial vowel of e<u>la</u> sounds much like the
        <u>e</u> of 'bed,' while the initial vowel of e<u>le</u> sound more like
        the <u>ay</u> of English 'say,' but clipped short, without the
        glide. Compare again.

                    ela   ( )x   ( )x
                    ele   ( )x   ( )x

Exchange ≠ 12   a-f

In these exchanges the first line (the question) is constant.
Practice altering the second line (the response).

Question: O senhor conhece esse rapaz?

Response a) Conheço sim, é o Luís.

       b) Conheço sim, é o meu amigo Luís.

       c) Claro, é o Luís.

       d) Claro, é o nosso professor!

       e) Conheço, é o Marcos.

       f) Conheço claro, é o Paulo.

Question: Do you know that young man?

Response a) Yes, I do, it's Luís.

       b) Yes, I do, it's my friend, Luís.

       c) Certainly, it's Luís.

       d) Certainly, it's our teacher!

       e) Yes, I know him. It's Marcos.

       f) Certainly I know him. It's Paulo.

3.20

93.   In the next few exchanges you will be asking 'Who is she
(he, it)?' Here is the word for 'who?' Just listen.

               quem   ( )   ( )

94.   The word quem rhymes with bem and tem. Mimic.

               bem   ( )x   ( )x

               tem   ( )x   ( )x

               quem   ( )x   ( )x

95.   As you observed, the word quem begins with a k sound.

               quem   ( )x   ( )x

96.   Now you can ask 'Who is she (he, it)?

             Quem é?   ( )x   ( )x

97.   Make sure the verb é sounds similar to the e of 'bed.'

              é   ( )x   ( )x

            Quem é   ( )x   ( )x

Exchange ≠ 13

____ O senhor conhece esse rapaz?

____ Não, quem é ele?

                               ____ Do you know that young man?

                               ____ No, who is he?

Exchange ≠ 14

____ A senhora conhece essa moça?

____ Não, quem é ela?

                               ____ Do you know that young girl?

                               ____ No, who is she?

Exchange ≠ 15

____ Quem é esse rapaz?

____ É o Paulo.

        ____ Who is that young man?

        ____ It's Paulo.

Exchange ≠ 16

____ Quem é essa moça?

____ É a Maria.

        ____ Who is that young girl?

        ____ It's Maria.

Exchange ≠ 17

____ Quem é?

____ É o meu amigo Marcos.

        ____ Who is it?

        ____ It's my friend, Marcos.

Exchange ≠ 18

____ Quem é?
____ É o nosso professor.

                              ____ Who is it?
                              ____ It's our teacher.

Exchange ≠ 19

____ Quem é?
____ É o meu filho.

                              ____ Who is it?
                              ____ It's my son.

Unit 4

1. Recall the word for 'tomorrow.'

    amanhã   ( )x   ( )x

2. Recall that the final syllable of the word has a nasal vowel.

    -nhã   ( )x   ( )x

3. This nasal vowel is a common one. You also came across it
    in the first syllable of the name <u>Sandra</u>.

    San-   ( )x   ( )x

    Sandra   ( )x   ( )x

4. Here it is again in the first syllable of the word for
    'band.'

    ban-   ( )x   ( )x

    banda   ( )x   ( )x

5. Because of the influence of English, it is easy to think
    you hear an <u>n</u> sound in <u>Sandra</u> and <u>banda</u>. But there is none
    there. What you hear in the first syllable of each word is
    a Portuguese nasal vowel, the same nasal vowel you hear in
    the last syllable of <u>amanhã</u>. Compare, and mimic.

    amanhã   ( )x   ( )x

    -ã   ( )x   ( )x

    San-   ( )x   ( )x

    Sandra   ( )x   ( )x

    ban-   ( )x   ( )x

    banda   ( )x   ( )x

4.1

6.   Listen for the same vowel in the first syllable of this new
      word, the verb 'to dance.'

                dançar   ( )x   ( )x

7.   Again, the influence of English may lead you to think there
      is an n̲ sound in the first syllable. But there is none
      there. What you hear is a nasal vowel. Mimic carefully.

                dan-   ( )x   ( )x
                dançar   ( )x   ( )x

8.   Here are several more words with which you can practice this
      nasal vowel. We will not bother you with their meanings.
      Ignore the n̲ and concentrate on the nasal vowel.

                ando   ( )x
                dando   ( )x
                falando   ( )x
                dançando   ( )x
                quando   ( )x
                antes   ( )x
                santos   ( )x
                tantos   ( )x

9.   Now listen to the word for 'samba.'

                samba   ( )   ( )

10.   It is the m̲ that may get in the way here. The influence of
      English may lead you to think you hear an m̲ sound in this word,
      but there is none there. What you hear is the same nasal vowel.
      Listen and mimic.

                samba   ( )x   ( )x

                            4.2

11. Here is another name. It has this same nasal vowel. Just
     listen.

               Santos   ( )   ( )

12. Mimic the first syllable of the name.

               San-   ( )x   ( )x

13. Now mimic both syllables.

               Santos   ( )x   ( )x

14. Here is another name with the same nasal vowel. Just
     listen.

               Ângela   ( )   ( )

15. The nasal vowel is in the first syllable. Listen and mimic.

               Ân-   ( )x   ( )x

16. The second syllable begins with the s̲ sound of English
     'leis̲ure,' 'pleas̲ure' and 'treas̲ure,' or the z̲ sound of
     'azure.' Mimic carefully.

               -ge-   ( )x   ( )x

17. Be sure you do n̲o̲t̲ say the j̲ sound of English 'job,'
     'Jack,' etc. Mimic the syllable again.

               -ge-   ( )x   ( )x

18. Now say the whole name.

               Ângela   ( )x   ( )x

Exchange ≠ 1

_____ Quem é essa moça?

_____ É a Sandra.

                                               _____ Who is that girl?

                                               _____ It's Sandra.

Exchange ≠ 2

_____ O senhor conhece essa moça?

_____ Conheço sim. É a Ângela.

                                               _____ Do you know that girl?

                                               _____ Yes, I do. It's Ângela.

Exchange ≠ 3

_____ Quem é esse rapaz? A senhora conhece?

_____ Claro. É o Santos.

                                               _____ Who is that young man? Do
you know him?

                                               _____ Certainly. It's Santos.

4.4

19.　　Observe and mimic this item.

　　　　do Marcos　　( )x　　( )x

20.　　The above item means 'of Marcos.'

　　　　do Marcos　　( )x　　( )x

21.　　Now observe and mimic this item.

　　　　a filha do Marcos　　( )x　　( )x

22.　　The above item literally means 'the daughter of Marcos.'
In everyday English we would translate it as 'Marcos's
daughter.'

　　　　a filha do Marcos　　( )x　　( )x

23.　　Using the same pattern you can now say 'Luís's daughter.'

　　　　a filha do Luís　　( )x　　( )x

24.　　Likewise you can say 'Santos's daughter.'

　　　　a filha do Santos　　( )x　　( )x

25.　　And you can say 'Paulo's daughter.'

　　　　a filha do Paulo　　( )x　　( )x

26.　　Also, you can substitute 'son' in the above phrases.

　　　　o filho do Marcos　　( )x

　　　　o filho do Luís　　( )x

　　　　o filho do Santos　　( )x

　　　　o filho do Paulo　　( )x

27.　　Observe and mimic this item.

　　　　da Yara　　( )x　　( )x

28.　　The above item means 'of Yara.'

　　　　da Yara　　( )x　　( )x

29.   Now observe and mimic this item.

        o filho da Yara   ( )x   ( )x

30.   The above item literally means 'the son of Yara.' In
        everyday English we would translate it as 'Yara's son.'

        o filho da Yara   ( )x   ( )x

31.   Using the same pattern, you can also say 'Maria's son.'

        o filho da Maria   ( )x   ( )x

32.   You can say 'Sandra's son.'

        o filho da Sandra   ( )x   ( )x

33.   And you can say 'Ângela's son.'

        o filho da Ângela   ( )x   ( )x

34.   Also, you can substitute 'daughter' in the above phrases.

        a filha da Yara   ( )x   ( )x

        a filha da Maria   ( )x   ( )x

        a filha da Sandra   ( )x   ( )x

        a filha da Ângela   ( )x   ( )x

Exchange ⧣ 4

____ O senhor conhece essa moça?

____ Conheço sim. É a filha da Ângela.

> ____ Do you know that young girl?
>
> ____ Yes, I do. It's Ângela's daughter.

Exchange ⧣ 5

____ Quem é esse rapaz?

____ É o filho da Maria.

> ____ Who is that young man?
>
> ____ It's Maria's son.

Exchange ⧣ 6

____ Quem é esse rapaz? A senhora conhece?

____ Conheço sim. É o filho do Santos.

> ____ Who is that young man? Do you know him?
>
> ____ Yes, I do. It's Santos' son.

4.7

Exchange # 7

____ O senhor conhece a filha do Paulo?

____ Conheço sim.   Chama-se Sandra.

                                        ____ Do you know Paulo's daughter?

                                        ____ Sure.   Her name is Sandra.

Exchange # 8

____ Quem é?

____ É o Marcos, o filho do Santos.

                                        ____ Who is it?

                                        ____ It's Marcos, Santos' son.

4.8

35.   In the upcoming exchanges you will have the chance to
       practice the phrase 'Where is ....?' Here is the question-
       word 'Where?' First, just observe and listen.

                   onde   ( )   ( )

36.   The first syllable rhymes with the word <u>bom</u>. It has
       the same nasal vowel. Listen and mimic.

                   bom   ( )x   ( )x
                   on-   ( )x   ( )x

37.   Now mimic the word <u>onde</u>, meaning 'Where?'

                   onde   ( )x   ( )x

38.   Many speakers pronounce the word as you just heard it, with
       a recognizable <u>d</u> sound.   Many others will pronounce it
       with the <u>j</u> sound of 'jeep,' as in this frame. Listen and
       mimic.

                   onde   ( )x   ( )x

39.   For the moment we will use the <u>j</u> of 'jeep.'

                   onde   ( )x   ( )x

40   Now observe this item and repeat it.

                   onde está?   ( )x   ( )x

41.   The above item means 'Where is?'

                   Onde está?   ( )x   ( )x

42.   It is the way you will ask 'Where is Paul?', for example.

                   Onde está o Paulo?   ( )x   ( )x

43.   And 'Where is Sandra?'

                   Onde está a Sandra?   ( )x   ( )x

4.9

44.   And, indeed, 'Where is everybody and anybody?'

               Onde está a Yara?   ( )x

          Onde está a minha filha?   ( )x

       Onde está o meu professor?   ( )x

     Onde está o filho do Santos? ( )x

          Onde está a mais nova?   ( )x

         Onde está a mais velha?   ( )x

45.   Now we will give you a few of the responses. First, here
     is 'at home.'

          em casa   ( )x   ( )x

46.   Notice the z sound in casa.

          casa   ( )x   ( )x

47.   Notice also that there is no m sound in this phrase.

         em casa   ( )x   ( )x

48.   Now you can answer 'He (She) is at home.'

       Está em casa   ( )x   ( )x

49.   Here is 'in New York.' Just listen.

     em Nova Iorque ( )   ( )

50.   The word 'new' you have already had in the sense of 'young.'

          nova   ( )x   ( )x

       Nova Iorque   ( )x   ( )x

51.   Now you can answer 'Paulo is in New York.'

     O Paulo está em Nova Iorque ( )x   ( )x

52.   The word <u>em</u> meaning 'in' precedes quite a few place names.

             Está em Washington   ( )x
          Está em Filadélphia   ( )x
              Está em Denver   ( )x
           Está em Brasília   ( )x
            Está em Lisboa   ( )x

53.   By way of contrast, notice this item.

             na festa   ( )x   ( )x

54.   The above item means 'at the party.'

             na festa   ( )x   ( )x

55.   You will use the same pattern to say 'at school.'

             na escola   ( )x   ( )x

56.   Notice the <u>o</u> sound in <u>escola</u>. It resembles the <u>a</u> of
       English 'paws.'

             paw   ( )x   ( )x
            esco-   ( )x   ( )x
            escola   ( )x   ( )x
          na escola   ( )x   ( )x

57.   So now you can say 'Ângela is in/at school.'

       A Ângela está na escola   ( )x   ( )x

58.   And you can say 'Yara is at the party.'

       A Yara está na festa   ( )x   ( )x

59.   Here is the word 'here.'

             aqui   ( )x   ( )x

4.11

60.   And here is the phrase 'is here.'

        está aqui   ( )x   ( )x

61.   Now you can say 'Marcos is here.'

        O Marcos está aqui   ( )x   ( )x

62.   And you can say 'Maria is here.'

        A Maria está aqui   ( )x   ( )x

Exchange ≠ 9

____ Onde está Maria?

____ Está em casa.

____ Where's Maria?

____ She's at home.

Exchange ≠ 10

____ Onde está a Ângela?

____ Está na escola.

____ Where's Angela?

____ She's at school.

Exchange ≠ 11

____ Onde está a Sandra?

____ Está na festa.

____ Where's Sandra?

____ She's at the party.

Exchange ≢ 12

____ Onde está o professor?

____ Está em Washington.

         ____ Where's the teacher?

         ____ He's in Washington.

Exchange ≢ 13

____ Onde está a filha do Santos?

____ Está aqui.

         ____ Where is Santos' daughter?

         ____ She's here.

Exchange ≢ 14

____ Onde está o Luís?

____ Está em Nova Iorque.

         ____ Where is Luís?

         ____ He's in New York.

63. With the question-word <u>Onde</u> and the verb form <u>vai</u> you
     are now equipped to ask 'Where are you going?' First,
     just listen to the question.

                    Onde o senhor vai?   ( )   ( )

64. Now mimic.

                              vai   ( )x   ( )x
                     o senhor vai   ( )x   ( )x
               Onde o senhor vai?   ( )x   ( )x

65. Now substitute 'a senhora.'

                   a senhora vai   ( )x   ( )x
              Onde a senhora vai?   ( )x   ( )x

66. We will approach the response by recalling the verb form
     that corresponds to 'I go' or 'I am going.'

                              vou   ( )x   ( )x

67. You practiced this form in the phrase 'I'm going (doing)
     well, thanks.'

                  Vou bem obrigado   ( )x   ( )x

68. Now notice its use in this phrase. Just listen.

                  Vou a Nova Iorque   ( )   ( )

69. The phrase means 'I'm going to New York.' The English
     preposition 'to' often translates as <u>a</u> in Portuguese. Mimic.

                     a Nova Iorque   ( )x   ( )x
                 Vou a Nova Iorque   ( )x   ( )x

70. Here is 'to Lisbon.'

                          a Lisboa   ( )x   ( )x

                                 4.15

71.   Now you can say 'I'm going to Lisbon.'

Vou a Lisboa   ( )x   ( )x

72.   Here is 'to Brasília.'

a Brasília   ( )x   ( )x

73.   Now you can say 'I'm going to Brasília.'

Vou a Brasília   ( )x   ( )x

74.   You can also say 'I'm going to the party.'

Vou à festa   ( )x   ( )x

75.   Later on we will tell you the reason for the accent mark
       (ˆ) over the a. For now just repeat.

Vou à festa   ( )x   ( )x

76.   You can phrase questions such as the following.

O senhor vai a Nova Iorque?   ( )x

A senhora vai a Filadélfia?   ( )x

O senhor vai à festa?   ( )x

77.   And you can phrase answers such as the following.

Vou sim   ( )x

Não, não vou   ( )x

Vou, claro   ( )x

78.   The form vai accompanies o senhor and a senhora. It also
       accompanies Ângela, Marcos, filho, filha, etc., i.e. any
       third person item.

a Ângela vai   ( )x

o Marcos vai   ( )x

o Paulo vai   ( )x

4.16

a minha filha vai   ( )x

o professor vai   ( )x

79.   So you can also phrase questions such as these:

A Sandra vai?   ( )x

O Luís vai a Brasília?   ( )x

O amigo da Yara vai?   ( )x

80.   And you can phrase answers like these:

A Yara vai sim   ( )x

Não, o Marcos não vai   ( )x

Exchange # 15

____ Onde o senhor vai?

____ Vou à festa.

                              ____ Where are you going?

                              ____ I'm going to the party.

Exchange # 16

____ Onde o Luís vai?

____ Vai a Nova Iorque.

                              ____ Where is Luís going?

                              ____ He's going to New York.

Exchange # 17

____ Onde a Ângela vai?

____ Vai a Lisboa.

                              ____ Where is Ângela going?

                              ____ She's going to Lisbon.

4.18

Exchange ≠ 18

_____ A senhora vai a Denver?

_____ Não, não vou.

                           _____ Are you going to Denver?

                           _____ No, I'm not.

Exchange ≠ 19

_____ O senhor vai à festa?

_____ Vou sim.

                           _____ Are you going to the party?

                           _____ Yes, I am.

Exchange ≠ 20

_____ O Marcos vai?

_____ Vai sim.

                           _____ Is Marcos going?

                           _____ Yes, he is.

Exchange ≠ 21

____ A senhora vai?

____ Vou sim.

                            ____ Are you going?

                            ____ Yes, I am.

Exchange ≠ 22

____ A professora vai?

____ Não, não vai.

                            ____ Is the teacher going?

                            ____ No, she's not.

Unit 5

1. Listen to this item but do not repeat it yet.

    eu   ( )   ( )

2. Mimic just the first vowel.

    e-   ( )x   ( )x

3. Mimic the second vowel.

    -u   ( )x   ( )x

4. Now mimic the two together.

    eu   ( )x   ( )x

5. The above item is the pronoun 'I.'

    eu   ( )x   ( )x

6. Sometimes <u>eu</u> accompanies the verb form, as 'I' does in English. For example:

    'I am going' = eu vou   ( )x   ( )x

    'I know' = eu conheço   ( )x   ( )x

7. But since the verb form itself tells us who the actor is, the pronoun <u>eu</u> is often not said.

    vou   ( )x   ( )x

    conheço   ( )x   ( )x

8. Do not be concerned about when you should and when you should not say <u>eu</u>. There is really no strict 'right' or 'wrong' about it. There are guidelines, but we will talk about them later when they will be more meaningful to you. In the meantime, just repeat.

    eu   ( )x   ( )x

    eu vou ( )x ( )x

    eu conheço ( )x ( )x

9. Observe this item. First, just listen.

    chegar ( ) ( )

10. Mimic the first syllable. Notice it begins with an <u>sh</u>-type sound.

    che- ( )x ( )x

11. Mimic the second syllable. Notice it ends with the <u>r</u> sound that resembles a strong English <u>h</u>.

    -gar ( )x ( )x

12. Now mimic the word.

    chegar ( )x ( )x

13. The word means 'arrive.'

    chegar ( )x ( )x

14. Now observe this item. Just listen.

    vou chegar ( ) ( )

15. You know that <u>vou</u> means 'I am going.' The combination <u>vou</u> <u>chegar</u> therefore must mean 'I am going to arrive.' Mimic.

    vou chegar ( )x ( )x

16. At times you may want to use the pronoun <u>eu</u> with the above phrase.

    eu vou chegar ( )x ( )x

17. Now notice this combination. Mimic.

    vai chegar ( )x ( )x

18. The form <u>vai</u> is the form of 'going' that we use with <u>Maria</u>, <u>Paulo</u>, <u>o senhor</u>, etc. We may want to include an actor with this combination so we know who we are talking about. We can say, for example, 'Sandra is going to arrive.'

    A Sandra vai chegar   ( )x   ( )x

19. We can say 'The teacher is going to arrive.'

    O professor vai chegar   ( )x   ( )x

20. We can say 'My son is going to arrive.'

    O meu filho vai chegar   ( )x   ( )x

21. We can also say 'You are going to arrive.'

    O senhor vai chegar   ( )x   ( )x

    A senhora vai chegar   ( )x   ( )x

22. Now observe this word. Do not repeat yet.

    ficar   ( )   ( )

23. The above word means 'stay.' Now repeat.

    ficar   ( )x   ( )x

24. Notice the <u>h</u>-type quality to the <u>r</u> at the end of the word.

    ficar   ( )x   ( )x

25. Now observe this combination.

    vai ficar   ( )x   ( )x

26. That combination means 'going to stay.'

    vai ficar   ( )x   ( )x

27. We need to provide an actor so that we know who is going to stay. We can start with 'Paulo.' Here is 'Paulo is going to stay.'

    O Paulo vai ficar   ( )x   ( )x

5.3

28. We can say 'Maria is going to stay.'

   A Maria vai ficar   ( )x   ( )x

29. We can say 'the teacher is going to stay.'

   O professor vai ficar   ( )x   ( )x

30. We can ask questions, too. We can ask 'Are you going to stay?'

   A senhora vai ficar?   ( )x   ( )x

31. Now mimic this combination.

   vou ficar   ( )x   ( )x

32. The above combination means 'I am going to stay.' It can also be said with the pronoun eu.

   eu vou ficar   ( )x   ( )x

Observation:

   Both ficar and chegar are examples of Portuguese verbs in the infinitive form, the form that generally corresponds to English 'to + verb.' We will also call this form the 'neutral form.' It is 'neutral' in that it does not change its shape to correspond to person(s) doing the acting. By way of contrast, forms like conheço/conhece, and vou/vai show different shapes as the actors change. In this sense they are not neutral forms.

33. Here is the infinitive or neutral form of the verb 'study.'

   estudar   ( )x   ( )x

5.4

34.   Now you can practice these combinations where you say
        that somebody is going to study.

                        A Maria vai estudar   ( )x
                        A Sandra vai estudar   ( )x
                          Quem vai estudar?   ( )x
                        O senhor vai estudar?   ( )x
                  Onde o senhor vai estudar?   ( )x
                          (eu) vou estudar   ( )x

35.   Here is another infinitive or neutral form: 'dance.' You
        practiced it earlier when you were mimicking nasal vowels.

                  dançar   ( )x   ( )x

36.   Now practice these combinations.

                  A senhora vai dançar?   ( )x
                  A Sandra vai dançar?   ( )x
                    O Luís vai dançar?   ( )x
                    (eu) vou dançar   ( )x

Exchange # 1

____ O senhor vai ficar?

____ Vou sim.

              ____ Are you going to stay?

              ____ Yes, I am.

Exchange # 2

____ Quem vai ficar?

____ A Yara vai ficar.

              ____ Who is going to stay?

              ____ Yara is going to stay.

Exchange # 3

____ Quem vai estudar?

____ O Luís vai estudar.

              ____ Who is going to study?

              ____ Luís is going to study.

Exchange ≠ 4

_____ O senhor vai estudar?

_____ Não, não vou.

> _____ Are you going to study?
>
> _____ No, I'm not.

Exchange ≠ 5

_____ Quem vai chegar?

_____ A Ângela vai chegar.

> _____ Who is going to arrive?
>
> _____ Angela is going to arrive.

Exchange ≠ 6

_____ A senhora vai dançar?

_____ Vou sim.

> _____ Are you going to dance?
>
> _____ Yes, I am.

End of Tape 1B

5.7

37. Many neutral forms end in -ar, as do chegar and ficar.
     Others end in -er or -ir, and a very few end in -or. Here
     is the neutral form meaning 'know' or 'meet.' It is an
     example of a neutral form that ends in -er.

              conhecer   ( )x   ( )x

38. You already know the forms that correspond to 'I know' and
     'you know.'

              conheço   ( )x   ( )x
              conhece   ( )x   ( )x

39. Here is the neutral form again.

              conhecer   ( )x   ( )x

40. Practice these combinations.

                   O Paulo vai conhecer   ( )x
              a professora vai conhecer   ( )x
                   a Maria vai conhecer   ( )x
                   o senhor vai conhecer   ( )x
                      (eu) vou conhecer   ( )x

41. Here is an example of a neutral form that ends in -ir:
     the verb 'leave.' First, just listen.

              sair   ( )   ( )

42. Now mimic by syllables.

                   sa-   ( )x   ( )x
                   -ir   ( )x   ( )x
                   sair   ( )x   ( )x

                        5.8

43. Practice these combinations. They say that someone is
going to leave, or they ask if someone is going to leave.

    O senhor vai sair?   ( )x

    A Ângela vai sair?   ( )x

      Quem vai sair?   ( )x

      (Eu) vou sair   ( )x

    O Marcos vai sair   ( )x

44. Here is another common name that will be useful. First,
just listen.

    José ( )   ( )

45. Mimic the first syllable. Notice that the first sound is
like the s of English 'pleasure' and 'leisure.'

    Jo- ( )x ( )x

46. Mimic the second syllable. Notice that it begins with a
z sound. Notice also that the vowel is similar to the e
of 'bed.'

    -sé ( )x ( )x

47. Now mimic both syllables together.

    José ( )x ( )x

48. Practice these phrases.

    O José conhece ( )x

      O José vai ( )x

    O José vai sair ( )x

  O José vai chegar ( )x

  O José vai estudar ( )x

49.   Here is another name. First, just listen.

        Raquel   ( )   ( )

50.   Mimic the first syllable. The r is similar to a strong
English h sound.

        Ra-   ( )x   ( )x

51.   Mimic the second syllable. The l for many Portuguese
speakers sounds much like a w sound.

        -quel   ( )x   ( )x

52.   Now mimic both syllables together

        Raquel   ( )x   ( )x

53.   Practice these phrases.

        a Raquel conhece   ( )x

           a Raquel vai   ( )x

    a Raquel vai conhecer   ( )x

     a Raquel vai dançar   ( )x

      a Raquel vai sair   ( )x

54.   Here is another name that starts with the same r sound.
First, just listen.

        Roberto   ( )   ( )

55.   Now mimic the name by syllables.

          Ro-   ( )x   ( )x

        -ber-   ( )x   ( )x

         -to   ( )x   ( )x

   Together: Roberto   ( )x ( )x

56.   Practice these phrases.

        o Roberto conhece   ( )x

              o Roberto vai   ( )x

        o Roberto vai sair   ( )x

     o Roberto vai estudar   ( )x

     o Roberto vai chegar   ( )x

57.   Here is another name. First just listen.

                    Inês   ( )   ( )

58.   Mimic the first syllable.

                    I-   ( )x   ( )x

59.   Mimic the second syllable.

                    -nês   ( )x   ( )x

60.   Mimic the two syllables together. Notice that it is the
        second syllable which is stressed stronger than the first.

                    Inês   ( )x   ( )x

61.   Practice these phrases.

              a Inês conhece   ( )x

                    a Inês vai   ( )x

        a Inês vai conhecer   ( )x

        a Inês vai chegar   ( )x

        a Inês vai dançar   ( )x

62.   Here is another name. Just listen.

                    Lúcia   ( )   ( )

63.   Mimic the first syllable.

                    Lú-   ( )x   ( )x

64.　　Mimic the second syllable.　It begins with an s̲ sound.

　　　　　　-cia　　(　)x　　(　)x

65.　　Mimic the two syllables together.　Notice that the first
　　　　syllable has a stronger stress than the second.

　　　　　　Lúcia　　(　)x　　(　)x

66.　　Practice these phrases.

　　　　　　　a Lúcia conhece　　(　)x

　　　　　　　　a Lúcia vai　　(　)x

　　　　　a Lúcia vai chegar　　(　)x

　　　　a Lúcia vai estudar　　(　)x

　　　　　　a Lúcia vai sair　　(　)x

67.　　Practice saying these phrases containing the word não
　　　　meaning 'not.'

　　　　　　a Lúcia não conhece　　(　)x

　　　　　　　a Lúcia não vai　　(　)x

　　　　　a Lúcia não vai ficar　　(　)x

　　　　　o José não conhece　　(　)x

　　　　　　o José não vai　　(　)x

　　　　o José não vai estudar　　(　)x

68.　　Notice that não precedes verbs and combinations of verbs.

　　　　　　　a Inês não vai　　(　)x

　　　　　a Inês não vai dançar　　(　)x

　　　a Raquel não está na festa　　(　)x

　　a Raquel não está em Nova Iorque　　(　)x

                a Ângela não é casada   ( )x

            a Ângela não é professora   ( )x

                        eu não vou   ( )x

        eu não vou a Nova Iorque   ( )x

69.   Here is the word for 'but.'

                    mas   ( )x   ( )x

70.   Now you can make contrastive statements, such as 'Yara is

    not going, but I am (going).'

        A Yara não vai, mas eu vou   ( )x   ( )x

71.   Or 'Marcos is married, but Luís is not.'

        O Marcos é casado, mas o Luís não é   ( )x   ( )x

Exchange ≠ 7

____ O senhor vai?

____ Não, não vou. Mas a Raquel vai.

                                ____ Are you going?

                                ____ No, I'm not going. But

                                Raquel is.

Exchange ≠ 8

____ A Inês está em casa?

____ Não, não está. Mas a Lúcia está.

                                ____ Is Inês at home?

                                ____ No, she's not. But Lúcia is.

Exchange ≠ 9

____ O José é professor?

____ Não, não é. Mas o Paulo é.

                                ____ Is José a teacher?

                                ____ No, he's not. But Paulo is.

5.14

Exchange ≠ 10

____ A senhora conhece a Yara?

____ Não, não conheço.   Mas a Raquel conhece.

                           ____ Do you know Yara?

                           ____ No, I don't know her. But
                                     Raquel does.

Exchange ≠ 11

____ O Luís vai ficar?

____ Não, não vai.   Mas a Lúcia vai.

                           ____ Is Luís going to stay?

                           ____ No, he's not. But Lúcia is.

72.   Observe this item. Do not repeat yet.

        pretende   ( )   ( )

73.   The above item is a verb form meaning 'plan(s) to.' Mimic
        the first syllable. Notice the flapped r after the p.

            pre-   ( )x   ( )x

74.   Mimic the second syllable. You will hear a nasal vowel,
        but no n sound.

            -ten-   ( )x   ( )x

75.   Mimic the third syllable. Notice the j sound of 'jeep.'

            -de   ( )x   ( )x

76.   Now mimic the three syllables together. The form means
        'plan(s) to.'

        pretende   ( )x   ( )x

77.   It is the form used with Marcos, Ângela, o senhor, etc.
        Therefore, you can now express the thought 'Marcos plans
        to....'

            O Marcos pretende... ( )x   ( )x

78.   And you can say 'Ângela plans to....'

            A Ângela pretende... ( )x   ( )x

79.   And of course you can substitute other names and persons.

            A Lúcia pretende...   ( )x

        A professora pretende... ( )x

            O rapaz pretende...   ( )x

            A Raquel pretende... ( )x

80. You can use the form <u>pretende</u> with 'you' to say 'you plan to....'

    O senhor pretende...　( )x

    A senhora pretende...　( )x

81. To complete the thought we need an infinitive, a neutral form. For example, you might want to say 'José plans to leave.'

    O José pretende sair　( )x　( )x

82. Or you might want to say 'Ângela plans to study.'

    A Ângela pretende estudar　( )x　( )x

83. You might want to ask 'Do you plan to stay?'

    O senhor pretende ficar?　( )x　( )x

84. Or 'Do you plan to dance?'

    A senhora pretende dançar?　( )x　( )x

85. Now observe this item. Do not repeat yet.

    pretendo　( )　( )

86. This item is the verb form meaning 'I plan to.' Mimic the first syllable.

    pre-　( )x　( )x

87. And the second.

    -ten-　( )x　( )x

88. And the third.

    -do　( )x　( )x

89. The three syllables together mean 'I plan to.'

    pretendo　( )x　( )x

90.   At times you will use it with the pronoun <u>eu</u>.

      eu pretendo   ( )x   ( )x

91.   With this form you can say 'I plan to stay.'

      (eu) pretendo ficar   ( )x   ( )x

92.   You can say 'I plan to leave.'

      (eu) pretendo sair   ( )x   ( )x

93.   You can say 'I plan to study.'

      (eu) pretendo estudar   ( )x   ( )x

94.   And you can say 'I plan to dance.'

      (eu) pretendo dançar   ( )x   ( )x

Exchange ≠ 12

____ O senhor pretende ficar?

____ Não, não pretendo. Eu vou sair.

        ____ Do you plan to stay?

        ____ No, I don't. I'm going to leave.

Exchange ≠ 13

____ O Luís pretende sair?

____ Pretende.

        ____ Does Luís plan to leave?

        ____ He does.

Exchange ≠ 14

____ A Raquel pretende sair?
____ Não, não pretende.

                                  ____ Does Raquel plan to leave?
                                  ____ No, she doesn't.

Exchange ≠ 15

____ A senhora pretende estudar?
____ Pretendo, sim.

                                  ____ Do you plan to study?
                                  ____ Yes, I do.

95.   Here is the question-word 'When?' Do not mimic it yet.

      Quando   ( )   ( )

96.   Now mimic the first syllable. Try to pronounce a nasal

      vowel, and not an n.

      Quan-   ( )x   ( )x

97.   Here is the second syllable.

      -do   ( )x   ( )x

98.   The two syllables together constitute the word 'When?'

      Quando   ( )x   ( )x

99.   In response to the question Quando? you will need the

      word 'today.' Here it is. Just listen.

      hoje   ( )   ( )

100. Mimic the first syllable. An h appears in print, but not

      in speech.

      ho-   ( )x   ( )x

101. The second syllable begins with the s sound of English

      'pleasure' and 'leisure.' Mimic carefully.

      -je   ( )x   ( )x

102. Together the two syllables constitute the word 'today.'

      hoje   ( )x   ( )x

103   You will also need the word 'now.' Here it is. Just listen.

      agora   ( )   ( )

104. Here is the first syllable.

      a-   ( )x   ( )x

105.   And the second. The o is like the a of 'paws.'

        -go-   ( )x   ( )x

106.   The third syllable has the flapped r.

        -ra   ( )x   ( )x

107.   Here they are together, forming the word 'now.'

        agora   ( )x   ( )x

108.   Now you can say 'He's at home now.'

        Está em casa agora   ( )x   ( )x

109.   You can say 'Sandra is going to New York today.'

        A Sandra vai a Nova Iorque hoje   ( )x   ( )x

110.   You already know the word for 'tomorrow.'

        amanhã   ( )x   ( )x

111.   So you can say 'Inês is going to leave tomorrow.'

        A Inês vai sair amanhã ( )x   ( )x

112.   Here is the word for 'early.'

        cedo   ( )x   ( )x

113.   Practice cedo in these phrases.

        O Paulo vai estudar cedo   ( )x

        Eu vou chegar cedo   ( )x

        O senhor pretende sair cedo?   ( )x

        O Santos pretende chegar cedo   ( )x

114.   Here is a more specific time reference: 'at two o'clock.'

        às duas   ( )x   ( )x

115. For example, you might want to say 'I'm going to arrive
     at two o'clock.'

        Eu vou chegar às duas   ( )x ( )x

116. Here is 'at three o'clock.'

        às três   ( )x ( )x

117. Here is 'at four o'clock.'

        às quatro ( )x ( )x

118. Repeat the number 'four' by syllables.

        qua-   ( )x ( )x

        -tro   ( )x ( )x

119. Again, here is 'at four.'

        às quatro ( )x ( )x

120. And here is 'at five.'

        às cinco ( )x ( )x

121. The first syllable of <u>cinco</u> rhymes with the word <u>sim</u>
     'yes.'

        sim   ( )x ( )x

        cin-   ( )x ( )x

        cinco   ( )x ( )x

122. Again, here is 'at five.'

        às cinco ( )x ( )x

123. Finally, here is 'at ten.'

        às dez   ( )x ( )x

124.   Practice these phrases containing time references.

O Paulo vai chegar às duas   ( )x

A Ângela vai chegar às três   ( )x

O Marcos pretende sair às quatro   ( )x

A Inês pretende sair às cinco   ( )x

Eu vou sair às dez   ( )x

Ela vai sair às duas   ( )x

Exchange ≠ 16

_____ Quando o senhor vai a Nova Iorque?

_____ Vou hoje.

> _____ When are you going to New
> York?
>
> _____ I'm going today.

Exchange ≠ 17

_____ Quando o Luís vai chegar?

_____ Vai chegar hoje.

> _____ When is Luís going to arrive?
>
> _____ He's going to arrive today.

Exchange ≠ 18

_____ O Luís vai chegar hoje?

_____ Vai sim. Vai chegar cedo, às duas.

> _____ Is Luís going to arrive today?
>
> _____ Yes, he is. He's going to
> arrive early, at two.

5.25

Exchange ≠ 19

____ A Ângela vai chegar às quatro?

____ Não, não vai. Vai chegar às cinco.

> ____ Is Ângela going to arrive
> at four?
>
> ____ No, she's not. She's going
> to arrive at five.

Exchange ≠ 20

____ Quando a senhora pretende estudar?

____ Eu vou estudar agora.

> ____ When are you planning to
> study?
>
> ____ I'm going to study now.

Exchange ≠ 21

____ Quando o senhor pretende sair?

____ Eu vou sair agora.

> ____ When are you planning to leave?
>
> ____ I'm going to leave now.

5.26

Exchange ≠ 22

____ O senhor vai a Nova Iorque?

____ Vou, sim.

____ Quando?

____ Hoje, às três.

            ____ Are you going to New York?

            ____ Yes, I am.

            ____ When?

            ____ Today at three.

Exchange ≠ 23

____ A senhora pretende estudar?

____ Pretendo.

____ Quando?

____ Agora.

            ____ Do you plan to study?

            ____ I do.

            ____ When?

            ____ Now.

Exchange # 24

_____ O Marcos vai sair?

_____ Vai.

_____ Quando?

_____ Hoje, às quatro ou às cinco.

> _____ Is Marcos going to leave?
>
> _____ Yes, he is.
>
> _____ When?
>
> _____ Today, at four or five.

Exchange # 25

_____ A Raquel pretende sair?

_____ Pretende sim.

_____ Quando?

_____ Hoje cedo, às duas.

> _____ Does Raquel plan to leave?
>
> _____ Yes, she does.
>
> _____ When?
>
> _____ Today, early, at two.

Unit 6

1.   Recall this word from a previous exchange.

Qual   ( )x   ( )x

2.   When qual is said alone, the l, for many speakers, has a
quality almost like a w sound.

Qual   ( )x   ( )x

3.   We pointed out the same feature about the l in the name
Raquel. For many speakers it sounds very much like a w.

Raquel   ( )x   ( )x

4.   This w-like pronunciation of the l is typical when the l
is the last sound uttered in a word or phrase. Another
example is the l in the word Brasil.

Brasil   ( )x   ( )x

5.   You may also have noticed this kind of l in the word
solteiro.

solteiro ( )x   ( )x

6.   In solteiro the l is not at the end of a word, but it is at
the end of a syllable. In that location too it is likely
to be pronounced with a w-like quality.

sol-   ( )x   ( )x
solteiro ( )x   ( )x

7.   Listen for the l in the name Silva.

Silva   ( )x   ( )x

8.   Here too the l is at the end of a syllable and is likely to
resemble a w.

Silva   ( )x   ( )x

6.1

9.   Practice the <u>l</u> in these additional words, whose meanings
      we can omit for now.

mal	falta	talco
sal	calda	alvo
sol	alma	selva
mel	calmo	
tal		
vil		

10.   Also, practice it in these names.

Nilza	Elza	Celso
Vilma	Olga	Wilson
Telma	Ilze	Nelson
Silva	Alma	Gilson

11.   Now observe and repeat this item.

      dona   ( )x   ( )x

12   Do the same with these items.

      dona Nilza   ( )x
      dona Telma   ( )x
      dona Ângela   ( )x
      dona Lúcia   ( )x
      dona Inês   ( )x

13.   The word <u>dona</u> is a title of respect commonly used with
      feminine names.

      A dona Inês está em casa   ( )x
      A dona Nilza vai ficar   ( )x

A dona Ângela não vai sair   ( )x

Como vai, dona Raquel?   ( )x

Tudo bem, dona Lúcia?   ( )x

14.   Now observe this item. Do not repeat yet.

     o senhor Silva   ( )   ( )

15.   You know <u>o senhor</u> with the meaning 'you.' It can also

     serve as a title of repect for men. Its closest English

     equivalent is 'Mister.' Mimic.

     o senhor Silva   ( )x   ( )x

     o senhor Santos   ( )x   ( )x

     o senhor Paulo   ( )x   ( )x

     o senhor José   ( )x   ( )x

16.   Practice these phrases.

     O senhor Silva está em Brasília ( )x

     O senhor Santos é casado ( )x

     O senhor Paulo vai sair ( )x

     O senhor Luís não vai estudar ( )x

17.   Observe this item. Do not mimic yet.

     quero   ( )   ( )

18.   This is the verb form 'I want.' Mimic the first syllable.

     que-   ( )x   ( )x

19.   Mimic the second syllable.

     -ro   ( )x   ( )x

20.   Now say the two syllables together. The <u>r</u> is the flapped
        <u>r</u>.

                quero   ( )x   ( )x

21.   The form means 'I want.' At times you will precede it
        with the pronoun <u>eu</u>.

                eu quero   ( )x   ( )x

22.   Now you can add the infinitive or neutral form <u>sair</u> and
        say 'I want to leave.'

                eu quero sair   ( )x   ( )x

23.   Or you could add the neutral form <u>ficar</u> and say 'I want
        to stay.'

                eu querc ficar   ( )x   ( )x

24.   Practice these additional combinations that say 'I want
        to ....'

                eu quero dançar   ( )x   ( )x

                eu quero conhecer   ( )x   ( )x

                eu quero estudar   ( )x   ( )x

                eu quero chegar   ( )x   ( )x

25.   Practice these combinations that say 'I don't want to....'

                eu não quero ficar   ( )x   ( )x

                eu não quero sair   ( )x   ( )x

            eu não quero estudar   ( )x   ( )x

                eu não quero chegar   ( )x   ( )x

            eu não quero conhecer   ( )x   ( )x

26.   Now observe this form.

             quer   ( )   ( )

27.   Notice the h-type quality of the r. Mimic.

             quer   ( )x   ( )x

28.   This is the verb form for 'want(s),' the form that goes with José, Nilza, o senhor, etc.

         o José quer   ( )x

         a Nilza quer   ( )x

        o senhor quer   ( )x

     o senhor Silva quer   ( )x

      a professora quer   ( )x

      a dona Inês quer   ( )x

29.   Now you can add the neutral form ficar and say 'José wants to stay.'

        o José quer ficar   ( )x   ( )x

30.   And you can add the neutral form dançar and say 'Nilza wants to dance.'

       a Nilza quer dançar   ( )x   ( )x

31.   Practice these combinations that say somebody 'wants to...' or 'doesn't want to....'

      a dona Raquel quer sair ( )x

        o Marcos quer ficar ( )x

       a Ângela quer estudar ( )x

6.5

a Lúcia não quer ficar   ( )x

o senhor Luís não quer sair   ( )x

o Paulo não quer conhecer a professora   ( )x

32.   At this juncture we can supply several additional neutral forms. Here is the form for 'work.' Do not repeat it yet.

       trabalhar   ( )   ( )

33.   Mimic the first syllable.

         tra-   ( )x   ( )x

34.   Mimic the second syllable.

         -ba-   ( )x   ( )x

35.   Mimic the third syllable. It begins with a sound similar to the <u>ll</u> of William.

         -lhar   ( )x   ( )x

36.   Here is the infinitive again.

       trabalhar   ( )x   ( )x

37.   Practice these phrases.

       o Marcos vai trabalhar   ( )x

         o Yara quer trabalhar   ( )x

    o senhor pretende trabalhar?   ( )x

         eu não quero trabalhar   ( )x

         eu não vou trabalhar   ( )x

38.   Here is the neutral form for the verb 'come.'

       vir   ( )x   ( )x

39.   It consists of the sound <u>v</u> followed by the -<u>ir</u> ending.

vir   ( )x   ( )x

40.   Practice these phrases which contain the verb 'come.'

o senhor quer vir? ( )x

a senhora pretende vir? ( )x

o Luís não quer vir hoje ( )x

eu quero vir amanhã ( )x

Exchange ≠ 1

____ A Lúcia quer vir?
____ Não, não quer.

                    ____ Does Lúcia want to come?
                    ____ No, she doesn't.

Exchange ≠ 2

____ A dona Inês quer sair?
____ Quer sim.

                    ____ Does Inês want to leave?
                    ____ Yes, she does.

Exchange ≠ 3

____ O senhor quer trabalhar hoje?
____ Quero sim.

                    ____ Do you want to work today?
                    ____ Yes, I do.

Exchange ≠ 4

_____ O senhor Santos quer sair hoje?

_____ Quer sim. Quer sair agora.

> _____ Does Santos want to leave
> today?
>
> _____ Yes, he does. He wants to
> leave now.

Exchange ≠ 5

_____ Quem quer ficar?

_____ Eu quero ficar.

> _____ Who wants to stay?
>
> _____ I want to stay.

Exchange ≠ 6

_____ Quem quer trabalhar?

_____ A Lúcia quer trabalhar.

> _____ Who wants to work?
>
> _____ Lúcia wants to work.

6.9

Exchange ≠ 7

____ Quem quer conhecer o senhor Silva?

____ Eu quero.

                         ____ Who wants to meet Mr. Silva?

                         ____ I want to.

Exchange ≠ 8

____ O senhor pretende trabalhar hoje?

____ Pretendo.

                         ____ Do you plan to work today?

                         ____ I do.

Exchange ≠ 9

____ O José pretende vir?

____ Pretende.

                         ____ Does José plan to come?

                         ____ He does.

Exchange ≠ 10

____ O Paulo vai trabalhar hoje?

____ Vai, claro.

        ____ Is Paulo going to work today?

        ____ Certainly he's going to.

Exchange ≠ 11

____ A senhora quer trabalhar em casa?

____ Não, não quero.

        ____ Do you want to work at home?

        ____ No, I don't want to.

41.   Observe this item. Do not repeat it yet.

        posso   ( )   ( )

42.   This is the verb form for 'I can.' Mimic the first
      syllable. The vowel is the a of 'paws.' There is no puff
      of air on the p.

        po-   ( )x   ( )x

43.   Mimic the second syllable.

        -sso   ( )x   ( )x

44.   Mimic the two together. The form means 'I can.'

        posso   ( )x   ( )x

45.   There will be times that you will want to use the pronoun
      eu.

        eu posso   ( )x   ( )x

46.   Now you can add the infinitive ficar and say 'I can stay.'

      eu posso ficar   ( )x   ( )x

47.   And you can add the infinitive sair and say 'I can leave.'

      eu posso sair   ( )x   ( )x

48.   Practice these additional combinations in which you say
      that you can or cannot do something.

        eu posso chegar   ( )x

        eu posso estudar   ( )x

    eu não posso dançar   ( )x

    eu não posso ficar   ( )x

49.   Observe this item. Do not repeat it yet.

                pode   ( )   ( )

50.   This is the verb form for 'can' that accompanies José,

        Maria, a senhora, etc. Mimic the first syllable. Notice

        the a of 'paws.'

                po-   ( )x   ( )x

51.   Mimic the second syllable. Notice the j sound of English

        'jeep.'

                -de   ( )x   ( )x

52.   Here is the complete form.

                pode   ( )x   ( )x

53.   Now you can say 'Maria can.'

            a Maria pode   ( )x   ( )x

54.   And 'José can.'

            o José pode   ( )x   ( )x

55.   And 'you can.'

            o senhor pode   ( )x   ( )x

56.   Now add the neutral form estudar to say 'Jose can study.'

            o José pode estudar   ( )x   ( )x

57.   And add the neutral form sair to say 'Maria can leave.'

            a Maria pode sair   ( )x   ( )x

58.   Practice these additional combinations in which you say

        that somebody can or cannot do something.

            a dona Lúcia pode ficar   ( )x

            a dona Lúcia não pode dançar   ( )x

6.13

                    a Inês pode estudar   ( )x
                    a Inês não pode sair   ( )x
          o senhor Silva não pode dançar   ( )x
             o senhor Silva pode ficar   ( )x
                   a Ângela pode chegar   ( )x
             a Ângela não pode estudar   ( )x
               a senhora não pode ficar   ( )x
                   a senhora pode sair   ( )x

                            6.14

Exchange ≠ 12

____ O senhor pode ficar?

____ Posso sim.

               ____ Can you stay?

               ____ Yes, I can.

Exchange ≠ 13

____ A senhora pode estudar?

____ Não, não posso.

               ____ Can you study?

               ____ No, I can't.

Exchange ≠ 14

____ O senhor pode dançar?

____ Não, não posso.

               ____ Can you dance?

               ____ No, I can't.

Exchange ≠ 15

____ Quem pode ficar?

____ Eu posso.

                              ____ Who can stay?

                              ____ I can.

Exchange ≠ 16

____ Quem pode estudar?

____ Eu não posso.

                              ____ Who can study?

                              ____ I can't.

Exchange ≠ 17

____ A Ângela pode sair?

____ Pode, claro.

                    ____ Can Ângela come out?

                    ____ Of course she can.

Exchange ≠ 18

____ Quando ela pode sair?

____ Pode sair agora.

                    ____ When can she come out?

                    ____ She can come out now.

59. You already know the question-words <u>Quem</u>?, <u>Onde</u>?, <u>Quando</u>?, and <u>Como</u>?

   Quem?   ( )x   'Who?'

   Onde?   ( )x   'Where?'

   Quando?   ( )x   'When?'

   Como?   ( )x   'How?'

60. Here is the question-word 'Why?' Just listen.

   Por que?   ( )   ( )

61. It is written as two words. Mimic the first portion.

   por   ( )x   ( )x

62. Mimic the second portion.

   que   ( )x   ( )x

63. Now mimic it in its entirety.

   Por que?   ( )x   ( )x

64. Now you can ask, for example, 'Why are you going?'

   Por que o senhor vai?   ( )x   ( )x

65. Or 'Why are you going to study?'

   Por que o senhor vai estudar?   ( )x   ( )x

66. Or 'Why does Ângela want to study?'

   Por que a Ângela quer estudar?   ( )x   ( )x

67. Practice these additional questions, all asking 'Why?'
   Be sure you know what they mean.

   Por que a Lúcia está em casa?   ( )x

   Por que o Marcos vai a Brasília?   ( )x

6.18

Por que o Paulo quer ficar?   ( )x

Por que a Maria pretende sair?   ( )x

Por que a Inês não quer dançar?   ( )x

Por que o Luís não pode chegar?   ( )x

Por que a senhora está aqui?   ( )x

Por que a senhora não vai hoje?   ( )x

68.   The answer 'because' uses the same words, said with a
       slightly different intonation within the sentence.   The
       words are written as one.

porque   ( )x   ( )x

69.   Now you can answer 'Because I want to,' for example.

porque eu quero   ( )x   ( )x

70.   Or 'because I'm married.'

porque sou casado   ( )x   ( )x

71.   Or 'because Marcos is in New York.'

porque o Marcos está em Nova Iorque   ( )x   ( )x

72.   Practice these additional phrases beginning with 'because.'

porque está chovendo   ( )x

porque o dia está lindo   ( )x

porque a minha filha não quer   ( )x

porque o meu filho não pode   ( )x

porque eu não posso   ( )x

porque a senhora não quer   ( )x

porque a dona Nilza vai sair   ( )x

porque o senhor Santos pretende ficar   ( )x

6.19

Exchange # 19

____ Por que o senhor vai a Filadélfia?

____ Porque não conheço.

> ____ Why are you going to
> Philadelphia?
> ____ Because I don't know it.

Exchange # 20

____ Por que o senhor vai ficar?

____ Porque está chovendo.

> ____ Why are you going to stay?
> ____ Because it's raining.

Exchange # 21

____ Por que a senhora quer sair agora?

____ Porque a tarde está linda.

> ____ Why do you want to go out
> now?
> ____ Because the afternoon is
> beautiful.

6.20

Exchange ǂ 22

____ Por que o senhor vai a Nova Iorque?
____ Porque a Yara vai chegar.

                        ____ Why are you going to New
                              York?
                        ____ Because Yara is going to
                              arrive.

Exchange ǂ 23

____ Por que o Luís vai a São Paulo?
____ Porque vai estudar.

                        ____ Why is Luís going to São
                              Paulo?
                        ____ Because he's going to study.

Exchange ǂ 24

____ Por que a senhora vai à festa?
____ Porque eu quero dançar.

                        ____ Why are you going to the party?
                        ____ Because I want to dance.

6.21

Exchange # 25

____ Por que a Inês quer ficar em casa?

____ Porque quer ficar com a filha.

          ____ Why does Inês want to stay home?

          ____ Because she wants to stay with her daughter.

Exchange # 26

____ Por que a senhora não pode sair?

____ Porque sou casada!

          ____ Why can't you go out?

          ____ Because I'm married!

Exchange # 27

____ Por que o senhor não vai?

____ Porque não quero!

          ____ Why aren't you going?

          ____ Because I don't want to !

73. Here is the preposition 'with.'

   com ( )x ( )x

74. It rhymes with <u>bom</u>. In other words, it has the same nasal vowel.

   bom ( )x ( )x

   com ( )x ( )x

75. Practice these phrases that say 'with somebody.'

    com Santos ( )x

   com o Santos ( )x

    com Marcos ( )x

   com o Marcos ( )x

     com Yara ( )x

    com a Yara ( )x

     com Inês ( )x

    com a Inês ( )x

   com a senhora ( )x

   com o senhor ( )x

  com a minha filha ( )x

   com o meu filho ( )x

76. Notice this special form for 'with me.'

   comigo ( )x ( )x

77. Here is the preposition 'without.'

   sem ( )x ( )x

78.   It rhymes with <u>bem</u>.

                    bem   ( )x   ( )x

                    sem   ( )x   ( )x

79.   Practice these phrases containing 'without.'

                    sem   Marcos   ( )x

                    sem o Marcos   ( )x

                      sem Yara   ( )x

                    sem a Yara   ( )x

                    sem Paulo   ( )x

                    sem o Paulo   ( )x

                    sem professor   ( )x

                    sem o professor ( )x

                    sem o meu filho ( )x

                    sem a minha filha ( )x

80.   Here are some longer phrases with <u>com</u> and <u>sem</u>.

                    A Inês está com a Ângela   ( )x

                    O Luís está com a Lúcia?   ( )x

                    Quem está com a Raquel?   ( )x

            Quem vai a Brasília com o senhor?   ( )x

         Quem vai ficar em casa com essa moça?   ( )x

                    Quem vai sair comigo?   ( )x

                    O senhor quer estudar comigo?   ( )x

            A senhora quer sair com o Marcos?   ( )x

            O Santos quer vir com o senhor?   ( )x

                    Eu não posso sair sem a Ângela   ( )x

Eu não posso sair sem a minha filha ( )x

Eu não quero ficar aqui sem o Marcos ( )x

Eu não posso ficar aqui sem o Luís ( )x

A Yara não quer dançar sem o José ( )x

O Santos não vai trabalhar sem o Paulo ( )x

A Raquel vai sair sem a Lúcia ( )x

O senhor vai sair sem a Ângela? ( )x

6.25

Exchange ≠ 28

____ A Ângela está com o senhor?

____ Não, ela está com a Sandra.

                 ____ Is Ângela with you?

                 ____ No, she's with Sandra.

Exchange ≠ 29

____ O senhor quer estudar comigo?

____ Não, não quero.

                 ____ Do you want to study with me?

                 ____ No, I don't.

Exchange ≠ 30

____ Quem vai com a Lúcia?

____ A Nilza vai.

                 ____ Who's going with Lúcia?

                 ____ Nilza's going.

Exchange ≠ 31

____ O Luís vai sair sem a Lúcia?

____ Vai sim.

                      ____ Is Luís going to leave

                              without Lúcia?

                      ____ Yes, he is.

Exchange ≠ 32

____ A Inês vai à festa?

____ Não, ela não vai sem o Paulo.

                      ____ Is Inês going to the party?

                      ____ No, she's not going without

                              Paulo.

6.27

Exchange ≠ 33

____ Quem vai trabalhar com o Marcos?
____ Eu vou.

　　　　　　　　____ Who's going to work with
　　　　　　　　Marcos?
　　　　　　　　____ I am.

Exchange ≠ 34

____ O senhor vai trabalhar?
____ Não, eu não posso trabalhar sem ela.

　　　　　　　　____ Are you going to work?
　　　　　　　　____ No, I can't work without her.

End of Tape 2A

6.28

Unit 7

1. Review these verb forms.

                        posso   ( )x
                      pretendo   ( )x
                        quero   ( )x
                       conheço   ( )x

2. The above verb forms all say 'I' do something. We will
    call them 'I-forms.' Repeat them again, this time preceded
    by eu.

                     eu posso   ( )x
                   eu pretendo   ( )x
                     eu quero   ( )x
                    eu conheço   ( )x

3. The unstressed -o ending is typical of I-forms. Listen for
    it in the additional examples below. The examples are
    new to you. You need not memorize their meanings. You will
    probably recognize them, though, because they are related
    to infinitive forms that you have already practiced.

                       chego   ( )x   'I arrive'
                        fico   ( )x   'I stay'
                      estudo   ( )x   'I study'
                    trabalho   ( )x   'I work'
                        saio   ( )x   'I leave'

4. You have had several other I-forms that do not have this
    typical ending and which therefore can be said to be
    irregular.

                        vou   ( )x
                        sou   ( )x

5. Now review these verb forms.

                        pode   ( )x
                    pretende   ( )x
                     conhece   ( )x
                         vai   ( )x
                        está   ( )x
                          é   ( )x

6. You have learned to use the above verb forms with Paulo,
    Ângela, o senhor, o professor, o dia, etc.

                o Paulo pode...   ( )x
            a Ângela pretende...   ( )x
             o senhor conhece...   ( )x
              o professor vai...   ( )x
             o dia está lindo...   ( )x
             o Paulo é casado...   ( )x

7. We could call these forms 'He-forms,' 'You-forms,' 'third
    person singular forms,' etc., etc. We will simplify matters
    and settle on just one designation. Henceforth, we will
    call all such forms 'He-forms.' Practice these he-forms
    again.

                              7.2

a Inês pode...   ( )x

o Paulo não pode...   ( )x

a professora pretende...   ( )x

o professor não pretende...   ( )x

o Marcos está em Washington   ( )x

a Ângela não está aqui   ( )x

o senhor vai?   ( )x

a senhora não vai?   ( )x

8.   He-forms, like I-forms, have typical endings, but these
involve more patterns than we want to get into at this
point. Instead, we want to introduce the concept of the
'We-form,' the form of the verb that says 'we' do something.
For example, here is the form for 'we know.'

conhecemos   ( )x   ( )x

9.   Here is the form for 'we can.'

podemos   ( )x   ( )x

10.   Here is 'we plan.'

pretendemos   ( )x   ( )x

11.   And here is 'we want.'

queremos   ( )x   ( )x

12.   The unstressed -mos ending always signals a we-form. Repeat
again.

conhecemos   ( )x

podemos   ( )x

pretendemos   ( )x

queremos   ( )x

7.3

13.   The word for 'we' often precedes these forms. Here is
        the word for 'we.'

                nós   ( )x   ( )x

14.   Practice saying <u>nós</u> together with the we-form.

                nós conhecemos   ( )x

                    nós podemos   ( )x

                nós pretendemos   ( )x

                    nós queremos   ( )x

15.   Now you can say 'We know Yara,' for example.

        Nós conhecemos a Yara   ( )x

16.   And you can say 'We know Lisbon.'

        Nós conhecemos Lisboa   ( )x

17.   You can combine the last three of the above we-forms with
        infinitives. For example, here is 'We want to stay.'

                Nós queremos ficar   ( )x   ( )x

18.   And here is 'We want to leave.'

                Nós queremos sair   ( )x   ( )x

19.   Here is 'We plan to arrive.'

                Nós pretendemos chegar   ( )x   ( )x

20.   And here is 'We plan to work.'

                Nós pretendemos trabalhar   ( )x   ( )x

21.   Here is 'We are able to stay.'

                Nós podemos ficar   ( )x   ( )x

22.   And here is 'We are able to study.'

        Nós podemos estudar   ( )x ( )x

23.   Practice the following combinations. They incorporate the
      negative element não.

          Nós não queremos sair   ( )x

       Nós não pretendemos ficar   ( )x

       Nós não podemos dançar   ( )x

    Nós não podemos trabalhar   ( )x

    Nós não queremos estudar   ( )x

24   Remember how you say 'the day.'

        o dia   ( )x ( )x

25   The word dia is preceded by the definite article o.

        o dia   ( )x ( )x

26.   Now listen to how you say 'a day.' Do not mimic yet.

       um dia   ( )   ( )

27.   The word dia is preceded by the indefinite article, um.
      Again, just listen to 'a day.'

       um dia   ( )   ( )

28.   Listen to the contrast between o and um, i.e., the
      difference between 'the' and 'a.'

        o   ( )   ( )   'the'

       um   ( )   ( )   'a'

29.   The difference is a matter of nasalization. The o is not
      nasalized. The um is nasalized. Mimic the contrast.

        o   ( )x ( )x   'the'

       um   ( )x ( )x   'a'

30.   Indeed, <u>um</u> can be pronounced by nasalizing the <u>o</u> sound.
       Try it.

                    o   ( )x   ( )x   'the'

                   um   ( )x   ( )x   'a'

31.   Now mimic the contrast between 'the day' and 'a day.'

                 o dia   ( )x   ( )x

                um dia   ( )x   ( )x

32.   Mimic the contrast between 'the young man' and 'a young
       man.'

                o rapaz   ( )x   ( )x

               um rapaz   ( )x   ( )x

33.   Here is a new word, the word for 'car.' Just listen.

                 carro   ( )   ( )

34.   The <u>rr</u> represents the <u>r</u> sound which is similar to the
       strong English <u>h</u> sound. Mimic.

                 carro   ( )x   ( )x

35.   Now mimic the contrast between 'the car' and 'a car.'

                o carro   ( )x   ( )x   'the'

               um carro   ( )x   ( )x   'a'

36.   Here is the word for 'phone call.'

               telefonema ( )x   ( )x

37.   Mimic the contrast between 'the phone call' and 'a phone
       call.'

              o telefonema ( )x   ( )x   'the'

             um telefonema ( )x   ( )x   'a'

38. Let us take another look at the so-called flapped r. By
     this time you may feel rather comfortable saying this r
     between vowels.

                   Yara   ( )x
                  quero   ( )x
                  claro   ( )x
                senhora   ( )x
                  Maria   ( )x
             professora   ( )x
               solteiro   ( )x

39. But when the r is the second element of a consonant cluster,
     you may be experiencing a bit more trouble with it. Practice
     saying these isolated syllables, all of which have the
     flapped r clustered with another consonant.

                   bri   ( )x   ( )x
                   bre   ( )x   ( )x
                   pri   ( )x   ( )x
                   pre   ( )x   ( )x
                   dro   ( )x   ( )x
                   dru   ( )x   ( )x
                   tra   ( )x   ( )x
                   tre   ( )x   ( )x
                   gro   ( )x   ( )x
                   gri   ( )x   ( )x
                   cro   ( )x   ( )x

                              7.7

```
              cri    (  )x    (  )x
              fra    (  )x    (  )x
              fre    (  )x    (  )x
```

40.   Now practice the r clusters in these familiar words.

```
      pretendo    (  )x    (  )x
      professor   (  )x    (  )x
      trabalhar   (  )x    (  )x
      obrigado    (  )x    (  )x
```

41.   Here is the tr cluster in a new word.

```
              outra    (  )x    (  )x    'other'
```

42.   Here it is in another new word.

```
              metro    (  )x    (  )x    'meter'
```

43.   Recall the question 'Where is?'

```
      Onde está?    (  )x    (  )x
```

44.   You have used this pattern in asking, for example, 'Where
      is Luís?'

```
      Onde está o Luís?    (  )x    (  )x
```

45.   Portuguese speakers commonly use a variation of this
      pattern to ask 'Where is?' They insert é que between
      Onde and está. Just listen.

```
      Onde é que está?    (  )    (  )
```

46.   The é que portion means 'it is that.' Repeat.

```
              é que    (  )x    (  )x
```

7.8

47. Thus the question <u>Onde é que está</u>? asks 'Where is it that
    is?'

           Onde é que...   ( )x   ( )x

        Onde é que está?   ( )x   ( )x

48. You can use this new formula to ask 'Where is Luís?'

        Onde é que está o Luís?   ( )x   ( )x

49. Or 'Where is Inês?', or anybody else, of course.

        Onde é que está a Inês?   ( )x   ( )x

     Onde é que está a professora?   ( )x   ( )x

50. Compare the two patterns.

        Onde está o professor?   ( )x   ( )x

     Onde é que está o professor?   ( )x   ( )x

           Onde está a Yara?   ( )x   ( )x

        Onde é que está a Yara?   ( )x   ( )x

51. It is time to introduce another way of addressing someone,
    another way of saying 'You.' Thus far you have seen <u>o</u>
    <u>senhor</u> and <u>a</u> <u>senhora</u>. Generally, these are the forms that
    are used when one is talking with persons that one does
    not know too well and with whom one does not feel
    particularly close. This will almost always be the case
    in your initial contacts with a Portuguese speaker. After
    a degree of familiarity or friendship has been established,
    the Portuguese speaker may feel that it is appropriate to
    switch to another form of address. He will suggest that
    both of you begin to use <u>você</u>.

        Você   ( )x   ( )x

52. <u>Você</u> is the form for both sexes.

    Bom dia Paulo. Você vai bem?   ( )x

    Bom dia Yara. Você vai bem?   ( )x

53. Practice these additional phrases with <u>você</u>.

                  Você pode   ( )x

             Você pode sair   ( )x

              Você pretende?   ( )x

       Você pretende ficar?   ( )x

                  Você quer?   ( )x

       Você quer trabalhar?   ( )x

             Você é solteiro   ( )x

          Você é professora   ( )x

This ends the programming section of this unit. You should now go to the dialog, which appears on the next page and which is also recorded on tape. Look over the English translation of the dialog so that you know what you are dealing with. Then go to the tape. The dialog is recorded in two steps, Pronunciation and Fluency. In the Pronunciation step the sentences of the dialog are broken down into smaller units to make it easier for you to mimic and repeat. In the Fluency step the entire sentence is voiced for you to repeat. In recording both steps we have carefully timed the presentation of material, so that you should be able to let the tape run while you are repeating. However,

if you need to stop or listen to something again, do so. Keep
your book open and refer to the English or Portuguese as necessary.
Your goal is to know the sentences well enough so that you can
participate in the dialog with your instructor in the check-out
session.

Dialog

Paulo

fome	hunger
Estou com fome.	I'm hungry.
é que?	is it that?
onde é que está?	where (is it that) is?
a comida	the food
Onde é que está a comida?	Where's the food?

Sandra

na	in the
outra	other

7.11

a sala	the room
em cima	on top
da	of the
a mesa	the table

Na outra sala, em cima da mesa.   In the other room, on the table.

Paulo

vai	go (he-form)
comer	eat (neutral form)

Você não vai comer?   Aren't you going to eat?

Sandra

só	only
tarde	late

Só mais tarde.   Not until later.

agora	now
vou	go (I-form)
dar	give (neutral form)
vou dar	I'm going to give
dar um telefonema	to make a phone call

Agora vou dar um telefonema.   Right now I'm going to make a

                                 phone call.

Paulo

falar	speak, talk (neutral form)
nisso	of that
por falar nisso	speaking of that

Por falar nisso, Maria quer falar com você.

By the way, Maria wants to talk with you.

Sandra

pretendemos	plan (we-form)
visitar	visit (neutral form)
o parque	the park

Ah! Eu e ela pretendemos visitar o parque amanhã.

Oh! She and I plan to visit the park tomorrow.

Paulo

Ah, é?! Eu não conheço o parque.

Oh, really?! I'm not familiar with the park.

Sandra

quiser	wish
se você quiser	if you wish
ir	go (neutral form)
conosco	with us

Se você quiser, você pode ir conosco.

If you wish, you can go with us.

7.13

Supplementary Practice

A. Additional work with I-forms in combination with neutral
    forms.

        Practice repeating the following combinations. Be
sure you know what they mean.

        1. Eu quero vir.

            Eu quero visitar.

            Eu quero ir.

            Eu quero falar.

        2. Eu pretendo dar.

            Eu pretendo comer.

            Eu pretendo visitar.

            Eu pretendo ir.

        3. Eu não posso falar.

            Eu não posso ficar.

            Eu não posso comer.

            Eu não posso ir.

        4. Eu não vou falar.

            Eu não vou dar.

            Eu não vou comer.

            Eu não vou sair.

7.14

5. Eu vou ficar até as três hoje.

    Eu não posso ficar aqui amanhã.

6. Eu quero dar um telefonema.

    Eu quero falar com a Yara.

7. Eu vou trabalhar até as cinco.

    Eu não vou sair às três.

8. Eu não vou sair com o senhor.

    Eu vou sair com o Marcos.

9. Eu pretendo sair cedo.

    Eu quero chegar às cinco.

10. Eu não posso trabalhar hoje.

    Eu vou ficar em casa.

B. Additional work with we-forms in combination with neutral
    forms.

    Practice repeating the following combinations.

    1. Nós queremos visitar.

        Nós queremos sair.

7.15

Nós queremos ir.

Nós queremos trabalhar.

2. Nós não pretendemos ficar.

Nós não pretendemos falar.

Nós não pretendemos vir.

Nós não pretendemos sair.

3. Nós não podemos ficar.

Nós não podemos ir.

Nós não podemos vir.

Nós não podemos dar.

4. Nós não queremos trabalhar hoje.

Nós pretendemos ficar em casa.

5. Nós não pretendemos sair agora.

Nós queremos sair mais tarde.

6. Nós pretendemos visitar o parque.

Nós queremos ir hoje.

7. Nós não podemos vir cedo.

Nós queremos vir às sete.

7.16

C. Additional work with he-forms in combination with neutral forms.

Practice repeating the following combinations.

1. A Inês pode falar.

A Inês pode ir.

A Inês pode visitar.

A Inês pode trabalhar.

2. Você pode vir.

Você pode ficar.

Você pode dar.

Você pode comer.

3. O senhor não quer ficar?

O senhor não quer trabalhar?

O senhor não quer sair?

O senhor não quer ir?

4. O José quer ir.

O José quer vir.

O José quer falar.

O José quer dar.

5. O Marcos pretende ir.

    O Marcos pretende trabalhar.

    O Marcos pretende sair.

    O Marcos pretende ficar.

6. A Nilza pretende ir hoje.

    E a Raquel quer ir amanhã.

7. A Lúcia vai visitar o parque hoje.

    Mas a Ângela vai trabalhar.

8. O Marcos pode sair às três.

    Mas o Luís vai ficar até as quatro.

9. Você pode ir conosco.

    E o Paulo pode ir com a Yara.

10. A Sandra vai trabalhar até as cinco.

    Mas a Inês só vai trabalhar até as duas.

11. O Paulo vai sair às sete.

    Mas o José não quer ficar até tarde.

D. Practice in Asking Questions.

Using the first sentence of each group as a model, how would you express these questions in Portuguese?

I.   1. Do you plan to stay?   (Você pretende ficar?)

2. Do you plan to eat?

3. Do you plan to leave?

4. Do you want to leave?

5. Do you want to come?

6. Do you want to stay?

II. 1. Does Yara want to talk?   (Yara quer falar?)

2. Does Yara want to eat?

3. Does Yara want to stay?

4. Does Yara plan to stay?

5. Does Yara plan to visit?

6. Does Yara want to visit?

III. 1. Can Mr. Silva stay?   (O senhor Silva pode ficar?)

2. Can Mr. Silva leave?

3. Can Mr. Silva speak?

4. Is Mr. Silva able to speak?

5. Is Mr. Silva able to eat?

6. Is Mr. Silva able to leave?

7.19

E.   Practice in Answering Questions.

  Follow along visually as you listen to and <u>repeat</u> these questions and answers on the tape. This will give you additional practice in answering questions <u>affirmatively</u>.

   1. Do you plan to leave?

    Yes, I do.

   2. Do you want to leave?

    Yes, I do.

   3. Do you want to make a phone call?

    Yes, I do.

   4. Do you want to speak with Yara?

    Yes, I do.

   5. Does Yara want to leave?

    Yes, she does.

   6. Does Yara want to stay?

    Yes, she does.

   7. Does Yara plan to leave?

    Yes, she does.

   8. Does José plan to leave?

    Yes, he does.

   9. Does José want to eat?

    Yes, he does.

   10. Does José want to speak?

    Yes, he does.

11. Is José able to speak?

Yes, he is.

12. Is José able to stay?

Yes, he is.

13. Can José stay?

Yes, he can.

F. Practice with só.

Só a Lúcia

Só a Inês

Só o Afonso

Só o Afonso e a Ângela

Só ela

Só nós

Só o José vai

Só a Maria quer

Só nós podemos

Só ele conhece

- - - - - - - -

Só até as três

Só até amanhã

7.21

Só com o senhor

Só com a Sandra

Eu vou ficar só até as quatro

A Yara vai ficar só até amanhã

Eu quero ir só com o senhor

Ele pode dançar só com a Maria

- - - - - - - - - - - - - -

A Ângela só vai estudar

A Sandra só vai dar um telefonema

O Marcos só quer trabalhar

O Luís só quer ficar em casa

- - - - - - - - - - - - - -

só translatable as 'only' or 'not...until.'

só mais tarde

só às cinco

só às quatro

só amanhã

só hoje

- - - - - - -

Eu vou comer só mais tarde

O Paulo vai sair só às duas

A Raquel vai chegar só às três

A Nilza pode sair só amanhã

G. Practice with the special form <u>quiser</u>

Se você quiser, você pode dar um telefonema

Se você quiser, você pode falar com a Inês

Se você quiser, você pode ir com a Yara

Se você quiser, você pode trabalhar amanhã

Se você quiser, você pode estudar aqui

Se você quiser, você pode ficar em casa

- -

Se a Sandra quiser, ela pode sair hoje

Se a Sandra quiser, ela pode ficar até as três

Se a Sandra quiser, ela pode vir com você

Se a Sandra quiser, ela pode chegar amanhã cedo

Se a Sandra quiser, ela pode ir comigo

H. Translation Practice

Practice putting the following questions, answers and commentaries into Portuguese.

1. A. Are you planning to leave tomorrow?

    B. Yes, I am. At ten o'clock.

2. A. Are you planning to stay here?

    B. Yes, I am. But only until five o'clock.

3. A. Are you planning to stay until tomorrow?

    B. Yes, I am.

4. A. Are you planning to eat now?

    B. Yes, I am. I'm hungry.

5. A. I'm planning to eat at five.

    B. At five?

    A. Certainly! I'm hungry.

6. A. I plan to visit the park.

    B. When? Today?

    A. No. Tomorrrow.

7.24

7. A. Yara and I plan to leave early today.

     B. Why?

     A. Because the party is tomorrow.

8. A. Yara and I want to leave early tomorrow.

     B. Why?

     A. Because the party is tomorrow.

9. A. If you want, you can visit the park today.

     B. Can I?

     A. Of course. You can leave early.

10. A. If you want, you can make a phone call now.

      B. Thanks. I want to talk with Yara.

11. A. If you want, you can stay until later.

      B. No, thanks. I want to leave now.

12. A. If you want, you can stay here with me.

      B. Can I? Thanks. Can I make a phone call?

13. A. I'm hungry. I want to eat.

      B. The food is on the table.

14. A. Mary is hungry. She wants to eat now.

    B. The food is in the other room.

15. A. Aren't you going to eat?

    B. Later. Right now I want to talk with Paulo.

16. A. Aren't you going to speak with Yara?

    B. Later. Right now I want to eat.

17. A. Aren't you going to stay?

    B. Of course. I'm hungry.

18. A. Aren't you going to make a phone call?

    B. Of course. I want to talk with Joe.

19. A. The food is in the other room.

    B. Where is Joe?

    A. In the other room, with the food.

20. A. Where is Yara?

    B. In the other room, with Joe.

21. A. Do you want to leave now?

    B. Yes, I do.

22. A. Do you want to eat now?

    B. Yes, I do. I'm hungry.

23. A. Do you want to make a phone call?

    B. Yes, I do. Where's the phone?

       (phone = o telefone)

    A. It's in the other room.

24. A. Do you want to talk with Yara?

    B. Yes, I do. Where is she?

    A. She's in the other room.

25. A. Do you want to go out (leave) with that girl?

    B. Yes, I do. What's her name?

    A. Her name is Maria.

26. A. I want to go out with that girl.

    B. She's married.

    A. Oh, really?! (Ah, é?!)

27. A. I'm hungry.

    B. The food is on the table.

    A. Oh, is that right?! (Ah, é?!)

7.27

28. A. By the way, can I go with you?

    B. Yes you can.

29. A. By the way, you can go with us.

    B. Thanks, but I'm going to stay here.

30. A. Aren't you going to stay?

    B. No, I can't.

Unit 8

Programming

1. Listen to this new word.

    tráfego   ( )   ( )

2. Listen again. Its stressed syllable is the first one.

    tráfego   ( )   ( )

3. Now mimic the first syllable of the word, i.e., the stressed
    syllable.

    trá-   ( )x   ( )x

4. Now mimic the whole word.

    tráfego   ( )x   ( )x

5. Here is another word. It is stressed on the first of two
    syllables.

    vamos   ( )   ( )

6. If the word is stressed on the last syllable it sounds like
    an English slang word meaning 'scram.'

            ( )   ( )

7. But stressed on the first syllable it is standard Portuguese,
    and it means 'we are going.' Mimic.

    vamos   ( )x   ( )x   ( )x

Comment

    In the next few frames we are going to talk about 'diphthongs.'
The word 'diphthong' literally means 'two tones.' As applied to

Portuguese, however, the word is best interpreted as meaning 'two
vowel sounds.'

   The label 'diphthong' has been traditionally given to the
combination of sounds that results when a <u>stressed</u> vowel sound
and an <u>unstressed</u> <u>i</u> or <u>u</u> come together, in that order, in the same
sentence.

8.   Here are the diphthongs you have had thus far.

   (1)   Stressed <u>a</u> + unstressed <u>i</u> (as in <u>mais</u>, <u>vai</u>)
         Repeat: ai   ( )x   ( )x

   (2)   Stressed <u>a</u> + unstressed <u>u</u> (as in <u>Paulo</u>)
         Repeat: au   ( )x   ( )x

   (3)   Stressed <u>e</u> + unstressed <u>i</u> (as in <u>solteiro</u>)
         Repeat: ei   ( )x   ( )x

   (4)   Stressed <u>e</u> + unstressed <u>u</u> (as in <u>eu</u>)
         Repeat: eu   ( )x   ( )x

   (5)   Stressed <u>o</u> + unstressed <u>u</u> (as in <u>estou</u>, <u>outra</u>)
         Repeat: ou   ( )x   ( )x

   (6)   Stressed <u>o</u> + unstressed <u>i</u> (as in <u>noite</u>)
         Repeat: oi   ( )x   ( )x

9.   Now, repeat these items. Listen for the unstressed <u>u</u> sound.

             <u>Paulo</u>   ( )x   ( )x

               <u>eu</u>   ( )x   ( )x

             <u>estou</u>   ( )x   ( )x

             <u>outra</u>   ( )x   ( )x

8.2

10. Now try these. Listen for the unstressed i sound.

<u>mais</u>   ( )x   ( )x

<u>vai</u>   ( )x   ( )x

<u>solteiro</u> ( )x   ( )x

<u>noite</u>   ( )x   ( )x

11. Here is a diphthong that appears in the dialog of this unit.

Stressed <u>o</u> + unstressed <u>i</u>

Repeat: <u>oi</u>   ( )x   ( )x

12. Here is the word it appears in.

<u>oito</u>   ( )x   ( )x   ( )x

13. Some diphthongs can be nasalized.

(1) The combination of stressed <u>e</u> + unstressed <u>i</u> is nasalized in the word <u>bem</u>. The spelling of the word tends to obscure this fact.

Repeat: <u>bem</u>   ( )x   ( )x

(2) The combination of the sound we have freely symbolized as stressed <u>uh</u>, plus the unstressed <u>u</u>, is nasalized in the word <u>não</u>. Again, the spelling tends to obscure this fact.

Repeat: <u>não</u>   ( )x   ( )x

8.3

14. In the dialog for this unit there is a word which has the
     same nasal diphthong as the one you hear in the word não.
     Here is the word.

                    vão   ( )x   ( )x

15. Repeat não and vão one after the other. They rhyme.

               1. não   ( )x   ( )x
               2. vão   ( )x   ( )x

16. You will find this nasal diphthong in stressed syllables.

               salão   ( )x   ( )x
              portão   ( )x   ( )x
             grandão   ( )x   ( )x

17. And you will find it in unstressed syllables (where,
     incidentally, it is written differently).

              chegam   ( )x   ( )x
             estudam   ( )x   ( )x
               ficam   ( )x   ( )x

18. Here is a three syllable word. It is a new form of a
     familiar verb. Just listen.

            pretendem   ( )   ( )

19. The last syllable of this verb form has the same nasal
     diphthong as the word bem, but the syllable is not stressed.
     Here is the syllable in isolation.

                    -em   ( )x   ( )x   ( )x

8.4

20.   Here is the whole form again. Repeat, being sure not to
stress the -em at the end of it.

        pretendem   ( )x   ( )x

21.   Here are several more verb forms that end with the same
unstressed nasal diphthong.

          comem   ( )x   ( )x

          querem   ( )x   ( )x

       conhecem   ( )x   ( )x

          podem   ( )x   ( )x

22.   Let us leave diphthongs and return to a familiar vowel
sound. Repeat these words; then go on to the
Observation immediately following.

      a. festa   ( )x   ( )x

      b. até   ( )x   ( )x

      c. ela   ( )x   ( )x

      d. é   ( )x   ( )x

      e. José   ( )x   ( )x

Observation

You recall that the words in frame 22 all have the 'e' of
English bed. In order to simplify discussion of this
vowel sound, we will use the standard traditional
terminology and call it the 'open E sound.'* Similarly, we
will refer to the 'e' of você as the 'closed e.' The terms

8.5

'open' and 'closed' have to do with tongue position. In producing
the open E the tongue is lower in the mouth, with the result that
there is more of an 'opening' between the tongue and the roof of
the mouth. In producing the closed e, the tongue is higher in the
mouth; i.e., the space between the tongue and the roof of the
mouth is more 'closed.' Whether or not you are conscious of
actually feeling this variation in tongue position is not so
important. What matters is that you are able to hear and mimic the
two sounds. With the practice you have had thus far the chances
are good that you can already do so with considerable accuracy.
Still, the terms 'open' and 'closed' are convenient ones, and for
many they are useful in their descriptiveness, so we shall use
them henceforth.

23.   Here is a new word containing the open E sound, the word
        for 'seven.'
                sete   ( )x   ( )x   ( )x
24.   The word may also be pronounced another way, with a ch
        sound preceding the final i sound.
                sete   ( )x   ( )x   ( )x

*The capital E will regularly be used in this text to symbolize
 this sound.

25.   Either way is correct. The <u>t</u> sound and the <u>ch</u> sound alternate with each other before an <u>i</u> sound, the choice depending on the dialect of the native speaker.

          a.   ( )   ( )x   ( )x

          b.   ( )   ( )x   ( )x

26.   Recall that the pronoun 'she' has the open <u>E</u>.

          ela   ( )x   ( )x

27.   Listen to how 'she' contrasts with 'he.'

        (ela)x   (ele)x   (ela)x   (ele)x

28.   The final vowels of the two words are different, and so are the initial vowels. The initial vowel of 'she' is the <u>open</u> <u>E</u>; the initial vowel of 'he' is the <u>closed</u> <u>e</u>.

        (ela)x   (ele)x   (ela)x   (ele)x

29.   If we pluralize <u>ela</u> and <u>ele</u>, we have <u>elas</u> and <u>eles</u>, which are the words for 'they.' There is an open <u>E</u> in <u>elas</u>, and a closed <u>e</u> in <u>eles</u>.

          elas   ( )x ( )x

          eles   ( )x ( )x

30.   The word <u>elas</u> refers to a group of females, the word <u>eles</u> to a group of males.

             Ângela e Lúcia: elas   ( )x   ( )x

             Marcos e Luís: eles   ( )x   ( )x

<u>End of Tape 2B</u>

8.7

Tape 3A

Dialog

(Sandra has told Paulo that she and Maria are planning to visit the park tomorrow).

Sandra

vamos	go (we-form)
nós vamos sair	we're going to leave
às sete	at seven
a manhã	the morning
às sete da manhã	at seven in the morning
Nós vamos sair às sete da manhã.	We're going to leave at seven in the morning.

Paulo

vocês	you (plural)
pretendem	plan (they-form)
chegar	arrive (neutral form)
vocês pretendem chegar	you plan to arrive
lá	there
bem cedo	real early
Vocês pretendem chegar lá bem cedo?	Do you plan to get there real early?

8.8

Sandra

isso	that
mesmo	exactly
Isso mesmo.	That's right.
oito	eight
meia	half
Às oito e meia, mais ou menos.	At eight thirty, more or less.

Paulo

vão	go (they-form)
evitar	avoid (neutral form)
vão evitar	you're going to avoid
o tráfego	the traffic
todo	all
todo o tráfego	all the traffic
Vocês vão evitar todo o tráfego.	You're going to avoid all the traffic.

Sandra

Vamos...	We're going to... (Right!)
levantar	get up (neutral form)
quer levantar	you want to get up
você não quer levantar?	don't you want to get up?
também	also, too
Você não quer levantar cedo também?	Don't you want to get up early too?

8.9

A LOOK AT THE GRAMMAR

Practice Exercises

Part I: The 'they-form'

There is one more shape of the verb that you must become familiar with. We call it the 'they-form'. It is the shape the verb takes when 'they' or 'you-plural' is the actor. The they-form would be used in the Portuguese equivalents of the following sentences:

They have five minutes left.

They don't know where to go from here.

The twins are sick.

You two are going with us.

The mechanics refuse to work.

All four cars ran off the road.

Opposites attract.

Did you (plural) work hard over the weekend?

Practice 1: (Recorded)

Here is a group of ten they-forms. Listen to them while paying particular attention to their endings.

Practice 2: (Recorded)

Now listen to the difference between the he-form and the they-form of the same verbs.

He-form	They-form		He-form	They-form
1. ( )	( )	6. ( )	( )
2. ( )	( )	7. ( )	( )
3. ( )	( )	8. ( )	( )
4. ( )	( )	9. ( )	( )
5. ( )	( )	10. ( )	( )

The above they-forms all end with the same unstressed nasal diphthong -em.

Practice 3:   (Recorded)

Which of the following are he-forms and which are they-forms?
Mark an x in the appropriate column. Answers are on last page.

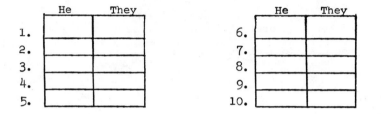

	He	They
1.		
2.		
3.		
4.		
5.		

	He	They
6.		
7.		
8.		
9.		
10.		

Practice 4:   (Recorded)

Now practice saying several they-forms.

1. ( ) ( )x ( )x   6. ( ) ( )x ( )x
2. ( ) ( )x ( )x   7. ( ) ( )x ( )x
3. ( ) ( )x ( )x   8. ( ) ( )x ( )x
4. ( ) ( )x ( )x   9. ( ) ( )x ( )x
5. ( ) ( )x ( )x   10. ( ) ( )x ( )x

Practice 5:   (Recorded)

a. Practice saying these noun and pronoun actors that might
    accompany they-forms.

    o Paulo e a Yara

    a Inês e a Ângela

    o Marcos e o Luís

    a Nilza e a Raquel

8.11

A Lúcia e você

os professores

as professoras

Vocês

Os senhores (plural of o senhor)

As senhoras (plural of a senhora)

Eles

Elas

b. Now practice saying these noun and pronoun actors followed
   by they-forms.

O Paulo e a Yara querem. (want)

A Inês e a Ângela pretendem. (plan to)

O Marcos e o Luís podem. (can)

A Nilza e a Raquel vão. (are going)

O Paulo e a Yara não vão. (are not going)

Vocês vão?

Os senhores querem?

As senhoras não podem?

Eles pretendem?

Elas querem?

Os professores vão?

As professoras não querem?

8.12

Practice 6:   (Recorded)

Practice saying the following combinations of they-form
plus infinitive until you can say them easily.

A. 1. They (masc.) want to eat.   ( ) ( )x ( )x

    2. They (masc.) want to leave.   ( ) ( )x ( )x

    3. They (masc.) want to get up.   ( ) ( )x ( )x

    4. They (masc.) want to avoid the   ( ) ( )x ( )x
        traffic.

B. 1. They (fem.) plan to eat.   ( ) ( )x ( )x

    2. They (fem.) plan to leave.   ( ) ( )x ( )x

    3. They (fem.) plan to arrive.   ( ) ( )x ( )x

    4. They (fem.) plan to avoid the   ( ) ( )x ( )x
        traffic.

C. 1. Are you (pl.) planning to stay?   ( ) ( )x ( )x

    2. Are you (pl.) planning to leave?   ( ) ( )x ( )x

    3. Are you (pl.) planning to get up?   ( ) ( )x ( )x

    4. Are you (pl.) planning to speak?   ( ) ( )x ( )x

D. 1. You (pl.) can come.   ( ) ( )x ( )x

    2. You (pl.) can get up.   ( ) ( )x ( )x

    3. You (pl.) can leave.   ( ) ( )x ( )x

    4. You (pl.) can eat.   ( ) ( )x ( )x

E. 1. Paulo and Yara are planning to   ( ) ( )x ( )x
        leave early.

    2. Paulo and Roberto are planning to ( ) ( )x ( )x
        arrive early.

    3. Paulo and Roberto are planning to ( ) ( )x ( )x
        come early.

    4. Yara and Maria are planning to get ( ) ( )x ( )x
        up early.

Practice 7: (Recorded)

     How would you say the following in Portuguese? Check the
tape for confirmation after you have made your response aloud.

     1. Are you (plural) planning to stay?

     2. Are you (plural) planning to leave?

     3. Do you (plural) want to avoid the traffic?

     4. Do you (plural) want to get up early?

     5. They (masc.) want to stay.

     6. They (masc.) want to eat.

     7. They (fem.) want to visit the park also.

     8. Paulo and Yara want to visit Washington too.

     9. Yara and Maria can get up early.

    10. Yara and Maria can arrive early.

    11. Yara and Santos want to make a phone call.

    12. Yara and Santos can avoid the traffic.

Part II. 'Going to' in Portuguese

In this section we expand upon another combination of verb
plus neutral form. It is the equivalent of English 'going to'
plus verb. ('He's going to retire.', 'She's going to faint.',
etc.) In both English and Portuguese this construction is
commonly used to talk about the future. Traditionally it is not
labelled the future tense in either language, but it might well
be called the 'substitute future' in both.

Here are several Portuguese examples you have had.

    1. Nós vamos sair às sete.

       (We are going to leave at seven.)

    2. Vocês vão evitar todo o tráfego.

       (You are going to avoid all the traffic.)

    3. Você não vai comer?

       (Aren't you going to eat?)

    4. Agora vou dar um telefonema.

       (I'm going to make a phone call now.)

Practice 8: We-forms and They-forms   (Recorded)

Listen to the following short sentences, then repeat as
indicated. Be sure you know what they mean.

A. 1. We're going to leave.   ( ) ( )x ( )x

    2. We're going to arrive.   ( ) ( )x ( )x

    3. We're going to stay.   ( ) ( )x ( )x

4. We're going to speak.   ( ) ( )x ( )x

B. 1. They're going to avoid the traffic.( ) ( )x ( )x
    2. They're going to visit.   ( ) ( )x ( )x
    3. They're going to get up.   ( ) ( )x ( )x
    4. They're going to arrive.   ( ) ( )x ( )x

C. 1. They (masc.) are going to visit   ( ) ( )x ( )x
        the park.
    2. They (fem.) are going to visit   ( ) ( )x ( )x
        the park.
    3. They (masc.) are going to avoid   ( ) (·)x ( )x
        all the traffic.
    4. They (fem.) are going to avoid   ( ) ( )x ( )x
        all the traffic.

D. 1. Are we going to make a phone call? ( ) ( )x ( )x
    2. Are we going to avoid the traffic? ( ) ( )x ( )x
    3. Are we going to get up late?   ( ) ( )x ( )x
    4. Are we going to stay?   ( ) ( )x ( )x

Practice 9: Comprehension exercises. (Recorded)

All of the following sentences on the tape say either 'We're
going to do something,' or 'They're going to do something.'
Listen to the sentences, determine the meaning of each, and make

8.16

a check in the appropriate column in the chart below. Number 1
is done for you. The answers appear on the last page of this
unit.

	We're going to:				They're going to:			
	get up	leave	arrive	stay	get up	leave	arrive	stay
1.		✔						
2.								
3.								
4.								
5.								
6.								
7.								
8.								
9.								
10.								
11.								
12.								

Practice 10:   (Recorded)

How would you say these thoughts in Portuguese? Check the
tape for verification after you make your response.

1. We're going to leave.

2. We're going to leave tomorrow.

3. We're going to stay.

4. We're going to stay until ten.

5. They're going to visit the park too.

6. They're going to get up at eight thirty.

7. They're going to eat.

8. They're going to make a phone call.

9. We're going to avoid the traffic.

10. We're going to arrive there quite early.

11. We're going to arrive at seven.

12. They're going to arrive at eight-thirty.

In the preceding exercises you have practiced the we-form
and the they-form. In the next several exercises you will practice
the I-form and the he-form.

Practice 11: (Recorded)

A. First, recall the I-form in these excerpts from an
    earlier dialog. Listen and repeat.

    1. vou   ( )x   ( )x
    2. vou dar   ( )x   ( )x
    3. Vou dar um telefonema.   ( )x   ( )x

B. Now, recall the he-form in these excerpts from an earlier
    dialog. Listen and repeat.

    1. vai   ( )x   ( )x
    2. vai comer   ( )x   ( )x
    3. Você não vai comer?   ( )x   ( )x

Practice 12:   (Recorded)

Listen to the following short sentences, then repeat as
indicated. Be sure that you associate the corresponding English
equivalent with each sentence.

A. 1. I am going to make a phone call.   ( ) ( )x ( )x
   2. I am going to leave early.   ( ) ( )x ( )x
   3. I am going to stay.   ( ) ( )x ( )x
   4. I am going to visit the park.   ( ) ( )x ( )x

B. 1. He is going to talk.   ( ) ( )x ( )x
   2. He is going to eat.   ( ) ( )x ( )x
   3. He is going to get up.   ( ) ( )x ( )x
   4. He is going to visit the park.   ( ) ( )x ( )x

C. 1. Yara is going to arrive tomorrow.   ( ) ( )x ( )x
   2. Yara is going to leave tomorrow.   ( ) ( )x ( )x
   3. Yara is going to stay.   ( ) ( )x ( )x
   4. Yara is going to make a phone call. ( ) ( )x ( )x

D. 1. Are you going to leave?   ( ) ( )x ( )x
   2. Are you going to get up?   ( ) ( )x ( )x
   3. Are you going to visit the park?   ( ) ( )x ( )x
   4. Are you going to make a phone call? ( ) ( )x ( )x

E. 1. I am going to talk with Santos.   ( ) ( )x ( )x

   2. I am going to leave with Yara.   ( ) ( )x ( )x

   3. I am going to stay with you.   ( ) ( )x ( )x

   4. I am going to avoid the traffic.   ( ) ( )x ( )x

F. 1. Is Santos going to stay?   ( ) ( )x ( )x

   2. Is Santos going to get up?   ( ) ( )x ( )x

   3. Is Santos going to talk?   ( ) ( )x ( )x

   4. Is Santos going to visit the park? ( ) ( )x ( )x

Practice 13: Comprehension exercise.   (Recorded)

Listen to the following sentences, determine the meaning of
each (either 'I' or 'he' is going to do something), then put a
check mark in the appropriate column below. Verify at the end of
this unit.

	I'm going to:				He's going to:			
	get up	leave	arrive	stay	get up	leave	arrive	stay
1.								
2.								
3.								
4.								
5.								
6.								
7.								
8.								
9.								
10.								
11.								
12.								

Practice 14:   (Recorded)

How would you say the following in Portuguese? Check the tape for verification after you make your response aloud. In this practice the voice on the tape omits the pronoun for 'I' but not for 'he' and 'you.'

1. I'm going to leave.

2. I'm going to leave now.

3. He's going to stay.

4. He's going to stay until 10.

5. He's going to arrive late.

6. I'm going to arrive early.

7. I'm going to make a phone call.

8. Paulo is going to avoid the traffic.

9. I'm going to speak with Yara, too.

10. Yara is going to speak with me.

11. You are going to speak with Paulo.

12. Are you going to speak with Paulo?

13. Maria is going to leave at 8:30 in the morning.

14. Maria is going to leave with Roberto.

15. Is Maria going to get up early?

Part III.   'Not' in Portuguese

The Portuguese word for 'not' (não) always comes immediately before verbs and verb combinations. Thus:

1. É casada.   (She's married)

   Não é casada.   (She's not married)

2. Posso.   (I can)

   Não posso.   (I can not)

3. Eu pretendo ir.   (I plan to go)

   Eu não pretendo ir.   (I do not plan to go)

Practice 15:   (Recorded)

Listen to these groups of sentences. In each case an affirmative utterance is followed by a negative one.

Practice 16:   (Recorded)

In this exercise you are to make the sentences negative. Listen first to the sentence in the affirmative, then during the silence on the tape, convert it orally to the negative by inserting 'não' in front of the verb. You will then hear your response confirmed.

1. _____   7. _____

2. _____   8. _____

3. _____   9. _____

4. _____   10. _____

5. _____   11. _____

6. _____   12. _____

Practice 17: (Recorded)

How would you say these short sentences in Portuguese? You should be able to do these rapidly. In this practice you should use the Portuguese pronouns. Check the tapes for confirmation.

1. He's not home.	9. She can't stay.
2. She's not married.	10. She doesn't want to stay.
3. She's not the oldest.	11. She doesn't plan to stay.
4. I'm not hungry.	12. She isn't going to stay.
5. I can't.	13. She isn't going to eat.
6. I can't leave.	14. He isn't going to arrive.
7. Paulo can't leave.	15. They aren't going to arrive.
8. Paulo can't get up.	16. They aren't going to talk.

Part IV: Answering questions in the negative

Listen to these groups of questions and answers as given by the instructors on the tape. In each case the second instructor will give a negative answer.

Practice 18: (Recorded)

In this group, Instructor A asks something about Instructor B, and Instructor B answers in the negative. Just listen.

Practice 19: (Recorded)

In this group, Instructor A will ask you something about yourself. Answer in the negative. Check the tape for confirmation.

Practice 20:   (Recorded)

In this group Instructor A will ask Instructor B something about somebody else, and Instructor B will answer in the negative. Just listen.

Practice 21:   (Recorded)

Now Instructor A will ask you similar questions about somebody else. You should answer in the negative.

Comprehension   (Recorded)

Listen to these sentences and write down the numbers of any that you do not understand. Your instructor will help you.

Translations

I.   Responding Affirmatively and Negatively

Follow along visually below as you listen to these questions and answers. Then see if you can participate in the exchanges just by looking at the English.

1. Are you going to get up early?

Yes, I am.

2. Are you going to get up at 7:00?

No, I'm not.

3. Are you going to leave now?

   Yes, I am.

4. Is Yara going to stay?

   Yes, she is.

5. Is Yara going to speak with José?

   Yes, she is.

6. Is Yara going to get up early?

   No, she's not.

7. Are we going to eat well?

   Yes, we are.

8. Are we going to avoid the traffic?

   No, we're not.

9. Are we going to arrive early?

   Yes, we are.

10. Are they going to visit the park?

    Yes, they are.

11. Are they going to talk with you?

    Yes, they are.

12. Are they going to stay?

    No, they are not.

13. Do they plan to stay?

    Yes, they do.

14. Do they plan to visit the park?
    No, they don't.

15. Do they want to leave?
    No, they don't.

16. Do they want to eat now?
    Yes, they do.

17. Are they able to get up early?
    No, they're not.

18. But do they want to get up early?
    Yes, they do.

19. Can they avoid the traffic?
    Yes, they can.

20. Do they want to?
    Yes, they do.

II.   Here are some more of the same sort, but expanded a
    bit. The same instructions apply. See if you can do these
    with another student.

1. A. Are you planning to leave early?
   B. No, I'm not. I'm planning to leave at 10:00.

2. A. Are you going to leave now?
   B. No, I'm not. I'm going to stay until 05:00.

3. A. Is Yara going to get up early?
   B. No, she's not. She's going to get up at 10:00.

4. A. Do you want to visit the park?
   B. No, I don't. I want to stay here.

5. A. Do you want to speak with Paulo?
   B. Yes, I do. And I want to speak with Yara, too.

6. A. Do you want to speak with Yara?
   B. Yes, I do. Does Yara want to speak with me?

7. A. Is José going to leave with you?
   B. No, he's not. He's going to leave with Yara.

8. A. Is José going to avoid the traffic?
   B. Yes, he is. He's planning to leave early.

9. A. Can José get up early?
    B. No, he can't. He's going to arrive late.
10. A. Does José want to make a phone call?
    B. Yes, he does. He wants to talk with Yara.
11. A. Are we going to eat now?
    B. No, we're not. We're going to eat later.
    A. But I'm hungry now.
12. A. Are we going to eat now?
    B. Yes, we are. Why?
    A. Because I'm hungry.
13. A. Are we going to get up at 05:30?
    B. No, we're not. Why?
    A. Because I'm not able to get up at 05:30.
14. A. Can we leave now?
    B. No, we can't. We're going to eat now.
    A. I don't want to eat. I'm not hungry.

ANSWERS:

Practice 3:   1. He   6. He

              2. They   7. They

              3. They   8. They

              4. They   9. He

              5. He   10. They

Practice 9:   1. We're going to leave.

              2. We're going to get up.

              3. They're going to get up.

              4. They're going to leave.

              5. We're going to stay.

8.27

6.   They're going to arrive.

7.   We're going to get up.

8.   They're going to stay.

9.   They're going to leave.

10. We're going to arrive.

11. They're going to get up.

12. They're going to arrive.

Practice 13:   1.   I'm going to stay.

2.   I'm going to arrive.

3.   He's going to get up.

4.   I'm going to get up.

5.   He's going to leave.

6.   He's going to stay.

7.   I'm going to leave.

8.   He's going to get up.

9.   He's going to arrive.

10. I'm going to stay.

11. I'm going to arrive.

12. I'm going to get up.

End of Tape 3A

Tape 3B

Unit 9

Programming

Pronunciation

1. Review these words.

          noite   ( )x   ( )x
          sete   ( )x   ( )x

2. We have suggested that you pronounce these words with a
    ch-type sound.

          noite   ( )x   ( )x
          sete   ( )x   ( )x

3. However, you will hear many Portuguese speakers say these
    words with a t sound.

          noite   ( )x   ( )x
          sete   ( )x   ( )x

4. Here are some additional words that can be said with a ch
    or a t. On the tape we are using the ch. Do not be
    concerned about the meaning of these words. Just follow
    along and mimic.

          gaste   ( )x   ( )x   dente   ( )x   ( )x
          goste   ( )x   ( )x   sente   ( )x   ( )x
          bate   ( )x   ( )x   vinte   ( )x   ( )x
          bote   ( )x   ( )x   antes   ( )x   ( )x
          sorte   ( )x   ( )x
          forte   ( )x   ( )x

9.1

5. Here is an example from the upcoming dialog, the word for
    'this.'

    este   ( )x   ( )x

6. Here is another example from the dialog, the expression
    'likewise.'

    igualmente   ( )x   ( )x

7. Now review the following words.

    dia   ( )x   ( )x
    tarde   ( )x   ( )x
    onde   ( )x   ( )x
    pode   ( )x   ( )x
    pretende ( )x   ( )x

8. The above words are commonly said with a j-type sound ....
    the j of 'jeep' or the dg of 'fudge.'

    dia   ( )x
    tarde   ( )x
    onde   ( )x
    pode   ( )x
    pretende ( )x

9. You will often hear the above words said with a d-type
    sound.

    dia   ( )x
    tarde   ( )x
    onde   ( )x
    pode   ( )x
    pretende ( )x

                    9.2

10.   Here are some additional words that can be said with
       either a j sound or a d sound. On the tape we are using
       the j sound.

grande	( )x	diga	( )x
mande	( )x	diurno	( )x
vende	( )x	diálogo	( )x
rende	( )x	disso	( )x
balde	( )x		
pede	( )x		

11.   Here is an example from the dialog of this unit, the word
       'city.'

              cidade   ( )x   ( )x

12.   The word de, meaning 'from' or 'of,' also has the j-type
       sound, but normally only when it is part of a longer phrase.
       You will hear it in the dialog in the question De onde?,
       meaning 'From where?'.

              De onde?   ( )x   ( )x

13.   You will also hear it in the response Sou de ..., meaning
       'I am from ....'

              Sou de ... ( )x   ( )x

9.3

DIALOG

Sandra

o amigo	the friend
meu	my
o meu amigo	my friend
este	this

Yara, este é o meu amigo Bill.

Yara, this is my friend Bill.

Bill

o prazer	the pleasure
muito prazer	much pleasure

Muito prazer.

Glad to meet you.

Yara

igualmente	equally, likewise
americano	American

Igualmente. O senhor é americano?

Likewise. Are you an American?

Bill

sou	I am (I-form of 'being')

Sou, sim.

Yes, I am.

Yara

de	of, from
de onde	from where

De onde o senhor é?

Where are you from?

Bill

sou de   I am from

Sou de Nova Iorque.   I am from New York.

Yara

da   from the

a cidade   the city

Da cidade?   From the city?

Bill

do   from the

o estado   the state

Não, do estado.   No, from the state.

9.5

A LOOK AT THE GRAMMAR

Practice Exercises

Classification of Nouns: Gender

All Portuguese nouns can be grouped into two categories. Traditionally these two categories have been labeled 'masculine' and
'feminine', and all nouns are said to have either 'masculine' gender
or 'feminine' gender. We will use this traditional terminology, but
we must quickly point out that other labels such as 'x' and 'y' or
'black' and 'white' might do just as well, since in the case of most
nouns masculinity and femininity have nothing whatsoever to do with
their classification. Such items as 'house', 'wheel', 'ear', 'moti-
vation' and 'fame' are all classifiable together as feminine nouns,
even though femininity, as we normally think of the term, is not
a characteristic of any of them. Similarly, 'program', 'eye', 'car',
'shoe' and 'book' fall together in the 'masculine' category, although
there is really nothing masculine about any of them.

In the case of nouns referring to people (and many animals) the
classifications generally do correspond to the sex of the person (or
animal) referred to. This is certainly reassuring, because it would
seem strange indeed to us if 'brother', 'uncle','nephew' and 'bull'
were not masculine, if 'sister', 'aunt', 'niece' and 'cow' were not
feminine, and if 'student', 'teacher' and 'cat' could not be either
one.

It is wise to keep in mind, nevertheless, that it is not the item
or the person that is classified as masculine or feminine; it is the
noun itself. Native speakers know what classification a noun falls into.
They don't struggle over the decision. Of course they have the advantage of having grown up with the language, so that for them gender
selection is pretty much automatic. We English speakers must make a
deliberate and conscious effort to sort out the nouns according to
their gender.

Fortunately, it is often not nearly so difficult as it may seem
to identify a noun as being masculine or feminine. The exercises that
follow will show you some of the things to look for.

9.6

Practice 1: (Recorded)
      Listen to the following group of familiar nouns. They are all
feminine.

1. ( ) ( )		**5.** ( ) ( )
2. ( ) ( )		**6.** ( ) ( )
3. ( ) ( )		**7.** ( ) ( )
4. ( ) ( )		**8.** ( ) ( )

      Notice that all of these nouns end in an unstressed a sound.

Practice 2: (Recorded)
      Here are the same feminine nouns again. This time you should
repeat them aloud.

1. ( )x ( )x		**5.** ( )x ( )x
2. ( )x ( )x		**6.** ( )x ( )x
3. ( )x ( )x		**7.** ( )x ( )x
4. ( )x ( )x		**8.** ( )x ( )x

      It is helpful to know that most nouns that end in an unstressed
a sound are feminine.

Practice 3: (Recorded)
      Now listen to the following group of familiar nouns. All of
these are masculine.

1. ( ) ( )		**5.** ( ) ( )
2. ( ) ( )		**6.** ( ) ( )
3. ( ) ( )		**7.** ( ) ( )
4. ( ) ( )		

      You have probably noticed that all of these nouns end in an
unstressed u sound.

Practice 4: (Recorded)

Here are the same masculine nouns again. This time you should
repeat them aloud.

1. (   )x   (   )x   5. (   )x   (   )x
2. (   )x   (   )x   6. (   )x   (   )x
3. (   )x   (   )x   7. (   )x   (   )x
4. (   )x   (   )x

It is helpful to know that most nouns that end in an unstressed
u sound are masculine.

Observation

Probably 80% of all nouns in Portuguese end either with an
unstressed a sound or an unstressed u sound. Since most of those
that end in an unstressed a sound are feminine, and most of those
that end in an unstressed u sound are masculine, it will pay you
to be extra alert to the presence of these two sounds at the ends
of nouns.

You may notice that with some speakers the unstressed u at
times seems to be a bit more like an unstressed o. Just accept
this as one more of the many variations to be found in
Portuguese.

Practice 5: (Recorded)

Listen to the following group of nouns. Some of them you have heard before, and some are new to you. Indicate which are feminine and which are masculine by making a check in the appropriate column in the chart below. The answers are at the end of this unit.

	Masculine	Feminine
1.	( )	( )
2.	( )	( )
3.	( )	( )
4.	( )	( )
5.	( )	( )
6.	( )	( )
7.	( )	( )
8.	( )	( )
9.	( )	( )
10.	( )	( )
11.	( )	( )
12.	( )	( )
13.	( )	( )
14.	( )	( )
15.	( )	( )
16.	( )	( )
17.	( )	( )
18.	( )	( )
19.	( )	( )
20.	( )	( )
21.	( )	( )
22.	( )	( )
23.	( )	( )
24.	( )	( )
25.	( )	( )
26.	( )	( )

Observation

The gender of the noun determines how we will say 'the (+ noun)'.
That is, there is one way to say 'the' if the noun is masculine,
another if the noun is feminine. We refer to this as <u>gender agree-</u>
<u>ment</u>. The word for 'the' <u>agrees in gender</u> with the noun that it
accompanies.

Practice 6: (Recorded)

The following items on the tape all say 'the (something <u>feminine</u>)'
Listen and repeat.

    1. ( ) ( )x ( )x
    2. ( ) ( )x ( )x
    3. ( ) ( )x ( )x
    4. ( ) ( )x ( )x
    5. ( ) ( )x ( )x
    6. ( ) ( )x ( )x
    7. ( ) ( )x ( )x

Practice 7: (Recorded)

The following items all say 'the (something <u>masculine</u>)'. Listen
and repeat. Several of the items are new to you.

    1. ( ) ( )x ( )x
    2. ( ) ( )x ( )x
    3. ( ) ( )x ( )x
    4. ( ) ( )x ( )x
    5. ( ) ( )x ( )x
    6. ( ) ( )x ( )x
    7. ( ) ( )x ( )x

Practice 8: (Recorded)

You will hear a series of nouns on the tape. After each one
decide quickly if it is masculine or feminine; then say, in Portuguese,
'the (noun)'. Be sure the gender of 'the' agrees with the noun. Your
response will be confirmed.

    (1-22)

Practice 9: (Recorded)

Learn to say these items in Portuguese. Do them in order.

1. the car
2. He wants the car.
3. the house
4. He wants the house too.
5. He wants the car and the house.
6. the table
7. He wants the table too.
8. When is the party?
9. The party is tomorrow.
10. Where is the food?
11. The food is on the table.
12. We're going to avoid the traffic.
13. Do you know the girl?
14. Do you know the American?
15. Do you know Yara?*
16. Do you know Paulo?*
17. Yara* wants to talk with me.
18. Paul* wants to talk with me.
19. Santos* is in New York.

Observation

English 'the' and its Portuguese counterparts are traditionally referred to as the _definite_ _articles_. English 'a' or 'an' and their Portuguese equivalents are called the _indefinite_ _articles_. This is useful terminology.

Just as the gender of a noun determines how we say the definite article, so does it determine how we say the indefinite article. That is, the indefinite article is said one way if the noun is masculine, and another way if the noun is feminine. This is another manifestation of _gender_ _agreement_. Observe this in the following practices.

*Portuguese frequently uses the word 'the' in front of names.

Practice 10: (Recorded)

The following items on the tape all say 'a/an (something
feminine)'. Listen and repeat.

    1. (   )   (   )x   (   )x
    2. (   )   (   )x   (   )x
    3. (   )   (   )x   (   )x
    4. (   )   (   )x   (   )x
    5. (   )   (   )x   (   )x
    6. (   )   (   )x   (   )x
    7. (   )   (   )x   (   )x

Practice 11: (Recorded)

The following items on the tape all say 'a/an (something
masculine)'. Just listen this time. Do not repeat yet.

    1. (   )   (   )
    2. (   )   (   )
    3. (   )   (   )
    4. (   )   (   )
    5. (   )   (   )
    6. (   )   (   )

Observation

The masculine definite article 'the' and the masculine indefinite
article 'a/an' sound somewhat similar. The difference is a matter
of nasalization. 'A/an' is nasalized and 'the' is not nasalized.
Listen to the difference in the next practice exercise.

9.12

Practice 12: (Recorded)

Listen to these pairs. In each case the first member of the pair is the indefinite article ('a/an') plus a masculine noun and the second member of the pair is the definite article ('the') plus the same masculine noun.

1. (a/an)   (the)
2. (a/an)   (the)
3. (a/an)   (the)
4. (a/an)   (the)
5. (a/an)   (the)
6. (a/an)   (the)
7. (a/an)   (the)

Practice 13: (Recorded)

Listen carefully to these masculine nouns. Some of them you have not heard before. Decide in each case whether you hear the indefinite article ('a/an') or the definite article ('the') before the noun. Indicate which one you hear by making a mark in the appropriate column below. You can check your answers at the end of this unit. Remember, all of these nouns are masculine.

	a/an	the
1.	___	___
2.	___	___
3.	___	___
4.	___	___
5.	___	___
6.	___	___
7.	___	___
8.	___	___
9.	___	___
10.	___	___
11.	___	___
12.	___	___

Practice 14: (Recorded)

Now repeat these masculine nouns. Numbers 1-6 say 'a/an' plus a noun, and numbers 7-12 say 'the' plus a noun.

      1-6 'a/an' something masculine (   )x (   )x

      7-12 'the' something masculine (   )x (   )x

Practice 15: (Recorded)

This practice deals only with the indefinite articles, but it involves <u>both</u> genders, masculine and feminine. Practice these words and phrases until you can say them with relatively little effort.

    1. a room
    2. a friend
    3. a daughter
    4. a house
    5. He wants a house.
    6. a car
    7. He wants a car.
    8. He wants a car and a house.
    9. a table
  10. He wants a table too.
  11. New York is a state.
  12. New York is a city too.
  13. a phone call
  14. He's going to make a phone call.

Observation

Many nouns do not end in an unstressed <u>u</u> sound or an unstressed <u>a</u> sound. In these instances it is often possible to know the gender via other clues; at other times there is no pattern to guide you and you must find out what the gender is and simply memorize it. In <u>all</u> cases it is highly desirable to train yourself to memorize the gender of a noun when you first begin to use it.

9.14

Comprehension

Listen to these items on the tape and tell your instructor the number of any that you cannot understand.

Translations

A. Follow along with these questions and answers as they are given on the tape. Then be sure that you can do them **live** with your instructor or a fellow student.

1. Where are you from?
   I'm from Minnesota.

2. Where is Paul from?
   He's from Minnesota also.

3. Where is Alice from?
   She's from Utah.

4. And Kathy, where is she from?
   She's from Maryland.

5. And Bill, where is he from?
   He's from Vermont.

6. Are you from New York?
   Yes, I am.

7. Is Bill from New York?
   Yes, he is.

8. Is Frank from New York too?
   No, he's not.

9. Is she from Boston?
   No, she's not. She's from Detroit.

9.15

B. How would you say the following thoughts in Portuguese? Take
    them in order. Do not translate items in parentheses.

    1. I am (an) American.

    2. I am from New York.

    3. I am not from the city; I'm from the state.

    4. This is my friend, Bill.

    5. Bill is (an) American too.

    6. But he's not from New York.

    7. He's from Washington.

    8. He's not from the state; he's from the city.

    9. And you? Where are you from?

  10. I'm from _____.

  11. Oh, really? Mr. Jones is from there too.

  12. But Mr. Jones' daughter isn't from there.

  13. Which one? Linda?

  14. No, the other daughter. The oldest one. Betty.

  15. Where is she from?

  16. She's from Boston.

C. Be prepared to engage in these dialogs with your instructor.

    1. A. Do you know Bill White?

        B. The American? Yes, I know him.

        A. Where is he from?

        B. He's from New York. From the city!

        A. Oh, really?! I know the city well.

2. A. Do you know Fred Marks?
   B. Sure, he's my friend.

   A. Is he an American?
   B. Yes, he is. He's from Pittsburgh.

   A. From <u>where</u>?
   B. From Pittsburgh. A city in Pennsylvania.

3. A. I'm hungry. Let's go eat! (<u>Vamos</u> <u>comer</u>!)
   B. So am I! (I, too). Do you want to leave now?

   A. Sure!.......this is my car.
   B. Let's go!

Answers:

   Practice 5.

1.	F	14.	F
2.	F	15.	M
3.	F	16.	F
4.	M	17.	F
5.	M	18.	M
6.	M	19.	F
7.	F	20.	F
8.	M	21.	F
9.	M	22.	M
10.	F	23.	M
11.	F	24.	M
12.	M	25.	F
13.	M	26.	F

   Practice 13.

1.	a/an	7.	the
2.	a/an	8.	a/an
3.	the	9.	a/an
4.	the	10.	the
5.	the	11.	the
6.	a/an	12.	a/an

Unit 10

In this unit you will find a number of frames that require an
oral response on your part. You might be asked, for example,
'How do you say ....?' You should give your answer <u>aloud</u>. Check
the left hand margin and you will find there, in parentheses, a
written verification of your response, of what it was that we
intended you to say. You should then further verify, and
strengthen, the correct response by listening to it as it is said
by the voice on the tape, and by repeating it aloud as indicated.

Programming

Part I.   The Contractions <u>na</u> and <u>no</u>.

1.   Recall the word for 'room.'

              sala   ( )x   ( )x

2.   Recall also how you would say 'the room.'

              a sala   ( )x   ( )x

3.   Now notice how you say '<u>in</u> the room.'

              na sala   ( )x   ( )x

4.   The word <u>na</u> is a combination of the word <u>em</u> (meaning 'in'
       and 'on') and the word <u>a</u> (the definite article 'the'). That
       is, <u>em</u> + <u>a</u> = <u>na</u>.

              na   ( )x   ( )x

10.1

5.   The word <u>na</u> is a contraction, an obligatory one, one that
      you must make every time <u>em</u> and <u>a</u> come together.

                     na   ( )x   ( )x
                  na sala   ( )x   ( )x

6.   Here is the phrase 'in the city.' Here again <u>em</u> and <u>a</u> come
      together and contract to <u>na</u>.

                  na cidade   ( )x   ( )x

7.   You should now be able to say 'in the house.' How would you
      say it?

(na casa)

                     Verify and repeat: ( )x   ( )x

8.   How would you say 'in (at) the party'?

(na festa)

                     Verify and repeat: ( )x   ( )x

9.   Here is a new word, the word for 'avenue.'

                  avenida   ( )x   ( )x

10.   The word is feminine, so here is the way to say 'the
      avenue.'

                  a avenida   ( )x   ( )x

11.   How would you say '<u>on</u> the avenue'?

(na avenida)

                           Verify: ( )x   ( )x

10.2

12.   <u>Em</u> + <u>a</u> always contract to <u>na</u>. Similarly, <u>em</u> + the definite
        article <u>o</u> always contracts to <u>no</u>.

                        no   ( )x   ( )x

13.   Here, for example, is 'in the park.'

                    no parque   ( )x   ( )x

14.   Here is 'in the traffic.'

                    no tráfego   ( )x   ( )x

15.   And here is 'in the state.'

                    no estado   ( )x   ( )x

16.   Here is a new word, the word for 'center' or 'downtown.'

                    centro   ( )x   ( )x

17.   How would you say 'in the downtown'?
(no centro)

                        Verify: ( )x   ( )x

18.   Portuguese speakers, when referring to Brazil, say '<u>the</u>
        Brazil,' much as we say '<u>the</u> United States.' Here is '<u>the</u>
        Brazil.'

                    o Brasil   ( )x   ( )x

19.   So how would you say '<u>in</u> (the) Brazil'?
(no Brasil)

                        Verify: ( )x   ( )x

20. Similarly, when speaking of the city of Rio de Janeiro, a Portuguese speaker says 'the Rio.'

        o Rio   ( )x   ( )x

21. How would you say 'in (the) Rio'?

(no Rio)

               Verify: ( )x   ( )x

22. How would you say 'in the car'?

(no carro)

               Verify: ( )x   ( )x

23. How about 'in the afternoon'? It's feminine.

(na tarde)

               Verify: ( )x   ( )x

24. In an item like 'I'm at home,' there is no possibility of a contraction since the article 'the' is not present to contract with anything.

     estou em casa   ( )x   ( )x

25. However, if you want to say 'I'm in the home of ...,' the article 'the' is present and must be contracted.

     estou na casa de...   ( )x   ( )x

Part II.   Descriptive Adjectives

1.   Observe this phrase.

         casa linda   ( )x   ( )x

2.   The phrase says 'pretty house.' The word order is 'house
      pretty,' just the reverse of the normal English order.

         casa linda   ( )x   ( )x

3.   Generally, Portuguese descriptive adjectives, such as <u>linda</u>,
      come after a noun.

         casa linda   ( )x   ( )x

4.   Here is 'pretty evening.'

         noite linda   ( )x   ( )x

5.   And here is 'pretty afternoon.'

         tarde linda   ( )x   ( )x

6.   If we wish to say 'pretty car' we have to change the ending
      of <u>linda</u> and say <u>lindo</u>, since <u>carro</u> is a masculine noun.
      This is a manifestation of gender agreement.

         carro lindo   ( )x   ( )x

7.   How would you say 'pretty park'?
(parque lindo)

                              Verify: ( )x   ( )x

8.   How would you say 'pretty state'?
(estado lindo)

                              Verify: ( )x   ( )x

9.   How about 'pretty city'?

(cidade linda)

                              Verify: ( )x   ( )x

10.   Here is 'American city.'

        cidade americana   ( )x   ( )x

11.   How would you say 'American car'?

(carro americano)

                              Verify: ( )x   ( )x

12.   How would you say 'American friend' if the friend is a male?

(amigo americano)

                              Verify: ( )x   ( )x

13.   And if the friend is female?

(amiga americana)

                              Verify: ( )x   ( )x

14.   Here is the word 'consulate,' a new item in the dialog of

        this unit.

                consulado   ( )x   ( )x

15.   How would you say 'American Consulate'?

(Consulado Americano)

                              Verify: ( )x   ( )x

16.   And here is the word 'embassy,' also a new item in the dialog

        of this unit.

                embaixada   ( )x   ( )x

17.   So how would you say 'American Embassy'?

(Embaixada Americana)

                              Verify: ( )x   ( )x

                        10.6

18.   Here is 'married daughter.'

     filha casada   ( )x   ( )x

19.   How would you say 'single daughter'?

(filha solteira)

                  Verify: ( )x   ( )x

20.   How would you say 'married son'?

(filho casado)

                  Verify: ( )x   ( )x

DIALOG

Yara

desde quando	since when
o Brasil	Brazil
no Brasil	in Brazil

Desde quando o senhor está no Brasil?*   How long have you been in Brazil?

Bill

estou	I am
aqui	here
a semana	the week

há uma semana	for a week

Estou aqui há uma semana.   I have been here (I am here) for a week.

Yara

trabalha	work (he-form.)
o Rio	Rio (de Janeiro)
no Rio	in Rio

O senhor trabalha aqui no Rio?   Do you work here in Rio?

Bill

trabalho	work (I-form)
o consulado	the consulate
no consulado	in the consulate

Trabalho, sim. No Consulado Americano.   Yes, I do. In the American Consulate.

Yara

Onde é o Consulado?   Where is the Consulate?

* Literally, 'Since when are you in Brazil?'

10.8

Bill

o centro	the center, downtown
no centro	in the center of town, downtown
a avenida	the avenue
na avenida	on the avenue
Presidente Wilson	President Wilson

É no centro, na avenida Presidente Wilson.

It's downtown, on President Wilson Avenue.

Yara

embaixada	embassy
que	that
fica	is, stays (he-form)

Mas, não é a Embaixada que fica na avenida Presidente Wilson?

But, isn't it the Embassy that is on President Wilson Avenue?

Bill

Não, a Embaixada é em Brasília.

No, the Embassy is in Brasília.

End of Tape 3B

Tape 4A

A LOOK AT THE GRAMMAR

Practice Exercises

Part I. Contractions

Practice 1: (Recorded)

In this exercise you will hear a group of feminine nouns.
In the pause after each noun you are to say na plus the noun. Thus
if you hear sala you will respond with na sala, 'in the room'. You
will hear your response confirmed.

Practice 2. (Recorded)

In this exercise you will work with a group of masculine
nouns. Respond to each with no plus the noun. Confirm your
response.

Practice 3: (Recorded)

In this exercise the masculine and feminine nouns appear in
mixed order. Respond with no or na plus the noun.

Part II. 'Being'

Observation

By this time it is becoming more and more obvious to you that
Portuguese is not a mirror image of English. The language handles
a number of things much differently from the way we handle them in
our own language. You can recall several instances where the
Portuguese grammatical construction is not a direct 'reflection'
of the English counterpart. For example, Portuguese often has
endings on verb forms whose English equivalents have none. Also,
you have learned that Portuguese groups its nouns into two categories, masculine and feminine. English, of course, has no such
categorization for gender.

10.10

Frequently Portuguese does not record the events of the everyday world from the same point of view as English. For example,
Portuguese has two ways of expressing the concept of 'being'. That
is, Portuguese has two ways of saying 'I am', 'he is', 'she was',
'they were', etc. Portuguese does this by using two different verbs.
In their neutral forms these verbs are:

ser and estar

They both translate into English as 'to be'.

The choice of ser or estar is very carefully dictated by
circumstances. There are certain situations which require a form
of ser, and there are others that require a form of estar. It is
a rare situation which will allow either one indiscriminately.

You have already learned to use some of the forms of these
two verbs, probably without knowing quite 'why'. In this and
subsequent units we will explain some of the 'whys'.

The two forms of ser that you know so far are sou and é.
The two forms of estar that you know are estou and está.

Recall the following examples:

ser	estar
De onde o senhor é?	Estou aqui.
Sou de Nova Iorque.	Você está no Brasil.
Onde é o Consulado?	Onde está o Santos?
É na Avenida P. Wilson.	Está em casa.

The above examples serve to illustrate several points:
1. If you want to say or ask where somebody or something is
   from, use the proper form of ser.

> Sou de Nova Iorque. (I am from New York.)
> Ela é de Washington. (She is from Washington.)
> De onde o senhor é? (Where are you from?)
> O carro é do Brasil. (The car is from Brazil.)

10.11

2. If you want to say or ask where somebody or something is
   (i.e. its location, not its origin) then you will have to
   choose between ser and estar. If the item you are talking
   about is by its very nature permanently fixed in its
   location, you will use a form of ser. If the item (or
   person) you are talking about can be moved from its
   location, that is if it's not permanently fixed, you will
   use a form of estar.

Examples with ser:

        Onde é o Consulado?

        É no centro.

(The Consulate building is immovable; it is fixed in
its location.)

        O Rio é no Brasil.

(Likewise, Rio cannot be removed from Brazil.)

Examples with estar:

        Onde está o Santos?

        Está em casa.

        Estou aqui no Brasil.

(People are always movable; they are never fixed in
their location, at least not in the sense that a
building or a city is.)

        A mesa está na sala.

        O carro está no centro.

(Tables and cars are examples of things which are not
normally fixed geographically.)

Practice 4. (Recorded)

    Listen to this exercise. Instructor A will ask Instructor B
where he is, and the latter will respond with a variety of answers.
Since Instructor B is movable, the forms está and estou (from estar)
are used in these interchanges. These are recorded with você.

Practice 5: (Recorded)

This time Instructor A will ask you where _you_ are. You are
to reply using the cues suggested in brackets below. Start each
answer with the form _estou_. You will hear your response confirmed.

1.   (...................?)   [in the living room]
2.   (...................?)   [in the Embassy]
3.   (...................?)   [in (the) downtown]
4.   (...................?)   [in (the) Brazil]
5.   (...................?)   [at the party]
6.   (...................?)   [in the park]
7.   (...................?)   [on (the) President Wilson Ave.]
8.   (...................?)   [in the city]
9.   (...................?)   [here]

Practice 6: (Recorded)

In this exercise one instructor will ask the other where
somebody or something is, and the latter will reply with a
variety of answers. In each case the person or thing talked
about is movable, so _está_ is used. Just listen.

Practice 7: (Recorded)

Now you will hear a similar set of questions and _you_ are to
provide the answers during the pause following each one. Use the
locations suggested in the brackets.

1.   (...................?)   [in the park]
2.   (...................?)   [in the Embassy]
3.   (...................?)   [in the living room]
4.   (...................?)   [in the city]
5.   (...................?)   [downtown]
6.   (...................?)   [here]
7.   (...................?)   [in Rio]
8.   (...................?)   [in the living room]
9.   (...................?)   [at the party]
10. (...................?)   [in Brazil]
11. (...................?)   [on President Wilson Ave.]

10.13

Practice 8:

If you were to ask the location or whereabouts of the following, which verb form--é or está--would you use? Remember, mova-
bility is the key. Indicate your choice by writing either é or
está in the blanks. You can check your answers below, preferably
after you have done them all.

1. Onde _____ [the American Embassy]?
2. Onde _____ [New York]?
3. Onde _____ [President Wilson Avenue]?
4. Onde _____ [my friend]?
5. Onde _____ [Paulo]?
6. Onde _____ [the car]?
7. Onde _____ [the park]?
8. Onde _____ [the museum]?
9. Onde _____ [my hat]?
10. Onde _____ [my sister]?
11. Onde _____ [your sister]?
12. Onde _____ [your office]?
13. Onde _____ [the cafeteria]?
14. Onde _____ [Yara]?
15. Onde _____ [São Paulo]?
16. Onde _____ [the president]?

Answers: 1.é 2.é 3.é 4.está 5.está 6.está 7.é 8.é 9.está
           10.está 11.está 12.é 13.é 14.está 15.é 16.está

10.14

<u>Practice 9</u>: (Recorded)

   Now, ask these questions in Portuguese. Check the tape for
verification.

   1. Where is Paul?
   2. Where is the car?
   3. Where is José?
   4. Where is the Embassy?
   5. Where is President Wilson Avenue?
   6. Where is Maria?
   7. Where is my friend?
   8. Where is Brazil?
   9. Where is the living room?
  10. Where is the traffic?
  11. Where is the food? [Refer to practice 10 below.]

<u>Practice 10</u>: (Recorded)

   You originally learned to say No. 11 above by inserting the
phrase <u>é que</u> after the question word <u>onde</u>. That is, you learned
'<u>Onde</u> <u>é</u> <u>que</u> está <u>a</u> <u>comida</u>?' (Where is it that is the food?). Listen
now as your tape instructor goes through all of the questions in
Practice 9 and inserts <u>é que</u> in each one of them. This means that
in addition to hearing the sequence <u>Onde é que está</u>?, as in No. 11,
you will also hear the sequence <u>Onde é que é</u>?, as in No. 4 where the
obviously fixed location of the living room requires the use of the
form <u>é</u>. These two sequences, <u>Onde é que está</u>? and <u>Onde é que é</u>?
are two longer, and very common, ways of asking 'Where is?' Listen
carefully.

<u>Practice 11</u>: (Recorded)

   Now <u>you</u> do the same thing. Go through the questions of
Practice 9 above and insert <u>é que</u> in each. Check the tape for
confirmation.

Practice 12:

Prepare the following brief dialogs so that you can participate
in them with your instructor or a fellow student.

1. A. Where is Paul today?
   B. He's at the American Embassy.

   A. And where's the American Embassy?
   B. It's in Brasilia.

2. A. Where is Maria from?
   B. She's from Washington.

   A. Where is she now?
   B. She's at home.

3. A. My friend is from New York.
   B. Does he work in Rio?

   A. Yes, he does. Downtown. But he's not in Rio now.
   B. Where is he?

   A. He's in Washington.

4. A. Where's the car?
   B. It's on President Wilson Avenue.

   A. Is President Wilson Avenue downtown?
   B. It is.

Practice 13: (Recorded)

Here are some questions that can be answered either 'yes' or
'no'. Answer them in the affirmative, using the appropriate verb
form followed by sim. Sample answers:

> Está, sim.
> É, sim.

Your response will be confirmed.

Practice 14: (Recorded)

Here are the same questions. This time answer them in the
negative. Sample answers:

> Não, não está.
> Não, não é.

Part III: More contractions

Observation:

You have seen how the word em combines with the definite
articles o and a to form the contractions no and na.

The word em may also combine with the indefinite articles to
form contractions. These contractions are not obligatory, however.
They are optional. Sometimes they are made and sometimes they
are not.

> You may recall that the indefinite articles look like this:
> um for masculine items
>
> uma for feminine items

When em combines with them, this is what happens:

> em + um = num
>
> em + uma = numa

For example, the phrase 'in a house' brings em and uma
together. If the Portuguese speaker contracts them, the resulting
phrase is:

> numa casa 'in a house'

Likewise, the phrase 'in a car' brings em and um together.
If the Portuguese speaker contracts them, the resulting phrase is:

> num carro 'in a car'

Practice 15: (Recorded)

Here are some examples of the contractions <u>num</u> and <u>numa</u>.
Repeat after your instructor as indicated.

1. 'in a house'   (   )   (   )x   (   )x
2. 'in a city'   (   )   (   )x   (   )x
3. 'in a car'   (   )   (   )x   (   )x
4. 'in a state'   (   )   (   )x   (   )x
5. 'at a party'   (   )   (   )x   (   )x
6. 'on an avenue'   (   )   (   )x   (   )x
7. 'in an embassy'   (   )   (   )x   (   )x
8. 'in a park'   (   )   (   )x   (   )x

Recorded portion continues on page 256.

10.18

Comprehension

Listen to these items on the tape and make a note of those that you do not understand. Note: Practice I is not included on the cassette.

Translations

I.   Practice putting these exchanges into Portuguese.

1.   How long have you been in Washington?
     I've been here for a week.

2.   How long have you been in Brazil?
     I've been here for five weeks.

3.   How long have you been in Rio?
     I've been here for eight days.

4.   Do you work in the American Embassy?
     Yes, I do.

5.   Do you work downtown?
     Yes, I do. The Embassy is downtown.

6.   Do you work with José?
     No, I don't. I work with Paulo.

7.   Does Yara work in Washington?
     Yes, she does. She works downtown.

8.   Does Bill work in Washington?
     No, he works in New York.

9.   I work in Washington. Where do you work?
     I work in Washington too.

10. Paulo works in the Embassy. Where does Yara work?
     She works in the Embassy too.

11. Are you going to work in Brazil?
     Of course. I'm going to work in the Embassy.

12. Where are you going to work?
     I'm going to work in the Embassy too.

13. I'm going to work in São Paulo.
     Really?! You're not going to work in the Embassy?

10.19

14. Are <u>you</u> going to work in Brasilia too?
    No, I'm not. I'm going to work in Rio.

15. We are going to work in Rio, in the Consulate General.
    Really?! (<u>Ah</u>, <u>é</u>?!) I'm going to work there too.

16. They aren't going to stay in Rio?!
    No, they're not.

17. They aren't going to work today.
    Why not?
    They don't want [to].

18. Where's the American Embassy?
    It's in Brasilia.

19. Where's Joe?
    He's at home.

20. Where's Paul?
    He's at a party. (<u>numa</u>)

21. Maria isn't here. Where is she?
    She's going to stay at home today.

22. Is Bill going to arrive tomorrow?
    Yes, he is. Very early.

23. When is Sandra going to arrive?
    She's going to arrive today.

II.   Practice saying these groups of sentences in Portuguese.

   A.   1.   We're not going to leave now.
        2.   We're going to leave later.
        3.   We're going to leave at ten o'clock.
        4.   We're going to avoid the traffic.

   B.   1.   We're not going to arrive at eight.
        2.   We're going to arrive early.
        3.   We're going to arrive at seven thirty.

   C.   1.   I want to stay here.
        2.   I'm going to stay here until tomorrow.
        3.   I'm going to leave tomorrow.
        4.   And I'm going to leave early, at 7:30.

   D.   1.   Yara wants to visit the park.
        2.   But she does not want to visit the park today.
        3.   She can not visit the park today.
        4.   But she can visit the park tomorrow.
        5.   And she is going to visit the park tomorrow.

   E.   1.   I don't want to get up early.
        2.   I don't want to get up at seven.
        3.   I can't get up at seven!
        4.   I want to get up at ten.
        5.   And I'm going to get up at ten!

   F.   1.   I want to avoid the traffic, of course.
        2.   But I don't want to get up at seven.
        3.   I'm going to get up at ten.
        4.   I'm going to leave at 10:30.
        5.   And I'm going to avoid the traffic!

   G.   1.   They want to leave now.
        2.   They don't want to leave later.
        3.   They are going to leave now.

UNIT 11

Part I. Pronunciation

1. Repeat these familiar words.

só	( )x	( )x
posso	( )x	( )x
pode	( )x	( )x
agora	( )x	( )x
senhora	( )x	( )x

2. All of the above words have a vowel sound in common, the vowel sound of the word só. Henceforth we will use traditional terminology and refer to this sound as the 'open O'. The capital letter O is our choice of a convenient symbol to represent this sound; it is not standard spelling. Recall our choice of capital E to represent another open vowel.

3. The other kind of o sound, the kind heard in hoje, você and moça, is traditionally referred to as a 'closed o.' We have already discussed the terms 'open' and 'closed' as they apply to the E and e sounds. The application to the O and o sounds is similar. The tongue is farther away from the roof of the mouth for the open O than it is for the closed o. That is, for the O there is a relatively larger space or 'opening' between the tongue and the roof of the mouth. For the o there is a relatively smaller opening; the space is more 'closed'. Thus the terms 'open' and 'closed' have their origins in the physical realities of speech. You may not be able to actually feel the difference between the open O and the closed o. Many people cannot. But you should be able

to hear the difference, and through careful mimicry and
practice you should be able to maintain it in your own
speech.

4. Listen to these pairs of contrasting words. In each case,
the first word of the pair has the open <u>o</u>, and the second
word has the closed <u>o</u>.
    1. ( ) ( )
    2. ( ) ( )
    3. ( ) ( )
    4. ( ) ( )
    5. ( ) ( )

5. Here are the same pairs again. Repeat each word right
after you hear it. Do this frame several times until
you are reasonably sure you are making the correct
distinction.
    1. ( )x ( )x
    2. ( )x ( )x
    3. ( )x ( )x
    4. ( )x ( )x
    5. ( )x ( )x

6. Now here are the new words from this unit that contain the
open <u>o</u>. Listen and repeat.
    1. ( ) ( )x ( )x ( )x
    2. ( ) ( )x ( )x ( )x
    3. ( ) ( )x ( )x ( )x
    4. This five-syllable word is built up gradually
       on the tape.

7. Recall these two words, paying particular attention to
the underlined consonant sound, the familiar <u>gn</u> of 'cognac.'
    a. co<u>nh</u>eço ( )x ( )x
    b. se<u>nh</u>or ( )x ( )x

11.2

8. Likewise, recall these two words, each of which contains this same sound.

    a. tenho   ( )x (   )x
    b. minha   ( )x (   )x

9. Recall the nasal diphthong -em in this item.

          tem   ( )x (   )x

Part II. Plurals

10. Most nouns ending in a vowel are made plural by adding an s sound. Listen to these examples, and repeat the last two times as shown.

    a. casa (   ): casas (   ) ( )x (   )x
    b. carro (   ): carros (   ) ( )x (   )x
    c. parque (   ): parques (   ) ( )x (   )x

11. How would you say the plural of 'party' in Portuguese?
(festas)

        Verify: ( )x (   )x

12. How would you say 'cities'?
(cidades)

        Verify: ( )x (   )x

13. How would you say 'weeks'?
(semanas)

        Verify: ( )x (   )x

14. In the speech of many people from the Rio area (and some
    other areas as well) this final s̲ sound may closely
    resemble the English s̲h̲ sound. Listen closely to these
    examples spoken by a Rio speaker:

    casa̲s̲   (   )   (   )
    carro̲s̲   (   )   (   )
    cidade̲s̲ (   )   (   )
    parque̲s̲ (   )   (   )
    semana̲s̲ (   )   (   )

15. The definite and indefinite articles also become plural
    when the noun that they accompany is plural. Observe
    these plural forms below and listen to them on the tape.
    Repeat where shown.

    1. o̲ (   ): o̲s̲ (   )   (   )x   (   )x
    2. a̲ (   ): a̲s̲ (   )   (   )x   (   )x
    3. um̲ (   ): un̲s̲ (   )   (   )x   (   )x
       (The spelling changes from m̲ to n̲)

    4. uma̲ (   ): uma̲s̲ (   )   (   )x   (   )x

16. Now, observe these examples with the definite articles.
    Follow along on the tape and repeat the last two times
    as shown.

    1. the cars - o̲s̲ carro̲s̲ (   )   (   )x   (   )x
    2. the parties - a̲s̲ festa̲s̲ (   )   (   )x   (   )x
    3. the cities - a̲s̲ cidade̲s̲ (   )   (   )x   (   )x
    4. the parks - o̲s̲ parque̲s̲ (   )   (   )x   (   )x

    This illustrates the process known as number agreement.
    A singular noun requires a singular form of 'the'; a
    plural noun requires a plural form of 'the'. The noun
    and the word 'the' thus agree in number.

11.4

17. Now observe these examples with the indefinite articles.
When the indefinite articles are pluralized the usual
English equivalent is 'some'. Observe the following
examples and follow along on the tape.
1. some cars – <u>uns carros</u> ( ) ( )x ( )x
2. some parties – <u>umas festas</u> ( ) ( )x ( )x
3. some cities – <u>umas cidades</u> ( ) ( )x ( )x
4. some parks – <u>uns parques</u> ( ) ( )x ( )x
Again, these examples illustrate <u>number agreement</u>.
Singular nouns are preceded by a singular form of the
indefinite article, and plural nouns are preceded by a
plural form. The plural forms are translatable as
English 'some'.

18. How would you say 'the weeks'?
(as semanas)
Verify: ( )x ( )x

19. How would you say 'some weeks'?
(umas semanas)
Verify: ( )x ( )x

20. How would you say 'the rooms'?
(as salas)
Verify: ( )x ( )x

21. How would you say 'some rooms'?
(umas salas)
Verify: ( )x ( )x

22. Many Rio speakers will pronounce the following plural
forms with the 'sh' – type sound we mentioned earlier
in frame No. 14. Listen to the Rio speaker on the tape.
You need not repeat.

(frame 22 continued)
    1. <u>os</u> (   ) <u>as</u> (   ) <u>uns</u> (   ) <u>umas</u> (   )
    2. <u>os carros</u> (   ) <u>as festas</u> (   )
    3. <u>uns carros</u> (   ) <u>umas festas</u> (   )

Comment

     In order to continue with this examination of plurals it is
necessary that you be familiar with the terms <u>voiced</u> and <u>unvoiced</u>.

     Any speech sound which is produced with the vocal cords
vibrating is said to be <u>voiced</u>. Any speech sound which is pro-
duced with the vocal cords at rest is said to be <u>unvoiced</u>.

     Your first impression may be that the vocal cords are in
operation for <u>all</u> speech sounds and that therefore all speech
sounds are voiced. Such is not the case, however.

     English has several sounds that are unvoiced. The <u>f</u> is a
good example. The vocal cords do not vibrate as you produce the <u>f</u>
sound. You do not use your voice. You have to whisper the sound.
There's simply no other way to say it. If you do force the vocal
cords to vibrate, you are no longer producing the <u>f</u>. You are
producing the <u>v</u>. The <u>v</u> is a <u>voiced</u> sound. With a bit of careful
self-examination you will realize that the principal phonetic
difference between our words <u>fat</u> and <u>vat</u> is that the vocal cords
are vibrating for the <u>v</u> but not for the <u>f</u>.

     You can notice similar distinctions in the following pairs
of English words. Read them aloud in pairs, and notice that the
presence or the absence of voicing on the first consonant sound
makes all the difference in the world.

bet	pet	veal	feel
ban	pan	van	fan
den	ten	zip	sip
dare	tear	zeal	seal
god	cod		
game	came		

     Portuguese has voiced and unvoiced sounds too. It is not
necessary for us to sort them all out, but it is helpful to realize
that the presence or absence of voicing often affects the way

11.6

adjacent sounds are pronounced. We will show you how this works
with regard to the pluralization of the definite and indefinite
articles, which is, after all, what we are dealing with here.

In frames 10-21 above we pluralized the definite and indefinite articles by adding an s sound. The s is unvoiced. It is
significant that the first sound of each of the nouns is also
unvoiced (the p of parque, the f of festa, the s sound of cidade
and sala, and the k sound of carro). It is because these sounds
are unvoiced that the plural forms of the articles have the
unvoiced s. The two unvoiced elements form a kind of pair.

> os parques
> as festas
> os carros
> as cidades
> as salas

By way of contrast, you will notice in the examples that
follow that when the first sound of the noun is voiced, the
definite and indefinite articles do not have the unvoiced s sound.
They have the voiced z sound instead. For example, you will hear
'oz amigos' (the friends) and 'az mesas' (the tables), both with
a z sound rather than the s sound you might have expected. The
a of amigos and the m of mesas are both voiced and each of them
colors the preceding sound (the pluralizing s) to the point where
it too becomes voiced and changes from an s to a z. (All of this
happens in speech. In the writing system this z sound is still
written with an s.)

23. Listen for the z sound in these examples where the
     noun begins with a voiced vowel sound. The z is
     indicated here by an underlined s.
     1. as avenidas   ( )x   ( )x
     2. as embaixadas ( )x   ( )x
     3. os americanos ( )x   ( )x
     4. os estados   ( )x   ( )x

    5. uma<u>s</u> avenidas ( )x ( )x
    6. uma<u>s</u> embaixadas ( )x ( )x
    7. un<u>s</u> americanos ( )x ( )x
    8. un<u>s</u> estados ( )x ( )x

24. How would you say 'the friends'?
(o<u>s</u> amigos)

          Verify: ( )x ( )x

25. How would you say 'some friends'?
(un<u>s</u> amigos)

          Verify: ( )x ( )x

26. How would you say 'the Americans'?
(o<u>s</u> americanos)

          Verify: ( )x ( )x

27. How would you say 'some Americans'?
(un<u>s</u> americanos)

          Verify: ( )x ( )x

28. Listen for the <u>z</u> sound in these examples where the
      noun begins with a voiced consonant sound.
    1. a<u>s</u> mesas ( )x ( )x
    2. a<u>s</u> moças ( )x ( )x
    3. a<u>s</u> velhas ( )x ( )x
    4. a<u>s</u> vistas* ( )x ( )x
    5. o<u>s</u> dias ( )x ( )x

    6. uma<u>s</u> mesas ( )x ( )x
    7. uma<u>s</u> moças ( )x ( )x
    8. uma<u>s</u> velhas ( )x ( )x
    9. uma<u>s</u> vistas ( )x ( )x
    10. un<u>s</u> dias ( )x ( )x

*'The views'. New in this unit.

29. So, how do you say 'the tables'?
(a<u>s</u> mesas)

        Verify: ( )x   (   )x

30. And how do you say 'the girls'?
(a<u>s</u> moças)

        Verify: ( )x (   )x

31. How would you say '<u>some</u> girls'?
(uma<u>s</u> moças)

        Verify: ( )x   (   )x

32. Finally, how do you say 'the days'?
(o<u>s</u> dias)

        Verify: ( )x   (   )x

33. The Rio speaker is very likely to give the <u>z</u> sound before
voiced consonants a slightly different treatment. You
can expect him to pronounce it in a way that resembles
our English <u>z</u> of <u>azure</u> or our <u>s</u> of <u>pleasure</u>. But note
that he will do this only in front of voiced consonants,
not in front of vowels. Listen to these samples spoken
by a Rio speaker. You need not repeat.

               (1 - 4)

34. Now, recall these four contractions.

       <u>no</u> ( )x   (   )x
       <u>na</u> ( )x   (   )x
       <u>num</u> ( )x   (   )x
       <u>numa</u> ( )x   (   )x

35. These contractions are made plural when the noun they
go with is plural.

       <u>nos</u> ( )x   (   )x
       <u>nas</u> ( )x   (   )x
       <u>nuns</u> ( )x   (   )x
       <u>numas</u> ( )x   (   )x

               11.9

36. Here are some examples. Listen for the z sound in
    2 and 4 where the noun begins with a voiced sound.
    1. nas cidades (   )x (   )x 'in the cities'
    2. nos estados (   )x (   )x 'in the states'
    3. nuns carros (   )x (   )x 'in some cars'
    4. numas mesas (   )x (   )x 'on some tables'

37. Give the English equivalents of these items that you
    hear on tape.
            1. (   ) (   )
(in the parks)
            2. (   ) (   )
(at the parties)
            3. (   ) (   )
(in the cars)
            4. (   ) (   )
(in some cars)
            5. (   ) (   )
(on some tables)
            6. (   ) (   )
(on some avenues)
            7. (   ) (   )
(on the tables)
            8. (   ) (   )
(in the embassies)
            9. (   ) (   )
(in some embassies)

38. In unit 7 you learned that the phrase é que may be
    inserted after a question-word. We noted that the
    question 'Where is Santos?' can be asked in two ways.
            Onde está o Santos?
            Onde é que está o Santos?
    In this unit we will again insert é que after a question-
    word. The question word in this case is 'What?'. In

11.10

Portuguese it is 'O que?' Listen and repeat.

    O que? ( )   ( )x   ( )x   ( )x

39. By inserting é que imediately afterwards we have a longer but
equally common way of asking 'What?'. It is not really so
much a tongue twister as it seems.

    O que é que? ( )   ( )x   ( )x   ( )x

40. 'What do you want?' (What is it that you want?) is said
like this: O que é que o senhor quer?

    ( )   ( )x   ( )x   ( )x

Special Pre-dialog Practice   (Recorded)

When a Portuguese speaker feels it is appropriate he will
ask you to switch from the formal 'you' to the informal 'you.'
There is no single linguistic formula for accomplishing this. The
variations are endless. However, we are illustrating two common
ways in the brief exchanges presented below. We suggest you
practice these. They are recorded for you on tape.

The American's question or statement is picked at random.
It could be anything. The Brazilian's response is what we are
interested in.

Exchange No. 1

	por favor	please
American:	A senhora trabalha no Rio?	Do you work in Rio?
Brazilian:	'A senhora, não. Você, por favor.	Not 'a senhora.' Please (use) 'você.'
American:	Está bem.	Okay.

Exchange No. 2

	Me chame	Call me
American:	Eu quero falar com o senhor.	I want to talk with you.
Brazilian:	'O senhor', não. Me chame de 'você'.	Not 'o senhor'. Call me 'você'.
American:	Está bem.	Okay.

DIALOG

Yara and Bill have switched to 'você'.

Yara

Você é casado?   Are you married?

Bill

minha   my
a esposa   the wife
a minha esposa   my wife
a criança   the child

Sou. A minha esposa está em   Yes, I am. My wife is in
Washington com as crianças.   Washington with the children.

Yara

quantos?   how many?
o filho   the child
tem   have (he-form)

Quantos filhos você tem?   How many children do you have?

Bill

tenho   have (I-form)
dois   two
três   three
nove   nine
o menino   the little boy
a menina   the little girl

Tenho dois. Um menino de   I have two. A boy nine
nove e uma menina de três.   and a girl three.

11.13

Yara

o que?	what?
o que é que?	what is it that?
acha	think (he-form)
O que é que você acha do Rio?	What do you think of Rio?
gosta	like (he-form)
Você gosta?	Do you like it?

Bill

gosto	like (I-form)
muito	much, a lot
Gosto muito.	I like it a lot.
a vista	the view
umas vistas	some views
maravilhosa	marvelous
Tem umas vistas maravilhosas.	It has some marvelous views.

End of Tape 4A

Tape 4B

SOME NUMBERS

1.	um, uma	9.	nove
2.	dois, duas	10.	dez
3.	três	11.	onze
4.	quatro	12.	doze
5.	cinco	13.	treze
6.	seis	14.	catorze
7.	sete	15.	quinze
8.	oito		

A LOOK AT THE GRAMMAR

Practice Exercises

Part I. Plural Nouns

Practice 1: (Recorded)

Listen to your tape instructor say this group of nouns in their plural forms. The word for 'the', which precedes each one, is pluralized by adding the s sound. Repeat each one after the instructor.

11.14

Practice 2: (Recorded)

Now here are more nouns given in their plural forms. Again the word for 'the' precedes each one, but this time it is pluralized by adding the z sound since the nouns begin with a vowel or with a voiced consonant. Repeat each one.

Practice 3: (Recorded)

In this exercise you are to make the nouns plural. Listen to the noun in its singular form, then say it in the plural. Be sure to pluralize the word for 'the'. (In 1-10 add the s sound; in 11-20, add the z sound). Check your response with the tape.

Practice 4: (Recorded)

This is a group of plural nouns preceded by the appropriate word for 'some'. Repeat each one. Notice how 'some' is pluralized with an s sound in Group 1, and with a z sound in Group 2.

Practice 5: (Recorded)

Listen to the following singular nouns and then make them plural by saying 'some' followed by the plural noun. 'Some' is pluralized with an s sound in 1-9, with a z sound in 10-18.

Practice 6: (Recorded)

How would you say these items in Portuguese? You should be able to respond rapidly. Verify your responses with the tape.

1.	the parks	6.	the Americans
2.	the states	7.	the views
3.	the houses	8.	the cities
4.	the tables	9.	the phone calls
5.	the friends		

- -

10.	some parties	15.	some parks
11.	some cars	16.	some states
12.	some cities	17.	some mornings
13.	some young girls (meninas)	18.	some friends
14.	some wives		

11.15

Practice 7: (Recorded)

Listen to and repeat these plural contractions, all of them combinations of em plus the plural forms os, as, uns, umas.

1. in the states   (   )   (   )x   (   )x
2. in the embassies   (   )   (   )x   (   )x
3. in the cities   (   )   (   )x   (   )x
4. at the parties   (   )   (   )x   (   )x
5. in the cars   (   )   (   )x   (   )x
6. in the parks   (   )   (   )x   (   )x
7. on the tables   (   )   (   )x   (   )x

- -

8. in some states   (   )   (   )x   (   )x
9. in some embassies (   )   (   )x   (   )x
10. in some cities   (   )   (   )x   (   )x
11. at some parties   (   )   (   )x   (   )x
12. in some cars   (   )   (   )x   (   )x
13. in some parks   (   )   (   )x   (   )x
14. in some houses   (   )   (   )x   (   )x

Practice 8: (Recorded)

This is an exercise in changing contractions from singular to plural. Listen to the singular contractions on the tape, then change the contraction and the accompanying noun to the plural forms. For example, na festa will become nas festas. Verify your response with the response given on the tape.

Part II. More on gender agreement

Observation

Recall the sentence: Quantos filhos você tem? ('How many children do you have?'). Notice what happens to the word Quantos if we ask 'How many houses do you have?'.

Quantas casas você tem?

11.16

The -os of Quantos changes to -as and the word becomes Quantas.
This is because casas is feminine. The word for 'how many', since
it is an adjective used in association with the feminine word
casas, must itself be feminine. It must agree. Thus the masculine
ending -o (unstressed u sound) of Quantos gives way to the
feminine ending -a of Quantas, and we say that there is gender
agreement between the noun casas and its accompanying adjective.

Practice 9: (Recorded)
    Instructor A will ask Instructor B 'How many _____ do you
have?', and Instructor B will answer 'I have _____'. Just listen.
Pay particular attention to whether you hear Quantos or Quantas.
Notice also that here too the s sound becomes a z sound before a
vowel or a voiced consonant.

Practice 10: (Recorded)
    Now the instructor will ask you the same questions. In your
answer you may pick any number that you wish.

Practice 11: (Recorded)
    This time you ask the questions. Ask how many of the following
items your friend has, following the same pattern used in the
previous practice. The tape will not answer your question, but
it will confirm how you should have asked the question.

1.	filhas	5.	salas
2.	crianças	6.	casas
3.	carros	7.	meninos
4.	amigos	8.	festas

Observation
    Recall the sentence Este é o meu amigo, Bill. Notice in
particular:

        o meu amigo = my friend

In this unit you have learned this sentence: A minha esposa
está em Washington com as crianças. Notice in particular:

a minha esposa = my wife

This is another case of gender agreement. Since amigo is masculine,
the expression for 'my', which is closely linked to it, assumes the
masculine form o meu. Since esposa is feminine the expression for
'my' assumes the feminine form a minha. (The o and the a in these
expressions are the words for 'the'. Thus we are literally saying
'the my friend, the my wife', etc.)

All three elements change for the plural.

O meu amigo becomes os meus amigos = my friends.

A minha esposa becomes as minhas esposas = my wives.

The os and as have the z sound in the above examples because
they precede the voiced m sound.

Practice 12: (Recorded)

Listen to your tape instructor say a series of 'my____'.
The first part of the series, Group A, will be singular; the
second part, Group B, will be plural. Repeat each item after the
instructor.

Practice 13: (Recorded)

How would you say these short phrases in Portuguese? Check
the tape for verification.

1. my party	10. my girl (menina)
2. my living room	11. my girls
3. my car	12. my house
4. my daughter (filha)	13. my cars
5. my wife	14. my state
6. my friend	15. my children (crianças)
7. my friends	16. my view
8. my boy (menino)	17. my city
9. my boys	18. my phone call

Observation

The numbers 'one' and 'two' also show gender agreement. The
masculine and feminine forms for 'one' are synonymous with the
indefinite articles; that is,

> um estado = 'a state', or 'one state'
>
> uma casa = 'a house', or 'one house'

The masculine form for 'two' appears in the sentence Tenho
dois; it refers to the masculine word filhos. The feminine form
is duas. It is used when one is referring to feminine words,
as in the sentence Tenho duas casas.

Practice 14: (Recorded)

Listen to your tape instructor saying this series of nouns
preceded by the number 'two'. Notice the masculine and feminine
forms. Repeat each one after him.

Part III. More contractions

Observation

You have learned that em combines with the definite and
indefinite articles to form certain contractions.

The word de (meaning 'of', or 'from') also combines with
the definite and indefinite articles to form another set of
contractions. You have already learned a few of these.

> da cidade, a contraction of de a cidade
>
> da mesa, a contraction of de a mesa
>
> do estado, a contraction of de o estado
>
> do Sr. Silva, a contraction of de o Sr. Silva.

Practice 15: (Recorded)

Listen to these contractions and repeat as indicated.
1. (of/from the embassy)

>   da embaixada   (   )   (   )x   (   )x   (   )x
2. (of/from the daughter)

>   da filha   (   )   (   )x   (   )x   (   )x

3. (of/from the car)
       <u>do</u> <u>carro</u>   (   )   (   )x   (   )x   (   )x
4. (of/from the friend)
       <u>do</u> <u>amigo</u>   (   )   (   )x   (   )x   (   )x
5. (of/from the week)
       <u>da</u> <u>semana</u>   (   )   (   )x   (   )x   (   )x
6. (of/from the American)
       <u>do</u> <u>americano</u> (   )   (   )x   (   )x   (   )x

Numbers 7-12 show contractions used with plural nouns. Listen particularly for the <u>z</u> sound (starred*) in 9, 10 and 11.

7. (of/from the children)
       <u>das</u> <u>crianças</u>   (   )   (   )x   (   )x   (   )x
8. (of/from the cities)
       <u>das</u> <u>cidades</u>   (   )   (   )x   (   )x   (   )x
9. (os/from the states)
       <u>dos</u>* <u>estados</u>   (   )   (   )x   (   )x   (   )x
10. (of/from the wives)
       <u>das</u>* <u>esposas</u>   (   )   (   )x   (   )x   (   )x
11. (of/from the embassies)
       <u>das</u>* <u>embaixadas</u>   (   )   (   )x   (   )x   (   )x
12. (of/from the parks)
       <u>dos</u> <u>parques</u>   (   )   (   )x   (   )x   (   )x

The next group consists of contractions of <u>de</u> with 'a/an'.

13. (of/from) a friend)
       <u>dum</u> <u>amigo</u>   (   )   (   )x   (   )x   (   )x
14. (of/from) an embassy)
       <u>duma</u> <u>embaixada</u>   (   )   (   )x   (   )x   (   )x
15. (of/from) a wife)
       <u>duma</u> <u>esposa</u>   (   )   (   )x   (   )x   (   )x
16. (of/from a child)
       <u>dum</u> <u>menino</u>   (   )   (   )x   (   )x   (   )x
17. (of/from a city)
       <u>duma</u> <u>cidade</u>   (   )   (   )x   (   )x   (   )x
18. (of/from a daughter)
       <u>duma</u> <u>filha</u>   (   )   (   )x   (   )x   (   )x

The following are all contractions of <u>de</u> with 'some'.

19. (of/from some girls)

   <u>dumas moças</u>   (   )   (   )x   (   )x   (   )x

20. (of/from some wives)

   <u>dumas esposas</u>   (   )   (   )x   (   )x   (   )x

21. (of/from some friends)

   <u>duns amigos</u>   (   )   (   )x   (   )x   (   )x

22. (of/from some Americans)

   <u>duns americanos</u>   (   )   (   )x   (   )x   (   )x

23. (of/from some states)

   <u>duns estados</u>   (   )   (   )x   (   )x   (   )x

24. (of/from some children)

   <u>dumas crianças</u>   (   )   (   )x   (   )x   (   )x

Practice 16: (Recorded)

The following two questions will be repeated several times on the tape. Be sure you can say each one effortlessly before going on to Practice 17.

O que é que você acha do Rio?   What do you think of Rio?

O que é que você acha da sala?   What do you think of the
                                     living room?

Practice 17: (Recorded)

Ask these questions in Portuguese, checking the tape for verification after each one. The emphasis at this point is once again on the contractions formed with <u>de</u>.

1. What do you think of (the) Rio?
2. What do you think of (the) car?
3. What do you think of (the) living room?
4. What do you think of (the) city?
5. What do you think of (the) embassy?
6. What do you think of (the) downtown?
7. What do you think of (the) park?
8. What do you think of (the) children? (<u>crianças</u>)
9. What do you think of (the) Americans?

10. What do you think of (the) girls? (moças)
11. What do you think of (the) views?
12. What do you think of (the) cities?
13. What do you think of (the) boys? (meninos)
14. What do you think of (the) parties?

Comprehension

Listen to these utterances recorded on the tape and make a note
of any that you do not understand.

Translations

Part I.

How would you say these thoughts in Portuguese? In numbers
1-13 you might assume that you are talking about a letter.

1. It's from a friend.
2. It's from some friends.
3. It's from an American.
4. It's from the American.
5. It's from the American Embassy.
6. It's from some Americans.
7. It's from a girl.
8. It's from some girls.
9. It's from Mr. Silva.
10. It's from my wife.
11. It's from my friend.
12. It's from the children.
13. It's from Rio.
14. Paul is from Rio.
15. Yara is from Brazil too, but she's from (do) Recife.
16. Mr. Clayton is from the American Embassy.

11.22

Part II.

1. My wife is in New York.
2. My wife is not in Washington.
3. My wife is with the children.
4. My wife wants to stay with the children.
5. The children can stay with my wife.
6. The children don't want to leave now.
7. I have two children.
8. A boy six and a girl four.
9. I have two houses, one in New York and one in Washington.
10. The house in New York is old.
11. Paul has two cars.
12. How many cars does Yara have?
13. How many friends does Yara have?
14. What do you think of the view?
15. What do you think of the cars?
16. What do you think of the two cars?
17. What do you think of the two houses?
18. The girls are going to stay.
19. The children plan to get up early.
20. I'm going to get up early with the children.
21. My little boy is downtown.
22. My daughter is at home.
23. My car is in Rio.
24. My house is in New York.
25. My party is tomorrow.
26. My house has a marvelous view.
27. I have a marvelous view from the living room.
28. I have a marvelous view from my house.
29. I have a marvelous view of the city.
30. I have a marvelous view of Rio.
31. But Yara only has a view of President Wilson Avenue.

Part III.

Prepare these brief dialogs in Portuguese.

1. A. How long has Susanna been here?
    B. She has been here 3 weeks, more or less.

    A. Does she like [it]?
    B. Yes, she does. A lot.

    A. Does she work?
    B. Yes. In the downtown [section].

2. A. How many children do you have?
    B. I have one. A boy twelve. And you?

    A. I have one also. A girl six.
    B. Is she here in Brasilia with you?

    A. Yes, she is. She's at home with my wife.

3. A. What do you think of the food?
    B. I don't like it.

    A. Aren't you going to eat?
    B. I can't. I'm not hungry. I'm going to eat at home.

UNIT 12

Preliminary Note

    You will need to have your pencil or pen in hand to work several of the frames in this unit.

Observation

    Cognates are words which are easily recognizable across language boundaries because of the close resemblance they bear to each other. The Portuguese word presidente and the English word president are cognates. The two words sound (and look) so much alike that a speaker of one language does not normally have any trouble recognizing and understanding the counter-word in the other language. The Portuguese word americano is an obvious cognate of the English word American. Chances are that it was very easy for you to learn to recognize this word and what it meant.

    Although recognition of cognates is a relatively simple matter accurate mimicry of them may present problems. The deeply ingrained speech habits of one's own native tongue are very comfortable and resist change. They interfere with the attempt to pronounce the cognate word in the target language as it should be pronounced. Almost invariably vowel and consonant qualities are different and must be reckoned with. Many times stress patterns are different too.

    To illustrate the significance of the difference in stress patterns we call your attention once again to the two pairs of cognates cited above. Notice that the strong stress falls on different vowels in the two languages. We are indicating strong stress here by underlining.

English	Portuguese
American	americano
president	presidente

    This unit contains additional cognates which illustrate the difference in stress patterns.

12.1

1. Listen to this word. Is it stressed on the first, second or last vowel?

     ( ) ( ) ( )

(last)

2. This was the word for 'Portuguese'. In English, is the word 'Portuguese' stressed on the first, second or last vowel?

(first)

3. Let's divide the Portuguese word for 'Portuguese' into syllables and practice it. Repeat.

     a. ( )x ( )x
     b. ( )x ( )x
     c. ( )x ( )x
     d. ( )x ( )x ( )x

4. Which of these two renditions is the correct one?

     (1) (2)   (1) (2)

(2)

5. Now listen to these next two renditions. Although both are stressed correctly, one is still mispronounced. Which one is mispronounced?

     (1) (2)   (1) (2)

(2)

6. The mispronunciation you just heard is quite common among English speakers learning Portuguese. All of us who are native speakers of English will invariably pronounce the word in <u>English</u> like this:

     Pór-chu-guese

   Notice the <u>ch</u> sound. That <u>ch</u> sound is very comfortable for us, and if we are not careful we will carry it over into Portuguese, where it definitely does not belong.

7. Here is the word pronounced correctly. Repeat as indicated.

( )x ( )x
( )x ( )x ( )x

8. Now we will examine another set of cognates. First, say the English word 'opportunity' aloud and notice which vowel the strong stress is on.

(opport<u>u</u>nity)

9. Now listen to the Portuguese cognate.

( ) ( ) ( )

10. Listen again; then with your pencil underline the vowel which has the strong stress.

oportunidade ( ) ( ) ( )

(oportunid<u>a</u>de)

11. Now practice saying the word by repeating the sequence you hear next on the tape.

(Follow tape)

12. Here is the Portuguese word for 'grammar'. Just listen.

( ) ( ) ( )

13. Here it is again. Underline the vowel of the syllable that has the strong stress.

gramática ( ) ( ) ( )

(gram<u>á</u>tica)

14. Now practice saying the word by repeating the sequence given on the tape.

(Follow tape)

15. Here is the word for 'English'.

( ) ( )

12.3

16. Here it is again. Underline the vowel that has the strong stress.

inglês ( ) ( ) ( )

(inglês)

17. Now practice the word as you hear it presented on the tape.

(Follow tape)

18. Here is the Portuguese word for 'Spanish'.

( ) ( ) ( )

19. Here it is again. As before, take your pencil and underline the stressed vowel.

espanhol ( ) ( ) ( )

(espanhol)

20. Now practice saying it. Follow the sequence on the tape and repeat. Observe that the final l sound is the type that closely resembles our English w; also that the o is 'open'.

(Follow tape)

21. The very first vowel sound of espanhol is often whispered by many Portuguese speakers. It may sound to you as if it is not there at all, but it is.

( ) ( )x ( )x

22. Another cognate appears in the dialog for this unit. It is the neutral form of 'practice'. Just listen.

( ) ( ) ( )

23. Now listen again, and underline the stressed vowel.

praticar ( ) ( )

(praticar)

24. Now practice saying it. Repeat everything that you hear on the tape.

> (Follow tape)

25. The noun <u>oportunidade</u> is feminine. Therefore how would you say '<u>the</u> opportunity'?

(a oportunidade)

26. The plural form is <u>as</u> <u>oportunidades</u>. Will the word <u>as</u> have an <u>s</u> sound or a <u>z</u> sound in this case?

(<u>z</u> sound)

27. Listen and repeat.

> as oportunidades   ( ) ( )x ( )x ( )x

28. If we want to say 'much opportunity', the word for 'much' will have a feminine ending because it must reflect its .close association with 'opportunity'. This is one more example of gender agreement.

> a. muita   ( ) ( )x ( )x
>
> b. muita oportunidade   ( ) ( )x ( )x

29. The word for 'day', you may remember, is masculine in spite of the fact that it ends in an unstressed <u>a</u> sound. Therefore 'the day' is said like this:

> o dia   ( ) ( )x ( )x ( )x

30. The plural form is <u>os dias</u>. Will the word <u>os</u> have an <u>s</u> sound or a <u>z</u> sound in this case?

sound)

31. Listen and repeat.

> os dias   ( ) ( )x ( )x ( )x

32. Recall this he-form of a verb you learned in the last unit.

> gósta   ( ) ( )

33. And this I-form of the same verb.

> gosto   ( ) ( )

34. Here is the he-form of a new verb.

     fala   ( )   ( )   ( )x   ( )x

35. And here is the I-form of that verb.

     falo   ( )   ( )   ( )x   ( )x

36. Here is another new verb. Is it the he-form or the I-form?

     ( )   ( )

(he-form)

37. Which form is this?

     ( )   ( )

(I-form)

38. Here is still another new verb. Which form is it?

     ( )   ( )

(he-form)

39. Recall the I-form of the verb 'have'.

     tenho   ( )   ( )   ( )x   ( )x

40. It is possible to combine this I-form with various neutral forms as we do in English in order to express such thoughts as the following:

          I have to leave
          I have to eat
          I have to study

41. In Portuguese, combinations of this sort require the insertion of the small word que between the I-form and the neutral form. Listen to the word que, and repeat.

     que   ( )   ( )   ( )x   ( )x   ( )x

42.   Therefore 'I have to leave' would be said as follows:

Tenho que sair   ( )   ( )

The que is untranslatable into English, but it must be present in Portuguese.

43.   Repeat again.

Tenho que sair   ( )   ( )x   ( )x   ( )x

44.   'I have to eat' would be said like this:

Tenho que comer   ( )   ( )x   ( )x   ( )x

45.   How would you say 'I have to stay'?

(Tenho que ficar)   Verify: ( )x   ( )x

46.   How would you say 'I have to speak'?

(Tenho que falar)   Verify: ( )x   ( )x

47.   And 'I have to visit'?

(Tenho que visitar)   Verify: ( )x   ( )x

48.   The he-form (tem) is also used in combination with the neutral form. Again, que must link the two. Thus 'He has to leave' consists of these elements:

tem + que + sair

49.   Now listen to and repeat 'He has to leave'.

( )   ( )x   ( )x   ( )x

50.   Here is 'He has to stay'.

( )   ( )x   ( )x   ( )x

51.   How would you say 'He has to eat'?

(Tem que comer)   Verify: ( )x   ( )x

52.   How about 'He has to make a phone call'?

(Tem que dar um telefonema)   Verify: ( )x   ( )x

End of Tape 4B

(Go on now to the dialog).

Tape 5A

DIALOG

Yara

fala	speak (he-form)
o português	Portuguese
Você fala português muito bem.	You speak Portuguese very well.

Bill

nota	notice (he-form)
o sotaque	accent
espanhol	Spanish
Você não nota um sotaque espanhol?	Don't you notice a Spanish accent?

Yara

pouco	little (in quantity)
Um pouco. Por quê? Você fala espanhol também?	A little. Why? Do you speak Spanish too?

Bill

falo	speak (I-form)
atrapalha	(it) causes confusion (he-form)
a palavra	word
a gramática	grammar
etcetera	etcetera

12.8

Falo. E atrapalha muito.   I do. And it causes lots
As palavras, a gramática, etc.   of confusion. The words,
                                         the grammar, etc.

Yara

a oportunidade   opportunity

praticar   practice (neutral form)

Você tem muita oportunidade   Do you have much chance to
de praticar português?   practice Portuguese?

Bill

tenho que falar   I have to speak

o escritório   office

todos   all, every

todos os dias   every day

Tenho que falar[1] no escritório   I have to speak it[1] in the
todos os dias.   office every day.

que tal?   how?, how about?

o seu   your

o inglês   English

E que tal o seu inglês?   And how's your English?

Yara

Péssimo!   Terrible!

---

1. Portuguese has a word to express the direct object 'it'
   but frequently does not use the word.

12.9

A LOOK AT THE GRAMMAR

Practice Exercises

Part I. Verbs of the -ar type

Practice 1. **Review** (Recorded)

Let us review some of the I-forms that you have learned thus far. Repeat after the voice on the tape while following along on this page.

posso ( )x	falo ( )x
tenho ( )x	trabalho ( )x
pretendo ( )x	gosto ( )x
quero ( )x	

All of these end in an unstressed u sound (written as o). With a few important exceptions, the I-forms of every verb in the language end in this unstressed u sound.

Practice 2. **Review** (Recorded)

Now let us re-examine some of the he-forms that you have learned. Repeat them from the tape and follow along on this page.

A.	fala ( )x	B.	pretende ( )x
	trabalha ( )x		pode ( )x
	nota ( )x		
	gosta ( )x		
	atrapalha ( )x		
	acha ( )x		

The he-forms of Group A all end in an unstressed a sound. Those in Group B end in an unstressed i sound (written as e).

It is important to be able to associate these forms with their respective neutral forms. You may recall that earlier we talked about three types or categories of neutral forms: those that end in -ar, those that end in -er, and those that end in -ir. We called them the -ar type, the -er type and the -ir type.

The he-forms <u>fala</u>, <u>gosta</u>, <u>trabalha</u>, <u>nota</u>, <u>acha</u>, and <u>atrapalha</u>, all ending in unstressed <u>a</u>, are of the -<u>ar</u> type. That is their neutral forms end in -<u>ar</u>. We will postpone actively practicing these neutral forms until a later time, but we are listing them below.

he-form	neutral form
fala	falar
gosta	gostar
trabalha	trabalhar
nota	notar
acha	achar
atrapalha	atrapalhar

The he-forms <u>pode</u> and <u>pretende</u>, which end in an unstressed -<u>i</u> sound, are of the -<u>er</u> type. Their neutral forms end in -<u>er</u>.

he-form	neutral form
pode	poder
pretende	pretender

Many times you will have to work this association in reverse. You will learn the neutral form first and from that you will be able to determine the shape of the he-form. That is what you will do in the practices that immediately follow.

Practice 3. Review (Recorded)

The following are all neutral forms of the -<u>ar</u> type. You have learned them in previous dialogs. Repeat them now to refresh your memory.

```
ficar      ( )x  ( )x
falar      ( )x  ( )x
levantar   ( )x  ( )x
visitar    ( )x  ( )x
chegar     ( )x  ( )x
evitar     ( )x  ( )x
praticar   ( )x  ( )x
```

Practice 4. (Recorded)

Listen to this group of I-forms of the -ar verbs listed in
Practice 3.

Practice 5. (Recorded)

Now listen to this group of he-forms of the same verbs.

Practice 6. (Recorded)

Now listen to the neutral form, the I-form, and the he-form
of these verbs side by side.

(neutral-form) (I-form) (he-form)

Practice 7. (Recorded)

Listen to the items presented on the tape and indicate which
form you hear by putting a check mark in the appropriate column in
the chart below. The answers are given at the end of this unit.

	Neutral form	I-form	He-form
1.			
2.			
3.			
4.			
5.			
6.			
7.			
8.			
9.			
10.			
11.			
12.			
13.			
14.			

12.12

Practice 8   (Recorded)

Now practice these I-forms. Be sure that you can associate them
with their respective neutral forms, which are shown in brackets.

[falar]	1.	( )	( )x	( )x
[ficar]	2.	( )	( )x	( )x
[levantar]	3.	( )	( )x	( )x
[chegar]	4.	( )	( )x	( )x
[visitar]	5.	( )	( )x	( )x
[evitar]	6.	( )	( )x	( )x
[praticar]	7.	( )	( )x	( )x
[trabalhar]	8.	( )	( )x	( )x

Practice 9. (Recorded)

Now practice the he-forms, once again associating them with the
neutral forms given in brackets.

[falar]	1.	( )	( )x	( )x
[ficar]	2.	( )	( )x	( )x
[levantar]	3.	( )	( )x	( )x
[chegar]	4.	( )	( )x	( )x
[visitar]	5.	( )	( )x	( )x
[evitar]	6.	( )	( )x	( )x
[praticar]	7.	( )	( )x	( )x
[trabalhar]	8.	( )	( )x	( )x

Practice 10. (Recorded)

Here are some he-forms and I-forms in print. Listen to them on
tape and underline the vowel that has the strong stress.

1.	fala	falo
2.	fica	fico
3.	pratica	pratico
4.	levanta	levanto

5. visita	visito
6. gosta	gosto
7. trabalha	trabalho
8. evita	evito
9. nota	noto
10. acha	acho

(If you marked those correctly, you underlined the next-to-the-last vowel).

Practice 11. (Recorded)

Paying particular attention to the strong stress, practice the above cited he-forms and I-forms as they are given now on the tape.

Practice 12. (Recorded)

One of the instructors will ask the other if he does something, and the latter will answer either that he does or that he does not. Listen, and repeat the answer that the second instructor gives.

Practice 13. (Recorded)

Now the first instructor will ask the second instructor if a third party does something, and the second instructor will answer either that the third party does or that he does not. Repeat just the answer.

Practice 14. (Recorded)

These questions are directed at you. Answer them affirmatively.

Practice 15. (Recorded)

Listen to the tape and, following the model of the example given, ask the questions which are suggested there.

Practice 16. (Recorded)

You have not yet had an opportunity to say the neutral form of several verbs that you have been working with. We will give you that opportunity in this practice.

        <u>trabalhar</u> ( ) ( )x ( )x ( )x
        <u>achar</u> ( ) ( )x ( )x ( )x
        <u>atrapalhar</u> ( ) ( )x ( )x ( )x

Practice 17. (Recorded)

Observation

You also have not yet had an opportunity to say the neutral forms of 'notice' and 'like'. They both have the closed <u>o</u>, in contrast to the he- and I-forms which, as you know, have the open <u>o</u>. Later you will learn more verbs in which this kind of vowel shift occurs.

        1. nota ( ) ( )x ( )x
            noto ( ) ( )x ( )x
            notar ( ) ( )x ( )x

        2. gosta ( ) ( )x ( )x
            gosto ( ) ( )x ( )x
            gostar ( ) ( )x ( )x

Part II. <u>Gostar</u> plus <u>de</u>

Observation

Forms of the verb <u>gostar</u> must be followed by <u>de</u> if what is liked is actually stated in the sentence. In Portuguese you like 'of' somebody or something.

        I like Mary = Gosto <u>de</u> Maria.

        Mary likes Paul = Maria gosta <u>de</u> Paulo.

Sometimes it is not necessary to actually say what is liked because the item has already been mentioned in the context. In that case there is no <u>de</u>. Recall these lines from the previous dialog.

        Q. Você gosta? (Referring back to Rio)
        A. Gosto, sim.

When the definite article 'the' accompanies the liked object
the de enters into the appropriate contraction.

I like the city. = Gosto da cidade.   [de + a cidade]
I like the car. = Gosto do carro.   [de + o carro]

I like the cities. = Gosto das cidades.   [de + as cidades]
I like the cars.   = Gosto dos carros.   [de + os carros]

Remember that the definite article 'the' may also accompany proper
names. Thus the first two examples cited above might also be said with
the appropriate contractions.

I like Mary.   = Gosto da Maria.   [de + a Maria]
Mary likes Paul. = Maria gosta do Paulo. [de + o Paulo]

The liked object may be the neutral form of a verb, as is often
the case in English. In such instances there are no contractions.

I like to eat.   = Gosto de comer.
She likes to talk. = Gosta de falar.

Practice 18. (Recorded)

Listen to your instructor say what he likes, then repeat after
him. The items he likes are listed on the left below.

a. (Without contractions)

1.	Maria	( )	( )x	( )x
2.	to talk	( )	( )x	( )x
3.	Yara	( )	( )x	( )x
4.	Paulo	( )	( )x	( )x
5.	to practice	( )	( )x	( )x
6.	to eat	( )	( )x	( )x
7.	to get up early	( )	( )x	( )x
8.	English	( )	( )x	( )x
9.	Washington	( )	( )x	( )x
10.	you	( )	( )x	( )x
11.	Bill	( )	( )x	( )x
12.	Portuguese	( )	( )x	( )x
13.	to work	( )	( )x	( )x

12.16

b. (With contractions)

1.	Maria	( )	( )x	( )x
2.	Paulo	( )	( )x	( )x
3.	Yara	( )	( )x	( )x
4.	the president	( )	( )x	( )x
5.	the city	( )	( )x	( )x
6.	the views	( )	( )x	( )x
7.	the children	( )	( )x	( )x
8.	(the) Rio	( )	( )x	( )x
9.	the Embassy	( )	( )x	( )x
10.	the parks	( )	( )x	( )x
11.	the living-room	( )	( )x	( )x
12.	the words	( )	( )x	( )x
13.	the accent	( )	( )x	( )x
14.	the party	( )	( )x	( )x
15.	the food	( )	( )x	( )x

Practice 19. (Recorded)

In this exercise your instructor will ask 'Do you like _____?'
Repeat the questions after him. Do not answer them. All of the
questions contain contractions. Again, the items are listed for you.

1. o Rio
2. a cidade
3. o carro
4. o parque
5. os meninos
6. a comida
7. os americanos
8. o escritório

9. o meu amigo
10. os meus amigos
11. a minha espôsa
12. as minhas festas
13. o tráfego
14. a Yara
15. o Paulo

Practice 20.   (Recorded)

Say that you like the following things. Check the tape for
confirmation. Do this exercise several times, if necessary, until
you can do it smoothly.

1.   to talk
2.   to eat
3.   to leave early
4.   to stay until late
5.   to speak Portuguese
6.   to avoid the traffic
7.   to arrive early
8.   to visit Washington
9.   to practice Portuguese
10. to work here

Practice 21.   (Recorded)

Say that you don't like the following. Check the tape for
confirmation. Do these several times, if necessary, to assure a
smooth performance.

1.   to get up early
2.   to speak Spanish
3.   to practice English
4.   to arrive at seven
5.   to visit Paul
6.   to leave early
7.   to speak with a Spanish accent
8.   to work in Washington
9.   to stay in New York
10. to confuse you

Practice 22. (Recorded)

Now say that Paul likes the following items. Check the tape for confirmation.

1. the embassy
2. the city
3. the downtown
4. Maria
5. Carlos
6. Rio
7. Brazil
8. my friends
9. my view
10. my house
11. the car
12. my daughter
13. the little boy

Practice 23. (Recorded)

Now say that Maria does not like the following items.

1. Bill
2. Yara
3. the traffic
4. the party
5. my car
6. my wife
7. the food
8. the park
9. the living room
10. the view
11. my son (filho)
12. my parties
13. the little girl

12.19

<u>Practice 24</u>. (Recorded)
   Ask your friend if he likes the following items.

   1. Brazil
   2. the city
   3. to speak Portuguese
   4. to arrive early
   5. to get up early
   6. the view
   7. the children
   8. the car
   9. to work here
   10. the food

<u>Part III</u>. 'have to'

<u>Reminder</u>: In phrases like 'I have to leave', 'he has to leave',
           and the like, Portuguese inserts the word <u>que</u> between
           'have (has)' and the neutral form. Practices 25 through
           28 deal with this pattern.

<u>Practice 25</u>. (Recorded)

   In this practice you will hear your instructor say that he has
to do certain things. Listen to him, and repeat after him where
indicated by the <u>x</u>. The things he has to do are indicated to the
left below.

   1. to talk   ( )   ( )x   ( )x
   2. to practice   ( )   ( )x   ( )x
   3. to get up   ( )   ( )x   ( )x
   4. to stay   ( )   ( )x   ( )x
   5. to work   ( )   ( )x   ( )x
   6. to leave   ( )   ( )x   ( )x
   7. to visit   ( )   ( )x   ( )x
   8. to eat   ( )   ( )x   ( )x
   9. make a phone call ( )   ( )x   ( )x

Practice 26. (Recorded)

    Now listen to him say that someone else has to do certain things, and repeat after him.

1.	to get up	( )	( )x	( )x
2.	to practice	( )	( )x	( )x
3.	to speak Portuguese	( )	( )x	( )x
4.	to stay	( )	( )x	( )x
5.	to leave early	( )	( )x	( )x
6.	to work	( )	( )x	( )x
7.	to eat	( )	( )x	( )x
8.	to avoid the traffic	( )	( )x	( )x
9.	to arrive early	( )	( )x	( )x

Practice 27. (Recorded)

    In this exercise you will hear your instructor ask 'Do you have to _____?'. Repeat after him.

1.	to leave	( )	( )x	( )x
2.	to work	( )	( )x	( )x
3.	to practice	( )	( )x	( )x
4.	to stay	( )	( )x	( )x
5.	to get up	( )	( )x	( )x
6.	to speak English	( )	( )x	( )x
7.	to make a phone call	( )	( )x	( )x
8.	to come	( )	( )x	( )x
9.	to arrive early	( )	( )x	( )x

Practice 28. (Recorded)

    How would you say these brief thoughts in Portuguese? Again, check the tape for verification.

1. I have to work more.
2. I have to practice more.
3. I have to get up at six o'clock.

12.21

4. She has to get up at seven o'clock.
5. She has to leave early.
6. I have to leave early too.
7. I have to eat less.
8. Paul has to eat more.
9. Paul has to practice Spanish.
10. Yara has to work today.
11. Do you have to work tomorrow?
12. I have to arrive early tomorrow.
13. I have to speak Portuguese in the Embassy.
14. Carlos has to come at 5 o'clock.
15. But he has to stay until 10.

Part IV. Negative questions

Negative questions are questions that have the negative element 'not' (não) in them. Here are some examples.

Mas ela não é casada?

Você não vai comer?

Você não quer levantar cedo também?

Você não nota um sotaque espanhol?

Practice 29. (Recorded)

A. Listen to your instructor ask these negative questions in Portuguese.

1. Isn't she married?
2. Isn't he American?
3. Aren't you the oldest?

B. Now how would you say these? Check the tape for confirmation.

1. Isn't she single?
2. Isn't he from New York?
3. Isn't he Portuguese?

12.22

4. Isn't he English?
5. Aren't you married?
6. Aren't you single?
7. Isn't he [está] at home?
8. Isn't she in the Embassy?

Practice 30: (Recorded)

A. Now listen to these questions.

1. Aren't you going to eat?
2. Aren't you going to work?
3. Aren't you planning to leave?
4. Isn't he planning to arrive early?
5. Doesn't he want to arrive early?
6. Doesn't he have to arrive tomorrow?

B. How would you say these? Check the tape after each one.

1. Aren't you going to leave?
2. Aren't you going to get up?
3. Aren't you going to make a phone call?
4. Isn't he going to work?
5. Doesn't he want to work?
6. Doesn't she want to stay?
7. Doesn't she have to stay?
8. Doesn't Yara have to work?
9. Isn't Yara planning to work?

Practice 31: (Recorded)

A. Listen to these questions.

1. Don't you notice a Spanish accent?
2. Don't you work in Washington?
3. Don't you speak Spanish?

4. Doesn't he speak Portuguese?

5. Doesn't she practice a lot?

B. How would you say these? Check the tape.

1. Don't you arrive early?

2. Doesn't Bill arrive early?

3. Doesn't Paul stay until 5:00?

4. Doesn't Paul like Rio?

5. Don't you like Yara?

6. Doesn't Yara like you?

7. Doesn't Spanish get in the way?

8. Don't you notice an English accent?

Comprehension (Recorded)

Listen to these sentences on the tape and write down the numbers of any that are not clear to you.

End of Tape 5A

Translations

Part I.

How would you say the following in Portuguese? These sentences are numbered separately, but they constitute a running narrative. You should practice them until you can go through them smoothly. Feel free to make alterations to fit your own personal situation.

1. I get up early every day.
2. I have to get up early because I have to leave early.
3. I get up at six.
4. I arrive at the office at eight, and I work until five.
5. I don't like to get up early.
6. My wife stays at home with the children.
7. My office is in Washington; my home is in Bethesda.
8. Tomorrow I have to arrive at seven.
9. When I arrive at seven I avoid the traffic.
10. Tomorrow I'm going to work only until four.
11. But Paulo has to work until six.
12. Paulo speaks English very well.
13. But I note a Portuguese accent.
14. I don't have much opportunity to practice my Portuguese.
15. I like my office very much.
16. It has a marvelous view of the city.
17. Also it has a view of the river.
18. And how is my Portuguese?

19. It's not terrible, nor is it [também não é] very good.
20. I have been here only two weeks.
21. I like to speak Portuguese.
22. I practice every day with my friends.
23. My friend Tom speaks Portuguese very well.
24. He's not married and he has more opportunity to practice.

Part II.

Prepare these dialogs.

1. A. How is Betty?
   B. Fine. She works in Washington now.

   A. Every day?
   B. No, only three days a (por) week.

   A. Where does she work?
   B. In an office downtown.
      She has to leave home (de casa) at seven.
      She arrives more or less at eight.

   A. Does she like to get up early?
   B. Yes, she does, but I don't.

2. A. Do you speak Portuguese?
   B. A little. Why?

   A. I want to talk with Yara but I don't speak Portuguese
      very well.
   B. Doesn't Yara speak English?

   A. No, she doesn't.
   B. Why don't you speak Portuguese to her?
      It's an opportunity to practice your Portuguese.

3. A. How's your Portuguese?
   B. Terrible!

   A. Terrible? Why?
   B. I don't have the opportunity to practice. I have
      to stay in the office until eight o'clock every day.

   A. But can't you practice with Carla?
   B. She speaks Spanish, and Spanish gets in the way.

Answers to Practice 7: Neutral form: 4, 5, 14
                        I-form: 1, 6, 7, 9, 10, 12
                        He-form: 2, 3, 8, 11, 13

UNIT 13

Pronunciation Review

1. These words from previous units all contain the same nasal
    vowel. Just listen.

    a. ( ) ( )
    b. ( ) ( )
    c. ( ) ( )
    d. ( ) ( )

2. Here they are again, with the nasal vowel underlined. Repeat
    as indicated.

    a. c_entro   ( )x ( )x
    b. pret_ende   ( )x ( )x
    c. igualm_ente   ( )x ( )x
    d. _embaixada   ( )x ( )x

3. The sight of the printed _n or _m may lead you to think that
    you hear an _n or _m in these words, but what you are really
    hearing (and should be saying) is a nasalized vowel sound.
    Here are some new examples from this unit.

    e. ( ) ( )x ( )x
    f. ( ) ( )x ( )x

4. Here they are again with the nasal vowel underlined.

    e. s_ente   ( )x ( )x
    f. chov_endo   ( )x ( )x

5. Here are familiar examples of another nasal vowel.

    g. ( ) ( )
    h. ( ) ( )
    i. ( ) ( )
    j. ( ) ( )

13.1

6. Now repeat them.

g. lev<u>a</u>nto   ( )x ( )x
h. qu<u>a</u>ndo   ( )x ( )x
i. qu<u>a</u>nto   ( )x ( )x
j. amanh<u>ã</u>   ( )x ( )x

7. Here are new examples. Just listen.

k. ( ) ( )
l. ( ) ( )
m. ( ) ( )

8. Now repeat.

k. m<u>a</u>ndo   ( )x ( )x
l. b<u>a</u>nda   ( )x ( )x
m. c<u>a</u>nso   ( )x ( )x

9. The following are familiar examples of still <u>another</u> nasal
    vowel.

n. ( ) ( )
o. ( ) ( )
p. ( ) ( )

10. Now repeat them.

n   b<u>o</u>m   ( )x ( )x
o. c<u>o</u>m   ( )x ( )x
p. <u>o</u>nde   ( )x ( )x

11. Here are several new examples, one of which appears in this
    unit. Just listen.

q. ( ) ( )
r. ( ) ( )
s. ( ) ( )

12. Now look, listen and repeat.

q. <u>o</u>nça   ( )x ( )x
r. l<u>o</u>nge   ( )x ( )x
s. <u>o</u>nda   ( )x ( )x

13.2

13. Here are familiar examples of a <u>fourth</u> nasal vowel.

       t. ( ) ( )
       u. ( ) ( )
       v. ( ) ( )

14. Now repeat.

       t. s<u>i</u>m ( )x ( )x
       u. c<u>i</u>nco ( )x ( )x
       v. <u>i</u>nglês ( )x ( )x

15. Here are two new examples. Just listen.

       w. ( ) ( )
       x. ( ) ( )

16. Now repeat.

       w. m<u>i</u>m ( )x ( )x
       x. v<u>i</u>m ( )x ( )x

17. Here is another example, taken from this unit, and said a little slower then normal.

       y. ( ) ( )

18. Now, here it is said at normal speed. Repeat.

       y. ( )x ( )x ( )x

19. This is what the last word looks like: <u>ainda</u>.

20. Say it again. Pronounce the nasal vowel but don't pronounce the <u>n</u>.

       a<u>i</u>nda ( )x ( )x ( )x

21. Now let's move on to a nasal diphthong. Recall these words, repeating as indicated.

       não ( )x ( )x
       vão ( )x ( )x

22. Now repeat just the nasal diphthong.

    ão: ( )x ( )x

23. This nasal diphthong appears in the second syllable of the following word, but it is <u>not stressed</u>. Just listen.

    ( ) ( )

24. Since it is not stressed, it may not sound quite like the same diphthong, but it is.

    ( ) ( )x ( )x ( )x

25. The following is the <u>wrong</u> way to say the word; it is wrong because the speaker has stressed the diphthong.

    (w) (w)

26. This time he says it <u>right</u>, by stressing the first syllable and not the diphthong.

    ( ) ( )x ( )x

- -

27. The word you have just practiced in No. 26 is the they-form of 'speaking'; that is, it is the way you say 'they speak' or 'they talk'. The <u>unstressed</u> nasal diphthong ão is the marker or indicator which signals the they-form.

28. Here are several additional they-forms of familiar verbs. Note the <u>unstressed</u> diphthong.

    1. ( ) ( )x ( )x
    2. ( ) ( )x ( )x
    3. ( ) ( )x ( )x
    4. ( ) ( )x ( )x

29. In Unit 8 you learned several they-forms that ended with a different kind of unstressed nasal diphthong. They were all they-forms of -<u>er</u> type verbs. Recall them below.

    1. pretendem ( ) ( )x ( )x
    2. podem ( ) ( )x ( )x
    3. querem ( ) ( )x ( )x

13.4

30. In this unit we are dealing with -ar type verbs, whose they-forms end with the unstressed ão diphthong. Here are several more examples:

          1. ( ) ( )x ( )x
          2. ( ) ( )x ( )x
          3. ( ) ( )x ( )x

31. And here, finally, is the they-form of a new -ar verb that appears in this unit. It means 'they live'. Notice the open O.

     ( )   ( )   ( )x   ( )x   ( )x

32. In this unit you are also going to work with we-forms of -ar verbs. Remember that you have already learned the we-forms of several -er verbs.

          1. pretendemos   ( )x ( )x
          2. podemos   ( )x ( )x
          3. queremos   ( )x ( )x

33. And you know the we-form of 'going'.

          vamos   ( )x ( )x

34. But here we will be working with -ar verbs. Practice these we-forms. Notice the -mos ending.

          1. ( ) ( )x ( )x
          2. ( ) ( )x ( )x
          3. ( ) ( )x ( )x
          4. ( ) ( )x ( )x
          5. ( ) ( )x ( )x

35. This is what they look like in print. Repeat again.

          1. chegamos   ( )x ( )x
          2. falamos   ( )x ( )x
          3. trabalhamos   ( )x ( )x
          4. visitamos   ( )x ( )x
          5. evitamos   ( )x ( )x

13.5

36. Here is the we-form of a new -ar verb. It means 'we live'. Notice the closed o.

$$( ) \quad ( ) \quad ( )x \quad ( )x$$

37. Here it is in print.

moramos   ( )x   ( )x

38. How would you say 'we talk'?

(falamos)

Verify: ( )x   ( )x

39. How would you say 'we arrive'?

(chegamos)

Verify: ( )x   ( )x

40. How about 'we avoid'?

(evitamos)

Verify: ( )x   ( )x

41. And 'we work'?

(trabalhamos)

Verify: ( )x   ( )x

42. A number of -ar verbs that have the open o in the I-form, he-form and they-form have the closed o in the we-form and the neutral form. Listen to the tape and follow along with the examples shown below. Repeat each item.

I-form	He-form	They-form	We-form	Neutral form
1. gOsto	gOsta	gOstam	gostamos	gostar
2. nOto	nOta	nOtam	notamos	notar
3. mOro	mOra	mOram	moramos	morar

43. Repeat the following pairs. Be sure you are distinguishing between O and o.

1. gOstam ( )x   gostamos ( )x
2. nOtam ( )x   notamos ( )x
3. mOram ( )x   moramos ( )x

13.6

44. In an earlier unit you learned that <u>ficar</u> means 'to stay',
'to remain'. It can have other meanings too. Frequently
it takes the place of <u>ser</u> in sentences which give the
permanent location of objects. Thus the sentence

<u>O consulado</u> <u>é</u> <u>no</u> <u>centro</u>

could also be said

<u>O consulado</u> <u>fica</u> <u>no</u> <u>centro</u>.

Repeat: ( ) ( )x ( )x

45. Using a form of <u>ficar</u>, how would you say 'Recife is in
Brazil'?

(Recife fica no Brasil.)

Verify: ( )x ( )x

46. Again, using <u>ficar</u>, how would you ask 'Where is the
American Consulate?'

(Onde fica o Consulado Americano?)

Verify: ( )x ( )x

47. And how would you answer that question?

(Fica na Avenida Presidente Wilson.)

Verify: ( )x ( )x

DIALOG

Yara

é que	it is that
como é que?	how is it that?
se sente	feel (he-form)
Como é que o senhor se sente hoje?	How do you feel today?

Mr. Clayton

cansado	tired
Um pouco cansado.	A little tired.
ainda	still, yet
resfriado	cold
Ainda estou resfriado.	I still have a cold.

Yara

lógico	logical
É lógico!	No wonder! (It's logical)
chovendo	raining
a vez	time
outra vez	again (another time)
Está chovendo outra vez.	It's raining again.

13.8

Mr. Clayton

parece (1) | appears, looks (he-form)

parece que | it appears that, it looks like

chover | rain (neutral form)

o dia todo (2) | all day

E parece que vai chover o dia todo. | And it looks like it's going to rain all day.

horrível | horrible

O tráfego está horrível hoje. | The traffic is terrible today.

- - - - - - - - - -

Yara

os senhores | you (masculine plural)

moram | live (they-form)

Onde os senhores moram? | Where do you live?

Mr. Clayton

nós | we

moramos | live (we-form)

Leme | Leme (section of Rio)

Nós moramos no Leme. | We live in Leme.

Yara

longe | far

É longe? | Is it far?

Mr. Clayton

perto | near

o túnel | tunnel

Não, fica perto do túnel. | No, it's near the tunnel.

---

(1) Notice the open E sound in this verb: parEce.

(2) Note that the adjective todo appears after o dia. It is also possible to say todo o dia.

A LOOK AT THE GRAMMAR

Practice Exercises

Part I. They-forms of -ar verbs

Practice 1. (Recorded)

In the following series you will hear the he-form of a verb, a pause for repetition, then the they-form of the same verb, and again a pause for repetition.

Practice 2. (Recorded)

Indicate with a check mark in the appropriate column whether you hear a he-form or a they-form.

	He-form	They-form
1.	_____	_____
2.	_____	_____
3.	_____	_____
4.	_____	_____
5.	_____	_____
6.	_____	_____
7.	_____	_____
8.	_____	_____
9.	_____	_____
10.	_____	_____

Answers are at the end of this unit.

Practice 3. (Recorded)

Listen to these questions and answers containing they-forms. The word for 'they' accompanies the they-form in the questions. In the first four 'they' is feminine; in the second four 'they' is masculine.

(1-8)

13.10

Practice 4. (Recorded)

Answer these questions affirmatively. If you have any
doubt as to what the questions are, check below.

1. Do they like the view?
2. Do they work in the city?
3. Do they live in Washington?
4. Do they practice a lot?
5. Do they get up at seven?
6. Do they speak English at home?
7. Do they stay here?

Practice 5. (Recorded)

Ask these questions in Portuguese. Check the tape for
confirmation of your response, <u>not</u> for the answers. Let 'they'
be masculine in all cases.

1. Do they live in Rio?
2. Do they like Rio?
3. Do they work in Rio?
4. Do they speak Portuguese?
5. Do they get up late?
6. Do they arrive early?
7. Do they practice at home?
8. Do they stay at the office?

Part II. We-forms of -ar verbs

Practice 6: (Recorded)

In this exercise the questionner is asking for information about os senhores (you all), so the answers will be given in the we-form. Listen to the we-form, then repeat it.

(1-8)

Practice 7: (Recorded)

In this exercise the questionner will ask you and your friend if you do one thing or if you do another. Answer for yourself and your friend in the we-form. Then check the response on the tape.

    Example: Q. Do you work in Rio or in Recife?

                   A. We work in Recife.

On the tape the second choice (the one after 'or') is always given as the response.

(1-8)

Practice 8:

How would you say the following?

1. We get up early every day.
2. We live in Leme.
3. We like to live there.
4. We work in the American Embassy.
5. We practice Portuguese in the office.
6. We don't notice an accent.
7. We don't live far from the city.
8. We don't like grammar.
9. We don't like to get up early.
10. We don't work well together.

Part III.   The conjunction que

Observation

  Notice the word que (meaning 'that') in the sentence Parece
que vai chover. Literally the sentence says 'It appears that it's
going to rain'. The word que is frequently used to join two clauses
together. Another example: Acho que Paulo vai ficar 'I think
that Paul is going to stay'. American students sometimes forget to
use the que in sentences of this sort since in English we can easily
dispense with the word 'that'. We can say with equal facility
either

I think that Paul is going to stay

or

I think Paul is going to stay.

  In Portuguese, however, the que must be said.

Practice 9:   (Recorded)

  Listen to your instructor say a series of sentences, each one of
which begins with 'I think that...'. After each number below, write
the letter of the sentence on the right which correctly translates
what it is that the instructor is thinking. The answers are at the
end of the unit.

1. _____	a.	It's going to rain.
2. _____	b.	It's raining again.
3. _____	c.	They live in Leme.
4. _____	d.	They work in Leme.
5. _____	e.	I'm going to leave.
6. _____	f.	I'm going to like her.
7. _____	g.	He's tired.
8. _____	h.	He has a cold.

13.13

Practice 10: (Recorded)

How would you say the following? Don't forget to put <u>que</u> in
each one. Check the tape for confirmation.

1. I think she's hungry.
2. I think he's married.
3. I think he's an American.
4. I think he knows Maria.
5. I think he works in Washington.

- -

6. Do you (<u>o senhor</u>) think she speaks Portuguese?
7. Do you think she is married?
8. Do you think she has an accent?
9. Do you think she has to practice?
10. Do you think she plans to stay?

- -

11. We think they live near.
12. We think they speak English.
13. We think she's married.
14. We think she's from Texas.
15. We think it's going to rain.

Practice 11: (Recorded)

The following should all begin with <u>parece que</u>. Check the tape
for confirmation.

1. It looks like the party is tomorrow.
2. It looks like Yara is hungry.
3. It looks like Yara knows the city well.
4. It looks like Yara speaks well.
5. It looks like Yara cannot arrive early.
6. It looks like it is not going to rain today.
7. It looks like it's raining now.

13.14

Part IV. Review

   A.   Asking questions with é que

Practice 12: (Recorded)

   Practice asking the following questions by inserting é que after
the interrogative word. Start the questions as indicated. Use
o senhor in each.

   a.   (Onde é que...?)

                    1.   Where do you live?
                    2.   Where do you work?
                    3.   Where do you practice?
                    4.   Where do you stay?
                    5.   Where do you plan to stay?
                    6.   Where do you plan to be (estar)?
                    7.   Where do you want to be?

   b.   (Por que é que...?)

                    1.   Why do you work in Washington?
                    2.   Why do you live in Leme?
                    3.   Why do you practice all day?
                    4.   Why do you avoid the tunnel?
                    5.   Why do you arrive early?
                    6.   Why do you want to arrive early?
                    7.   Why are you going to arrive early?

   c.   (Quando é que...?)

                    1.   When do you practice?
                    2.   When do you get up?
                    3.   When do you arrive?
                    4.   When do you plan to arrive?
                    5.   When do you want to arrive?
                    6.   When do you want to leave?
                    7.   When do you have to leave?

d. (O que é que...?)

1. What do you think?
2. What do you think of the food?
3. What do you think of Rio?
4. What do you want?
5. What do you want to be (ser)?
6. What do you have?
7. What do you have to practice?
8. What do you like?
9. What do you like to eat?

B. Contractions with de

The words longe and perto are frequently followed by the preposition de. Longe de is the equivalent of 'far from' and perto de
is the equivalent of 'near to'. The de will always form a contraction with definite articles which follow immediately after, and it
may form a contraction with indefinite articles.

perto da cidade   = near (to) the city

longe do Rio   = far from Rio

perto dum parque   = near (to) a park

longe duma embaixada   = far from an embassy

Practice 13: (Recorded)

Practice saying these short phrases after your tape instructor.

1. near the car   ( )x ( )x
2. near the avenue   ( )x ( )x
3. near the embassies   ( )x ( )x
4. near the tunnel   ( )x ( )x
5. near a tunnel   ( )x ( )x
6. near a city   ( )x ( )x
7. near the cities   ( )x ( )x
8. near some cities   ( )x ( )x
9. near Rio   ( )x ( )x

- -

13.16

10. far from Rio   ( )x ( )x
11. far from Brazil   ( )x ( )x
12. far from the city   ( )x ( )x
13. far from my wife   ( )x ( )x
14. far from the children   ( )x ( )x
15. far from the Americans   ( )x ( )x
16. far from my car   ( )x ( )x
17. far from my friends   ( )x ( )x
18. far from the embassy   ( )x ( )x

Comprehension

Listen to the sentences on the tape and make a note of any that are not clear to you.

Translations

A. Prepare these brief exchanges for your instructor.

1. Where do you live? (<u>os senhores</u>)
   We live in Brasilia, near the Embassy.

2. Where do you live?
   We live in Washington, near the river.

3. Where do they live?
   They live in Rio, near the Consulate.

4. How do you feel now? (<u>o senhor</u>)
   I'm still tired.

5. How do you feel today?
   Very well. But I'm still a little tired.

6. How do you feel?
   Not very well. I have a cold.

7. How does Bill feel today?
    He's still a little tired.

8. Doesn't Bill feel well?
    No, he has a cold.

9. Don't you feel well today?
    No, I have a cold.

10. Aren't you going to eat?
    No, I'm not hungry. I'm tired.

11. Is it going to rain today?
    Yes, it is.

12. Is it going to rain all day today?
    Yes, it is. The traffic is going to be (<u>estar</u>) terrible.

13. How long have you lived here?
    I have lived here for six weeks.

14. How long have you worked in the Embassy?
    I have worked here for only five days.

15. Do you still live in Brasilia? (<u>os senhores</u>)
    Yes, we do.

16. Do you still work in São Paulo? (<u>os senhores</u>)
    Yes, we do.

17. Do you still speak Spanish? (<u>você</u>)
    Yes, I do. And it still gets in the way.

18. Is the Embassy near? (use <u>fica</u>)
    No, it's far.

19. We can talk in my office.
     Is it near? (use <u>fica</u>)
     Yes, it is.

20. She lives in Leme.
     Is it far from the Consulate? (use <u>fica</u>)
     Yes, it is.

21. He lives far from the office.
     Really? Where does he live?
     In Copacabana.

22. I'm very tired today.
     Really? Why don't you stay home? (use <u>é que</u>)

23. I'm real hungry. When are we going to eat? (use <u>é que</u>)
     We can eat now, if you want to.

24. I like Rio very much.
     Why don't you stay here? (use <u>é que</u>)
     I can't. I work in Brasilia.

B.   Prepare these brief dialogs for display to your instructor.

   1. A. How do you feel today?
       B. I'm still a little tired.

       A. Are you going to work all day?
       B. No, I'm not (going to). I'm going to leave early.

       A. Do you still have a cold?
       B. Yes, I do. (estou)
           [I've had it] for a week.

   2. A. Do you (pl.) live in Washington?
       B. No, we live in Virginia.

       A. Near the river?
       B. No, near the city of Falls Church.

       A. Do you like to live there?
       B. Yes, we do. But it's (fica) far from the office.

   3. A. How's the traffic today? (Use que tal)
       B. Terrible! It's raining again.

       A. And it looks like it's going to rain tomorrow, too.
       B. Of course! The party is tomorrow!

Answers to Practice 2:   He-form: 1, 4, 7, 8
                       They-form: 2, 3, 5, 6, 9, 10
Answers to Practice 9:   1-e, 2-g, 3-f, 4-b, 5-a, 6-h, 7-c, 8-d

UNIT 14

1. Here again is a familiar nasal diphthong.

     ( )x ( )x

2. It appears in two new words in this unit.

        1. ( )   ( )x ( )x

        2. ( )   ( )x ( )x

3. Recall the non-nasal diphthong in solteiro.

        1. ei   ( )x ( )x

        2. solteiro   ( )x ( )x

        3. (again) ei ( )x ( )x

4. Now try these words, all of which end with the same ei
   diphthong. Here, however, it is stressed.

        1. ( )   ( )x ( )x

        2. ( )   ( )x ( )x

        3. ( )   ( )x ( )x

5. When the stressed ei diphthong is added to the stem of
   -ar verbs, as in the examples just given, the verb is
   transformed into the PAST TENSE of the I-form. That is,
   this stressed ei diphthong signals to the listener that
   the speaker did something in the PAST.

   Thus: 1. ( )x ( )x = I talked (past)

               2. ( )x ( )x = I worked (past)

               3. ( )x ( )x = I visited (past)

6. This is what the last three words look like. Look,
   listen and repeat.

        1. falei   ( )x ( )x

        2. trabalhei   ( )x ( )x

        3. visitei ( )x ( )x

14.1

7. This is the way you say 'I got up'.

    ( ) ( )x ( )x

8. Write it in this space. [   ]

(levantei)

9. How do you say 'I lived'?

    Verify: ( )x ( )x

10. How do you say 'I liked'?

    Verify: ( )x ( )x

11. 'I avoided' would be...?

    Verify: ( )x ( )x

12. What does this word mean?

    ( ) ( )

(I arrived)

13. What does this word mean?

    ( ) ( )

(I stayed)

14. And this one?

    ( ) ( )

15. Here is the neutral form of the verb 'study': <u>estudar</u>.

    ( ) ( )x ( )x ( )x

16. How would you say 'I studied'?

    Verify: ( )x ( )x

17. And here is the neutral form of the verb 'pass': <u>passar</u>.

    ( ) ( )x ( )x ( )x

14.2

18. So, how would you say 'I passed'?

Verify: ( )x ( )x

19. Repeat 'I studied' and 'I passed'.

1. ( )x ( )x
2. ( )x ( )x

20. What does this word mean? Be careful!

( ) ( )

(I study: <u>present</u> tense)

21. The distinction between present tense and past tense is
just as essential in Portuguese as it is in English.
In the case of most Portuguese verbs this distinction
is maintained by means of the verb endings.

22. Which of these verbs is present tense, No. 1 or No. 2?

(1) (2)   (1) (2)

(1)

23. Which two of these verbs are <u>past</u> tense?

(1) (2) (3) (4)   (1) (2) (3) (4)

(2,4)

24. The present and past endings have different vowel sounds,
and they have different stresses, too. The <u>ei</u> of <u>falei</u>
is stressed; the <u>o</u> of <u>falo</u> is not stressed.

(falei) (falo)   (falei) (falo)

25. The past tense of the he-form of an -<u>ar</u> verb is signalled
by another diphthong: <u>ou</u>. Recall this diphthong in
these familiar words.

1. <u>sou</u>   ( )x ( )x
2. <u>pouco</u> ( )x ( )x

26. Try the diphthong by itself this time.

<u>ou</u> ( )x ( )x ( )x

27. Now add it to the stem of several -ar verbs. Be sure to
    stress it.

      1. <u>falou</u>   ( ) ( )x ( )x
      2. <u>chegou</u>   ( ) ( )x ( )x
      3. <u>trabalhou</u> ( ) ( )x ( )x
      4. <u>achou</u>   ( ) ( )x ( )x

28. This stressed <u>ou</u> signals that 'he (she, you) <u>did</u> something',
    in the <u>past.</u> Thus <u>chegou</u> would be the form you would
    use to express 'he arrived', 'she arrived' and 'you
    arrived'. As always the native speaker will use a noun
    or pronoun if the identity of the actor is not already
    clear. He may say <u>ele chegou</u>, <u>Yara chegou</u>, etc.

29. What does this mean in English?

                    ( ) ( )

(he got up)

30. What does this mean?

                    ( ) ( )

(you lived)

31. And this?

                    ( ) ( )

(she avoided)

32. How would you say 'she visited'? Use the pronoun.

           Verify: ( )x ( )x

33. How would you say 'she talked'?

           Verify: ( )x ( )x

34. How about 'he stayed'? Use the pronoun.

           Verify: ( )x ( )x

35. And 'he practiced?

           Verify: ( )x ( )x

14.4

36. Here is 'you noticed!

( )x   ( )x

37. How would you say 'you studied'?   Use the pronoun.

Verify: ( )x   ( )x

38. How would you say 'you passed'?

Verify: ( )x   ( )x

39. Here is another new -ar verb: the neutral form of
'prepare'.

( )   ( )x   ( )x   ( )x

40. Here is 'he prepared'

( )x   ( )x

41. What does this mean?

( )   ( )

(I prepared)

42. The past tense verb forms that you have just been practicing all fall into regular, predictable patterns. In
the dialog of this unit you will find several past tense
forms that do not seem to follow a pattern. They are
said to be irregular.

End of Tape 5B

Tape 6A

43. For example, here is the past tense of the I-form of
'going', that is, 'I went'.

( )   ( )x   ( )x   ( )x

44. And here is the past tense of the he-form of 'going', that
is, 'he went'.

( )   ( )x   ( )x   ( )x

45. Listen to them side by side.

(I went)   (he went)   (I went)   (he went)

46. Now repeat.

(I went)x   (he went)x   (I went)x   (he went)x

14.5

47. Which one is this?

( ) ( )

(he went)

48. Which one is 'I went'?

(1) (2)   (1) (2)

(2)

49. The past tense of the verb 'have' is also irregular in the
past. Here is the I-form ('I had').

( ) ( )x ( )x ( )x

50. Now listen to the he-form ('he had'). Do not repeat yet.

( ) ( ) ( )

51. Here are the he-form and the I-form, one after the other.
Observe that it is the first vowel, not the final one,
that distinguishes them.

(I had) (he had)   (I had) (he had)

52. Now repeat the he-form.

he had ( )x ( )x ( )x

53. Now repeat the he-form and the I-form.

he had ( )x   I had ( )x   he had ( )x   I had ( )x

54. You will remember that in the present tense you must
insert the word que between a form of 'having' and a
neutral form. Thus you have learned to say, for example,
Tenho que ficar 'I have to stay'. This same que must
again be inserted when you are dealing with the past
tense. Therefore, 'I had to stay' is said as follows:

a. ( ) ( )

Likewise, 'He had to stay' is said as follows:

b. ( ) ( )

55. Repeat 'I had to stay'.

( ) ( )x ( )x

56. Now repeat 'He had to stay'.

( ) ( )x ( )x

57. What does this sentence mean in English?

( ) ( )

(He had to leave)

58. What does this sentence mean?

( ) ( )

(I had to leave)

59. What does this one mean?

( ) ( )

(I had to work)

60. And this one?

( ) ( )

(He had to work)

(For items 61-64 check the tape for confirmation _after_ making your response aloud).

61. How would you say 'I had to work'?

( ) ( )

62. How would you say 'I had to practice'?

( ) ( )

63. How would you say 'He had to practice'?

( ) ( )

64. And finally how would you say 'He had to talk'?

( ) ( )

65. In this unit you will meet two more obligatory contractions.
When the preposition <u>a</u> ('to', 'at') is followed by a
definite article ('the'), the two items always combine to
form a contraction. Thus, for example:

<u>a</u> + <u>o</u> contracts to <u>ao</u>.

66. Listen to <u>ao</u>, then repeat.

( ) ( )x ( )x ( )x

67. Here is the way to say 'to the tunnel'.

( ) ( )x ( )x

68. Here is 'to the office'.

( ) ( )x ( )x

69. This is 'to the downtown'.

( ) ( )x ( )x

70. How would you say 'to the park'?

Verify: ( )x ( )x

71. How would you say 'to (the) Rio'?

Verify: ( )x ( )x

72. When <u>a</u> is followed by the feminine definite article <u>a</u>,
the resulting contraction is simply a slight lengthening
of the <u>a</u> sound. In normal speech this is sometimes very
difficult to hear. The contraction is written with just
one <u>a</u>, over which is placed a grave accent ( ). Thus:

<u>a</u> ('to') + <u>a</u> ('the') = <u>à</u> ('to the')

73. Here is the way to say 'to the city'. (Lengthen the <u>a</u>
sound just a bit.)

( ) ( )x ( )x ( )x

74. Here is 'to the party'.

( ) ( )x ( )x ( )x

75. This is 'to my wife'.

( ) ( )x ( )x ( )x

14.8

76. How would you say 'to the room'?

                 Verify: ( )x ( )x

77. How would you say 'to the Embassy'?

                 Verify: ( )x ( )x

78. Here is 'in the afternoon'. Literally, 'at the after-
     noon'.

              ( ) ( )x ( )x

Observation

    We are coming to another contraction, one which occurs
much less frequently than the others you already know. It
is the sequence 'in it', or 'on it'. First of all, let us explain
that after a preposition ('in', 'at', 'for', 'to', etc.) the word
'it' assumes either a masculine form (ele) or a feminine form
(ela), thereby reflecting the gender of the item being talked
about. When the preposition is em, a contraction always results.

              Em + ele = nele   on it (masc.)
              Em + ela = nela   on it (fem.)

79. Here, then, is nela.   (Notice the open E sound.)

              ( ) ( )x ( )x ( )x

80. And here is nele. (There is no open E sound.)

              ( ) ( )x ( )x ( )x

81. Is this item referring to something masculine or something
     feminine?

              ( ) ( )

(masc.)

82. Which of these items refers to something feminine?

              (1) (2) (3)   (1) (2) (3)

(1)

14.9

83. And here, on paper only, are two English words, the
    Portuguese counterparts of which appear for the first
    time in this unit. We want to remind you of where these
    English words are stressed, and we have done so by
    writing a stress mark over the stressed vowels. Say
    these words to yourself.

       1. díalog

       2. dífficult.

84. Now listen to the Portuguese counterparts.

       1. ( ) ( )

       2. ( ) ( )

85. Here they are again. Listen, then with your pencil
    write a stress mark over the stressed vowel of each.
    Don't repeat yet.

       1. ( ) ( )   dialogo

       2. ( ) ( )   dificil

(diálogo)
(difícil)

86. Now continuing to be mindful of the stress, repeat
    these two words as indicated.

       1. ( ) ( )x ( )x ( )x

       2. ( ) ( )x ( )x ( )x

Dialog

o professor, a professora	teacher
o aluno	student

- - - - - - - - - -

O professor

fazer	do, make (neutral form)
a tarde	afternoon
à tarde	in the afternoon
hoje à tarde	this afternoon
O que é que o senhor vai fazer hoje à tarde?	What are you going to do this afternoon?
estudar	study (neutral form)
a lição	lesson
treze	thirteen

O aluno

Vou estudar a lição treze.	I'm going to study lesson thirteen.
estudou	studied (he-form: past)
ontem	yesterday

O professor

O senhor não estudou ontem?	Didn't you study [it] yesterday?

14.11

estudei	studied (I-form: past)
doze	twelve
a doze	the [lesson] twelve

O aluno

Não. Estudei a doze.

No. I studied number twelve.

tão	so
difícil	difficult

E é tão difícil!

And it's so difficult!

passei	spent (I-form: past)
a hora	hour
nela	on it [i.e., the lesson]

Passei três horas nela.

I spent three hours on it.

Nossa!	Gosh! *
então	then
foi	went (He-form: past)
ao	to the
ao cinema	to the movies

O professor

Nossa! Então o senhor não foi ao cinema com os outros.

Gosh! Then you didn't go to the movies with the others.

fui	went (I-form: past)
fiquei	stayed (I-form: past)

---

*Literally, short for Nossa Senhora! (Our Lady!), a mild oath.

14.12

<u>O aluno</u>

<u>Não</u>, <u>não</u> <u>fui</u>. <u>Fiquei</u> em   <u>No</u>, <u>I</u> <u>didn't</u> <u>go</u>. <u>I</u>
<u>casa</u>.   <u>stayed</u> <u>at</u> <u>home</u>.

    tive   had (I-form: past)

    preparar   prepare (neutral form)

    tive que preparar   I had to prepare

    o diálogo   dialog

<u>Tive</u> <u>que</u> <u>preparar</u> <u>os</u>   <u>I</u> <u>had</u> <u>to</u> <u>prepare</u> <u>the</u>
<u>diálogos</u>.   <u>dialogs</u>.

A LOOK AT THE GRAMMAR

Practice Exercises

Part I. Past tense of -ar verbs

Practice 1: (Recorded)

Listen to these I-forms of -ar verbs in the past. In each case
the instructor is saying 'I did something.' Repeat after him. The
pronoun for 'I' is deliberately omitted.

1. studied
2. spoke
3. practiced
4. noticed
5. liked
6. got up
7. avoided
8. visited
9. arrived
10. worked
11. passed
12. prepared

Practice 2: (Recorded)

Now listen to these he-forms of -ar verbs in the past. In each
case the instructor is saying that 'somebody else' did something.
However, 'somebody else' remains nameless for the sake of this
practice. Repeat each one.

1. studied
2. spoke
3. practiced
4. noticed
5. liked
6. got up
7. avoided
8. visited
9. arrived
10. worked
11. passed
12. prepared

14.14

Practice 3: (Recorded)

In this practice you are to determine whether the instructor
is saying 'I did something' or 'he did something'. You have only
the verb endings to guide you. Mark your choice in the appropriate
column in the chart below. Answers are at the end of this unit.

'_I_ did'   '_He_ did'

1		
2		
3		
4		
5		
6		
7		
8		
9		
10		
11		
12		
13		
14		

Practice 4: (Recorded)

Determine which of these forms say 'he _did_ something' (past)
and which ones say 'I _do_ something' (present). Mark the chart
accordingly.

'He _did_   'I _do_'

1		
2		
3		
4		
5		
6		
7		
8		
9		
10		
11		
12		
13		
14		

14.15

Practice 5: (Recorded)

In this practice you will again hear your instructor mix I-forms and he-forms at random, but this time he is putting them all in the past. Furthermore, he is preceding each one with a noun or pronoun. Listen, and repeat each one.

(1-24)x

Practice 6: (Recorded)

The English voice on the tape will ask you to give certain information about yourself, and you are to give it immediately afterwards in the pause provided. For example, in No. 1. the English voice will say, 'Tell me that you arrived', and you will answer in Portuguese, 'I arrived'. Use the pronoun eu in your response. The correct response appears on the tape.

(1-12)

Practice 7: (Recorded)

This time the English voice will ask you to tell what others did, and you are to respond as directed, using nouns and pronouns as appropriate. For example, if the English voice says, 'Tell me that Yara arrived', you will respond in Portuguese, 'Yara arrived'. The correct response appears on the tape.

(1-14)

Practice 8: (Recorded)

Instructor A will ask Instructor B if he (Instructor B) did something, and Instructor B will answer either that he did or that he did not. Just listen; do not repeat.

(1-8)

Practice 9: (Recorded)

This time instructor A will ask you if you did something. Answer affirmatively in numbers 1-6; answer negatively in numbers 7-12. You will then hear your response confirmed. (Note: instructor A is using o senhor in his questions. If you are female, you should mentally convert this to a senhora.)

14.16

Practice 10: (Recorded)

In this exercise instructor A will ask instructor B if <u>somebody</u>
<u>else</u> did something, and instructor B will answer either affirmatively
or negatively. Just listen; do not repeat.

(1-8)

Practice 11: (Recorded)

In this exercise the instructor will ask <u>you</u> if somebody else
did something, and you should reply, affirmatively in 1-6, and
negatively in 7-12. You will hear your answer confirmed.

Practice 12: (Recorded)

In this exercise you are to ask the questions, rather than
give the answers. Using <u>O senhor</u>, practice asking the following
questions. (The questions, not the answers, are recorded on the
tape. Check them to confirm your response.)

1.   Did you study?
2.   Did you work?
3.   Did you practice?
4.   Did you get up?
5.   Did you like [it]?*
6.   Did you notice [it]?*
7.   Did you speak Portuguese?
8.   Did you avoid the traffic?
9.   Did you visit Paul?
10. Did you arrive yesterday?
11. Did you prepare the dialog?
12. Did you spend three hours?

Practice 13: (Recorded)

In this exercise you are to ask the questions about another
person, either Yara or Paulo, as indicated. Again, you should
confirm your question by checking with the tape.

1.   Did Yara get up?
2.   Did Yara get up at seven?
3.   Did Yara practice?
4.   Did Yara practice the dialog?
5.   Did Paul study?
6.   Did Paul study (the) lesson thirteen?

_____

*Do not try to put 'it' into Portuguese.

14.17

7. Did Paul work?
8. Did Paul work yesterday?
9. Did Paul work this afternoon?
10. Did Yara prepare?
11. Did Yara prepare well?
12. Did Yara arrive?
13. Did Yara arrive early?
14. Did Yara speak English?
15. Did Yara speak English with you?
16. Did Yara spend (pass) the day with you?

Practice 14: (Recorded)

This exercise contrasts the past tense with the future construction that you have learned. Below you will find a list of 'actions'.
In each case you are to say that Paulo didn't do the action yesterday
but that he is going to do it today. Number 1, for example, would
be as follows:

O Paulo não estudou ontem, mas ele vai estudar hoje.
     (Paul didn't study yesterday, but he's going
     to study today.)

Check your answer with the tape.

1. study   5. prepare the dialog
2. work   6. get up early
3. practice   7. speak Portuguese
4. arrive

Part II: Past tense of 'having'

Practice 15: (Recorded)

On the tape you will hear your instructor say 'I had to work',
then 'I had to practice', then a number of other actions that he
had to perform and indeed did perform. Repeat each short phrase
after him, imagining that you yourself had to perform the action
and did so. Observe the word que preceding the neutral form.

(1-9)x

Practice 16: (Recorded)

This time you will hear your instructor say that somebody
else (whose name is omitted here) had to perform a number of actions.
As before, repeat each short phrase.

(1-9)x

14.18

<u>Practice 17</u>:   (Recorded)

In this practice Instructor A will ask Instructor B if he
(Instructor B) had to do something, and B will answer either that
he had to or that he did not have to.   Notice that Instructor B
does not need to repeat the neutral form in his answer.   Just listen.

(1-8)

<u>Practice 18</u>:   (Recorded)

This time Instructor A's questions are directed at <u>you</u>, (and
he is using the familiar <u>você</u>!)   Answer affirmatively, then check
your response with the tape.

(1-8)

<u>Practice 19</u>:   (Recorded)

Listen to the tape.   An English voice will instruct you to say
that you had to do such-and-such.   Make your response, then check
with the tape for confirmation.

(1-7)

<u>Practice 20</u>:   (Recorded)

This time the English voice will instruct you to say that
<u>somebody else</u> had to do something.   Again, make your response
and confirm with the tape.

(1-7)

<u>Practice 21</u>:   (Recorded)

Now <u>ask the questions</u> which are requested by the voice on the
tape.   After responding, check the tape for confirmation.   (Use
<u>você</u> in numbers 1-5).

(1-9)

Part III: More obligatory contractions with a

Practice 22: (Recorded)

Practice repeating these contractions.

A. a + o = ao   Usual English equivalent is 'to the, at the'.

1. ao Rio: ( ) ( )x ( )x
2. ao centro: ( ) ( )x ( )x
3. ao parque: ( ) ( )x ( )x
4. ao túnel: ( ) ( )x ( )x
5. ao Brasil: ( ) ( )x ( )x
6. ao Carlos: ( ) ( )x ( )x
7. ao cinema: ( ) ( )x ( )x

B. a + a = à   Usual equivalent is 'to the, at the'.

1. à avenida: ( ) ( )x ( )x
2. à festa: ( ) ( )x ( )x
3. à embaixada: ( ) ( )x ( )x
4. à mesa: ( ) ( )x ( )x
5. à cidade: ( ) ( )x ( )x
6. à sala: ( ) ( )x ( )x

Practice 23: (Recorded)

Listen to these brief questions and answers as spoken by two instructors on the tape. Do not repeat.

(1-7)

Practice 24: (Recorded)

How would you say these short utterances?

1. I'm going to the party.
2. I'm going to the movies.
3. I'm going to (the) Rio.
4. He's going to the embassy.

14.20

    5. He's going to (the) Brazil.
    6. He's going to the park.
    7. He's going to the city.
    8. Are you going to the other room? (Use o senhor.)
    9. Are you going to the city?
   10. Are you going to the office?

Part IV: Past tense of 'going'

Practice 25: (Recorded)

     Your tape instructor will say a series of sentences beginning
with 'I went'. Repeat each one after him.

                         (1-10)x

Practice 26: (Recorded)

     In this series the instructor tells you that 'somebody else
went'. Repeat after him.

                         (1-10)x

Practice 27: (Recorded)

     Listen to these brief questions and answers. Do not repeat.

                    (1-8)   End of Tape 6A

[Note: Practices 28-33 are not recorded.]
Practice 28: (Recorded)

     In this exercise the voice on the tape requests that you ask
him a number of questions. Do so, then check the tape for confirmation of your questions. Use você for 'you'.

Practice 29: (Recorded)

     In this exercise you are to answer the questions you hear on
the tape. Answer 1-5 affirmatively, 6-10 negatively. The answers
are recorded for you.

Part V: More on the conjunction que.

In the last unit you practiced using the conjunction que ('that') in such sentences as these:

Acho que vai chover.   (I think that it's going
                                         to rain.)

Parece que vai chover.   (It seems that it's going
                                         to rain.)

Now, you will see that you will also have frequent occasions to use the que after various forms of the verb falar.

Ele fala que vai chover.   (He says that it's going
                                         to rain.)

Ele falou que estudou muito.   (He said that he studied
                                         a lot.)

In such instances it is best to think of falar as meaning 'to say', rather than 'to speak' or 'to talk'.

Practice 30: (Recorded)

Listen to these short sentences, all of which begin with Ele fala que (He says that). Repeat each one.

(1-11)x

Practice 31: (Recorded)

All of these sentences begin with Ele falou que (He said that). Repeat each one.

(1-11)x

Practice 32: (Recorded)

All of these sentences begin with Eu falei que (I said that). Repeat each one.

(1-10)x

Practice 33: (Recorded)

In this practice you will hear instructor A ask instructor B, 'Did you say that you did such-and-such?' Instructor B will answer either, 'I said so', or 'I didn't say so'. Listen to both the questions and the answers, and repeat only the answers.

(1-7)

14.22

UNIT 15

1. Recall the R sound in these words from past units.

    a. senhoR   ( )x ( )x
    b. fazeR   ( )x ( )x
    c. poRque   ( )x ( )x
    d. peRto   ( )x ( )x
    e. taRde   ( )x ( )x

2. Now here are several words from this unit which have the R sound. Listen, then repeat.

    a. poRta   ( ) ( )   ( )x ( )x
    b. caloR   ( ) ( )   ( )x ( )x
    c. veR   ( ) ( )   ( )x ( )x
    d. inteRvalo ( ) ( )   ( )x ( )x

3. Now, recall these words, all of which have a t sound followed by an i sound.

    a. presidente ( )x ( )x
    b. sente   ( )x ( )x
    c. igualmente ( )x ( )x

4. These three words can also be pronounced differently, by giving the t a ch-type quality.

    a. presidente ( )x ( )x
    b. sente   ( )x ( )x
    c. igualmente ( )x ( )x

5. Here are two new words from the present unit which have this same feature of pronunciation. First, practice pronouncing them this way:

    a. frente   ( ) ( )x ( )x
    b. restaurante ( ) ( )x ( )x

6. Now, practice pronouncing them this way:

    a. fren<u>te</u>   ( ) ( )x ( )x

    b. restauran<u>te</u> ( ) ( )x ( )x

7. The second word above (<u>restaurante</u>) is sometimes difficult for English speakers. Try practicing it syllable by syllable.

    a. res   ( )x ( )x

    b. tau   ( )x ( )x

    c. restau   ( )x ( )x

    d. ran   ( )x ( )x

    e. restauran   ( )x ( )x

    f. restaurante ( )x ( )x

8. Which vowel is the stressed vowel? Underline it.
    restaurante ( ) ( )

(restau<u>ra</u>nte)

9. Notice the diphthong <u>au</u> in the syllable <u>tau</u>.

    rest<u>au</u>-   ( )x ( )x

10. Now do the whole word again.

    restaurante: ( )x ( )x ( )x

11. Here is a familiar <u>nasal</u> diphthong.

    ão: ( )x ( )x

12. Recall it in these words:

    a. Stressed.

        1. <u>não</u> ( )x ( )x

        2. <u>vão</u> ( )x ( )x

        3. <u>então</u> ( )x ( )x

        4. <u>lição</u> ( )x ( )x

15.2

b. Unstressed (spelled _am_)

    1. <u>moram</u>.   ( )x ( )x
    2. <u>trabalham</u>   ( )x ( )x
    3. <u>ficam</u>   ( )x ( )x

13. As shown in (b) above, the unstressed ão diphthong
    (spelled _am_) signals the they-form of -_ar_ verbs in
    the present tense. Other familiar examples of this
    form are:

    <u>praticam</u>   ( )x ( )x
    <u>estudam</u>   ( )x ( )x
    <u>preparam</u>   ( )x ( )x

14. This same unstressed ão diphthong is also part of
    the ending which signals the they-form of -_ar_ verbs
    in the _past_ tense. Compare these present and past
    tense forms. Do not repeat yet.

Present	Past
a. <u>estudam</u> ( )	<u>estudaram</u> ( )
b. <u>falam</u> ( )	<u>falaram</u> ( )
c. <u>ficam</u> ( )	<u>ficaram</u> ( )
d. <u>trabalham</u> ( )	<u>trabalharam</u> ( )

15. As you can see and hear, the ending which signals the
    they-form of -_ar_ verbs in the past is -_aram_. The first
    syllable (-_a_-) is stressed; the second syllable (-_ram_)
    is not stressed. The familiar unstressed ão diphthong
    is, of course, part of the second syllable. Now, repeat
    this two-syllable ending.

    -<u>aram</u>   ( ) ( )x ( )x ( )x

16. The _r_ in the ending is the single-flap _r_ of <u>Yara</u>, <u>Maria</u>,
    etc. Repeat this sequence:

    a. <u>Yara</u> ( )x ( )x
    b. -<u>aram</u> ( )x ( )x ( )x

17. Now try this sequence.

    a. -aram   ( )x ( )x
    b. falaram   ( )x ( )x : they spoke

18. And this sequence.

    a. -aram   ( )x ( )x
    b. estudaram   ( )x ( )x : they studied
    c. ficaram   ( )x ( )x : they stayed
    d. trabalharam   ( )x ( )x : they worked

19. Here is 'they practiced'.

    ( )   ( )x ( )x ( )x

20. Here is 'they prepared'.

    ( )   ( )x ( )x ( )x

21. How would you say 'they lived'?

    Verify: ( )x ( )x

22. How would you say 'they passed'?

    Verify: ( )x ( )x

23. Remember that the they-form is also used when 'you'
(plural) is the actor. Therefore, what is the form
for 'you (all) arrived'?

    Verify: ( )x ( )x

24. How would you say 'you (all) got up'?

    Verify: ( )x ( )x

25. This unit also deals with the we-form of -ar verbs in
the past. Fortunately, it is the same as the present
tense form, which you already know. Listen to these
we-forms of -ar verbs in the present and past tenses.
You will not hear any difference between present and
past.

15.4

1. a. (chegamos): we arrive   b. (chegamos): we arrived

2. a. (falamos): we speak   b. (falamos): we spoke

3. a. (trabalhamos): we work   b. (trabalhamos): we worked

4. a. (moramos): we live   b. (moramos): we lived

26. They sound the same. How do Portuguese speakers (and you) know which one has been said? The total context in which an utterance is said usually makes it clear which meaning is intended. Accompanying words such as ontem (yesterday) and hoje (today) will often provide unmistakeable clues as to which one the speaker has in mind.

27. Repeat these we-forms in the past tense.

> chegamos   ( )x ( )x
> praticamos ( )x ( )x
> ficamos   ( )x ( )x
> moramos   ( )x ( )x
> preparamos ( )x ( )x

28. Here is the we-form (past tense) of a new -ar verb in this unit. It means 'we took'.

> tomamos   ( ) ( ) ( )x ( )x ( )x

29. How would you say 'we take'?

> Verify: ( )x ( )x

30. How would you say the neutral form?

> Verify: ( )x ( )x

31. Here is the present tense, we-form, of another new -ar verb. It means 'we eat lunch'.

> almoçamos   ( ) ( ) ( )x ( )x ( )x

32. Since you know how to say 'we eat lunch', you also know how to say 'we ate lunch'. What is the form?

> Verify: ( )x ( )x

33. What is the neutral form?

    Verify: ( )x ( )x

34. 'We ate dinner', or 'we dined', is:

    <u>jantamos</u>   ( )   ( )   ( )x   ( )x   ( )x

35. The present tense form, i. e., 'we <u>eat</u> dinner', is
    therefore:

    <u>jantamos</u>   ( )   ( )   ( )x   ( )x   ( )x

36. What is the neutral form?

    Verify: ( )x ( )x

37. Recall from the previous unit the I-form and the he-form
    of 'go', in the past tense. Repeat.

        I went : <u>fui</u> ( )x ( )x
        he went: <u>foi</u> ( )x ( )x

38. Here is the they-form; i.e., 'they went'.

        ( )   ( )   ( )x   ( )x   ( )x

39. Again, notice the presence of the <u>ão</u> diphthong in the
    ending.

        ( )x ( )x

40. Here is the we-form; i.e., 'we went'.

        ( )   ( )   ( )x   ( )x   ( )x

41. Now, here are all four forms together.

        I went: <u>fui</u> ( )x ( )x
        he went: <u>foi</u> ( )x ( )x
        we went: <u>fomos</u> ( )x ( )x
        they went: <u>foram</u> ( )x ( )x

42. You will also recall from the last unit the irregular
    forms for 'I had' and 'he had'. Repeat.

      I had: <u>tive</u> ( )x ( )x
      he had: <u>teve</u>   ( )x ( )x

43. In this unit you will work with the forms for 'they had'
    and 'we had'. Here is 'they had'.

      ( ) ( ) ( )x ( )x ( )x

44. Again, notice the unstressed ão diphthong in the ending.

      ( )x ( )x ( )x

45. Here, now, is the we-form; i.e., 'we had'.

      ( ) ( ) ( )x ( )x ( )x

46. Now review all four forms together.

      I had: <u>tive</u> ( )x ( )x
      he had: <u>teve</u> ( )x ( )x
      we had: <u>tivemos</u> ( )x ( )x
      they had: <u>tiveram</u> ( )x ( )x

47. Here is the neutral form of the verb 'open'. It is an
    -<u>ir</u> verb. Listen and repeat.

      ( ) ( ) ( )x ( )x ( )x

48. Here is the we-form, present tense.

      ( ) ( ) ( )x ( )x ( )x

49. Notice the <u>i</u> sound in the ending. It is a sure clue
    that the verb form is an -<u>ir</u> type verb.

      abrimos   ( )x ( )x ( )x

50. You have had the neutral form of 'leaving'· i.e., <u>sair</u>.
    Now listen to 'we leave', and repeat.

      ( ) ( ) ( )x ( )x ( )x

51. In another unit we will deal with -ir type verbs in more
    detail. Right now, let us turn our attention to something
    else.

52. You remember how you say the 'good' of the greeting, 'good
    day'.

    a. bom   ( )x ( )x
    b. bom dia   ( )x ( )x

53. Bom is the masculine form of 'good'. Since the word for
    'day' is masculine, the accompanying adjective 'good'
    must also be masculine. This is another example of gender
    agreement.

54. Recall also the greeting 'good afternoon.'

        boa tarde   ( )x   ( )x   ( )x

55. Repeat just 'good'.

        boa   ( )x ( )x

56. This is the feminine form. Since tarde is feminine, the
    accompanying adjective 'good' must also be feminine.
    Observe and repeat.

        boa tarde   ( ) ( )x ( )x ( )x

57 Recall also the word for 'night' or 'evening.'

        noite   ( )x ( )x ( )x

58. It is feminine too. Thus, 'good evening' or 'good
    night' is said like this, you will recall.

        boa noite   ( )x ( )x

59. Repeat again.

        boa noite   ( )x ( )x ( )x

60. Listen to this diphthong.

        (Ei) (Ei)

61. It is different from this diphthong.

(ei) (ei)

62. It is different because it has the open E sound, not the
closed e sound which you hear in ei. Listen and mimic
as accurately as you can.

Ei   ( ) ( )x ( )x ( )x

63. Here is the word for 'idea'. Listen for the Ei diphthong.

idÉia   ( ) ( ) ( )

64. Now repeat.

idÉia   ( )x ( )x ( )x

65. You already know the I-form and the he-form of the neutral
form ser.

a. sou ( )x ( )x
b. é   ( )x ( )x

66. In this unit you will practice the we-form and the
they-form. Here is the they-form (i.e., 'they are').

são   ( ) ( ) ( )x ( )x ( )x

67. Here is the we-form (i.e., 'we are')

somos   ( ) ( ) ( )x ( )x ( )x

68. The form são appears in the expression which leads off
the dialog for this unit, namely: Que horas são?. This
is the equivalent of 'What time is it?' Literally, the
translation is, 'What hours are (they)?' Listen and
repeat.

Que horas são   ( ) ( ) ( )x ( )x ( )x

69. It also appears in the response: São dez horas. 'It's
ten o'clock' (they are ten hours).

São dez horas   ( ) ( ) ( )x ( )x ( )x

15.9

70. In this unit you will also work with the we-form and the
    they-form of the other verb which represents 'being':
    estar. You already know the I-form and the he-form.

        I am: estou ( )x ( )x
        he is: está ( )x ( )x

71. Here are the two new forms.

        We are: estamos ( )x ( )x
        They are: estão ( )x ( )x

72. Here are the I-form and the he-form of 'having' in the
    present tense. You already know both of these forms.

        I have: tenho ( )x ( )x
        he has: tem ( )x ( )x

73. Now here are the we-form and the they-form.

        we have: temos ( )x ( )x
        they have: têm ( )x ( )x

74. For Brazilians the he-form and the they-form sound
    the same. The circumflex accent (^) differentiates
    the two in standard spelling.
        a. tem ( )x ( )x
        b. têm ( )x ( )x
75. Here, finally, is the neutral form.

        ter ( )x ( )x ( )x

76. Recall the form conheço 'I know' from a previous dialog.

        conheço   ( )x .( )x

77. The neutral form of this verb is conhecer.

        conhecer   ( ) ( )x ( )x ( )x

78. Conhecer refers to 'knowing' in the sense of 'being
     acquainted with'. This usually means people, but it
     can also mean cities, books, buildings, and indeed
     anything else that we might be acquainted with.

        Conheço a Yara.   I know (am acquainted with) Yara.
        Conheço o Rio.   I know (am acquainted with) Rio.
        Conheço o livro.   I know (am acquainted with) the book.
        Conheço a Embaixada.   I know (am acquainted with) the Embassy.

79. Portuguese has another verb that covers our concept of
     'knowing'. The neutral form of this verb is saber. The
     I-form of saber, in the present tense, is sei.

        sei   ( )x   ( )x   ( )x

80. When one wishes to say that he possesses facts or information,
     he uses a form of saber.

     a. Ele é casado.   He's married.
         Eu sei.   I know.

     b. Vai chover?   Is it going to rain?
         Não sei.   I don't know.

81. Which verb, sei or conheço, would you use in this sentence?
        Não _____ os dois meninos.

(conheço)

82. Which one would you use in this sentence?
        Não _____ quando vamos jantar.

(sei)

83. Every once in a while the distinction becomes a little fine.

        Eu conheço o livro.   I'm acquainted with the book.
        Eu sei o livro.   I know the book (thoroughly).

     But these instances are not common and you should not worry
     too much about them.

DIALOG

Na escola (At school)

O professor

são	'being' (they-form, present)
Que horas são?	What time is it?

O aluno

sei	know (I-form, present)
Não sei.	I don't know.
deixe	let (command form)*
me	me
deixe-me	let me
ver	see (neutral form)
Deixe-me ver.	Let me see.
Ah! São dez horas.	Ah! It's ten o'clock.

O professor

já	already
Já? Nossa!	Already? Gosh!
está na hora	it's time
o intervalo	break period, interval
Está na hora do intervalo.	It's break time.

---

*Command forms are examined in a later unit.

15.12

trabalharam	work (they-form, past)
Vocês trabalharam muito esta hora.	You worked hard this hour.

O aluno

abrimos	open (we-form, present)
a porta	door
a janela	window
Por que não abrimos a porta e umas janelas?	Why don't we open the door and some windows?
fazendo	making
está fazendo	it's making
Está fazendo calor aqui.	It's hot in here.

O professor

boa	good
a idéia	idea
Boa idéia.	Good idea.

- -

O professor

já	already, yet
tomaram	take (they-form, past)
o café	coffee
Vocês já tomaram café?	Did you have (take) coffee yet?

O aluno

tomamos	take (we-form, past)
chegamos	arrive (we-form, past)

15.13

embaixo   below

lá embaixo   downstairs (there below)

Já.[1] Tomamos lá embaixo   Yes, we did. We had (took)
quando chegamos.   some downstairs when we
                                           arrived.

O professor

nada   nothing

ainda não   not yet

Eu ainda não tomei nada.[2]   I haven't had anything yet.

  jantei   eat dinner (I-form, past)

  a noite   night

  à noite   at night

  ontem à noite   last night (yesterday
                                                        at night)
  demais   too much

Jantei demais ontem à noite.   I ate too much (dinner) last
                                           night.

- -

O professor

Boa tarde.   Good afternoon.

  almoçaram   eat lunch (they-form, past)

Vocês almoçaram bem?   Did you have a good lunch?

_____

[1]Já, meaning 'already', is used here in response to the já in
the question just asked.

[2]Literally, 'I did not take nothing yet'. This kind of double
negative is standard in Portuguese.

15.14

<u>O aluno</u>

almoçamos	eat lunch (we-form, past)
fomos	go (we-form, past), i.e., 'we went'
o restaurante	restaurant
em frente	across the street

<u>Almoçamos, sim. Nós fomos ao restaurante em frente</u>.

<u>Yes, we did. We went to the restaurant across the street</u>.

15.15

A LOOK AT THE GRAMMAR

Practice Exercises

<u>Part I</u>. -<u>ar</u> verbs in the past; we-forms and they-forms

<u>Practice 1</u>: (Recorded)

Listen to this group of we-forms of -<u>ar</u> verbs in the past.
In each case, the voice says 'we <u>did</u> something'. Remember that
this form happens to be the same as the one that says 'we <u>do</u>
something' (in the present).

(1-14)

<u>Practice 2</u>: (Recorded)

Now practice repeating these we-forms.

(1-14)xx

<u>Practice 3</u>: (Recorded)

This is a comprehension check. After each lettered item is
presented on the tape, stop the tape and select the correct meaning
of that item from the list below. Write the corresponding number
in the blank. Answers are at the end of this unit.

a. _____   1. we worked

b. _____   2. we had lunch

c. _____   3. we ate dinner

d. _____   4. we prepared

e. _____   5. we lived

f. _____   6. we arrived

g. _____   7. we got up

h. _____   8. we practiced

i. _____   9. we took

15.16

j. _____	10. we noted
k. _____	11. we stayed
l. _____	12. we liked

Practiced 4: (Recorded)

Now listen to these they-forms of -ar verbs in the past. In each case the speaker is saying that 'they' or 'you-all' did something.

$$(1-14)x$$

Practice 5: (Recorded)

In this exercise you are to practice repeating the they-forms that appear on the tape.

$$(1-14)xx$$

Practice 6: (Recorded)

This is another comprehension check, similar to the one in Practice 3 above. Listen to the items on the tape and indicate in the blanks below the number of the correct English equivalent.

a. _____	1. they worked
b. _____	2. they liked
c. _____	3. they took
d. _____	4. they visited
e. _____	5. they ate lunch
f. _____	6. they arrived
g. _____	7. they studied
h. _____	8. they prepared
i. _____	9. they passed
j. _____	10. they had dinner
k. _____	11. they spoke
l. _____	12. they thought

15.17

Practice 7: (Recorded)

In this exercise one of the instructors will ask the other if some other people (eles or elas) did something. The second instructor will answer in the affirmative. You are to repeat the answer after the second instructor gives it.

(1-10)

Practice 8: (Recorded)

This exercise is similar to the preceding one. However, this time the questions are directed at you, and you are to answer affirmatively in the pause provided on the tape before the second instructor responds with the correct answer.

(1-10)

Practice 9: (Recorded)

Now the first instructor addresses both you and the second instructor, asking the two of you (os senhores) if you did something. Let the second instructor answer first, then you mimic his answer. Some answers will be affirmative, others negative.

(1-10)

Practice 10: (Recorded)

This time through, you answer first, then listen to the second instructor confirming your response. Answer affirmatively each time.

(1-10)

Practice 11: (Recorded)

Same procedure as in No.10 above, but this time answer in the negative.

(1-8)

End of Tape 6B

15.18

Practice 12: (Recorded)

Listen to the instructions given on the tape, and ask the
questions that are suggested there. Then check the tape for
confirmation. This exercise is in two parts.

(1-8)

Observation:

Since you are going from English into Portuguese, it is often
to your advantage to take English equivalents into special account.
Such is the case with the English equivalents of the past tense
forms you have been practicing. So far we have indicated the English
equivalents as simple pasts. For example:

trabalhei	=	I worked
ficou	=	he stayed
levantamos	=	we got up
falaram	=	they talked, or they spoke

But we could also have translated them as follows:

trabalhei	=	I _have_ worked
ficou	=	he _has_ stayed
levantamos	=	we _have_ gotten up
falaram	=	they _have_ talked, or they _have_ spoken.

There is no separate tense in Portuguese for translating the
English construction of the type (_have/has_ + past participial of main
verb), often referred to as the 'present perfect tense'. Portuguese
uses the simple past in most instances where English uses this kind
of construction. Thus, for example, in a situation where you might
be inclined to say 'He has eaten lunch', you will need to recast
your thoughts in terms of 'He _ate_ lunch' (_ele almoçou_). Similarly,
the question 'Has he eaten lunch?' would be reinterpreted as 'Did
he eat lunch?' (_ele almoçou?_).

Practice 13:   (Recorded)

How would you say the following in Portuguese? This time the
verification procedure is different.   Keep the response in the
right hand column below covered until after you have spoken aloud.
Then verify your response by checking the tape and the printed
answer below.

1.	Joe has worked a lot.	O José trabalhou muito.
2.	Joe has prepared the lesson.	O José preparou a lição.
3.	Has Joe arrived?	O José chegou?
4.	Has Joe gotten up?	O José levantou?
5.	I have had (taken) coffee.	Eu tomei café.
6.	I have studied two hours.	Eu estudei duas horas.
7.	We have had lunch.	Nós almoçamos.
8.	We have avoided the traffic.	Nós evitamos o tráfego.
9.	They have spoken well of you.	Eles falaram bem de você.
10.	Have they practiced?	Eles praticaram?

Observation:

The word já ('already', 'yet') very often appears with past
tense forms in those situations where the English equivalent might
likely be stated in the present perfect tense.

    a.   Já tomaram café?   (Have you taken coffee yet?)
    b.   Nós já jantamos.   (We have already eaten dinner.)

The já has the effect of bringing the action out of the past
right up into the present, which is more or less what the 'have'
does in the English construction.

We have already pointed out that a já in a question is often
echoed by a já in the answer.

            Já tomaram café?
            Já.   Tomamos lá embaixo.

15.20

Another example:

> Já almoçou?   (Have you eaten lunch yet?)
> Já.   (I did.)

If the answer is 'not yet', then you will most likely find this sequence:

> Já almoçou?
> Ainda não   (Not yet.)

Practice 14: (Recorded)

Ask the questions suggested by the tape, using the nouns and pronouns given (José, ele, etc.). Check the tape for confirmation.

(1-9)

Practice 15: (Recorded)

This time you will hear a series of questions of the sort 'Has so-and-so done such-and-such yet?' In each case you are to answer, 'Not yet, but he's going to do such-and-such now'. You will then hear your response confirmed on the tape.

Example:

> Q. O Paulo já preparou?
> A. Ainda não, mas ele vai preparar agora.

(1-8)

Practice 16: (Recorded)

Now, the question will be 'Have you (plural) done such-and-such yet?'. Your answer will be, 'Yes, we did such-and-such last night' Begin each answer with Já.

(1-6)

Practice 17: (Recorded)

How would you say these brief thoughts in Portuguese? Be
sure you can do these easily.

a. With já

1. He has already taken coffee.
2. He has already gotten up.
3. He has already spoken.
4. I have already practiced.
5. I have already eaten lunch.
6. We have already eaten dinner.
7. We have already studied.
8. They have already arrived.

b. With ainda não

1. I haven't studied yet.
2. I haven't lived there yet.
3. They haven't gone to the party yet.
4. They haven't gotten up yet.
5. We haven't eaten lunch yet.
6. We haven't eaten dinner yet.

Part II: We- and they-forms of 'having' and 'going', in the Past

Practice 18: (Recorded)

Repeat each of these short sentences after your instructor.
Group A says 'we had to do something', and Group B says 'they had
to do something'.

A. 1. Tivemos que praticar.
    2. Tivemos que trabalhar.
    3. Tivemos que almoçar.
    4. Tivemos que passar.
    5. Tivemos que ficar.

6. Tivemos que sair.

7. Tivemos que abrir.

8. Tivemos que jantar.

B. 1. Tiveram que tomar.

2. Tiveram que levantar.

3. Tiveram que comer.

4. Tiveram que sair.

5. Tiveram que ficar.

6. Tiveram que abrir.

7. Tiveram que almoçar.

8. Tiveram que jantar.

Practice 19: (Recorded)

Listen to these questions on the tape, then respond affirmatively.
Your answer will be either 'Yes, we had to' or 'Yes, they had to'.
Confirm with the tape.

(1-8)

Practice 20: (Recorded)

Now, how would you ask the following questions? Use eles and
vocês. Confirm with the tape and by checking below.

1.	Did they have to leave?	Eles tiveram que sair?
2.	Did they have to stay?	Eles tiveram que ficar?
3.	Did they have to study?	Eles tiveram que estudar?
4.	Did they have to prepare?	Eles tiveram que preparar?
5.	Did they have to get up?	Eles tiveram que levantar?
6.	Did you (plural) have to eat lunch?	Vocês tiveram que almoçar?
7.	Did you (plural) have to work?	Vocês tiveram que trabalhar?
8.	Did you (plural) have to arrive early?	Vocês tiveram que chegar cedo?
9.	Did you (plural) have to speak Portuguese?	Vocês tiveram que falar português?
10.	Did you (plural) have to talk a lot?	Vocês tiveram que falar muito?

15.23

Practice 21:   (Recorded)

Now make these negative statements, and confirm on the tape and below.

(1-7)

1.	We didn't have to work.	Não tivemos que trabalhar.
2.	We didn't have to leave.	Não tivemos que sair.
3.	We didn't have to study.	Não tivemos que estudar.
4.	We didn't have to prepare.	Não tivemos que preparar.
5.	We didn't have to speak.	Não tivemos que falar.
6.	We didn't have to stay.	Não tivemos que ficar.
7.	We didn't have to open.	Não tivemos que abrir.

Practice 22:   (Recorded)

Repeat each of these short sentences after your tape instructor. Group A says 'we went' somewhere; Group B says 'they went' somewhere.

A. 1. Fomos ao centro.

2. Fomos à embaixada.

3. Fomos ao restaurante.

4. Fomos lá embaixo.

5. Fomos ao Rio.

6. Fomos à cidade.

7. Fomos à escola.

B. 1. Foram à festa.

2. Foram à escola.

3. Foram a Nova York.

4. Foram ao túnel.

5. Foram ao Leme.

6. Foram à cidade.

7. Foram ao Rio.

15.24

<u>Practice 23</u>:   (Recorded)

    Respond to these questions in the negative, saying either 'No,
we didn't go', or 'No, they didn't go', whichever is appropriate.
Then check yourself with the correct response on the tape.

(1-9)

<u>Practice 24</u>:   (<u>Not</u> recorded)

    Give the Portuguese equivalents of these brief English sentences.
Uncover the right hand column only to check your answers. You will
find a variety of forms in this exercise.

1. Yara went to Boston yesterday.   A Yara foi a Boston ontem.
2. Maria and Paul went with her.   Maria e Paulo foram com ela.
3. Robert and Bill went to New York. Roberto e Bill foram a Nova York.
4. Santos and I didn't go with them. Eu e o Santos fomos com eles.
5. We went to have dinner in Bethesda. Fomos jantar em Bethesda.
6. But we didn't go to the movies.   Mas não fomos ao cinema.
7. I went home (<u>para</u> <u>casa</u>).   Eu fui para casa.
8. And Santos went to visit a friend. E o ·Santos foi visitar um
                                         amigo.

<u>Part III</u>. Present tense: We-forms and they-forms of <u>ter</u>, <u>ser</u>
                               and <u>estar</u>

    A. The verb <u>ter</u>

<u>Practice 25</u>: (Recorded)

    In this series of questions and answers an instructor will ask
'How many _____ do they have?' or 'How many _____ do you-all have?'.
A second instructor will answer appropriately either 'We have _____'
or 'They have _____'. There is space on the tape for you to repeat
questions and answers.

15.25

Practice 26: (Recorded)

Ask the following questions of your friends, whom you address as vocês. Follow the pattern Vocês têm que...? You can verify your questions by checking the column on the right or by listening to the tape.

1.	Do you have to study now?	Vocês têm que estudar agora?
2.	Do you have to get up early?	Vocês têm que levantar cedo?
3.	Do you have to speak English?	Vocês têm que falar inglês?
4.	Do you have to live in Rio?	Vocês têm que morar no Rio?
5.	Do you have to work today?	Vocês têm que trabalhar hoje?
6.	Do you have to stay in the school?	Vocês têm que ficar na escola?
7.	Do you have to leave with Joe?	Vocês têm que sair com José?

Practice 27: (Recorded)

Now try these. Verify on tape and below.

1.	We have two cars.	Temos dois carros.
2.	We have four daughters.	Temos quatro filhas.
3.	We have only one home.	Temos só uma casa.
4.	We have to prepare the dialog.	Temos que preparar o diálogo.
5.	We have to speak with you.	Temos que falar com você.
6.	We have to leave now.	Temos que sair agora.
7.	We have to spend the night.	Temos que passar a noite.
8.	We don't have to speak English.	Não temos que falar inglês.
9.	We don't have to do that (isso).	Não temos que fazer isso.

B. Ser and estar

Observation: You will recall that you learned to use forms of ser when speaking of one's origin, where one comes from.

De onde você é?	Where are you from?
Sou de Nova Iorque.	I'm from New York.

15.26

You also learned that you use forms of <u>ser</u> when speaking of
the permanent, geographically fixed location of something.

<u>A</u> <u>embaixada</u> é <u>no</u> <u>centro</u>.   The embassy is downtown.

<u>O</u> <u>Rio</u> é <u>no</u> <u>Brasil</u>.   Rio is in Brazil.

On the other hand, you learned that when the location is not
fixed, but temporary, forms of <u>estar</u> are called for. Recall such
sentences as these:

<u>O</u> <u>Paulo</u> está <u>no</u> <u>centro</u>.   Paul is downtown.

<u>Eu</u> <u>estou</u> <u>no</u> <u>Brasil</u>.   I'm in Brazil.

The above principles apply, of course, to the we-form and
they-form of each of these verbs too. Here are the new forms:

	<u>ser</u>	<u>estar</u>
We are:	somos	estamos
They are:	são	estão

Hence, in summary, the four present tense forms of each are:

	<u>ser</u>	<u>estar</u>
I-form	sou	estou
He-form	é	está
We-form	somos	estamos
They-form	são	estão

<u>Practice 28</u>: (Recorded)

Now practice the we-forms. Repeat these short utterances after
your instructor. In each case he says 'we are.....', first with
<u>somos</u>, then with <u>estamos</u>.

<u>Practice 29</u>: (Recorded)

This is a practice with the they-forms, first <u>são</u>, then <u>estão</u>.
Repeat after your instructor.

Practice 30: (Recorded)

Give the information requested on the tape.

Practice 31: (Recorded)

Answer affirmatively the questions given on the tape. Give just the appropriate verb form, followed by sim. Then check the tape for confirmation.

Part IV: The use of ser for identity

Observation:

Ser is used with nouns to identify or classify. When we say that Yara é solteira we are identifying or classifying her as a 'single girl'. Likewise, when we refer to another young lady and say that Ela é filha do Senhor Silva we are identifying or classifying her as a 'daughter', and very specifically, the daughter of Mr. Silva. In both cases the formula is the same: é (a form of ser) plus a noun (solteira and filha). You can easily observe the same formula in Este é o meu amigo. In the sentence É ele ('It is he') the pronoun ele replaces a noun, but the same principle is involved.

People are classified in many ways; among the more common are nationality, job or profession, and membership in groups.

O Paulo é americano.

O Paulo é professor.

O Paulo é aluno.

Additional assorted examples of identification, all requiring ser, would be the following:

I am a Republican.

This is a hammer.

Ed is a lawyer.

Ed's car is a Ford.

Is it you?

KLM is an airline.

It's a boy!

15.28

In the plural:

> We are housewives.
>
> The men are all actors.
>
> The passengers are children.
>
> You are fools!

In all such cases the verb that is used with the identifying noun or pronoun is a form of _ser_. Forms of _estar_ can never be used.

Practice 32: (Recorded)

A. Preliminary step

You need to know the Portuguese words for 'Brazilian', both masculine and feminine, in order to do this exercise and several of the following. Practice these words now.

> brasileiro   ( )   ( )x   ( )x   ( )x
>
> brasileira   ( )   ( )x   ( )x   ( )x

B. Listen to these questions and answers as given by Instructors A and B.

Practice 33: (Recorded)

Respond to these taped questions affirmatively, then check the tape for confirmation.

Practice 34: (Not recorded)

Practice making these statements and asking these questions until you can do them flawlessly. Use the right hand column only as a check.

1. Are you a teacher?   O senhor é professor?
2. No, I'm a student.   Não, sou aluno.
3. We all (todos) are students.   Todos somos alunos.
4. We all are americans.   Todos somos americanos.

5. Paul and Robert are Brazilians. Paulo e Roberto são brasileiros.
6. And they're not students. E não são alunos.
7. Where are they from? De onde eles são?
8. They're from Recife. São do Recife.
9. Are you (all) from the American Embassy? Os senhores são da Embaixada Americana?
10. We are, yes. Somos, sim.
11. Is this your car? Este é o seu carro?
12. No, it's not. Não, não é.

Practice 35: (Recorded)

The two short dialogs printed below are recorded on the tape. Listen to them and practice them with yourself or a fellow student until they flow freely.

1. A. Êles são brasileiros?

    B. Não, não são. São americanos.

    A. E os senhores? O que são?

    B. Somos americanos também.

    Somos da Flórida.

2. A. Todos somos alunos.

    E os senhores, são alunos também?

    B. Não, não somos.

    A. São professores?

    B. Somos, sim.

    A. De onde são?

    B. Somos do Brasil.

Observation:

The verb ser is also used in telling time, as you have observed in the dialog of this unit. This will be treated as a separate topic in the next unit.

15.30

Part V: The double negative <u>não</u>... <u>nada</u>

Practice 36:   (Recorded)

Practice these short sentences, all of which contain the
double negative <u>não</u>... <u>nada</u>.

1. Não sei nada. ( )x	I don't know anything.
2. Não tenho nada. ( )x	I don't have anything.
3. Ele não fala nada. ( )x	He doesn't speak anything.
4. Ele não pode fazer nada.( )x	He can't do anything.
5. Ela não vai preparar nada. ( )x	She's not going to prepare anything.
6. Ela não gosta de nada. ( )x	She doesn't like anything.
7. Ela não gosta de fazer nada. ( )x	She doesn't like to do anything.
8. Você não pretende fazer nada? ( )x	Don't you plan to do anything?
9. Você não falou nada? ( )x	Didn't you say anything?
10. Vocês não prepararam nada? ( )x	Didn't you all prepare anything?
11. Eu não tive que estudar nada. ( )x	I didn't have to study anything.
12. Eu não achei nada. ( )x	I didn't think anything.
13. Não é nada. ( )x	It's nothing. (It isn't anything).

Observation:

The double negative of the type illustrated above is
considered bad grammar in English ('I <u>don't</u> know <u>nothing</u>'),
but it has no such pejorative connotation in Portuguese.

15.31

Comprehension (Recorded)

Listen to these sentences on the tape. Tell your instructor which ones are not clear to you.

Translations

A. Practice putting these thoughts into Portuguese.

1. I know (<u>eu sei</u>) that he's married.
2. I know that he studies a lot.
3. I know what (<u>o que</u>) you can do.
4. I don't know what they can do.
5. I don't know what to do.
6. I don't know what to study.
7. I don't know what to prepare.
8. I don't know when to study.
9. I don't know when to leave.
10. I don't know where to live.
11. I don't know (<u>conheço</u>) your friend.
12. Good afternoon! Did you (<u>os senhores</u>) study a lot?
13. Good afternoon! Did you arrive OK?
14. Good afternoon! Did you eat lunch in the restaurant?
15. Good evening! Did you have dinner already?
16. Good evening! Did you work hard today?
17. Good idea! Let's (<u>vamos</u>) leave now!
18. Good idea! Let's get coffee later!
19. Good idea! Let's study tomorrow!
20. Good idea! Let's practice more!
21. It's two o'clock. Did she have lunch yet?
22. It's 9:00. Are you going to work now?
23. It's 5:00. Are we going to have dinner now?
24. It's 11:00. When are they going to study?
25. It's late. When are they going to leave?
26. It's early. Why is he going to get up now?

(The following are in the form of brief exchanges. Do these with a fellow student.)

27. Do you think it's a good idea?
     Sure! Let's go <u>now</u>!

28. Do you think it's a good idea?
     Sure! Let's eat dinner at home tonight.

15.32

29. Do you think it's a good idea?
No. I don't want to do that.

30. Do you think it's a good idea?
No. I don't like the idea.

31. Do you (os senhores) think it's a good idea?
No, we don't. We're tired. We have worked hard this
afternoon.

32. It's ten o'clock. Do you think they've arrived yet?
I don't know. We can make a phone call.

33. It's six o'clock. Do you think they went to the movies?
I don't know. We can talk to Paul.

34. Do you think they went downtown tonight?
No. They went there last night.

35. Do you think.....?
(Interrupting, because you're tired of these questions:)
No, I don't think!

B. Practice this tale (of woe), then recount it to your teacher. It's all in fun. The Portuguese version is on the tape, the English version below.

1. It's ten o'clock.

2. The teachers haven't arrived yet, and I think I know why.

3. They went to a party last night, and they stayed there until very late.

4. Gosh! And we, [the] students, we studied so much! (so much = <u>tanto</u>). We spent <u>hours</u> on the dialog. We studied all night.

5. And the teachers aren't here yet.

6. We can't do the dialog without the teachers.

7. Well—(<u>ôba!</u>) Here they are! Good afternoon!

C. Prepare this brief dialog for display to your instructor.

A. I'm hungry.

B. Me (<u>eu</u>) too. Where are we going to have lunch today?

A. I don't know. But I don't want to eat across the street (<u>lá</u> <u>em</u> <u>frente</u>) again.

B. Why don't we go to the Lucas restaurant?

A. Good idea! I haven't gone there yet.

B. Paulo and Yara ate dinner there last night. They said (that) they liked the food very much.

ANSWERS: <u>Practice 3</u>.   <u>Practice 6</u>.

a.	4.	g.	1	a.	3	g.	12
b.	12	h.	3	b.	5	h.	2
c.	6	i.	11	c.	9	i.	8
d.	7	j.	9	d.	10	j.	7
e.	2	k.	8	e.	1	k.	4
f.	10	l.	5	f.	11	l.	6

UNIT 16

1. Verbs of the -ar type have their own special set of endings in the past. You already know these endings, since you have been working with them in recent units. In this unit you will learn how to use -er type verbs in the past.

2. Recall the endings of a typical -ar verb in the past.

   trabalhei ( )x   'I worked'   trabalhamos ( )x   'we worked'
   trabalhou ( )x   'he worked'   trabalharam ( )x   'they worked'

3. Here is another example.

   falei ( )x   'I talked'   falamos ( )x   'we talked'
   falou ( )x   'he talked'   falaram ( )x   'they talked'

4. The endings of -er type verbs in the past are different. Take, for example, the verb which represents 'drinking'. The neutral form is beber.

   beber   ( )   ( )x   ( )x   ( )x

5. The I-form in the past ('I drank') is bebi. Notice the stressed i ending.

   bebi   ( )   ( )x   ( )x   ( )x

6. The neutral form of the verb which represents 'writing' is escrever.

   escrever   ( )   ( )x   ( )x   ( )x

7. The I-form in the past ('I wrote') is escrevi.

   escrevi   ( )   ( )x   ( )x   ( )x

8. Which of these two means 'I wrote'?

   (1) (2)   (1) (2)

(2)

9. No. 1 is not the right answer because the stress is not on
    the right syllable, i.e. the final syllable.

10. The neutral form for 'eating' is <u>comer</u>.

        <u>comer</u>   (   ) (   )x (   )x (   )x

11. You would expect then that 'I ate' would be <u>comi</u>. And that
    is indeed the form.

        <u>comi</u>   (   ) (   )x (   )x (   )x

12. The ending for the he-form is the stressed diphthong <u>-eu</u>.
    You will recognize this diphthong as the same one that is in
    the words <u>meu</u> and <u>seu</u>.

        <u>meu</u>   (   )x (   )x
        <u>seu</u>   (   )x (   )x

13. Here is the he-form of 'eating', in the past ('he ate').

        <u>comeu</u>   (   ) (   )x (   )x (   )x

14. This is the way you say 'he drank'.

        <u>bebeu</u>   (   ) (   )x (   )x (   )x

15. Remember that 'I wrote' is <u>escrevi</u>. How would you say
    'he wrote'?

(escreveu)
                Verify: (   )x (   )x

16. Repeat:

        <u>comeu</u>   (   )x (   )x
        <u>bebeu</u>   (   )x (   )x
        <u>escreveu</u>   (   )x (   )x

16.2

17. A verb that is very useful, because we all do it, is the verb 'forget' The neutral form is <u>esquecer</u>.

<u>esquecer</u>   (   )   (   )x   (   )x   (   )x

18. The form for 'he forgot' is:

<u>esqueceu</u>   (   )   (   )x   (   )x   (   )x

19. How would you say 'I forgot'?

(esqueci)   **Verify:**   (   )x   (   )x

20. Now repeat 'I forgot', then 'he forgot'.

<u>esqueci</u>   (   )x   (   )x
<u>esqueceu</u>   (   )x   (   )x

21. The we-form of <u>-er</u> type verbs in the past is the same as the we-form in the <u>present</u>. The form ends in <u>-emos</u>. You probably recall this ending from the present tense forms <u>podemos</u>, <u>pretendemos</u>.

22. Thus, the form <u>bebemos</u> can mean either 'we drink' or 'we drank'. Only the context makes clear which meaning is intended.

23. Repeat 'we drank'.

<u>bebemos</u>   (   )x   (   )x

24. How would you say 'we forgot'? (The neutral form is <u>esquecer</u>.)

(esquecemos)   Verify: (   )x   (   )x

25. How would you say 'we ate'? (The neutral form is <u>comer</u>.)

(comemos)   Verify: (   )x   (   )x

26. Repeat both 'we forgot' and 'we ate'.

<u>esquecemos</u> (   )x (   )x
<u>comemos</u> (   )x (   )x

27. Listen to the ending which marks the they-form.

(   ) (   ) (   )x (   )x (   )x

28. This is *'they ate'.

(   ) (   )x (   )x (   )x

29. This is 'they forgot'.

(   ) (   )x (   )x (   )x

30. Here are the above two items in print. Repeat again.

<u>comeram</u> (   )x (   )x
<u>esqueceram</u> (   )x (   )x

31. How would you say 'they drank'?

(beberam)

Verify: (   )x (   )x

32. Repeat:

<u>beberam</u> (   )x (   )x
<u>comeram</u> (   )x (   )x
<u>esqueceram</u> (   )x (   )x

33. In summary, the four forms of a typical <u>-er</u> type verb in the past are:

bebi (   )x   bebemos (   )x
bebeu (   )x   beberam (   )x

16.4

34. Another example:

$$
\begin{array}{ll}
\text{esqueci} & (\quad)\text{x} \\
\text{esqueceu} & (\quad)\text{x} \\
\text{esquecemos} & (\quad)\text{x} \\
\text{esqueceram} & (\quad)\text{x}
\end{array}
$$

35. Here is another example, using a new verb (ler) 'to read'. The stem is short (just l) but the pattern is the same.

$$
\begin{array}{lll}
\text{ler} & (\quad)\text{x} & (\quad)\text{x} \\
\hline
\text{li} & (\quad)\text{x} & (\quad)\text{x} \\
\text{leu} & (\quad)\text{x} & (\quad)\text{x} \\
\text{lemos} & (\quad)\text{x} & (\quad)\text{x} \\
\text{leram} & (\quad)\text{x} & (\quad)\text{x}
\end{array}
$$

36. The following frames deal with a concept we shall label reflexives. In the English sentence 'I cut myself', the pronoun 'myself' is sometimes referred to as a reflexive pronoun since it 'reflects' back upon the actor 'I'. The doer of the action and the receiver of the action are the same person.

37. Similarly, in the sentence 'He dragged himself out of bed.' the pronoun 'himself' can be considered a reflexive pronoun since it 'reflects' back upon the actor 'He'. The actor and the receiver are one and the same person.

38. Furthermore, it is common practice to label each of the verbs in the two sentences cited above reflexive verbs. They are directly involved in the reflexive relation between the actor and the receiver.

39. Hence, in the sentence, 'She fooled herself that time' the word 'herself' is properly called a r_____ p_____.
(reflexive pronoun)

40. In the same sentence, the word 'fooled' is properly called a r_____ v_____.
(reflexive verb)

41. Portuguese has numerous examples of reflexive verbs and reflexive pronouns similar to those just illustrated, where clearly the actor is doing something to himself.

42. Here are the reflexive pronouns in Portuguese.

me   ( ) ( )X ( )X = myself

nos ( ) ( )X ( )X = ourselves

se   ( ) ( )X ( )X = himself, herself, yourself, themselves, yourselves, itself

43. These reflexive pronouns frequently precede the verb. Thus, if you want to say 'I know myself', you may say:

Eu me conheço   ( ) ( )X ( )x

44. If you want to say 'I prepare myself', you can say:

Eu me preparo   ( ) ( )X ( )x

45. 'He prepares himself' can be said like this:

Ele se prepara   ( ) ( )X ( )x

46. How would you say 'He knows himself'?

Ele __ _____.

Verify: ( )X ( )X

47. How would you say 'She knows herself'?

Ela __ _____.

Verify: ( )X ( )X

48. 'He confuses himself' is:

Ele se atrapalha   ( )X ( )X ( )X

49. How do you say 'I confuse myself'?
(Eu me atrapalho)
Verify: ( )X ( )X

50. Sometimes you will find a reflexive construction where the reflexive pronoun comes after the verb.

Chama-se Yara   ( )X ( )X

16.6

51. Literally, this expression says 'She calls herself Yara'.
    In normal English we would avoid a reflexive and say some-
    thing like 'Her name is Yara.'

    Chama-se Yara   ( )X ( )X

52. You can also hear this said as follows:

    Ela se chama Yara   ( )X ( )X

53. Now, here is how you say 'My name is Joe'.

    Eu me chamo José   ( )X ( )X

54. Sometimes you will find that a Portuguese verb is reflexive
    even though the actor is not performing the action on himself.
    Such a case is the verb 'remember'. The neutral form is
    lembrar.

    lembrar   ( )X ( )X

55. When the Portuguese speaker wants to say 'I remember', he
    may say:

    Eu me lembro   ( ) ( )X ( )X

    It seems like he is saying 'I remember myself', but actually
    he is just saying the equivalent of 'I remember'.

56. Since 'remember' is an -ar type verb, how would you say 'he
    remembers'?

    Ele __ _____
    Verify: ( )X ( )X

57. The negative 'não precedes the reflexive pronoun. Thus, the
    way to say 'I don't remember' is:

    Eu não me lembro   ( ) ( )X ( )X

58. How do you say 'I don't call myself' or 'My name is not'?
(Eu não me chamo)   Verify: ( )X ( )X

59. How do you say 'She doesn't remember'?   (Answer aloud.)

    Ela n__ s_ l_____
    Verify: ( )X ( )X

60. How would you say 'He doesn't call himself Joe'?
(Ele não se chama José)
    Verify: ( )X ( )X

61. How would you say 'She doesn't confuse herself'?
(Ela não se atrapalha)   Verify: ( )X ( )X

62. How would you say 'I don't confuse myself'?
(Eu não me atrapalho)
                        Verify: ( )X ( )X

63. Another reflexive verb is <u>deitar</u> 'to go to bed'. Here is the
    way to say 'He goes to bed'.
                Ele <u>se</u> <u>deita</u>   ( ) ( )X ( )X

64. 'I go to bed' is:
                Eu <u>me</u> <u>deito</u>   ( ) ( )X ( )X

65. How would you say 'He doesn't go to bed'? Answer aloud.
                Ele ____ __ ____
                Verify: ( )X ( )X

66. How would you say 'I <u>went</u> to bed'?
                Eu ___ _____
                Verify: ( )X ( )X

67. How would you say 'He went to bed'?
                Verify: ( )X ( )X

68. In spite of what you have just been practicing, you will
    find that the reflexive element will often be omitted in the
    verbs 'remember' and 'go to bed' with no apparent change in
    meaning. Thus you may hear somebody say:
                Eu <u>lembro</u>   I remember
                Eu <u>deito</u>   I go to bed

    Either pattern is normal. We will recommend, however, that
    you practice the reflexive so that you feel comfortable with
    it and so that you recognize it when others use it.

16.8

69. The verb <u>levantar</u>, which you have already learned as a non-reflexive, can also be used reflexively, with no change in meaning. Thus, if you want to say 'I got up', you can say either:

    a. <u>Eu</u> <u>levantei</u>   ( )X ( )X, or

    b. <u>Eu</u> <u>me</u> <u>levantei</u>   ( )X ( )X

70. Using the reflexive, how would you say 'He got up'?

(Ele se levantou)   Verify: ( )X ( )X

71. Let us finish this section with a brief reference to contractions. You have already learned a number of con-tractions. In this unit you will learn several more, all of them involving the preposition <u>por</u> and a definite article. Here is the first one, the joining together of <u>por</u> and the definite article <u>a</u>. <u>por</u> + <u>a</u> = <u>pela</u>

    <u>pela</u> ( )X ( )X

72. Now let's look at another one. Here is the contraction for <u>por</u> + the definite article <u>o</u>. <u>por</u> + <u>o</u> = <u>pelo</u>

    <u>pelo</u> ( )X ( )X

73. It follows then that the combination of <u>por</u> plus the plural definite article <u>os</u> results in <u>pelos</u>.

    <u>pelos</u> ( )X ( )X

74. It also follows that the combination of <u>por</u> plus the plural definite article <u>as</u> results in <u>pelas</u>.

    <u>pelas</u> ( )X ( )X

75. Now, go on to the dialog but before doing so please take note of this summary of the new verbs presented in this section.

beber	deitar (-se)
escrever	lembrar (-se)
ler	
comer	
esquecer	

<u>End of Tape 7A</u>

16.9

Tape 7B

Dialog

Aluno

o sono	sleep
com sono	sleepy
(bocejo)	(yawn)
desculpe	excuse (command form)

Eu estou com sono. (Bocejo)   I'm sleepy. (Yawn)
Desculpe.   Excuse me.

Professor

nada	nothing
de nada	that's O.K., think
	nothing of it.

De nada. O senhor passou bem   That's O.K. Did you have a
a noite?   good night?

Aluno

acordado   awake

Passei, sim. Mas ainda não   Yes. I did. But I'm not
estou acordado.   awake yet.

16.10

Professor

a que horas?	At what time?
se deitou	went to bed (he-form,
	-ar type)

A que horas o senhor se deitou?　　What time did you go to
Às onze?　　　　　　　　　　　　bed? At eleven?

Aluno

me lembro	I remember (-ar type)

Não me lembro.　　　　　　　　I don't remember.

escrevi	I wrote (-er type)
a carta	letter
li	I read (-er type)
o jornal	newspaper
logo depois	shortly afterwards
me deitei	I went to bed (-ar type)

Escrevi uma carta, li o jornal,　　I wrote a letter, read the
e (bocejo), logo depois me　　　paper and (yawn) shortly
deitei.　　　　　　　　　　　afterwards I went to bed.

pòr	around, about
pela (contraction of por and a)	around, about the
meia	half, middle
a meia-noite	midnight

Lá pela meia-noite.　　　　　　Around midnight.

Professor

começar	begin (neutral form)

Bom, vamos começar!　　　　　Well, let's begin!

16.11

Aluno

Iiii !	(an expression of dismay roughly equivalent here to 'oh, no!')
esqueci	I forgot (-_er_ type)
o livro	book

Iiii... Esqueci o meu livro.   Oh, no! I forgot my book.

estava	I was
tanta	so much
a pressa	haste
deixei	I left (-_ar_ type)

Estava com tanta pressa que   I was in such a hurry that
deixei tudo em casa.   I left everything at home.

A LOOK AT THE GRAMMAR

Practice Exercises

Part I

Practice 1. (Recorded)
    Practice saying these past forms of -er type verbs.

a. He-forms
    1. comeu   ( )X   ( )X : ate
    2. bebeu   ( )X   ( )X : drank
    3. escreveu   ( )X   ( )X : wrote
    4. esqueceu   ( )X   ( )X : forgot
    5. leu   ( )X   ( )X : read
    6. choveu   ( )X   ( )X : rained

b. They-forms
    1. comeram   ( )X   ( )X : ate
    2. beberam   ( )X   ( )X : drank
    3. escreveram ( )X   ( )X : wrote
    4. esqueceram ( )X   ( )X : forgot
    5. leram   ( )X   ( )X : read

c. I-forms
    1. comi   ( )X   ( )X : ate
    2. bebi   ( )X   ( )X : drank
    3. escrevi   ( )X   ( )X : wrote
    4. esqueci   ( )X   ( )X : forgot
    5. li   ( )X   ( )X : read

d. We-forms
    1. comemos   ( )X   ( )X : ate
    2. bebemos   ( )X   ( )X : drank
    3. escrevemos ( )X   ( )X : wrote
    4. esquecemos ( )X   ( )X : forgot
    5. lemos   ( )X   ( )X : read

16.13

e. (And just to refresh your memory, here are the neutral forms.)

1. comer	( )X	( )X	:	idea of eating
2. beber	( )X	( )X	:	idea of drinking
3. escrever	( )X	( )X	:	idea of writing
4. esquecer	( )X	( )X	:	idea of forgetting
5. ler	( )X	( )X	:	idea of reading
6. chover	( )X	( )X	:	idea of raining

Practice 2: (Recorded)

In this practice Instructor A will ask Instructor B questions using the past forms you have just reviewed. Just listen this time through.

(1-13)

Practice 3: (Recorded)

In this practice you will hear a similar set of questions and answers. There is a space after each question and after each answer for you to repeat.

Practice 4: (Recorded)

In this set of questions you will be asked if Yara did something. You are to say that she didn't, but that you did. The verifying answer is on the tape.

Example:

Question: A Yara leu o livro?

Your answer: Não, não leu, mas eu li.

(1-7)

Practice 5: (Recorded)

In this set of questions you will be asked if they did something. You are to say that they didn't, but that we did. Confirm your answer with the tape.

16.14

Example:

Question: <u>Eles leram o livro?</u>

Your answer: <u>Não, não leram, mas nós lemos.</u>

(1 - 6)

Practice 6: (Recorded)

These questions all begin with 'What did you...?' Repeat the
answers which are supplied by the tape. Some contain -er type
verbs, others -ar type verbs.

Part II: Telling Time

The following exercise has been prepared to teach you a number
of useful time expressions. Repeat each one after the voice on the
tape and follow along with the Portuguese and English below. You
should do this practice several times.

Practice 7: (Recorded)

1.	São dez (horas)	( )X	( )X	It's ten o'clock.
2.	meia	( )X	( )X	half
3.	dez e meia	( )X	( )X	ten thirty (ten and a half)
4.	São dez e meia	( )X	( )X	It's ten thirty (half past ten)
5.	São dez e trinta	( )X	( )X	It's ten thirty.
6.	São seis e meia	( )X	( )X	It's six thirty.
7.	São seis e trinta	( )X	( )X	It's six thirty,
8.	São seis e cinco	( )X	( )X	It's 6:05.
9.	São seis e oito	( )X	( )X	It's 6:08.
10.	São seis e vinte	( )X	( )X	It's 6:20:
11.	São seis e vinte e dois	( )X	( )X	It's 6:22.
12.	São seis e quarenta	( )X	( )X	It's 6:40.
13.	São seis e quinze	( )X	( )X	It's 6:15.
14.	São seis e um quarto	( )X	( )X	It's a quarter past six.

16.15

15.	para	( )X ( )X	for, towards
16.	para as seis	( )X ( )X	'towards' six (to six)
17.	São dez para as seis	( )X ( )X	It's ten to six.
18.	São vinte para as seis	( )X ( )X	It's twenty to six.
19.	São cinco para as seis	( )X ( )X	It's five to six.
20.	São quinze para as seis	( )X ( )X	It's fifteen to six.
21.	É um quarto para as seis	( )X ( )X	It's a quarter to six.

- - - - - - - - - - - - -

22.	É meio-dia	( )X ( )X	It's twelve noon.
23.	É meia-noite	( )X ( )X	It's midnight.
24.	É uma hora	( )X ( )X	It's one o'clock.

- - - - - - - - - - - - -

25.	A que horas?	( )X ( )X	At what time?
26.	A que horas você janta?	( )X ( )X	(At) what time do you eat dinner?
27.	As oito	( )X ( )X	At eight.
28.	As oito em ponto	( )X ( )X	At eight sharp.
29.	A uma	( )X ( )X	At one.
30.	Ao meio-dia	( )X ( )X	At noon.
31.	A meia-noite	( )X ( )X	At midnight.
32.	Está na hora do intervalo	( )X ( )X	It's break time.
33.	Está na hora da festa	( )X ( )X	It's time for the party.
34.	Está na hora de sair	( )X ( )X	It's time to leave.
35.	Está na hora de trabalhar	( )X ( )X	It's time to work.

Notice that:

1. Time is generally given by stating the hour plus the minutes after the hour.

3:10	três e dez
4:29	quatro e vinte e nove
7:50	sete e cinqüenta

2. After the half hour, time is very commonly expressed by stating the number of minutes before the next hour.

4:40	vinte para as cinco
7:50	dez para as oito

3. a. The half hour is given either as <u>meia</u> or <u>trinta</u>.

                7:30   sete e meia/sete e trinta

    b. The quarter hour is given as <u>um quarto</u> or <u>quinze</u>.

                7:15   sete e um quarto/sete e quinze
                7:45   um quarto para as oito/
                                  quinze para as oito

4. When the time is not <u>exactly</u> on the hour, the word <u>hora(s)</u>
    is usually omitted from the time expression. When the time
    is on the hour, the word <u>hora(s)</u> is optional.

                São quatro e quinze
                São cinco para as três
                          (but)
                São quatro (horas)
                É uma (hora)

5. The singular form <u>é</u> is used when the item immediately fol-
    lowing is singular; the plural form <u>são</u> is used when the
    item immediately following is plural.

                1. É uma hora
                2. É meia-noite
                3. É meio-dia
                4. São três (horas)
                5. São cinco para as três
                6. São cinco para a uma

6. In Brazil the twenty-four hour clock is observed in many
    official contexts (radio announcements, time tables, etc.),
    but the twelve hour clock is adhered to in general conver-
    sation.

    <u>São vinte e três horas</u>   It's 11:00 p.m. (radio time)
    <u>São onze horas</u>   It's 11:00 p.m. (general conver-
                                                          sation)

                                16.17

7. The expression <u>está</u> <u>na</u> <u>hora</u> <u>de</u> (utilizing a form of <u>estar</u>
    rather than <u>ser</u>) is used as the equivalent of 'it is time
    (to) or (for)'.

<u>Está</u> <u>na</u> <u>hora</u> <u>de</u> <u>sair</u>   It's time to leave.

<u>Está</u> <u>na</u> <u>hora</u> <u>da</u> <u>festa</u>   It's time for the
                                     party.

Practice 8: (Recorded)

        Listen to these times as recorded on the tape. For each one
select the correct time from the list below and write the corresponding letter in the blank. Answers are given at the end of this
unit.

1. _____	a.	3:15
2. _____	b.	7:45
3. _____	c.	7:48
4. _____	d.	2:03
5. _____	e.	11:55
6. _____	f.	4:17
7. _____	g.	5:00
8. _____	h.	8:22
9. _____	i.	8:42
10. _____	j.	10:50
11. _____	k.	1:05
12. _____	l.	12:55
13. _____	m.	6:50

16.18

Practice 9: (Recorded)

Now practice saying these items. Repeat after the voice on the tape, and follow along visually below.

1. It's 8:07
2. It's 7:08
3. It's 7:53
4. It's midnight
5. It's 4:45
6. It's half past one
7. It's a quarter to eight
8. It's a quarter past eight
9. It's five after one
10. It's five till one
11. It's one o'clock sharp

- - - - - - - - - -

12. At 4:00
13. At 7:30
14. At 1:45
15. At noon
16. At 2:05
17. At 6:47
18. At 12:15 p.m.
19. At 8:17
20. At 11:20

Practice 10: (Recorded)

How would you say these items in Portuguese? Check the tape for confirmation after you have spoken aloud. Do this exercise several times to assure a rapid and accurate response.

1. It's four thirty.
2. It's quarter past four.   (quarter: um quarto)
3. It's fifteen past four.   (fifteen: quinze)
4. It's fifteen to four.

5. It's a quarter to four.
6. It's five past three.
7. It's five to three.
8. It's nine o'clock.
9. At nine o'clock.
10. At nine fifteen.
11. At a quarter to nine.
12. At midnight.
13. Today at three.
14. Tomorrow at ten.
15. Tomorrow at midnight.

Part III.   Reflexives

Practice 11:   (Recorded)

Practice saying these sentences and the follow-up questions. They will give you additional experience with reflexives.

1.	Eu me chamo José.	Como se chama o senhor?
2.	Eu me levanto cedo.	A que horas o senhor se levanta?
3.	Eu também me deito cedo.	A que horas o senhor se deita?
4.	Ontem eu me deitei tarde.	O senhor também se deitou tarde?
5.	Hoje eu me levantei às 9.	A que horas o senhor se levantou?
6.	Eu não me lembro.	O senhor se lembra?

Comprehension

A. Listen to these sentences and make a note of those that are not clear to you.

B. Listen to these brief dialogs on the tape. Run through each one several times until you are sure you understand them. If you find that you are helped by visual aids, follow along with the printed version below.

1. A. Estou com pressa.
    B. Outra vez! Por quê?
    A. Tenho muito que fazer.

16.20

B.   Você já tomou café?

A.   Não, mas agora não posso. Vou dar um tele-
     fonema.

2.   A.   O que é que você vai fazer hoje à noite?

     B.   Vou escrever umas cartas, ler o jornal e
          deitar cedo.

     A.   E você não vai estudar?

     B.   Vou estudar aqui hoje à tarde.

3.   A.   Como é que ele se chama? Não me lembro.

     B.   Acho que se chama...ah...ah...Esqueci..!

     A.   Esqueceu?!! Mas você falou.....

     B.   Esqueci, sim! É só que estou cansado.
          Deitei tarde ontem à noite.

                                        End of Tape 7B

                   Translations

A.   How would you say the following in Portuguese?

     1.   I'm sleepy.
     2.   I'm hungry.
     3.   I'm sleepy and hungry.
     4.   Are you sleepy?
     5.   Are you in a hurry?
     6.   I was in a hurry.
     7.   I was in such a hurry!
     8.   I was in such a hurry that I left my book at home.
     9.   I read the letter.
     10. Right afterwards I read the paper.
     11. I went to bed late.
     12. Around (lá pelas) two o'clock.
     13. What time did Paulo go to bed?
     14. I don't remember. Around one o'clock.
     15. I remember well. At three thirty!
     16. He wasn't (estava) sleepy last night, but he is today.
     17. I wasn't sleepy when I got up, but I am now.

                        16.21

18. I wasn't in a hurry when I got up, but I am now.
19. I'm not in a hurry now, but I'm going to be later.
20. I have a lot to do today.
21. It looks like we're going to have dinner very late.
22. I think we're going to have dinner around ten-thirty.
23. By the way, Maria, what time are we going to have dinner?
24. Let's see. Around about 8:30. Are you hungry?
25. No, I ate too much lunch. (almoçar)
26. Yes, I am [hungry]. I haven't eaten yet today. (comer)
27. No, I'm not hungry now, but I know that (que) I'm going to be at 8:30.
28. I was so hungry !
29. I was so hungry that I ate everything !
30. I was so hungry that I didn't leave anything !
31. I was so sleepy (tanto sono) that I didn't remember.
32. I forgot everything that he said.
33. He forgot everything that I said.
34. I don't remember if he studied or not.
35. I don't remember if I said that or not.
36. He doesn't remember what time he went to bed.
37. Well ! Let's study !
38. Well ! Let's work !
39. Well ! Let's practice more !
40. Well ! Let's leave !

B. Practice putting these brief dialogs into Portuguese.

    1. A. Did you have a good lunch?
       B. I ate too much.
       A. Are you sleepy?
       B. I am.
       A. Why don't we open some windows?
       B. Good idea.

    2. A. I left the book at home.
       B. Here is my book.
       A. Thanks. (yawn) Excuse me.

16.22

        B.   Aren't you awake yet?

        A.   Yes, but I'm still sleepy. I read until
            midnight.

3.   A.   Did you read the paper today?

        B.   No, why?

        A.   The president has arrived in Brazil. He is
            in Rio now.

        B.   When does he go to (a) Brasilia?

        A.   Tomorrow, and right after (logo depois) he
            goes to (a) Recife.

Answers to Practice 8:

      1.   f

      2.   b

      3.   a

      4.   c

      5.   i

      6.   j

      7.   d

      8.   k

      9.   m

     10.   l

     11.   e

     12.   g

     13.   h

Unit 17

Preliminary Note:

Beginning with this unit, the programming format will
include practice exercises appropriate to the point being developed.

17.1

Unit 17

1. You will remember from previous units that many Portuguese
    nouns ending in a vowel sound simply add an <u>-s</u> sound to
    form the plural.

<u>festa</u> ˃ <u>festas</u>	<u>escritório</u> ˃ <u>escritórios</u>
<u>semana</u> ˃ <u>semanas</u>	<u>noite</u> ˃ <u>noites</u>

2. Now, recall the word for 'lesson'. Recall that it has a
    stressed nasal diphthong in the last syllable.

    <u>lição</u>   ( )x   ( )x

3. When this word is made plural, something happens to its
    nasal diphthong before the <u>-s</u> is added. The nasal diphthong
    is replaced by another nasal diphthong, a blend of the
    nasal o̞ sound and the <u>i</u> sound. It is written õe.

    õe   ( ) ( ) ( )x ( )x ( )x

4. Thus, the plural of <u>licão</u> is

    <u>lições</u>   ( ) ( )x ( )x ( )x

5. Most other words that end in ão in the singular form will
    have the õe diphthong in the plural form. This includes a
    long list of words that are easily recognizable counterparts
    (cognates) of English words ending in <u>-tion</u> and <u>-sion</u>. For
    example, the English word <u>nation</u> is <u>nação</u> in Portuguese. (Be
    careful not to use the English <u>sh</u> sound. Instead, use the
    Portuguese <u>s</u> sound.)

    <u>nação</u>   ( ) ( )x ( )x

6. In the plural form, the nasalized diphthong ão is replaced
    by the nasalized diphthong õe.

    <u>nações</u>   ( ) ( )x ( )x

17.2

Practice 1. (Recorded)

Here are several words whose English counterparts end in '-tion' or '-sion'. You should look at them as you listen and repeat. They will all be fairly easy to recognize; hence we call them 'close cognates'. Notice that the English sh sound corresponds to the Portuguese s sound (numbers 1-9) and the English ž sound corresponds to the Portuguese z sound (numbers 10-12). Each Portuguese word is recorded twice.

English	Portuguese Singular	Plural
1. solution	solução	soluções
2. position	posição	posições
3. condition	condição	condições
4. situation	situação	situações
5. petition	petição	petições
6. communication	comunicação	comunicações
7. mission	missão	missões
8. session	sessão	sessões
9. expression	expressão	expressões
10. vision	visão	visões
11. invasion	invasão	invasões
12. decision	decisão	decisões

7. Here is the Portuguese word for 'formation'.

    <u>formação</u>   ( )x ( )x

8. How would you say the plural <u>formations</u>?
(formações)

    Verify: ( )x ( )x

9. Here is 'vibration'.

    <u>vibração</u> ( )x ( )x

17.3

10.   How would you say 'vibrations'?

(vibrações)

                          Verify: (   )x (   )x

11.   Here is an English plural form: 'intentions'. In Portuguese
      it is

                   intenções (   )x (   )x

12.   How would you say the singular, 'intention'?

(intenção)

                          Verify: (   )x (   )x

13.   Before we go on, let us hasten to warn you that not every
      -ion word in English converts to a word ending in ão in
      Portuguese, but very many of them do.

14.   Here's one more that does: 'opinion'.

                   opinião   (   )x (   )x
                   opiniões   (   )x (   )x

15.   There are several Portuguese singular nouns ending in ão
      whose plurals end in still another nasal diphthong. This
      diphthong is the 'last' nasal diphthong, the only one that
      you have not yet been formally introduced to. Here it is:

              ãe   (   ) (   )x (   )x (   )x

16.   Here are two common words which have ão in the singular and
      ãe in the plural. Notice that they are one syllable words.

              1. 'dog'   : cão   (   )x (   )x
                  'dogs'   : cães (   )x (   )x
              2. 'bread'   : pão   (   )x (   )x
                  'bread(s)' : pães (   )x (   )x

                              17.4

17. The ãe diphthong appears elsewhere, too, as in 'mother'.

'mother':   mãe ( )x ( )x

18. What happens to words that end in stressed -al (like jornal)
when they are made plural? They do not just add -s. Instead,
the -al is replaced by the non-nasal diphthong ai, and then
the -s is added. This gives the ending -ais. Remember, it's
not nasal.

ais ( ) ( )x ( )x

19. Thus the plural for jornal is jornais.

jornal   ( )x ( )x
jornais   ( )x ( )x

20. Portuguese has many words that go through this sort of change,
and again we can draw examples from words (both nouns and
adjectives) which closely resemble their English counterparts.
In repeating the singular form in the following practice be
sure to give the final -L that special 'w-like' quality we
mentioned in earlier units.

Practice 2. (Recorded)

	English	Portuguese				
		Singular		Plural		
a.	canal	canal ( )X ( )X		canais ( )X ( )X		
b.	final	final ( )X ( )X		finais ( )X ( )X		
c.	formal	formal ( )X ( )X		formais ( )X ( )X		
d.	signal	sinal ( )X ( )X		sinais ( )X ( )X		
e.	annual	anual ( )X ( )X		anuais ( )X ( )X		
f.	special	especial ( )X ( )X		especiais ( )X ( )X		
g.	legal	legal ( )X ( )X		legais ( )X ( )X		
h.	postal	postal ( )X ( )X		postais ( )X ( )X		

21. Here is the adjective 'local'.

        <u>local</u>   ( )X ( )X

22. How would you say the plural form?

(locais)

        Verify: ( )X ( )X

23. Here is the adjective 'normal'.

        <u>normal</u>   ( )X ( )X

24. What is the plural?

(normais)

        Verify: ( )X ( )X

25. The English plural form 'mortals' is given in Portuguese as:

        <u>mortais</u>   ( )X ( )X

26. What is the singular form?

(mortal)

        Verify: ( )X ( )X

27. Again we must warn you that not all English words ending in
     -al will convert into Portuguese as nicely as the examples
     given above. Many of them will, however.

28. Here is another that does, the word 'metal'.

        <u>metal</u>   ( )X ( )X

29. What is the plural?

(metais)

        Verify: ( )X ( )X

30. Here is a plural form: <u>capitais</u>. How would you say the singular?
(capital)

Verify: (   )X   (   )X

31. Now let's review another point. Recall these instances when
    the pluralizing -<u>s</u> sound of the definite article becomes a
    -<u>z</u> sound because a vowel sound follows immediately after-
    wards. Listen for the -<u>z</u> sound, and repeat.

    1. os͜ estados   (   )X   (   )X
    2. os͜ escritórios   (   )X   (   )X
    3. as͜ avenidas   (   )X   (   )X
    4. as͜ esposas   (   )X   (   )X
    5. as͜ horas   (   )X   (   )X

32. The same thing happens to the -<u>s</u> at the end of other words
    when these words are followed immediately by a vowel sound.
    The -<u>s</u> sound becomes a -<u>z</u> sound.

<u>Practice 3</u>.   (Recorded) Listen and repeat.

-s sound		-z sound	
a.	vamos ( )X	vamos͜ ao Rio ( )X	
b.	vamos ( )X	vamos͜ agora ( )X	
c.	vamos ( )X	vamos͜ almoçar ( )X	
d.	todos ( )X	todos͜ os͜ escritórios ( )X	
e.	todas ( )X	todas͜ as͜ esposas ( )X	
f.	fomos ( )X	fomos͜ ontem ( )X	
g.	chegamos ( )X	chegamos͜ amanhã ( )X	
h.	jantamos ( )X	jantamos͜ as͜ oito ( )X	
i.	temos ( )X	temos͜ uma ( )X	
j.	moramos ( )X	moramos͜ em Belém ( )X	
k.	abrimos ( )X	abrimos͜ a porta ( )X	
l.	mais ( )X	mais͜ ou menos ( )X	
m.	três ( )X	três͜ horas ( )X	
n.	quantos ( )X	quantos͜ escritórios ( )X	
o.	os senhores ( )X	os senhores͜ almoçaram ( )X	
p.	as senhoras ( )X	as senhoras͜ acham ( )X	

17.7

33. In the last unit you learned the past tense forms of a number of common -er type verbs. In this unit we will look at the past tense forms of some common -ir type verbs.

34. You remember that the neutral form for the verb 'open' is abrir. Here now is the form for 'I opened' (past tense).

$$( ) ( )X ( )X$$

35. Sair is the neutral form for 'leaving'. Here is the form for 'I left'.

$$( ) ( )X ( )X$$

36. Here is a new verb, the neutral form for 'sleeping'.

dormir ( ) ( )X ( )X

(One way to remember this verb is to associate it with the English word 'dormant'.)

37. Here is the form for 'I slept'.

$$( ) ( )X ( )X$$

38. Repeat again as shown.

I opened	abri	( )X ( )X
I left	saí	( )X ( )X
I slept	dormi	( )X ( )X

39. Preferir is the neutral form expressing the notion of 'preferring'.

preferir ( )X ( )X

40. How would you put <u>preferir</u> into the past and say 'I preferred'?
(preferi)

Verify: (   )X (   )X

41. <u>Repetir</u> expresses the notion of 'repeating'.

<u>repetir</u> (   )X (   )X

42. How would you say 'I repeated'?
(repeti)

Verify: (   )X (   )X

43. <u>Sentir</u> expresses the notion of 'feeling'. (Associate it with
English 'sentiment').

<u>sentir</u>   (   )X (   )X

44. What is the form for 'I felt'?
(senti)

Verify: (   )X (   )X

45. <u>Cair</u> expresses the notion of 'falling'.

<u>cair</u>   (   )X (   )X

46. How would you say 'I fell'?
(caí)

Verify: (   )X (   )X

47. Try these forms all together.

<u>abri</u>	( )X	I opened
<u>saí</u>	( )X	I left
<u>dormi</u>	( )X	I slept
<u>senti</u>	( )X	I felt
<u>preferi</u>	( )X	I preferred
<u>repeti</u>	( )X	I repeated
<u>caí</u>	( )X	I fell

17.9

48. Now let's go to the he-form. The ending for this form is the diphthong -iu. Repeat just the ending in this frame.

     -iu   ( ) ( )x ( )x ( )x

49. Now let's attach it to the end of some verbs. Here, for example, is 'he opened'.

     abriu   ( )x ( )x

50. Here is 'he slept'.

     dormiu   ( )x ( )x

51. What is the form for 'he left'?

(saiu)

          Verify: ( )x ( )x

52. What is the form for '[he] repeated'? (Neutral form: repetir)

(repetiu)

          Verify: ( )x ( )x

53. What is the form for '[she] preferred'? (Neutral form: preferir)

(preferiu)

          Verify: ( )x ( )x

54. What is the form for '[she] fell'? (Neutral form: cair)

(caiu)

          Verify: ( )x ( )x

55. What is the form for '[he] felt'? (Neutral form: sentir)

(sentiu)

          Verify: ( )x ( )x

56. Now review these forms.

preferiu   ( )x
saiu   ( )x
abriu   ( )x
sentiu   ( )x
dormiu   ( )x
repetiu   ( )x
caiu   ( )x

Practice 4. (Recorded)

Listen to this set of short questions and answers as delivered by speakers A and B.

Practice 5. (Recorded)

This time you are to answer the questions. Answer them all in the affirmative, then check the tape for confirmation.

57. In the we-form, -ir type verbs add the ending -imos.

-imos   ( ) ( )x ( )x

58. Thus 'we opened' would be said like this:

abrimos . ( )x ( )x

59. 'We slept' would be said like this:

dormimos   ( )x ( )x

60. How would you say 'we left'?

(saímos)

Verify: ( )x ( )x

61. How would you say 'we fell'?

(caímos)

Verify: ( )x ( )x

17.11

62. Repeat these three items.

>   <u>repetimos</u> ( )X ( )X : 'we repeated'
>   <u>preferimos</u> ( )X ( )X : 'we preferred'
>   <u>sentimos</u> ( )X ( )X : 'we felt'

63. The they-form of these verbs utilizes an ending which is deserving of a bit of special practice.

   a. First, repeat the already familiar <u>-eram</u> ending of <u>-er</u> verbs in the past.

   > <u>-eram</u>   ( )X ( )X ( )X

   b. Now, substitute the <u>-i</u> sound for the <u>-e</u> sound and you have the ending for <u>-ir</u> verbs. Listen and repeat.

   > <u>-iram</u>   ( )X ( )X ( )X ( )X

64. Therefore, the form for 'they left' must be:

   > ( ) ( )X ( )X

65. The form for 'they opened' is:

   > ( ) ( )X ( )X

66. 'They slept' is:

   > ( ) ( )X ( )X

67. Here are the above forms, plus some others, in print. Repeat as indicated.

>   saíram   ( )X ( )X
>   abriram   ( )X ( )X
>   dormiram   ( )X ( )X
>   repetiram ( )X ( )X
>   caíram   ( )X ( )X
>   preferiram ( )X ( )X
>   sentiram   ( )X ( )X

Practice 6. (Recorded)

Listen to this short set of questions and answers as given on the tape by two instructors. Numbers 1-4 ask 'Did you-all do something?'. Numbers 5-9 ask 'Did they do something?'.

Practice 7. (Recorded)

This time you are to answer the questions. Answer them all affirmatively. Check your answers with those given on the tape.

68. Notice this sentence:

      Saí de lá   ( )X ( )X 'I left there'.

69. Now notice this one:

      Saí do Rio   ( )X ( )X 'I left Rio'.

70. And this one:

      Saí da cidade   ( )X ( )X 'I left the city'.

71. The word de appears between the verb sair (or one of its forms) and the place left from. That is, Portuguese says 'I left from such-and-such a place', rather than 'I left such-and-such a place'. Where one of the definite articles is involved, the de enters into the appropriate contraction, as in No's 69 and 70 above.

72. So, if you wanted to say 'I left the party', you would say:

      Saí da festa   ( )X ( )X

73. How would you say 'I left the Embassy?' Make the contraction.
(Saí da Embaixada)

              Verify: ( )X ( )X

74. How would you say 'He left the school?
(Ele saiu da escola.)

              Verify: ( )X ( )X

75. Here is 'He left Joe's home' (the home of Joe).
    Ele saiu da casa do José ( )X ( )X

76. Contrast this with 'He left home', which contains no con-
    traction since there is no article ('the') to contract with de.

         Ele saiu de casa ( )X ( )X

77. How would you say 'He left the park'? Use do.
(Ele saiu do parque)
                    Verify: ( )X ( )X

78. How would you say 'He left the office'?
(Ele saiu do escritório)
                    Verify: ( )X ( )X

Practice 8. (Recorded)

    Put these brief utterances into Portuguese. Confirm with the
tape.
            1. He is going to leave Brazil.
            2. He is going to leave Rio tomorrow.
            3. He has already left the Embassy.
            4. He left there yesterday.
            5. He plans to leave home early.
            6. He left the restaurant early.

                         Pronunciation

79. Portuguese has a very few words beginning with the consonant
    cluster pn. This is a combination of sounds which English
    speakers do not have at the beginning of a word, so it may be
    troublesome at first. The word for 'automobile tire', which
    begins with this cluster, appears in the dialog for this unit.
         pneu ( ) ( )X ( )X

80. You pronounce both the p and the n, and follow with the
     familiar diphthong eu.

                    (   )   ( )x   ( )x

Note: Before going on to the dialog, take note of the new verbs
       presented in the section just concluded.

                         cair

                         dormir

                         sentir

                         preferir

                         repetir

Dialog

Sônia

ô	Hey!
o dorminhoco	sleepyhead
acorde	wake up (command form)

Ô dorminhoco, acorde!   Hey, sleepyhead.... wake up!

João

an	uh
ô	oh

An, o quê...? Ô! Desculpe!   Uh, what...? Oh! Excuse me.

Sônia

João	John
caiu	you fell (-ir type)

João! Você caiu no sono outra   John! Did you fall asleep again?
vez?

João

parece	it appears (-er type)

Parece.   Apparently so.

dormi	I slept (-ir type)
essa	that
essa noite	that night (used here in the sense of 'last night')

Eu não dormi muito essa noite.   I didn't sleep much last night.

Sônia

Não? Por quê?   No? Why?

João

voltamos	we returned (-ar type)
a praia	beach
Nós voltamos tarde da praia.	We returned late from the beach.

sabe	you know (-er type)
aconteceu	(it) happened (-er type)
E você sabe o que aconteceu?	And do you know what happened?

Sônia

| Não. O que é que aconteceu? | No. What happened? |

João

o pneu	tire
furou	it punctured (-ar type)
logo	precisely (used here in the sense of 'of all places')
a ponte	bridge
O pneu furou logo na ponte.	The tire blew out on the bridge, of all places.

Sônia

quem	who
dirigindo	driving (-ir type) *
E quem é que estava dirigindo?	And who was driving?

João

| Eu estava. | I was. |

* Supplementary note and practice. (Recorded)

The neutral form is dirigir. This verb fits into the same category as sair, dormir, etc, presented earlier in this unit. Thus,

```
        dirigi    ( )x ( )x   'I drove'
        dirigiu   ( )x ( )x   'He drove'
      dirigimos   ( )x ( )x   'We drove'
      dirigiram   ( )x ( )x   'They drove'
                 -----------
        dirigir   ( )x ( )x   (neutral form)
```

17.17

Expansion Exercises

Adverbial Time Expressions

Expansion Exercise 1 (Recorded)

Practice these time expressions.

a.	tonight	hoje à noite ( )X ( )X	
		hoje de noite ( )X ( )X	
b.	tomorrow night	amanhã à noite ( )X ( )X	
		amanhã de noite ( )X ( )X	
c.	last night	ontem à noite ( )X ( )X	
		ontem de noite ( )X ( )X	
d.	this afternoon	hoje à tarde ( )X ( )X	
		hoje de tarde ( )X ( )X	
e.	tomorrow afternoon	amanhã à tarde ( )X ( )X	
		amanhã de tarde ( )X ( )X	
f.	yesterday afternoon	ontem à tarde ( )X ( )X	
		ontem de tarde ( )X ( )X	
g.	this morning	hoje de manhã ( )X ( )X	
h.	tomorrow morning	amanhã de manhã ( )X ( )X	
i.	yesterday morning	ontem de manhã ( )X ( )X	

Notice that 'afternoon' and 'night' are preceded by either **à** or
de.

Expansion Exercise 2 (Recorded)

Identify these terms by placing the letter of the correct
translation in the blank. Stop the tape whenever necessary.

1. ( )_____	a.	This afternoon
2. ( )_____	b.	This morning
3. ( )_____	c.	Tomorrow morning
4. ( )_____	d.	Tonight
5. ( )_____	e.	Yesterday afternoon
6. ( )_____	f.	Last night
7. ( )_____	g.	Tomorrow night

Expansion Exercise 3 (Recorded)

   a. Practice putting these items into Portuguese.

      1. I left this morning.
      2. I'm going to leave tonight.
      3. She's going to leave tomorrow night.
      4. But Paul is going to leave tomorrow morning.
      5. I'm not going to study this afternoon.
      6. Because I already studied last night.
      7. Did you sleep well last night? (essa noite)*
      8. No, but I'm going to sleep well this morning.

   b. Prepare these brief questions and answers, either by
      yourself or with one of your fellow students. Use é que
      in the questions. For example, No.1 would be: Quando
      é que o senhor saiu?

1. When did you leave?	Yesterday morning.
2. When did you return?	Yesterday afternoon.
3. When did you fall?	This morning.
4. When did you fall asleep?	This morning.
5. When did you go home? (para casa)	Last night.
6. When did you write the letter?	This afternoon.
7. When are you going to sleep?	Tomorrow morning.
8. When are you going to drive?	Tonight.

---

* Essa noite refers to sleeping time. When the reference is to
time other than sleeping time, 'last night' is given as ontem
à noite or ontem de noite. 'I went to the movies last night'
would be Eu fui ao cinema ontem à noite or ontem de noite.

9.	When are you going to return?	Tomorrow morning.
10.	When are you going to practice?	Tomorrow night.
11.	When are you going to read the book?	Tonight.
12.	When are you going to arrive in Rio?	Tomorrow afternoon.

Comprehension

Listen to these sentences and make a note of any that are not clear to you.

Translations

I. <u>Practice in asking questions</u> (Recorded)

   A. Ask these questions beginning with <u>O que é que</u>.

     1. What happened?
     2. What fell?
     3. What did he eat?
     4. What did he drink?
     5. What did he take?
     6. What did he prepare?
     7. What did he prefer?
     8. What did he write?
     9. What did he feel?
    10. What did he open?

   B. These questions begin with <u>Como é que</u>.

     1. How did it happen?
     2. How did he fall? (Use <u>ele</u>)
     3. How did he begin?
     4. How did they begin?
     5. How did they sleep?
     6. How did they spend the night?
     7. How did they arrive?

C. These begin with <u>Quem é que</u>.
  1. Who fell?
  2. Who opened the window?
  3. Who prepared the food?
  4. Who drove?
  5. Who got up late?
  6. Who returned early?
  7. Who went out with Yara?
  8. Who wrote the book?
  ----
  9. Who wants to eat?
 10. Who wants to go?
 11. Who wants to begin?
 12. Who has to work?
 13. Who has to return?
 14. Who is going to return?
 15. Who is going to drive?
  ----
 16. Who remembers? (reflexive)
 17. Who knows Mary?
 18. Who is awake?
 19. Who is sleepy?
 20. Who is hungry?
  ----
 21. Who is driving?
 22. Who is dancing with Joe?

D. These begin with <u>Por que é que</u>.
  1. Why did they fall? (Use <u>eles</u>.)
  2. Why did they leave?
  3. Why did they stay?
  4. Why did they return?
  5. Why did they eat so much? (<u>tanto</u>)
  6. Why did they begin late?
  7. Why did they go to bed early?
  8. Why did they forget?

9. Why did they open the door?
10. Why did they fall asleep?
11. Why did they drive?

E. These begin with <u>Onde é que</u>.
1. Where did she eat lunch?   (Use <u>ela</u>.)
2. Where did she stay?
3. Where did she fall?
4. Where did she drive?
5. Where did she eat?
6. Where did she go?
7. Where did she leave the book?
8. Where did she begin?

II. Say these thoughts in Portuguese.
1. I'm sorry. I don't remember.
2. I'm sorry. I don't know what happened.
3. I'm sorry. I can't go today.
4. I'm sorry. I left the car at the (<u>na</u>) Embassy.
5. I'm sorry, but I'm sleepy.
6. I'm sorry, but it's time to go back.
7. I was driving when the tire blew out.
8. I was driving when we passed the Embassy. (Use <u>passar</u> <u>pela</u>)
9. It was raining when we left the Embassy.
10. I slept real well because it was raining.
11. I'm going to sleep real well because it's raining.
12. We're not going to leave now because it's raining.

III. Prepare these dialogettes for presentation to your instructor.
1. A. Do you know what happened today?
   B. No. What happened?
   A. I fell asleep in the office, of all places.

17.22

B. Sleepyhead! You'll have to go to bed earlier.

2. A. I arrived late today. I'm sorry.
    B. What happened?
    A. A tire blew out.
    B. Where? Near here?
    A. No. In the tunnel, of all places.

3. A. Did you like the beach, John?
    B. Not very much, no.
    A. Why?
    B. It rained all day.
    A. Why didn't you stay there another day? (mais um dia)
    B. I had to return because I have a lot of things to do.

4. A. Are we going to go back now?
    B. Why not? Don't you want to?
    A. Yes, but it's raining.
    B. But we're going in Yara's car.
    A. Hmm. I think I'm going to stay here.

5. A. At what time are you going to leave for New York?
    B. At 11:00. After the party.
    A. But isn't that late?
    B. Yes, it is. But I'm in a hurry.
    A. Drive carefully! (Dirija com cuidado!)

                                            End of Tape 8A

Unit 18

1. In past units you have seen that 'my' is given in Portuguese as either <u>meu</u> or <u>minha</u>, the choice depending on the gender of the item that follows. For example:

    a. <u>meu</u> <u>carro</u>   (   )X (   )X

    b. <u>minha</u> <u>esposa</u>   (   )X (   )X

2. You have also seen that the appropriate definite article very frequently appears before <u>meu</u> and <u>minha</u>.

    a. <u>o</u> <u>meu</u> <u>carro</u>   (   )X (   )X

    b. <u>a</u> <u>minha</u> <u>esposa</u>   (   )X (   )X

3. The phrases in No. 2 above mean exactly the same as those in No. 1: 'my car' and 'my wife'.

4. In English, if I want to remove the word 'car' from the sentence 'My car is a Chevrolet', I must also change something else. I must say,

    '<u>Mine</u> is a Chevrolet.'

    In such a case we assume, of course, that the word 'car', or its equivalent, has already been mentioned in a previous sentence. We would not be likely to say such a sentence if this were not true.

5. In Portuguese, if you wish to remove the word <u>carro</u> from the sentence <u>O</u> <u>meu</u> <u>carro</u> é um <u>Chevrolet</u>, you do so without changing anything else in the sentence.

    <u>O</u> <u>meu</u> é um <u>Chevrolet</u>.   (   )X (   )X

    This is the equivalent of 'Mine is a Chevrolet'. Again, common sense tells us that 'carro' was mentioned in a previous sentence.

6. Notice that you <u>must</u> have the definite article. You cannot say <s>Meu é um Chevrolet</s>. The <u>o</u> must be present.

7. If you are dealing with a feminine item, the procedure is the same. You omit the noun but retain the article and the possessive. Thus, if your Brazilian friend tells you---

    a. <u>A</u> <u>minha</u> <u>esposa</u> é <u>brasileira</u>   (   )X (   )X
        'My wife is Brazilian'

                                18.1

you may want to respond with---

   b. A <u>minha</u> <u>é</u> <u>americana</u>. ( )x ( )x
       'Mine is American'.

8. The plurals work the same way. For example, in response to
    the statement---

   a. <u>Os</u> <u>meus</u> <u>meninos</u> <u>estão</u> <u>no</u> <u>Rio</u>. ( )x ( )x
       'My children are in Rio'.

you might wish to say---

   b. <u>Os</u> <u>meus</u> <u>estão</u> <u>aqui</u>. ( )x ( )x
       'Mine are here'.

9. If you tell your Brazilian friend---

   a. <u>As</u> <u>minhas</u> <u>filhas</u> <u>são</u> <u>americanas</u>. ( )x ( )x
       'My daughters are American'.

he may respond with---

   b. <u>As</u> <u>minhas</u> <u>são</u> <u>brasileiras</u>. ( )x ( )x
       'Mine are Brazilian'.

Practice 1. (Recorded)

    How would you say 'mine' with reference to the following
items? Use the definite article. Confirm with the tape.

   a. car
   b. daughter
   c. house
   d. daughter<u>s</u>
   e. wife
   f. car<u>s</u>
   g. table
   h. newspaper
   i. window<u>s</u>
   j. tire<u>s</u>
   k. letter
   l. letter<u>s</u>
   m. party

Practice 2.   (Recorded)

In this exercise, your instructor will make short statements about items or persons that belong to him. You are to respond with, 'Mine is(are) such-and-such too.' For example, if you hear---

A minha esposa está em Washington.

you should respond with---

A minha está em Washington também.
                    (1-8)

10. Now let us continue. Recall this sentence:

E que tal o seu inglês? (   )x (   )x
        'And how's your English?

11. O seu (or just seu) is the form used for your when one is dealing with masculine nouns.

                (o) seu livro (   )x (   )x

                (o) seu menino (   )x (   )x

                (o) seu carro (   )x (   )x

12. When one is dealing with feminine nouns, a sua (or sua) is the appropriate form.

                a sua (   )x (   )x (   )x

13. Thus, 'your house' is---

    a. sua casa (   )x (   )x (   )x or

    b. a sua casa (   )x (   )x (   )x

14. 'Your wife' is---

            (a) sua esposa (   )x (   )x

15. How would you say 'your party'?

(a sua festa)
            Verify: (   )x (   )x

18.3

16. In the case of a plural noun, you must pluralize everything that goes with it. Thus, 'your parties' is---

    a. <u>as</u> <u>suas</u> <u>festas</u> (   )X (   )X, or simply

    b. <u>suas</u> <u>festas</u> (   )X (   )X

17. 'Your cars' would be----

    a. <u>Os</u> <u>seus</u> <u>carros</u> (   )X (   )X, or simply

    b. <u>seus</u> <u>carros</u> (   )X (   )X

18. How would you say 'your parties'?

(as suas festas)
              Verify: (   )X (   )X

19. How would you say 'your sons'?
(os seus filhos)
              Verify: (   )X (   )X

20. If we are talking about 'houses', and I want to refer to your house without actually saying the word 'house', I will simply say---

      <u>a</u> <u>sua</u>   (   )X (   )X

    In English, this translates as 'yours'.

21. How would you say 'yours' with reference to a 'party'?

(a sua)
              Verify: (   )X (   )X

22. How would you say 'yours' with reference to the <u>plural</u> item 'parties'?

(as suas)
              Verify: (   )X (   )X

23. How would you say 'yours' with reference to a car?

(o seu)
              Verify: (   )X (   )X

24. How would you say 'yours' with reference to the plural 'cars'?

(os seus)
              Verify: (   )X (   )X

Practice 3. (Recorded)

Say the following sentences, then give the equivalent of the
question 'And yours?' for each one. Confirm with the tape.

1. A minha filha é americana. (And yours?)
2. O meu carro é um Chevrolet. (And yours?)
3. Os meus pneus são velhos. (And yours?) [plural]
4. A minha casa é velha. (And yours?)
5. As minhas crianças são brasileiras. (And yours?) [plural]
6. A minha festa é amanhã. (And yours?)
7. O meu espanhol é péssimo. (And yours?)
8. Os meus filhos estão em Washington. (And yours?) [plural]

25. 'Our house' is---

a nossa casa   (   )X (   )X

26. 'Our book' is---

o nosso livro   (   )X (   )X

27. To say 'ours', with reference to 'house', just omit the word
casa.

a nossa   (   )X (   )X

28. Likewise, to say 'ours' with reference to 'book', you omit
the word livro.

o nosso   (   )X (   )X

29. With reference to the plural items 'houses' and 'books', the
forms are, respectively:

as nossas   (   )X (   )X
os nossos   (   )X (   )X

30. How would you say 'ours' with reference to 'daughter'?
(a nossa)
Verify: (   )X (   )X

31. How would you say 'ours' with reference to daughters'?
(as nossas)
Verify: (   )X (   )X

18.5

32. How would you say 'our' with reference to 'beaches'?
(as·nossas)

Verify: (   )X (   )X

33. With reference to 'parks'?
(os nossos)

Verify: (   )X (   )X

34. With reference to 'embassies'?
(as nossas)

Verify: (   )X (   )X

35. Thus far, you have learned how to say 'my' and 'mine', 'your'
and 'yours', and 'our' and 'ours'. But how about 'his'? And
how about 'her' and 'hers'?

36. The Portuguese equivalent of 'his book' is literally 'the
book of him'. The phrase 'of him' is <u>de</u> + <u>ele</u>, which always
contracts, as follows:

<u>dele</u>   (   )X (   )X (   )X

37. Thus, 'the book of him' or 'his book' is---

<u>o</u> <u>livro</u> <u>dele</u>   (   )X (   )X (   )X

38. How would you say 'his accent'?
(o sotaque dele)

Verify: (   )X (   )X

39. How would you say 'his wife'?
(a esposa dele)

Verify: (   )X (   )X

40. If the item possessed is plural, you simply use the plural
form of that item, as always. Thus, how would you say 'his
book<u>s</u>'?
(os livros d<u>e</u>le)

Verify: (   )X (   )X

41. How would you say 'his children'?
(as crianças dele)

Verify: (   )X (   )X

42. The Portuguese equivalent of 'her book' is literally 'the
book of her'. The phrase 'of her' is <u>de</u> + <u>ela</u>, which always
contracts, as follows:

<u>dela</u>   (   )X (   )X (   )X

43. Thus, 'the book of her' or 'her book' is

<u>o</u> <u>livro</u> <u>dela</u>   (   )X (   )X (   )X

44. How would you say 'her Portuguese'?
(o português dela)
                Verify: (   )x   (   )x

45. How would you say 'her newspaper'?
(o jornal dela)
                Verify: (   )x   (   )x

46. How would you say 'her letter'?
(a carta dela)
                Verify: (   )x   (   )x

47. If you wanted to say the plural, 'her letter__s', how would
     you say it?
(as cartas dela)
                Verify: (   )x   (   )x

48. And how would you say 'her children'?
(as crianças dela)
                Verify: (   )x   (   )x

Practice 4. (Recorded)

     Practice saying these items until you can do them freely and
easily.

1.	His friend	9.	His hous__es
2.	Her friend	10.	Her hous__es
3.	Her accent	11.	Her food
4.	Her tabl__es	12.	His room
5.	His friend__s	13.	His children
6.	His son__s	14.	His newspaper__s
7.	His wife	15.	Her dialo__gs
8.	His Chevrolet		

49. If we omit the word casa from the phrase a casa dela 'her
     house', we are left with a dela, which is the equivalent of
     'hers'. (Literally, 'the one of her'.)

            a casa dela   (   )x   (   )x
            a dela   (   )x   (   )x

50. Likewise, if we remove the word carro from the phrase o carro
     dela 'her car', we are left with o dela. This too translates
     as 'hers'.

o <u>carro</u> <u>dela</u>   (   )x (   )x

o <u>dela</u>   (   )x (   )x

51. Similarly, if we have already established that we are talk-
     ing about 'houses', and I want to say 'his' (as in 'his is
     old'), I will say <u>a</u> <u>dele</u>.

        a <u>casa</u> <u>dele</u>   (   )x (   )x

        a <u>dele</u>   (   )x (   )x

52. And, if I am referring to something masculine, such as <u>carro</u>, I
     will use the masculine definite article and say 'his' this
     way:

        o <u>dele</u>   (   )x (   )x

53. If we are speaking of plural items, I will use the appropri-
     ate plural definite article. Thus, 'hers', when it refers to
     the masculine plural, is as follows:

        <u>os</u> <u>dela</u>   (   )x (   )x

54. How would you say 'hers' with reference to 'letters'?
(as dela)
                Verify: (   )x (   )x

55. How would you say 'hers' with reference to 'dialogs'?
(os dela)
                Verify: (   )x (   )x

56. Now, how would you say 'his' with reference to 'dialogs'?
(os dele)
                Verify: (   )x (   )x

57. And how would you say 'his' when referring to 'parties'?
(as dele)
                Verify: (   )x (   )x

<u>Practice 5</u>. (Recorded)

     This practice is an easy one. All you need to do is listen
to the items on the tape and repeat each one <u>without</u> the noun.
Thus, if you hear <u>os</u> <u>livros</u> <u>dele</u>, you will repeat only <u>os</u> <u>dele</u>.

<u>Practice 6</u>. (Recorded)

     Repeat the following sentences from the tape, then translate
the English query that follows in parentheses.

                            18.8

1. A minha filha é americana. (And his?)
2. O meu carro é um Chevrolet. (And hers?)
3. Os meus pneus são velhos. (And his?)
4. A minha casa é velha. (And hers?)
5. A minha festa é amanhã. (And hers?)
6. Os meus filhos estão em Washington. (And his?)
7. O meu português é muito bom. (And hers?)

58. Instead of using the prounouns <u>ele</u>, <u>ela</u>, etc., we can use proper nouns. That is, instead of saying 'the book of her', we can say 'the book of Paul', i.e. 'Paul's book'.

o livro de Paulo   ( )X ( )X

59. If we use the definite article <u>o</u> with Paul's name, we have the contraction <u>do</u>. The meaning is still 'Paul's book'.

o livro do Paulo   ( )X ( )X

60. Using the contraction, how would you say 'Paul's office'?
(o escritório do Paulo)
Verify: ( )X ( )X

61. Using the contraction <u>da</u>, how would you say 'Yara's office'?
(o escritório da Yara)
Verify: ( )X ( )X

62. How would you say 'Yara's friends'?
(os amigos da Yara)
Verify: ( )X ( )X

63. How would you say 'Roberto's friends'?
(os amigos do Roberto)
Verify: ( )X ( )X

64. How would you say 'Roberto's grammar'?
(a gramática do Roberto)
Verify: ( )X ( )X

<u>Practice 7</u>. (Recorded)

Translate these brief phrases into Portuguese. The tape confirmations have the contractions <u>do</u> and <u>da</u>.

1. Paul's car   4. Joe's accent
2. Paul's cars   5. The teacher's words
3. Mary's Spanish   6. Rio's beaches

7. The Embassy's door   9. John's wife

8. John's newspaper   10. Yara's book

65. And, again, it is possible to leave out the noun in the above
phrases. If we omit the noun from the phrase <u>o escritório</u>
<u>da Yara</u>, for example, we are left with <u>o da Yara</u>, which
means 'Yara's' (referring to her office, of course).

<u>o da Yara</u>   (   )X (   )X

66. If we are talking about houses, and we want to say something
about Paul's house without actually saying the word <u>casa</u>, we
can say <u>a do Paulo</u>, which means 'Paul's'.

a ~~casa~~ <u>do Paulo</u> = <u>a do Paulo</u>   (   )X (   )X

67. The same procedure applies to the plural. The phrase <u>os livros</u>
<u>da Yara</u> ('Yara's books') can be shortened to <u>os da Yara</u>
('Yara's').

<u>os da Yara</u>   (   )X (   )X

68. Likewise, <u>as praias do Rio</u> ('Rio's beaches') can be shortened
to <u>as do Rio</u> ('Rio's').

<u>as do Rio</u>   (   )X (   )X

<u>Practice 8</u>.   (Recorded)

While referring to the nouns suggested at the left, practice
putting into Portuguese the statements at the right. Check with
the tape.

Example: <u>carro</u>   a. Yara's is a Chevrolet.

(You should say: <u>O da Yara é um Chevrolet</u>.)

1. <u>filha</u>   a. Paul's arrived yesterday.
                          b. Mine arrives today.
                          c. Maria's is going to arrive tomorrow.

2. <u>carro</u>   a. Mine is a Ford.
                          b. The teacher's is a Ford, too.
                          c. But Roberto's is a Volkswagen.

3. <u>filhos</u> (plural) a. Roberto's speak Portuguese.
                           b. Yara's speak Portuguese, too.
                           c. Do yours speak Portuguese, too?

18.10

4. <u>festa</u>   a. Mine is today.
                  b. Maria's is today too.
                  c. Is Sandra's going to be tomorrow?

5. <u>pneus</u> (plural)   a. Carlos's are old.
                  b. Mine are old, too.
                  c. And Bill's blew out.

6. <u>amigo</u>   a. Fred's is Brazilian.
                  b. Mine is too.
                  c. Yara's is American.

DIALOG

Professor

dona	(title of respect)
para	to, towards

Quando é que a senhora vai
para o Brasil, Dona Bárbara?

When are you going to Brazil,
Barbara?

Barbara

vinte e seis	twenty-six
maio	May
o sábado	Saturday
depois de	after
a formatura	graduation

No dia vinte e seis de maio.

On the 26th of May.

O sábado depois da minha
formatura.

The Saturday after my graduation.

Professor

direta	direct
diretamente	directly

A senhora vai diretamente
para o Rio?

Are you going directly to Rio?

Barbara

parar	stop (neutral form)
pais	parents

Bom, eu vou parar na Flórida
e passar uma semana com os
meus pais.

Well, I'm going to stop in Florida
and spend a week with my parents.

para	towards, for

E de lá, então, eu vou para
o Rio.

And from there, then, I'm going to
Rio.

<u>Professor</u>

Que bom!   That's good.

    a gente   we*
    receber   receive (neutral form)
    notícias   news
    suas   yours, of you

<u>A gente vai receber notícias</u> <u>Are we going to hear from you</u>?
<u>suas</u>?

<u>Barbara</u>

    mandar   send (neutral form)
    o cartão   post card

<u>Eu vou mandar um cartão do Rio</u>. <u>I'm going to send a card from Rio</u>.

<u>Professor</u>

    comprou   you bought (-<u>ar</u> type)
    as passagens   tickets

<u>A senhora já comprou as</u>   <u>Did you buy your tickets yet</u>?
<u>passagens</u>?

<u>Barbara</u>

    reservei   I reserved (-<u>ar</u> type)
    Varig   Varig (Brazilian International
                                      Airlines)

<u>Eu já reservei; de Washington</u>   <u>I've reserved them; from Washington</u>
<u>a Miami pela Eastern, e de</u>   <u>to Miami on Eastern, and from</u>
<u>Miami ao Rio pela Varig</u>.**   <u>Miami to Rio on Varig</u>.

---

*   <u>A gente</u> (literally, 'the people') is very commonly used in
    the sense of 'we' or 'us'.

** The definite article in this contraction is feminine since the
    reference is to the word <u>companhia</u> 'company', which is feminine.
    That is, the Portuguese concept is 'on the Eastern (or Varig)
    Company'. Notice that the meaning of <u>pela</u> here ('on') is quite
    different from its meaning in Unit 16 where it was equated with
    'around, about'. This is typical of the wide variety of
    equivalences that prepositions assume across language boundaries.

Supplementary Vocabulary   (Recorded)

The days of the week

segunda-feira	Monday
terça-feira	Tuesday
quarta-feira	Wednesday
quinta-feira	Thursday
sexta-feira	Friday
sábado	Saturday
domingo	Sunday

The months of the year

janeiro	January
fevereiro	February
março	March
abril	April
maio	May
junho	June
julho	July
agosto	August
setembro	September
outubro	October
novembro	November
dezembro	December

Expansion Exercise 1   (Recorded)

Practice saying these dates after your instructor's voice on the tape.

1. Sábado, dois de fevereiro

2. Domingo, vinte e seis de fevereiro

3. Quarta-feira, doze de janeiro

4. Quinta-feira, seis de junho

5. Segunda-feira, dez de abril

6. Sexta-feira, quinze de setembro

7. Terca-feira, trinta de maio

8. Sábado, dezesseis de julho

9. Domingo, vinte e sete de agosto

10. Quarta-feira, primeiro* de outubro

---

*   All dates except the 'first' are expressed with cardinal numbers.

Expansion Exercise 2. (Recorded)
  (Practice with the verb comprar)

Repeat: A senhora já comprou as passagens?

Translate:

1. Have you (already) bought the car?

2. I already bought the car.

3. Are you going to buy the car?

4. I'm not going to buy anything.

5. I want to buy a postcard.

6. We bought two tickets.

Expansion Exercise 3. (Recorded)
  (Practice with the verb mandar)

Repeat: Eu vou mandar um cartão.

Translate:

1. He's going to send a card from São Paulo.
2. He has already sent a card.
3. I sent a letter yesterday.
4. Did you send the letter to Brasilia?
5. Varig has already sent the tickets to New York.

Expansion Exercise 4. (Recorded)
  (Practice with a gente, meaning 'we')

Repeat: A gente vai receber notícias suas?

Translate:
1. Are we going to receive a letter?
2. Are we going to like [it]?
3. Are we going to work tomorrow?
4. Are we going to stop in Rio?
5. Are we going to sleep until late?
6. We drink a lot of coffee.
7. We eat a good lunch here.

18.15

Comprehension

Listen to these utterances and make a note of any that are
not clear to you.

Exchanges and Brief Dialogs

I. (Recorded) These are brief, 2 and 3 line exchanges in Portuguese. First, listen to them on tape for comprehension purposes.
Then look at them below, preferably while continuing to listen,
and familiarize yourself with them so that you can use them
readily, easily and understandingly with your teacher.

1. A. Eu esqueci os meus livros.
    B. E eu esqueci os meus também.

2. A. O senhor falou com os seus pais?
    B. Falei.
    A. Que bom! Eu vou falar com os meus amanhã.

3. A. Este é o meu livro. Qual é o seu?
    B. Este é o meu.

4. A. O filho do Paulo fala espanhol.
    B. O do Roberto fala inglês.

5. A. Eu estou com o carro da Sandra.
    B. Por que? O que é que aconteceu com o seu?
    A. Nada. O meu está em casa.

6. A. Eles já compraram as passagens.
    B. Eu ainda não comprei a minha.

7. A. Aqui está a minha passagem.
    B. Você sabe onde é que está a da Sandra?

8. A. A minha filha fala inglês. E a sua?
    B. A minha só fala português.

9. A. A nossa casa fica em Copacabana.
    B. A nossa fica em Ipanema, perto da praia.

10. A. O meu filho é americano.
    B. O da Yara é americano também.

18.16

II. Practice these brief dialogs. The first two are in Portuguese
     and are recorded for you.

     1. A. O meu carro está muito perto, na Avenida Rio Branco.
             Onde está o seu?
         B. O meu está lá também.
         A. Então vamos no meu, ou no seu?*
         B. O do Jorge está perto também. Por que não vamos no*
             dele?

     2. A. O senhor já comprou as passagens?
         B. Já, sim. Para o dia 28 de junho, pela Braniff.
         A. Por que pela Braniff? O senhor não gosta da Pan Am?
         B. Gosto, claro, mas a Pan Am vai diretamente ao Rio. A
             Braniff pára em Lima, e eu quero passar uns dias lá.
         A. O senhor conhece Lima?
         B. Conheço, sim. Eu tenho amigos lá.
         A. Que bom!

     3. A. Are you going by Varig?
         B. No, by Pan American.
         A. What time do you arrive in Rio?
         B. At 7:00 in the morning. Real early.

III. Now, how would you say these thoughts in Portuguese?

     1. I'm going to stop there.
     2. I'm going to stop in Belém.
     3. I'm going to spend two weeks in Belém.
     4. I'm going to spend Saturday in New York.
     5. When are you going to New York?
     6. Are you going after the graduation?
     7. From Rio, then, we are going to São Paulo.
     8. From Rio, then, he went to Fortaleza.
     9. From Rio, then, we went to Curitiba.
     10. And from Curitiba, we returned to Rio.

*Contraction: em + o = no

18.17

UNIT 19

Review Material - Pronunciation Practice

1. Here is the phrase 'with the car'.

    com o carro (   )x (   )x (   )x

2. You will remember that in the transition between com and o there is no m sound. There is, instead, the nasal vowel õ followed by the non-nasal vowel o.

    a. com (   )x (   )x
    b. o (   )x (   )x
    c. com o (   )x (   )x

3. For our purposes, com o might be rewritten like this, without an m:

    Kõ o (   )x (   )x

4. When saying com o, if you accidentally put an m sound after the õ, the Portuguese-speaking listener will very likely interpret what you say as como o, which means 'like the'.

5. Since 'with the' means something other than 'like the', it is important that you say this phrase so that you will be understood. For example, listen to the tape, and repeat 'with the car'.

    (   )x (   )x

6. Now listen to the tape, and repeat 'like the car'.

    (   )x (   )x

7. Repeat the one after the other.

    a. 'with the car' (   )x (   )x
    b. 'like the car' (   )x (   )x

8. Now do the same with the phrases 'with the president' and 'like the president'.

    a. 'with the president' (   )x (   )x
    b. 'like the president' (   )x (   )x

Practice 1.   (Recorded)

This is a chance to practice some more of the same. Below
is a list of items that appear on the tape in Portuguese. In
each case, item (a) is 'with somebody or something', and item (b)
is 'like somebody or something'. There is a pause for you to
repeat after each one.

	(a)	(b)
1.	with the traffic	like the traffic
2.	with the car	like the car
3.	with Bill	like Bill
4.	with the children	like the children
5.	with an accent	like an accent
6.	with a child	like a child
7.	with my friend	like my friend

9.   This same unwanted m sound can be a problem with other words
     ending in a nasal vowel or nasal diphthong when they are
     followed immediately by another vowel.

10. Thus, in falam espanhol, you must be sure that you go directly
     from the nasal diphthong ão to the following e without
     producing an m.

           falam espanhol ( )X ( )X (   )X

11. In this case, there is not much danger of your being mis-
     understood if you slip and put an m sound in the utterance.
     But to do so does constitute an error of pronunciation grave
     enough to hurt the native speaker's ears. So you will want
     to be careful. There is a nasal ão, but there is no m.

           falam espanhol ( )X ( )X

12. Here is another example.

           tem uns livros (   ) ( )X (   )X

13. In this case one goes directly from the nasal diphthong em
     to the nasal vowel ũ without saying an m sound. Now, try
     the first part of the utterance again.

           tem uns (   ) ( )X ( )X

Practice 2. (Recorded)

Here is a chance to practice more of the same. Repeat the following items, being very careful not to produce an m̲ sound where two vowel sounds are linked together. This linkage is shown here with the ⌣ . First listen to the tape, then repeat.

1. trabalham͜aqui   (   )x   (   )x

2. trabalham͜hoje   (   )x   (   )x

3. pretendem͜almoçar   (   )x   (   )x

4. querem͜amanhã   (   )x   (   )x

5. saíram͜ontem   (   )x   (   )x

6. abriram͜a porta   (   )x   (   )x

7. escreveram͜uma carta   (   )x   (   )x

8. leram͜um livro   )x   (   )x

9. repetiram͜outra vez   (   )x   (   )x

10. tem͜uma menina   (   )x   (   )x

11. tem͜um filho   (   )x   (   )x

12. tem͜o livro   (   )x   (   )x

13. sem͜o Paulo   (   )x   (   )x

14. sem͜a Yara   (   )x   (   )x

15. bom͜espanhol   (   )x   (   )x

14. Occasionally, there is a chance for misunderstanding. The way to say 'good hotel' is bom̲ hotel. There is no m̲ sound, nor is there an h̲ sound (the printed h̲ is silent). We could rewrite it like this:

    bõ otel   (   )x   (   )x

15. If you accidentally link the two words with an m̲ sound, instead of saying 'good hotel' you are saying 'good motel' (bom motel). Not a horrendous mistake, to be sure, but an interesting one, nonetheless.

    bom motel   (   )   (   )x   (   )x

19.3

16. Here are the two phrases, one after the other.

    a. bom hotel   ( )X   (   )X

    b. bom motel   ( )X   (   )X

End of Tape 8B

<u>Tape 9A</u>

<u>NEW MATERIAL</u>

1. In this unit we are going to examine the present tense of verbs of the -<u>ir</u> type. We have already examined the past tense of this type in Unit 17. In this unit we will use some of the same verbs we used in Unit 17, namely:

        abrir   ( )X

        sair   ( )X

        cair   ( )X

        sentir ( )X

        dirigir ( )X

2. First, recall from earlier units the present tense endings of a typical, regular -<u>er</u> type verb. The verb <u>pretender</u> is a good example.

        pretend<u>o</u>   ( )X   (   )X

        pretend<u>e</u>   ( )X   (   )X

        pretend<u>emos</u> ( )X   (   )X

        pretend<u>em</u> ( )X   (   )X

3. Verbs of the -<u>ir</u> type have a similar set of endings. Indeed, they are the very same except for the we-form. Take the verb <u>abrir</u> as an example.

        abr<u>o</u> ( )X   (   )X

        abr<u>e</u> ( )X   (   )X

        abr<u>imos</u> ( )X   (   )X

        abr<u>em</u> ( )X   (   )X

4. In the we-forms, -<u>er</u> type verbs have the -<u>emos</u> ending, while -<u>ir</u> type verbs have the -<u>imos</u> ending.

        pretend<u>emos</u> ( )X   (   )X : we plan

        abr<u>imos</u> ( )X   (   )X : we open

19.4

5. This -_imos_ ending is the same one that marks the past tense.
    Thus, _abrimos_ can also mean 'we opened'. The context tells
    us which meaning is intended.

6. Since 'we open' is _abrimos_, how would you say 'we feel'?
    Infinitive: _sentir_
(sentimos)
                    Verify: (   )x   (   )x

7. How would you say 'we drive'? Infinitive: _dirigir_
(dirigimos)
                    Verify: (   )x   (   )x

8. How would you say 'we leave'? Infinitive: _sair_
(saimos)
                    Verify: (   )x   (   )x

9. Now let us go to the 'they-form'. It has the same ending
    as the 'they-form' of an -_er_ type verb, namely -_em_. Thus,

    a. 'They open'   = _abr-em_   (   )x   (   )x
    b. 'they leave' = _sa-em_   (   )x   (   )x

10. How would you say 'they fall'? Infinitive: _cair_
(caem)
                    Verify: (   )x   (   )x

11. How would you say 'they drive'? Infinitive: _dirigir_
(dirigem)
                    Verify: (   )x   (   )x

12. How about 'they feel'? Infinitive: _sentir_
(sentem)
                    Verify: (   )x   (   )x

Practice 3. (Recorded)

    Listen to these short questions and answers as spoken by two
instructors on the tape. There is space for you to repeat the
answers aloud.

                              (1-8)

13. Now we will turn to the he-forms. Listen to 'he opens'.

                    (   )   (   )x   (   )x

14. What is the form for 'he feels'? Infinitive: _sentir_
(sente)
                    Verify: (   )x   (   )x

                              19.5

15. How do you say 'he drives'? Infinitive: <u>dirigir</u>
(dirige)
                   Verify: ( )x   ( )x

16. The form for 'he leaves' is a bit irregular. The unstressed
     <u>e</u> ending coalesces with the <u>a</u> of the stem and a diphthong
     results. The form is not <u>sa-e</u>. The form is <u>sai</u>.

          <u>sai</u> ( )   ( )x   ( )x   ( )x

17. The form for 'he falls' is irregular in exactly the same way.

          <u>cai</u> ( )   ( )x   ( )x   ( )x

18. And now we turn to the I-form which, as you would expect,
     is marked by an unstressed <u>o</u> ending. Thus, 'I drive' is

          <u>dirijo</u> * ( )   ( )x   ( )x

19. What is the form for 'I open'?
(abro)
                   Verify: ( )x   ( )x

20. The form for 'I leave' is a bit irregular. It is not <u>sa-o</u>,
     as you might expect. Listen to the correct form on the tape,
     and repeat.

          ( )   ( )x   ( )x   ( )x

21. This is the way it is written.

          <u>saio</u>   ( )   ( )x   ( )x

22. Can you guess what the form for 'I fall' is?
(caio)
                   Verify: ( )x   ( )x

23. The form for 'I feel', or 'I'm sorry', is also irregular.

          <u>sinto</u> ( )x   ( )x

24. It is irregular because the stem vowel has changed from the
     nasal <u>ẽ</u> of the infinitive to the nasal <u>ĩ</u>.

          <u>sentir</u> ( )x   ( )x
          <u>sinto</u>   ( )x   ( )x

*Note the spelling with 'j', instead of 'g'.

25. Here, in summary, are the four forms of a regular -ir type
    verb in the present.

    <u>abro</u> ( )X   <u>abrimos</u> ( )X
    <u>abre</u> ( )X   <u>abrem</u>   ( )X

26. And here in summary are the verbs <u>sair</u>, <u>cair</u> and <u>sentir</u>,
    some of whose forms are irregular in the present tense.

    <u>saio</u>   ( )X   <u>caio</u>   ( )X   <u>sinto</u>   ( )X
    <u>sai</u>   ( )X   <u>cai</u>   ( )X   <u>sente</u>   ( )X
    <u>saímos</u> ( )X   <u>caímos</u> ( )X   <u>sentimos</u> ( )X
    <u>saem</u>   ( )X   <u>caem</u>   ( )X   <u>sentem</u>   ( )X

<u>Practice 4</u>. (Recorded)

     Here are some more short questions and answers spoken by two
instructors on the tape. Listen to them, and repeat just the
answers.

<u>Practice 5</u>. (Recorded)

     Answer these questions using the present tense of the verbs
indicated. The questions (not the answers) are recorded on the
tape. If you wish, you can practice these questions with a
fellow student,

    1. Como é que ele dirige?
    2. Quando é que você sai?
    3. A que horas é que a embaixada abre?
    4. Quando é que ela cai no sono?
    5. Quem é que dirige até a praia?
    6. Quem é que sai comigo?
    7. Quem mais dirige?

27. The verb <u>sentir</u> is usually reflexive when it is used with
    reference to how one is feeling. Recall this sentence from
    a previous dialog.

        <u>Como é que o senhor se sente hoje</u>? ( )X ( )X

28. The answer to that question might be:

        <u>Eu me sinto bem</u> ( ) ( )X ( )X

29. Notice that the reflexive pronouns <u>se</u> and <u>me</u> precede the
     verb forms.

> <u>O</u> <u>senhor</u> <u>se</u> <u>sente</u>   ( )X   ( )X
>
> <u>Eu</u> <u>me</u> <u>sinto</u>   ( )X   ( )X

30. How would you say 'I feel tired'?
(Eu me
sinto cansado)
>   Verify: ( )X   ( )X

31. How would you say 'He feels tired'?
(Ele se sente
cansado)
>   Verify: ( )X   ( )X

32. How would you ask the question: 'Do you feel well?'

> Você ___ ___ ___?
(Você se
sente bem?)
>   Verify: ( )X   ( )X

33. Now, on to another topic. Recall these utterances.

> a. <u>Está</u> <u>chovendo</u> <u>outra</u> <u>vez</u>. ( )X   ( )X
>
> b. <u>Está</u> <u>fazendo</u> <u>calor</u> <u>aqui</u>. ( )X   ( )X
>
> c. <u>Quem</u> <u>é</u> <u>que</u> <u>estava</u> <u>dirigindo</u>?   ( )X   ( )X

34. The translations of the above sentences are:

> a. It is raining again.
>
> b. It is making heat (i.e., it's hot) here.
>
> c. Who was driving?

35. Notice:

> <u>chovendo</u> = raining
>
> <u>fazendo</u> = making
>
> <u>dirigindo</u> = driving

36. This <u>-ndo</u> ending on a verb generally equates with English
     '-ing'. This form is arrived at by removing the <u>r</u> of the
     infinitive, nasalizing the final vowel, and adding <u>-do</u>.
     In writing, the nasalization of the final vowel is indicated
     by the <u>n</u>; hence, it is common to say that one adds an <u>-ndo</u>
     ending, rather than a <u>-do</u> ending.

> chove-r / chove-ndo ( )X   dirigi-r / dirigi-ndo ( )X
>
> faze-r / faze-ndo   ( )X   fala-r / fala-ndo   ( )X

Practice 6.   (Recorded)

Practice saying the following forms, imitating the voice on the tape.

A. <u>-ar</u> type   morando   ( )x   ( )x
                 preparando ( )x   ( )x
                 estudando ( )x   ( )x
                 almoçando ( )x   ( )x
                 dando   ( )x   ( )x
                 levantando ( )x   ( )x
                 trabalhando ( )x   ( )x

B. <u>-er</u> type   comendo   ( )x   ( )x
                 bebendo ( )x   ( )x
                 escrevendo ( )x   ( )x
                 esquecendo ( )x   ( )x
                 lendo   ( )x   ( )x
                 sabendo ( )x   ( )x
                 pretendendo ( )x   ( )x

C. <u>-ir</u> type   dirigindo   ( )x   ( )x
                 abrindo ( )x   ( )x
                 saindo ( )x   ( )x
                 caindo ( )x   ( )x
                 repetindo ( )x   ( )x
                 preferindo ( )x   ( )x
                 dormindo ( )x   ( )x

Practice 7.   (Recorded)

Translate these English '-ing' forms into Portuguese.   Check with the tape for confirmation.

1. speaking   7. drinking
2. arriving   8. eating
3. working   9. sleeping
4. sending   10. feeling
5. buying   11. opening
6. writing   12. leaving

19.9

37. These -ndo forms are commonly preceded by a form of the verb
    estar. English has a direct parallel. The '-ing' form is
    often preceded by a form of the verb 'to be'.

eu estou trabalhando	(	)X	(	)X	I am working
ele está saindo	(	)X	(	)X	He is leaving
nós estamos bebendo	(	)X	(	)X	We are drinking
eles estão estudando	(	)X	(	)X	They are studying

38. The examples in 37 above all contain a present tense form of
    estar and thus refer to the present time. The use of this
    construction (present tense of estar + ndo form) underscores
    the continuing, progressive nature of an action in the
    present. For this reason it is often referred to as the
    present progressive construction.

39. The example estava dirigindo contains a past tense form of
    estar. We will deal with this construction in a later unit.

40. Thus, the phrase ele está dormindo means 'he is sleeping'.
    It would be used in the translation of these two utterances:

    a. Don't wake him; he's sleeping soundly. (At this moment)

    b. He's sleeping better these days. (Not necessarily at
       this very moment, but certainly during a time span
       which includes the present.)

41. However, this same phrase (ele está dormindo) would not be
    used in translating the following utterance:

    c. He's sleeping at Dave's tomorrow night.

    This is a normal sentence in English. It uses the present
    tense of 'to be' together with the '-ing' form of the main
    verb to refer to a future action. This cannot be done in
    Portuguese. The present tense of estar plus the -ndo form
    can be used only to describe actions occurring in the present,
    never in the future.

Practice 8. (Recorded)

    Listen to these recorded exchanges (questions and answers)
between two Brazilians. There is space on the tape for you to
mimic the replies of the second one.

(1-11)

19.10

Practice 9. Translation Exercise

Practice putting these short items into Portuguese. Check
the tape for verification.

1.	He's eating lunch.	(almoçar)
2.	He's making a phone call.	(dar)
3.	He's falling!	(cair)
4.	He's working.	(trabalhar)
5.	He's writing a letter.	(escrever)
6.	I'm returning.	(voltar)
7.	I'm receiving lots of news.	(receber)
8.	I'm living in Rio.	(morar)
9.	I'm studying.	(estudar)
10.	I'm planning.	(pretender)
11.	I'm planning to start.	(pretender)
12.	I'm starting.	(começar)

DIALOG

Paulo

Oi	Hi
Jorge	George
fazendo	doing (-er type)

Oi, Jorge! O que é que você
está fazendo?

Hi, George! What are you doing?

nunca	never
descansa	rest (-ar type)

Você nunca descansa?

Don't you ever rest?

Jorge

estudando	studying (-ar type)

Eu estou estudando.

I'm studying.

o exame	test, exam

Tenho exame amanhã.

I have a test tomorrow.

Paulo

há	there is
o que é que há?	what is there?
aquele	that
novo	new

O que é que há com aquele
novo professor Ferreira?

What is it with that new professor
Ferreira?

sempre	always
dando	giving (-ar type)
a prova	test (English 'proof')

Ele está sempre dando provas.

He's always giving tests.

19.12

Jorge

Eu sei lá! [1]   I don't know!

    viu?   you know?   (See Note 2)

Mas ele é bom, viu?[2]   But he's good, you know?

Paulo

    mesmo   indeed, really, surely[3]

É mesmo.   He sure is.

    olhe   look, say
    mudando   changing (-ar type)
    o assunto   subject
    vem   he comes (neutral form: vir)
    não é?   right? Is it not so?

Olhe, mudando de assunto,   Say, changing the subject, tomorrow
amanhã a gente vem no seu   we come in your car, don't we?
carro, não é?

Jorge

    a vez   time, turn

É, é minha vez.[4]   Yes, it's my turn.

    lembre   remember
    saio   I leave (-ir type)

E lembre que eu sempre saio   And remember that I always leave
cedo.   early.

_____

1. This very idiomatic expression has connotations roughly
    equivalent to 'How should I know?' and 'I don't have the
    slightest idea.' You will hear it frequently among close friends.
    Be careful to use it only in informal circumstances.
2. This use of viu? is common. The word is an abbreviation of
    ouviu? which means 'did you hear?' Thus this sentence says,
    'But he's good, do you hear me?' You should certainly be aware
    of this form, but you should be careful not to overuse it at
    first.
3. Mesmo has a variety of translations and shades of meaning, several
    of which are suggested here.
4. Notice that the first é echoes the é of the question just asked.
    Q. Is it not so? A. It is.

EXPANSION EXERCISES

Expansion Exercise 1. (Recorded)

Following the models given, ask the following questions in Portuguese. Verify with the tape.

A. Model: <u>O que é que você está fazendo</u>?

1. What are you studying?
2. What are you eating?
3. What are you preparing?
4. What are you drinking? (<u>beber</u>)
5. What are you buying?
6. What are you reading?
7. What are you saying?

B. Model: <u>Quem é que está falando</u>?

1. Who is practicing?
2. Who is leaving?
3. Who is driving?
4. Who is speaking?
5. Who is sleeping?
6. Who is studying?
7. Who is living?

C. Model: <u>Por que é que ele está praticando</u>?

1. Why is he sleeping?
2. Why is he resting?
3. Why is he leaving?
4. Why is he studying?
5. Why is he driving?
6. Why is he working?
7. Why is he reading?

D. Model: <u>Onde é que eles estão estudando</u>?
    1.   Where are they sleeping?
    2.   Where are they reading?
    3.   Where are they eating lunch?
    4.   Where are they living?
    5.   Where are they practicing?
    6.   Where are they working?
    7.   Where are they spending the night?

Expansion Exercise 2. (Recorded)

Study the following model, then prepare the four exchanges that follow.

Model: A. O que há com o Paulo? Ele sempre está cansado.
        B. Eu sei lá. Parece que ele está trabalhando demais.
----

  1.   A. What is it with Mr. Ferreira? He's always hungry.
        B. I don't know. It seems he likes to eat.

  2.   A. What is it with Maria? She's not awake yet.
        B. I don't know. It looks like she got to bed late.

  3.   A. What is it with Paul? He's always sleeping.
        B. I don't know. I think he's working at night.

  4.   A. What is it with him? He's always forgetting his book.
        B. I don't know. It looks like he doesn't like Portuguese.

Expansion Exercise 3. (Recorded)

Following the model given, prepare these short conversational exchanges.

Model: A. Mas ele é bom, viu?
        B. É mesmo.

  1.   A. But he is an American, you know?
        B. He is, indeed!

  2.   A. But he speaks well, you know?
        B. He does (speak), indeed!

3.   A.   But he drives well, you know?
      B.   He does, indeed!

4.   A.   But he likes to eat, you know?
      B.   He really does!

5.   A.   But he fell, you know?
      B.   He really did!

6.   A.   But he came back late, you know?
      B.   He really did!

7.   A.   But he left everything in the car, you know?
      B.   He really did!

Expansion Exercise 4. (Recorded)

By changing the intonation, phrases with _mesmo_, such as those you just practiced in Exercise 3, can be made into questions, with the meaning 'Really?', 'Is that so?', etc. Listen to the models given on the tape, then try the examples below. Pay particular attention to the question-type intonation of the phrases containing _mesmo_.

Models:

    Ele é brasileiro, viu? (He's Brazilian, you know?)
    É mesmo? (Is he really?)

    Ele trabalhou ontem, viu? (He worked yesterday, you know?)
    Trabalhou, mesmo? (Is that so?)

1. He's single, you know?
   Is he really?

2. He speaks Spanish, you know?
   Does he really?

3. He knows the president, you know?
   Is that so?

4. She's going directly to Rio, you know?
   Is she really?

5. She already bought the tickets, you know?
   Did she really?

6. She went by Pan Am, you know?
   Did she really?

19.16

7. It is difficult, you know?
    Is that so?

8. It was difficult, you know? ('was' = <u>foi</u>)
    Was it really?

9. They went to Florida, you know?
    Did they really?

10. His English is terrible (<u>péssimo</u>), you know?
    Is that so?

----

11. A. Paulo!.... It's time to get up!
    B. (Bocejo) Is it really?

12. A. Paulo!... Today is Monday!
    B. Is it really?

13. A. Paulo!... It's seven-thirty!
    B. Uh.. Is it really?

14. A. Paulo!... Wake up! We have a test today.
    B. (Bocejo)... Do we really?

15. A. Paulo!... Wake up!
    B. (Bocejo)... I'm awake!
    A. Are you really?

Expansion Exercise 5.

    Prepare these brief conversational exchanges.

A. Hi, George! What are you doing?
B. I'm eating lunch. Did you eat yet?
A. Yes. I ate downstairs.

A. Hi, George! What are you doing?
B. I'm leaving the party.
A. Why?
B. <u>Sh</u>! I don't like (I'm not liking) it!*

        ----

*   Frequently Portuguese uses the present progressive construction
    where English uses the simple present tense.

19.17

A. Hi George! What's going on? (<u>acontecendo</u>)
B. The president is speaking.
A. What's he saying?
B. I don't know. I'm sleeping.

A. Hi, George! What are you doing?
B. (Bocejo) I'm sleeping, see?!
A. Oh, Excuse me!........Sleepyhead!

<u>Expansion Exercise 6</u>. (Recorded)

(Note that an adverb like <u>sempre</u> may fall between <u>estar</u> and the <u>-ndo</u> form.)

Following the example of the model, put the following thoughts into Portuguese.

Model: <u>Ele está sempre dando provas</u>.

1. He's always making phone calls.
2. He's always studying.
3. Barbara is always talking with Mr. Ferreira.
4. Barbara is always going out with him.
5. I'm always doing that.
6. I'm always forgetting my book.
7. You're always saying that.
8. You're always eating.
9. You're always noticing my accent.
10. It's always raining there.

<u>Expansion Exercise 7</u>. (Recorded)

Again, follow the model and put these thoughts into Portuguese.

Model: <u>Você nunca descansa</u>?

1. Don't you ever work?
2. Don't you ever go to New York?
3. Don't you ever study?
4   Don't you ever arrive late?

5. Don't you ever open the windows?
6. Doesn't he ever leave early?
7. Doesn't he ever feel well?
8. Doesn't he ever go to bed early?
9. Doesn't he ever stop in Washington?
10. Doesn't he ever have to study?

Comprehension

Listen to these utterances and notify your instructor of any that are not clear to you.

Translations

How would you say the following utterances in Portuguese? In numbers 1-5 the present tense should be used, even though the reference is to future time. This use of the present tense is just as common in Portuguese as it is in English.

1. Tomorrow we (a gente) come early.
2. Tomorrow we rest.
3. Tomorrow we buy the tickets.
4. Remember that tomorrow we begin at 7:30 p.m.
5. Remember that tomorrow we go to the beach.
6. It's my turn.
7. It's never my turn.
8. It's my turn to rest. (Use de + descansar)
9. Remember that tomorrow it's my turn.
10. It's my turn to speak. (Use de + infinitive)
11. It's my turn to buy the food.
12. It's your turn to prepare the food.
13. It's your turn to buy the tickets.
14. It's your turn to eat lunch early.
15. It's your turn to repeat.
16. Changing the subject, what are we going to do tomorrow?
17. Changing the subject, where are we going to eat dinner?
18. Changing the subject, how are we going to get (receive) news of you?
19. Changing the subject, who is going to drive?
20. Changing the subject, when are we going to the movies?

21. I am a little tired. When are we going to leave?

22. I am very tired. I worked too much today.

23. If he is tired, why doesn't he go home?

24. If you are tired, why don't you stay home?

25. When I am tired, I always leave early.

26. I'm not tired. Let's go to the beach!

27. Yesterday I left early.

28. My friend Sam left with me. He lives in Alexandria also.

29. I always leave with Sam. He's a good friend.

30. Sam is a friend of the president.

31. Well, let's change the subject. Let's talk about Gloria.

32. Good idea! Who's Gloria?

33. Don't you know (her)? She's our teacher!

34. Of course. Now I remember. Excuse me.

End of Tape 9A

UNIT 20

1. Do you remember these present tense he-forms from earlier units?

<u>ele</u> <u>nota</u> (   )x (   )x   he notices
<u>ele</u> <u>mora</u> (   )x (   )x   he lives
<u>ele</u> <u>gosta</u> (   )x (   )x   he likes

2. All of them contain the open vowel <u>O</u>. Repeat them again and make sure that the vowel is an open <u>O</u>. Remember that it's similar to the vowel sound of English 'paws'.

n<u>O</u>ta (   )x (   )x
m<u>O</u>ra (   )x (   )x
g<u>O</u>sta (   )x (   )x

3. The same open <u>O</u> appears in the I-form.

<u>eu</u> n<u>O</u>to (   )x (   )x
<u>eu</u> m<u>O</u>ro (   )x (   )x
<u>eu</u> g<u>O</u>sto (   )x (   )x

4. It appears also in the they-form.

<u>eles</u> n<u>O</u>tam (   )x (   )x
<u>eles</u> m<u>O</u>ram (   )x (   )x
<u>eles</u> g<u>O</u>stam (   )x (   )x

5. But it does not appear in the we-form, where the <u>o</u> remains closed.

n<u>o</u>tamos (   )x (   )x
m<u>o</u>ramos (   )x (   )x
g<u>o</u>stamos (   )x (   )x

6. Nor does it appear in the infinitive, where again the <u>o</u> remains closed.

n<u>o</u>tar (   )x (   )x
m<u>o</u>rar (   )x (   )x
g<u>o</u>star (   )x (   )x

7. Observe that the open o appears in stressed syllables, the
    closed o in unstressed syllables:

    Stressed:

            nOto   nOta   nOtam   (   )X

            mOro   mOra   mOram   (   )X

            gOsto   gOsta   gOstam   (   )X

    Unstressed:

            notamos   notar   (   )X

            moramos   morar   (   )X

            gostamos   gostar   (   )X

8. A number of other -ar type verbs have the same distribution
    of o and O. Those that you have had thus far, in addition
    to the ones listed above, are almoçar and voltar.

9. Thus, 'I eat lunch' has the open O.

            eu almOço   (   )X (   )X

10. How do you say 'I return'?

(eu vOlto)

            Verify: (   )X (   )X

11. How do you say 'he returns'?

(ele vOlta)

            Verify: (   )X (   )X

12. How do you say 'they return'?

(eles vOltam)

            Verify: (   )X (   )X

13. How about 'they eat lunch'?

(eles almOçam)

            Verify: (   )X (   )X

14. The we-forms, as you know, do not have the open O; they have
    the closed o. Thus, 'we return' is---

            (   )X (   )X

15. How would you say 'we eat lunch'?

(nós almoçamos)

            Verify: (   )X (   )X

16. Several -ar type verbs have closed e and open E distributed
    in the same pattern as the o and the O, the closed e appearing
    in unstressed syllables and the open E appearing in stressed
    syllables. The only verb of this sort that you have had so
    far is começar 'begin'.

17. Thus, in 'I begin', the open E falls in the stressed syllable.
    comEço   (   )x (   )x

18. How would you say 'Sandra begins'?
(Sandra comEça)
              Verify: (   )x (   )x

19. How would you say 'they begin'?
(eles comEçam)
              Verify: (   )x (   )x

20. The phrase 'we begin' has the closed e sound. The syllable
    is not stressed. How do you say 'we begin'?
(nós começamos)
              Verify: (   )x (   )x

21. Another useful verb of this sort, and one that you have not
    run across in this book, is levar, which expresses the idea
    of 'carry'.
    levar   (   )x (   )x (   )x
22. The form 'I carry' requires the open E sound.
    eu lEvo (   )x (   )x

23. How, then, would you say 'Jorge carries'?
(Jorge lEva)
              Verify: (   )x (   )x

24. How would you say 'they carry'?
(eles lEvam)
              Verify: (   )x (   )x

25. 'We carry' requires the unstressed, closed e sound. So how
    do you say 'we carry'?
(nós levamos)
              Verify: (   )x (   )x   ‹

26. A number of -er type verbs also have the open E or open O
    sound in their stems, but only in the he- and they-forms.
    Verbs that have already appeared in this text and that
    follow this patterning are:

                    escrever

                    receber

                    beber

                    esquecer

                    conhecer

                    parecer

                    chover

27. Thus, when you hear the he-form for 'write', you will hear
    the open E sound in the stem. Listen and repeat.

    escrEve   ( ) ( )X ( )X

28. How would you say the he-form for 'drink'?
(bEbe)

           Verify: ( )X ( )X

29. How would you say the he-form for 'forget'?
(esquEce)

           Verify: ( )X ( )X

30. The he-form for 'know' is not new to you. You learned it
    early in the course, but you may not have been too careful
    about the open E sound.

           Repeat: conhEce   ( )X ( )X

31. The form parEce is another he-form that you already know.
    Be sure, however, that you say it with the open E sound.

           Repeat: parEce   ( )X ( )X

32. You already know how to say 'it is raining'. That expression
    is está chovendo. But do you know how to say 'it rains', with
    the he-form of chover? That form is chOve, with an open O.

    chOve   ( )X ( )X

33. All of the above verbs except chover have they-forms (you
    cannot say 'they rain' in Portuguese any more than you can
    say it in English) and all of those they-forms have the
    open E sound.

    escrEvem ( )X ( )X   parEcem ( )X ( )X
    bEbem   ( )X ( )X   recEbem ( )X ( )X
    esquEcem ( )X ( )X

34. However, in the I-form as well as the we-form the closed
    e̲ prevails (as underlined). Repeat in pairs.

       escr̲e̲vo/escr̲e̲vemos   ( )X

       b̲e̲bo/b̲e̲bemos   ( )X

       esqu̲e̲ço/esqu̲e̲cemos   ( )X

       par̲e̲ço/par̲e̲cemos   ( )X

       rec̲e̲bo/rec̲e̲bemos   ( )X

35. Here is the contrast between the open E̲ and the closed e̲.
    Imitate as well as you can, repeating in pairs. Do these
    several times if necessary.

       escrevo/escrEve ( )X ( )X

       bebo/bEbe ( )X ( )X

       esqueço/esquEce ( )X ( )X

       pareço/parEce ( )X ( )X

       recebo/recEbe ( )X ( )X

Practice 1. (Recorded)

This is a review and summary of the verb forms that you have
been working with thus far in this unit. You should repeat them
again in order to feel more comfortable with the contrasting open
and closed vowels. The voice on the tape will read these items
from left to right. There is space for you to repeat after each
one.

open O̲ or E̲			closed o̲ or e̲	

-a̲r̲ type

gOsto	gOsta	gOstam	gostamos	
nOto	nOta	nOtam	notamos	
vOlto	vOlta	vOltam	voltamos	
mOro	mOra	mOram	moramos	
almOço	almOça	almOçam	almoçamos	
comEço	comEça	comEçam	começamos	
lEvo	lEva	lEvam	levamos	

-e̲r̲ type

bEbe	bEbem	bebemos	bebo
recEbe	recEbem	recebemos	recebo
esquEce	esquEcem	esquecemos	esqueço
escrEve	escrEvem	escrevemos	escrevo
conhEce	conhEcem	conhecemos	conheço
parEce	parEcem	parecemos	pareço

20.5

Practice 2.   Put these brief dialogs into Portuguese.

    1. **A.** Do you know Sandra?
        B. Yes, I know her.
        A. Do you like her?
        B. I do.
        A. Where does she live?
        B. She lives nearby.
        A. Do you eat lunch with her?
        B. I do.
        A. What time does she get back?
        B. She always gets back at 1:30.

    2. **A.** Is he going to remember?
        B. Yes, he never forgets.

    3. **A.** Does he drink a lot?
        B. No. He doesn't like to drink.

    4. **A.** What time do you begin?
        B. I begin at 9:00.

    5. **A.** Is he going to take (_levar_) his son, too?
        B. He always takes his son.

36. Recall these sentences extracted from previous dialogs.

      <u>Vocês trabalharam muito esta hora</u>. ( )X ( )X

      <u>Este é o meu amigo, Carlos</u>. ( )X ( )X

37. Notice the two words for 'this': <u>esta</u> and <u>este</u>.

      <u>esta</u> ( )X ( )X
      <u>este</u> ( )X ( )X

38. <u>Esta</u> has an open <u>E</u> sound in the first syllable.

      <u>esta</u> ( )X ( )X

39. <u>Este</u> has a closed <u>e</u> sound in the first syllable.

      <u>este</u> ( )X ( )X

40. As you know, the <u>t</u> of this word is pronounced like a <u>ch</u> by many Brazilians.

      <u>este</u> ( )X ( )X

41. The final, unstressed vowel sounds of these two words are different, of course.

      <u>esta</u>/<u>este</u> ( )X ( )X

42. Which is the stressed syllable of <u>esta</u>, the first or the last? Listen again if you are not sure.

(first)

        ( ) ( ) 20.6

43. By contrast, which is the stressed syllable of the familiar verb form está, meaning '(he) is'?

(last)

( ) ( )

44. The location of the stress is one of the factors that make these two words different.

esta ( )X ( )X (this)
está ( )X ( )X (is)

45. The form esta is the word for 'this' which is used when one is referring to feminine items.

esta hora ( )X ( )X 'this hour'
esta comida ( )X ( )X 'this food'
esta lição ( )X ( )X 'this lesson'

46. The form este is the word for 'this' which is used when one is referring to masculine items. Notice in particular that the final syllable is an unstressed i sound, rather than the unstressed u sound that is usually the sign of the masculine.

este carro ( )X ( )X 'this car'
este exame ( )X ( )X 'this test'
este livro ( )X ( )X 'this book'

47. In other words, the word for 'this' has gender agreement with the noun that it refers to.

este diálogo ( )X ( )X 'this dialog'
esta palavra ( )X ( )X 'this word'

48. This gender agreement is maintained even if the word 'this' does not immediately precede the noun.

Este é o meu amigo. ( )X ( )X
'This is my friend'.

49. Amigo is masculine; hence the word for 'this' must appear in the masculine form, este, even though other words intervene.

50. Now let's introduce a female friend, Elsa.

Esta é a minha amiga, Elsa. ( )X ( )X
'This is my friend, Elsa'.

51. The word <u>amiga</u> is feminine since we are talking about Elsa;
    hence the word for 'this' must also be feminine. It doesn't
    matter that other words separate the two.

52. What about the plural? How do we change the singular 'this'
    to the plural 'these'? Answer: We simply add the pluralizing
    -<u>s</u> (which, as always, becomes -<u>z</u> or -ž before a vowel or a
    voiced consonant).

    a. este   (   )X   (   )X   'this'
        estes   (   )X   (   )X   'these'

    b. esta   (   )X   (   )X   'this'
        estas   (   )X   (   )X   'these'

53. Now try a few of these pairs. (<u>z</u> sound is starred*)

    a. este carro   (   )X
        estes carros   (   )X

    b. este livro   (   )X
        estes* livros (   )X

    c. este exame   (   )X
        estes* exames (   )X

    d. esta avenida   (   )X
        estas* avenidas (   )X

    e. esta casa   (   )X
        estas casas   (   )X

    f. esta passagem   (   )X
        estas passagens (   )X

54. How do you say 'this door'?
(esta porta)

          Verify: (   )X   (   )X

55. How do you say 'these doors'?
(estas portas)

          Verify: (   )X   (   )X

56. How do you say 'this office'?
(este escritório)

          Verify: (   )X   (   )X

57. How do you say 'these offices'?
(estes* escritórios)

          Verify: (   )X   (   )X

58. The words for 'this' and 'these' apply to items close at
    hand. Portuguese has other words, corresponding to English
    'that' and 'those', which apply to items not within the
    immediate reach of the speaker. These words too change their
    forms to agree in gender with the item they refer to.

59. Here is the word for 'that' which is used when one is
    referring to something masculine.

           ( )x ( )x

60. Here is the word for 'that' which is used when one is refer-
    ring to something feminine.

           ( )x ( )x

61. Here they are together.

           esse, with closed e   ( )x ( )x
           essa, with open E   ( )x ( )x

62. Here are some examples of the masculine form.

           esse carro   ( )x ( )x
           esse menino   ( )x ( )x
           esse escritório   ( )x ( )x
           esse pneu   ( )x ( )x

63. Here are some examples of the feminine form.

           essa moça   ( )x ( )x
           essa praia   ( )x ( )x
           essa carta   ( )x ( )x
           essa ponte   ( )x ( )x

64. How would you say 'that house'?
(essa casa)

           Verify: ( )x ( )x

65. How would you say 'that state'?
(esse estado)

           Verify: ( )x ( )x

66. How about 'that newspaper'?
(esse jornal)

           Verify: ( )x ( )x

20.9

67. How about 'that city'?
(essa cidade)

                    Verify: (   )X (   )X

68. And 'that day'? (Appearances aside, 'day' is masculine.)
(esse dia)

                    Verify: (   )X (   )X

69. Gender agreement is maintained even though the word 'that'
     does not immediately precede the noun.

                Esse é o meu carro.   (   )X (   )X That is my car.
                Essa é a minha casa. (   )X (   )X That is my house.

70. For the plural, we add, as usual, the pluralizing -s (which
     becomes -z is some cases.)

                esses   (   )X (   )X
                essas   (   )X (   )X

71. Here are some examples of plurals of masculine items. The
     -z sound is starred*.

                esses carros   (   )X (   )X
                esses* americanos   (   )X (   )X
                esses* exames   (   )X (   )X

72. Here are some examples of feminine items.

                essas casas   (   )X (   )X
                essas solteiras (   )X (   )X
                essas* avenidas (   )X (   )X
                essas palavras (   )X (   )X

73. Let us return to the singular forms again and compare two
     sets of minimal pairs.

     a. this car: este carro   (   )X
         that car: esse carro   (   )X
     b. this house: esta casa (   )X
         that house: essa casa (   )X

Comment

     The forms for 'this' differ from the forms for 'that' by
virtue of the presence of a t (or ch) sound. Why not seize upon
this t (or ch) to help you to remember which is which? Associate
the t of este and esta with the t of English touch. (If you are
a ch speaker, you can associate the ch sound of este with the ch

of <u>touch</u>.) Why <u>touch</u>? Because if the item you are talking
about is close enough for you to touch, either literally or
figuratively, you will normally use <u>este</u> or <u>esta</u>. <u>T</u> for <u>touch</u>!
On the other hand, if the item you are talking about is not
close enough for you to touch, you will normally refer to it
with <u>esse</u> or <u>essa</u>. No touch, no <u>t</u>!

    a.   <u>este carro</u>: this car (I can touch it)

    b.   <u>esta casa</u>: this house (I can touch it)

    c.   <u>esse carro</u>: that car (it's not within my reach)

    d.   <u>essa casa</u>: that house (it's not within my reach)

The same association of <u>t</u> for <u>touch</u> applies to the forms for
'these' and 'those'. If you can touch the items you are talking
about, use the appropriate form with <u>t</u> in it. If the items are too
far away for you to touch, use the appropriate form without the <u>t</u>.

    a.   <u>estes carros</u>: these cars (I can touch them)

    b.   <u>estas casas</u>: these houses (I can touch them)

    c.   <u>esses carros</u>: those cars (not within my immediate reach)

    d.   <u>essas casas</u>: those houses (not within my immediate reach)

There are areas of overlap, of course, and they tend to be
the same ones we have in English. If I know, for example, that
I can easily touch a picture on the wall beside me simply by
leaning to the right and stretching a bit, am I going to say
'<u>this</u> picture' or '<u>that</u> picture' when I refer to it? Doesn't
really matter, does it? The overlap is very common in the non-
concrete world of ideas, where spatial relationships are hard
to define. Does it make much difference whether I say '<u>this</u>
proposal' or '<u>that</u> proposal' when we are in the midst of a discussion on the proposal itself? Probably not. The point of all
this is that you would not concern yourself with such distinctions
in English and you should not do so in Portuguese either.

<u>Practice 3</u>. (Recorded)

Put these items into Portuguese. Omit items in brackets.

1. This car is [a] Chevrolet.   7. These cars are American.

2. That car is [a] Ford.   8. These girls speak English.

3. This house is old.   9. These boys are Brazilians.

4. This dialog is difficult.   10. Those girls are Americans.

5. That dialog is horrible.   11. These Brazilians work a lot.

6. This view is marvelous.   12. These teachers are from Brazil.

Practice 4. (Recorded)

> Following the example of the model, ask these questions in Portuguese.

> Model: <u>Você conhece essa moça?</u>
> 1. Do you know that teacher? (m.)
> 2. Do you know this restaurant?
> 3. Do you know this city?
> 4. Do you know this book?
> 5. Do you know those children? (<u>crianças</u>)
> 6. Do you know those Americans?
> 7. Do you know those states?

Practice 5. (Recorded) Same procedure as for Practice 4.

> Model: <u>A senhora estudou esta lição?</u>
> 1. Did you prepare these lessons?
> 2. Did you read this book?
> 3. Did you write those letters?
> 4. Did you work a lot this hour?
> 5. Did you prepare this food?
> 6. Did you buy this coffee in Brazil?
> 7. Did you notice that accent?!! Wow!

Practice 6. (Recorded) Same procedure.

> Model: <u>Este é o meu amigo, Carlos.</u>
> 1. This is my friend, Paulo.
> 2. This is my friend, Sandra.
> 3. This is my wife, Brünhilde.
> 4. This is my daughter, Ângela.
> 5. That is my daughter, Luísa.
> 6. That is my son, Roberto.
> 7. Those are my sons, Roberto and Paulo.
> 8. Those are my daughters, Ângela and Luísa.
> 9. These are my books.
> 10. These are my tires.
> 11. These are my tickets.

12. These are my children.

13. This is my car.

14. This is my office.

15. This is my break time (<u>intervalo</u>).

DIALOG

Luísa

Geraldo	Gerald, Jerry
entre	enter, come in (command form)

Entre, Geraldo. Tudo bom?   Come in, Jerry. How's it going?

Geraldo

ótimo	fine, wonderful
Luisa	Luisa

Tudo ótimo, Luísa. E com você?   Fine, Luísa. And you?

Luísa

Sente	sit (command form)

Também...Sente.   Same here...Have a seat.

Geraldo

o calor	heat
Ui!	whew!
que calor!	what heat!

Obrigado, Ui! Que calor!   Thanks. Whew! It sure is hot!

Luísa

aceita	(you) accept (-ar type)
o refrigerante	soft drink

Você aceita um refrigerante?   Will you have a soft drink?

Geraldo

aceito	(I) accept (-<u>ar</u> type)
por favor	please

<u>Aceito. Uma Coca-cola, por favor.</u>   <u>I will. A Coke, please.</u>

Luísa

faz	(he) does (irregular, -<u>er</u> type)
a gente faz	we do
o fim	end
o fim de semana	weekend

<u>O que é que a gente faz este fim de semana de 3 dias?</u>   <u>What are we going to do * this 3-day weekend?</u>

Geraldo

a certeza	certainty
tem certeza	(you) are sure (have certainty)
segunda-feira	Monday
o feriado	holiday

<u>Você tem certeza que segunda-feira é feriado?</u>   <u>Are you sure that Monday is a holiday?</u>

cai	(it) falls (-<u>ir</u> type)
terça-feira	Tuesday
ser	to be
comemorado	celebrated (commemorated)
segunda	(abbreviation of <u>segunda-feira</u>)

Luísa

<u>Tenho. O feriado cai na terça-feira, mas vai ser comemorado segunda.</u>   <u>Yes, I am. The holiday falls on Tuesday, but it's going to be celebrated on Monday.</u>

---

* Or ⌐What do we do?⌐. As in English, the present tense can sometimes be used when the reference is to future time.

20.15

Geraldo

a razão	reason, rationality
tem razão	you're right (have reason)

Você tem razão ... Bom!...   You're right...Well!...

dá	(it) gives (-ar type)
dá para	it's enough time to/for
ir	to go

Dá para ir a Williamsburg...   It's enough (time) to go to Williams-
ou...   burg...or...

Luîsa

caro	expensive

Dá. Mas fica caro.   Yes. But it's expensive.

Geraldo

fazemos	(we) do, make (-er type)
fazemos um passeio	(we) take a ride
a montanha	mountain

Por que não fazemos um   Why don't we take a drive to the
passeio até as montanhas?   mountains?

Luîsa

legal	fine, wonderful*
levo	(I) take (-ar type)
o sanduíche	sandwich

Legal! Eu levo uns   Wonderful! I'll take some sand-
sanduíches.   wiches.

---

* Notice this special use of the word legal. In other contexts
it is a cognate of the English word 'legal'.

EXPANSION EXERCISES

Comment Re Expansion Exercise 1

You have learned the following common greetings:

A. Bom dia   B. Alô
   Boa noite   Oi
   Boa tarde   Como vai? or Como é que vai?
                                 Tudo bom?
                                 Tudo bem?

To these expression in column B we can add the following.

     Você está bom?   (To a man)
     Você está boa?   (To a woman)

These two new ones and those in column B can be given literal
translations, but in the final analysis they are all greetings or
salutations and they all mean more or less the same thing, just
as the greetings 'Hi,' 'Hi ya,' 'How's it going?', 'How are you?',
etc., all mean more or less the same thing in English.

Expansion Exercise 1. (Recorded)

Listen to thse brief exchanges of greetings. From time to
time you can practice them, and variations of them, with your
instructor or a fellow student.

  I. A. Oi, Paulo. Como vai?
      B. Muito bem, e você?
      A. Muito bem.

 II. A. Bom dia, Luís. Tudo bom?
      B. Tudo bem, e com você?

III. A. Oi, Yara! Você está boa?
      B. Estou boa, e você?

 IV. A. Boa tarde, Luís. Você está bom?
      B. Estou bom, e você?

  V. A. Boa noite, Roberto. Você está bom?
      B. Vou bem, e você?

 VI. A. Oi, Roberto. Tudo bom?
      B. Tudo bom.

VII. A. Alô, Paulo. Tudo bem?
      B. Tudo bem, e com você?

20.17

Comment Re Expansion Exercise 2

The expression <u>dá para</u> (literally, 'it gives for') is very common. As used in the dialog of this unit, it means 'the circumstances give time for', i.e., 'there is enough time for'. In other contexts, the expression can mean 'the circumstances are appropriate for, convenient for, suitable for', etc.

In the exercise that follows, the expression refers primarily to time.

Expansion Exercise 2. (Recorded)

Repeat the several model sentences, then translate from English into Portuguese.

Model 1: <u>Dá para ir às montanhas.</u>
Model 2: <u>Dá para ir à praia.</u>
Model 3: <u>Dá para tomar café.</u>
Model 4: <u>Dá para fazer um passeio.</u>

1. There's enough time to write a letter.

2. There's enough time to go to the city.

3. There's enough time to eat lunch downtown.

4. There's enough time to speak with the teacher.

5. There's enough time to stop in Florida.

6. There's enough time to read the newspaper.

7. There's enough time to make a sandwich.

8. There's enough time to sleep an hour more.   (<u>mais uma hora</u>)

Comment Re Expansion Exercise 3

Expressions utilizing <u>Que</u> plus a noun are generally the equivalent of English 'what' or 'what a' plus a noun. They are exclamations, and they may be laudatory or depreciative. For example, <u>Que carro</u>! (What a car!) can mean either 'What a splendid automobile!' or 'What a lemon!' The circumstances and the tone of voice indicate which meaning is intended, just as they do in English.

In the dialog, <u>Que calor</u> is the equivalent of 'What heat!' or, as most of us would say, '<u>It sure is hot!</u>'.

Expansion Exercise 3. (Recorded)

Repeat the models, then translate from English to Portuguese. Verify with the tape.

Model 1: <u>Que calor</u>!
Model 2: <u>Que carro</u>!
Model 3: <u>Que festa</u>!
Model 4: <u>Que tráfego</u>!

1. What a teacher!

2. What a restaurant!

3. What a friend!

4. What a sandwich!

5. What a city!

6. What a view!

7. What a book!

8. What a word!

9. What a sleepyhead!

10. What food!

Comment Re Expansion Exercises 4 Through 8

Expansion Exercises 4 through 8 are designed to encourage you to seek out and use English cognates in your Portuguese. Portuguese has many English cognates. Some of them group themselves into fairly predictable patterns, thus making it relatively easy for English speakers to learn them. In this unit and in some of the units to follow you will have an opportunity to practice some of these patterns.

There are certain dangers involved in relying on cognates because every so often you will run across one that means something different from what its supposed counterpart means in English. These we call 'false cognates'. For example, the word <u>esquisita</u> looks and sounds like it ought to mean 'exquisite', but beware! It means 'strange', 'unusual', even 'freakish'. One could get himself into real trouble by telling an attractive young lady that she looks <u>esquisita</u>. One need only imagine her reaction! Better use another cognate — <u>elegante</u>. The latter is a 'true' cognate; it means what it seems to mean. Furthermore, it is almost guaranteed to bring forth the desired smile of appreciation on the lady's face.

Minor perils of this sort exist, and you must look out for them. But you should not let due caution deter you from healthy experimentation. Try cognates. They provide an excellent way to increase your vocabulary.

Expansion Exercise 4. (Recorded)

You will recall from an earlier unit that many English words that end in -tion and -sion have cognates in Portuguese that end in -ção and -são. All of them are stressed on the last syllable and all are feminine. Be wary, however, lest the sight of familiar letters lead you into English pronunciation habits. Note that numbers 12, 13, 14, and 15 have the -z sound, as underlined.

1. solução   ( )X ( )X   solution
2. situação   ( )X ( )X   situation
3. posição   ( )X ( )X   position
4. operação   ( )X ( )X   operation
5. repetição   ( )X ( )X   repetition
6. organização   ( )X ( )X   organization
7. promoção   ( )X ( )X   promotion
8. administração ( )X ( )X   administration
9. edição   ( )X ( )X   edition
10. missão   ( )X ( )X   mission
11. expressão   ( )X ( )X   expression
12. visão   ( )X ( )X   vision
13. decisão   ( )X ( )X   decision
14. invasão   ( )X ( )X   invasion
15. conclusão   ( )X ( )X   conclusion

Expansion Exercise 5. (Recorded)

Below you will find several model sentences. Using them as a starting point, put the English sentences that follow into Portuguese. Draw on the previous exercise for the necessary vocabulary. Verify on the tape.

Model Sentence A. Não gosto da cidade.

1. I don't like the situation.
2. I don't like the solution.
3. I don't like the organization.
4. I don't like the expression.
5. I don't like the mission.
6. I don't like the decision. (z sound)
7. I don't like the conclusion. (z sound)

Model Sentence B.   O que é que você acha da praia?

1. What do you think of the invasion?   (z sound)
2. What do you think of the solution?
3. What do you think of the expression?
4. What do you think of the situation?
5. What do you think of the repetition?
6. What do you think of the organization?
7. What do you think of the decision?   (z sound)

Model Sentence C.   A praia é boa.

1. The decision is good.   (z sound)
2. The situation is good.
3. The repetition is good.
4. The solution is good.
5. The position is good.
6. The administration is good.
7. The promotion is good.
8. The vision is good.   (z sound)

End of Tape 9B

Tape 10A

Expansion Exercise 6.   (Recorded)

In Unit 17 you learned that many English adjectives ending in -al have cognates in Portuguese that also end in -al. Review the ones listed below. Remember that in Portuguese the stress is on the last syllable. Take time to pronounce these well.

1.	formal	( )x ( )x	8.	local	( )x ( )x
2.	normal	( )x ( )x	9.	federal	( )x ( )x
3.	social	( )x ( )x	10.	regional	( )x ( )x
4.	oficial	( )x ( )x	11.	industrial	( )x ( )x
5.	legal	( )x ( )x	12.	anual	( )x ( )x
6.	final	( )x ( )x	13.	especial*	( )x ( )x
7.	nacional	( )x ( )x			

*Note that this word has an initial vowel e which is absent in the English cognate 'special'. This initial vowel is sometimes whispered.

20.21

Expansion Exercise 7. (Recorded)

Like all other descriptive adjectives, those ending in -al
are normally placed after the nouns they modify. Practice the
following sequences, repeating after each one on the tape.

A. 1. É uma festa boa.   (   )X
    2. É uma festa ótima.   (   )X
    3. É uma festa péssima. (   )X
    4. É uma festa maravilhosa.   (   )X
    5. É uma festa formal.   (   )X
    6. É uma festa anual.   (   )X
    7. É uma festa especial.   (   )X
    8. É uma festa oficial.   (   )X

B. 1. É um feriado americano.   (   )X
    2. É um feriado brasileiro.   (   )X
    3. É um feriado ótimo.   (   )X
    4. É um feriado local.   (   )X
    5. É um feriado nacional.   (   )X
    6. É um feriado industrial.   (   )X
    7. É um feriado legal.   (   )X
    8. É um feriado oficial.   (   )X

C. 1. É uma expressão americana.   (   )X
    2. É uma expressão brasileira.   (   )X
    3. É uma expressão formal.   (   )X
    4. É uma expressão local.   (   )X
    5. É uma expressão regional.   (   )X
    6. É uma expressão normal.   (   )X
    7. É uma expressão legal.   (   )X

D. 1. É uma situação maravilhosa.   (   )X
    2. É uma situação péssima.   (   )X
    3. É uma situação normal.   (   )X
    4. É uma situação formal.   (   )X
    5. É uma situação informal.   (   )X
    6. É uma situação legal.   (   )X
    7. É uma situação especial.   (   )X

E. 1. É uma organização americana.   (   )X
    2. É uma organização brasileira.   (   )X
    3. É uma organização nacional.   (   )X
    4. É uma organização industrial.   (   )X
    5. É uma organização legal.   (   )X
    6. É uma organização social.   (   )X
    7. É uma organização regional.   (   )X

F. 1. É a edição americana.   (   )X
    2. É a edição brasileira.   (   )X
    3. É a edição final.   (   )X
    4. É a edição anual.   (   )X
    5. É a edição local.   (   )X
    6. É a edição especial.   (   )X
    7. É a edição oficial.   (   )X

Expansion Exercise 8.   (Recorded)

    Using the nouns of exercise 4 and the adjectives of exercise
6, translate the following short phrases into Portuguese.   Verify
with the tape.

1. a legal solution
2. a legal decision
3. a legal organization
4. the final decision
5. the final conclusion
6. the annual promotion
7. my annual promotion   (admittedly, an unlikely phrase!)
8. my special mission
9. a normal operation
10. the final operation
11. the final repetition
12. the final solution
13. the final promotion
14. a normal promotion
15. the official position
16. the social position   20.23

Comprehension

On the tape are a total of ten, 2 and 3 line exchanges which have been prepared for your comprehension practice. Listen to them now and note any that are not clear to you.

Exchanges and Brief Dialogs

I. Prepare these brief exchanges for your teacher. Numbers 1-10 correspond to the ten exchanges recorded in the Comprehension section above.

1. A. Do you notice that I'm eating a lot for lunch?
    B. I notice, and I don't like it.

2. A. I live in Copacabana. And you? (plural), where do you live?
    B. We live there too.

3. A. What time do you begin?
    B. I begin early, at six.

4. A. Is this office mine?
    B. Yes, it's yours.
    A. Great! What a view!

5. A. Is this book yours?
    B. It's mine, yes. Thanks.

6. A. Is that book yours?
    B. No, it's Robert's.

7. A. Are these sandwiches yours?
    B. No, they're theirs.

8. A. Is that Coke yours?
    B. No, it's Sandra's.

9. A. This food is good, isn't it?
    B. No, I don't like it.
    A. You're not hungry!

10. A. Is this house yours?
    B. No, it's my parents'.

----

11. A. Are you sure it's my turn?
    B. I'm sure. My turn is tomorrow.

12. A. I'm sure I know that girl. But who is she?
    B. It's Sandra.

13. A. Are you sure he likes Sandra?
    B. Of course! He likes her a lot.
    A. Why doesn't he go out with her?

14. A. When is the holiday? Tuesday?
    B. Well, the holiday falls on Tuesday, but it's going to be celebrated on Monday.

15. A. But isn't tomorrow a holiday?
    B. It is. But it's going to be celebrated on Friday.
    A. Good. We work tomorrow, and Friday we go to the mountains.

16. A. Did you say that we're going to take a trip to the mountains?
    B. Yes, I did. Don't you like the idea?
    A. I do, indeed! This heat is too much!

17. A. Will you accept a Coke?
    B. Yes, thanks. It's very hot. (fazendo calor)

II. Prepare these short dialogs for your teacher. Numbers 3, 4 and 5 are recorded for you. Listen to them for comprehension practice before actively preparing them.

1. A. What are we (gente) going to do this Thursday?
   B. It's a holiday, isn't it?
   A. It is.
   B. Why don't we stay at home? I don't want to do anything. I'm tired.
   A. Good. We can sleep until late.

2. A. What are we (gente) going to do today?
   B. What do you want to do?
   A. I don't know. Let's see...Is it going to rain?
   B. I don't think so.
   A. Let's take a ride to the mountains.
   B. Good idea.

3. A. Oi, Geraldo. Tudo bom? Sente.
   B. Obrigado.
   A. Você aceita um café?
   B. Não, obrigado.
   A. Mesmo?! O café está muito bom hoje, viu?

4. (This dialog emphasizes the open O vowel. Practice it with your teacher or a fellow student. The open O is underlined.)

   A. A que horas você almoça?
   B. Almoço à uma hora.
   A. Você volta às duas?
   B. Volto, sim.
   A. Posso almoçar com você hoje?
   B. Pode, claro...Vamos sair agora.
   A. Vamos. Estou com fome.

5. (This dialog emphasizes both open vowels, O and E. They
are underlined. We have included several of the verbs that you
practiced earlier in this unit.)

A. Quando é a festa?
B. A festa é no dia dez.
A. Onde é que a Sônia mora?
B. Ela mora na Virginia.
A. A que horas a festa começa?
B. Às sete.
A. Você leva os sanduíches?
B. Levo.
A. E eu levo o café...e uns refrigerantes tambem. Você
    gosta de Coca-Cola?
B. Gosto.
A. Até quando você vai ficar lá?
B. Até às nove.
A. Só até às nove? (Party pooper!)*
B. Só.

*Translates as Chato or Chata.

UNIT 21

Part I

1. Listen to these verb forms.

      a. ( ) ( )

      b. ( ) ( )

      c. ( ) ( )

2. The stem of these forms may sound familiar to you, but the endings probably do not. The forms have not been used in this text before. Here they are again. Listen and repeat.

      a. ( ) ( )x ( )x

      b. ( ) ( )x ( )x

      c. ( ) ( )x ( )x

3. What we are doing is simple. We are adding the ending -ava, to the stems of three verbs that are well-known to you: ficar, falar and trabalhar. The situation looks like this.

      a. Stem fic→ plus ending ava = ficava

      b. Stem fal→ plus ending ava = falava

      c. Stem trabalh- plus ending ava = trabalhava

4. Repeat again.

      a. ficava ( )x ( )x

      b. falava ( )x ( )x

      c. trabalhava ( )x ( )x

5. The -ava ending on a verb signals a time reference which can be translated several ways in English. One frequent way is the phrase 'used to'. Thus, the form ficava often suggests the translation 'used to stay'. Likewise, the form falava often suggests the notion 'used to speak', and trabalhava the notion used to work'.

6. What is the notion suggested by this verb form?

                    (   )   (   )

(used to visit)

7. What is the notion suggested by this verb form?

                    (   )   (   )

(used to send)

8. How about this one?

                    (   )   (   )

(used to practice)

9. And this one?

                    (   )   (   )

(used to return)

10. Now, repeat the forms you heard in frames 6 through 9.

                    a. visitava   (   )x   (   )x
                    b. mandava   (   )x   (   )x
                    c. praticava (   )x   (   )x
                    d. voltava   (   )x   (   )x

11. How would you express the notion 'used to study'?

(estudava)
                    Verify: (   )x   (   )x

12. How would you express the notion 'used to arrive'?

(chegava)
                    Verify: (   )x   (   )x

13. How about 'used to prepare'?

(preparava)
                    Verify: (   )x   (   )x

14. And how would you say 'used to dance'?

(dançava)
                    Verify: (   )x   (   )x

15. The 'used to' forms that you have just been practicing are both
    I-forms and he-forms. That is, the ending for the I-form
    and the ending for the he-form is the same: ava. To avoid
    ambiguity it is often necessary to precede the verb form
    with the appropriate noun or pronoun. For example:

eu falava	( )x	( )x
ele falava	( )x	( )x
você falava	( )x	( )x
Maria falava	( )x	( )x
José falava	( )x	( )x

16. So, how would you say 'Mary used to stay'?
(Maria ficava)

               Verify: ( )x   ( )x

17. How would you say 'Sandra used to work'?
(Sandra trabalhava)

               Verify: ( )x   ( )x

18. How would you say 'George used to practice'?
(Jorge praticava)

               Verify: ( )x   ( )x

19. Using the pronoun, how would you say 'she used to eat lunch'?
(ela almoçava)

               Verify: ( )x   ( )x

20. Using the pronoun, how would you say 'I used to eat dinner'?
(eu jantava)

               Verify: ( )x   ( )x

21. Again, using the pronoun <u>você</u> how would you say 'you used
    to arrive'?
(você chegava)
               Verify: ( )x   ( )x

Practice 1. (Recorded)

Learn to say the following sentences well enough so that you do not have to refer to the Portuguese at the right.

1. I used to work a lot.   (Eu trabalhava muito.)
    I would work all day.   (Eu trabalhava o dia todo.)

2. I used to study too much.   (Eu estudava demais.)
    I would study all day.   (Eu estudava o dia todo.)

3. He used to speak English.   (Ele falava inglês.)
    He would speak [it] well.   (Ele falava bem.)

4. He used to eat lunch early.   (Ele almoçava cedo.)
    He'd always eat lunch at   (Ele sempre almoçava às onze.)
       eleven.

5. She used to eat dinner late.   (Ela jantava tarde.)
    She'd always eat at ten.   (Ela sempre jantava às dez.)

6. I used to stay home.   (Eu ficava em casa.)
    I'd stay with my son.   (Eu ficava com o meu filho.)

7. He used to get up early.   (Ele levantava cedo.)
    He'd get up at six.   (Ele levantava às seis.)

8. You used to arrive late.   (Você chegava tarde.)
    You'd arrive at nine.   (Você chegava às nove.)

9. I used to stop in Florida.   (Eu parava na Flórida.)
    I'd stop in Miami.   (Eu parava em Miami.)

10. She used to take the food.   (Ela levava a comida.)
    She'd always take sandwiches.   (Ela sempre levava sanduíches.)

Practice 2. (Recorded)

Now, learn how to participate in these question and answer exchanges without having to refer to the Portuguese.

1. Would you [habitually] stay home?   (Você ficava em casa?)
   Yes, I would.   (Ficava, sim.)

2. Would you [customarily] start   (Você começava às oito?)
      at eight?
   Yes, I would.   (Começava, sim.)

3. Would you [customarily] study   (Você estudava muito?)
      a lot?
   Yes, I would.   (Estudava, sim.)

4. Did you [habitually] rest on   (Você descansava nos fins
      weekends?   de semana?)
   Yes, I did.   (Descansava, sim.)

5. Did he [customarily] like the   (Ele gostava das festas?)
      parties?
   No, he didn't.   (Não, não gostava.)

6. Did you [ordinarily] notice his   (Você notava o sotaque
      accent?   dele?)
   Yes, I did.   (Notava, sim.)

7. Would she [usually] arrive late?   (Ela chegava tarde?)
   No, she wouldn't.   (Não, não chegava.)

8. Would she (usually) go to bed late?   (Ela deitava tarde?)
   Yes, she would.   (Deitava, sim.)

9. Did you use to live in Texas?   (Você morava no Texas?)
   Yes, I did.   (Morava, sim.)

10. Did you use to take sandwiches?   (Você levava sanduíches?)
    No, I didn't.   (Não, não levava.)

11. Would you buy the food?   (Você comprava a comida?)
    Yes, I would.   (Comprava, sim.)

12. Would you prepare the food?   (Você fazia a comida?)
    No, I wouldn't.   (Não, não fazia.)

13. Would Spanish get in the way?   (O espanhol atrapalhava?)
    Yes, it would.   (Atrapalhava, sim.)

14. Would it suit to go to the   (Dava para ir às montanhas?)
    mountains?
    Yes, it would.   (Dava, sim.)

Practice 3. (Recorded)
    Be sure you can translate these pairs of sentences. Notice
how easily _sempre_ and _nunca_ adapt themselves to these situations.

1. He used to stop in Brasilia.   (Ele parava em Brasília.)
   He wouldn't stop in Recife.   (Ele não parava em Recife.)

2. He used to stay till ten.   (Ele ficava até as dez.)
   He would never stay later.   (Ele nunca ficava até
                                        mais tarde.)

3. She would always speak Portuguese. (Ela sempre falava
                                        português.)
   She wouldn't speak English.   (Ela não falava inglês.)

4. She always used to go to bed early. (Ela sempre se deitava cedo.)
   She would never go to bed late.   (Ela nunca se deitava tarde.)

5. I always used to get back late.   (Eu sempre voltava tarde.)
   I'd never get back early.   (Eu nunca voltava cedo.)

6. I wouldn't take a Coke.   (Eu não aceitava Coca-cola.)
   I'd always take another soft drink. (Eu sempre aceitava outro
                                        refrigerante.)

7. I didn't (use to) like the mountains. (Eu não gostava das montanhas.)
   I always used to like the beach.   (Eu sempre gostava da praia.)

8. He'd never send a letter.   (Ele nunca mandava uma carta.)
   He'd always send a card.   (Ele sempre mandava um cartão.)

22. So much for the I and he-forms. Now let's go on to the
     we-form. Here is the <u>ending</u> for the we-form.
                 (   )   (   )   (   )

23. This ending has three syllables, the <u>first</u> one of which is
     stressed. Repeat as indicated; stress the first syllable.
                 (   )   (   )x   (   )x   (   )x

24. Now let's put that ending on a verb and see what we have.
     Let's use the verb 'talk'.
                 (   )   (   )x   (   )x   (   )x

25. That was the way you say 'we used to talk'. Now, here is
     the way you say 'we used to stay'.
                 (   )   (   )x   (   )x   (   )x

26. And here is 'we used to arrive'.
                 (   )   (   )x   (   )x   (   )x

27. So, how would you say 'we used to live'?
(morávamos)
                       Verify: (   )x   (   )x

28. How would you say 'we used to like'?
(gostávamos)
                       Verify: (   )x   (   )x

29. How about 'we used to take'? (<u>levar</u>)
(levávamos)
                       Verify: (   )x   (   )x

30. And how about 'we used to spend'?   (<u>passar</u>)
(passávamos)
                       Verify: (   )x   (   )x

31. Now let's leave the we-form for a moment and go on to the
    they-form: Here is the <u>ending</u> for the they-form.
        (   )   (   )x   (   )x

32. The last syllable of this ending is an <u>unstressed</u>, nasal
    diphthong that you are already familiar with.
        (   )x   (   )x

33. Here is the whole ending again. Be sure to stress the <u>first</u>
    syllable, <u>not</u> the diphthong.
        (   )   (   )x   (   )x

34. Now let's put that ending on the verb 'speak' in order to
    say 'they used to speak'.
        (   )   (   )x   (   )x

35. Now put it on another verb and say 'they used to live'.

        (   )   (   )x   (   )x

36. Here is the way you say 'they used to practice'.
        (   )   (   )x   (   )x

37. Now that you have the pattern, what is the form for 'they
    used to work'?
(trabalhavam)
           Verify: (   )x   (   )x

38. What is the form for 'they used to take'? (<u>tomar</u>)
(tomavam)
           Verify: (   )x   (   )x

39. How do you say 'they used to rest'?
(descansavam)
           Verify: (   )x   (   )x

21.8

40. And how do you say 'they used to begin'?
(começavam)

Verify: ( )x   ( )x

41. Notice this contrast between 'they speak' and 'they used
to speak'.

a.	falam	( )x ( )x	'they speak'
b.	falavam	( )x ( )x	'they used to speak'

42. Here are more contrasts of the same sort, the difference
between 'they do something' and 'they used to do something'.

(1)   a. moram   ( )x   ( )x
         b. moravam   ( )x   ( )x

(2)   a. tomam   ( )x   ( )x
         b. tomavam   ( )x   ( )x

(3)   a. começam   ( )x   ( )x
         b. começavam   ( )x   ( )x

(4)   a. jantam   ( )x   ( )x
         b. jantavam   ( )x   ( )x

(5)   a. preparam   ( )x   ( )x
         b. preparavam   ( )x   ( )x

(6)   a. levantam   ( )x   ( )x
         b. levantavam   ( )x   ( )x

(7)   a. atrapalham   ( )x   ( )x
         b. atrapalhavam   ( )x   ( )x

(8)   a. deixam   ( )x   ( )x
         b. deixavam   ( )x   ( )x

(9)   a. mudam   (   )x   (   )x
           b. mudavam   (   )x   (   )x

(10)   a. aceitam   (   )x   (   )x
           b. aceitavam   (   )x   (   )x

Observation

We have already indicated that the words 'used to' are only
one possible way of thinking about these verb forms. Another
useful way is the English word 'would'. Be not misled, however.
The word 'would' serves several purposes in English. In the
present context we are talking only about the 'would' which is
the equivalent of 'used to', the 'would' that we frequently use
when we are relating events that took place over and over again
in the past. It is the 'would' that occurs in these sentences:
   a. When I was a teenager I would go to bed much later
       than I do now.
   b. I would always say 'good morning' to her but she would
       never even smile.
   c. In those days we would ordinarily begin our day's work
       at 8:00.
In these instances we are talking about habitual, customary,
oft-repeated or continual actions in the past. Sometimes we feel
comfortable describing such actions with the phrase 'used to',
and sometimes we feel just as comfortable, or more so, using the
word 'would'. (Notice that you can substitute 'used to' for
'would' in the above sentences.) Both of these English terms are
useful in thinking about the Portuguese verb forms that we are
studying in this unit, for they too (the Portuguese forms) reflect
customary, habitual, oft-repeated or continual actions in the past.
    Sometimes it is a bit awkward to force the words 'used to'
or 'would' into the English translation, even though it is clear
from the context that this is indeed the sense of the Portuguese.
You will see some evidence of this in the dialogs and exercises
of this unit.

Practice 4.   (Recorded)

Learn how to say these sentences without having to refer to the right hand column.

1. They used to study a lot.   (Eles estudavam muito.)
   They would study all day.   (Eles estudavam o dia todo.)

2. They would speak English.   (Eles falavam inglês.)
   They'd speak [it] well.   (Falavam bem.)

3. They used to stop in Florida.   (Eles paravam na Flórida.)
   They'd stop in Miami.   (Paravam em Miami.)

4. They'd arrive real late.   (Eles chegavam muito tarde.)
   They'd arrive after eleven.   (Eles chegavam depois das onze.)

5. They used to live in Colorado.   (Eles moravam no Colorado.)
   They used to live in Denver.   (Moravam em Denver.)

6. We used to live in New York.   (Nós morávamos em Nova York.)
   We used to live in Albany.   (Morávamos em Albany.)

7. We used to begin real early.   (Nós começávamos bem cedo.)
   We'd begin at seven.   (Começávamos às sete.)

8. We used to stay till late.   (Nós ficávamos até tarde.)
   We'd stay until one o'clock.   (Ficávamos até uma hora.)

9. We would work a lot.   (Nós trabalhávamos muito.)
   We'd work day and night.   (Trabalhávamos dia e noite.)

10. We would eat dinner at home.   (Nós jantávamos em casa.)
    We'd eat well.   (Jantávamos bem.)

Practice 5. (Recorded)

　　Now, learn how to say these sentences.

1. We wouldn't stop in Baltimore. (Nós não parávamos em
   Baltimore.)

   We'd stop in Philadelphia. (Parávamos em Filadélfia.)

2. We wouldn't speak English. (Nós não falávamos inglês.)
   We'd speak Portuguese. (Falávamos português.)

3. We'd never get up late. (Nós nunca levantávamos tarde.)
   We'd always get up at six. (Nós sempre levantávamos às
   seis.)

4. We'd never eat lunch there. (Nós nunca almoçávamos lá.)
   We'd always eat lunch at home. (Nós sempre almoçávamos em casa.)

5. We'd never buy a Chevy. (Nós nunca comprávamos
   Chevrolet.)

   We'd always buy a Ford. (Sempre comprávamos Ford.)

6. They'd never eat dinner in the (Eles nunca jantavam no
   restaurant. restaurante.)
   They'd always eat dinner at (Sempre jantavam em casa.)
   home.

7. They'd never arrive late. (Eles nunca chegavam tarde.)
   They'd always arrive early. (Sempre chegavam cedo.)

8. They'd never stay in a hotel. (Eles nunca ficavam no hotel.)
   They'd always stay here. (Eles sempre ficavam aqui.)

9. They wouldn't take a Coke. (Eles não aceitavam Coca-cola.)
   They'd take another soft drink. (Aceitavam outro refrigerante.)

10. They didn't (use to) like (Eles não gostavam dos sábados.)
    Saturdays.
    They liked Sundays. (Eles gostavam dos domingos.)

Practice 6. (Recorded)

Practice asking and answering these questions.

1. Did you use to speak Spanish?　　Os senhores falavam espanhol?
   Yes, we did.　　　　　　　　　Falávamos, sim.

2. Did you use to return early?　　Os senhores voltavam cedo?
   Yes, we did.　　　　　　　　　Voltávamos, sim.

3. Would you practice a lot?　　　Os senhores praticavam muito?
   Yes, we would.　　　　　　　　Praticávamos, sim.

4. Would you stay at the Embassy?　Os senhores ficavam na
   　　　　　　　　　　　　　　　Embaixada?
   No, we wouldn't.　　　　　　　Não, não ficávamos.

5. Would you drink coffee?　　　　Os senhores tomavam café?
   No, we wouldn't.　　　　　　　Não, não tomávamos.

6. Did you [customarily] eat a　　Os senhores almoçavam bem?
   　a good lunch?
   Yes, we did.　　　　　　　　　Almoçávamos, sim.

7. Did you [usually] send cards?　Os senhores mandavam cartões?
   No, we didn't.　　　　　　　　Não, não mandávamos.

8. Did you [ordinarily] go to　　Os senhores se deitavam cedo?
   　bed early?
   Yes, we did.　　　　　　　　　Deitávamos, sim.

Part II

1. Recall the irregular formation of adjectives and nouns that
   end in stressed -al.

final	( )X	finais	( )X
canal	( )X	canais	( )X
normal	( )X	normais	( )X
local	( )X	locais	( )X
formal	( )X	formais	( )X
legal	( )X	legais	( )X
anual	( )X	anuais	( )X
federal	( )X	federais	( )X

2. Nouns that end in stressed -el (the open E) go through a
   similar process to form their plurals. The word 'hotel' is
   an example. First, repeat just the singular.

   ( ) ( )x ( )x

3. Now repeat the plural form, i.e., the equivalent of 'hotels'.

   ( ) ( )x ( )x

4. Here is the word for 'paper'. This is a new item for you.

   ( ) ( )x ( )x ( )x

5. Analogizing with the plural of 'hotel', how would you say the
   plural, 'papers'?

   Verify: ( )x ( )x

21.14

6. Here is the word for 'ring', the kind you put on your finger.
    It too is a new word for you.

$$(\quad)\quad(\quad)x\quad(\quad)x$$

7. Again, by analogy, you should be able to say the plural form
    'rings'. What is it?

Verify: $(\quad)x\quad(\quad)x$

8. Here is the word for something very tasty, a kind of small
    pie, or turnover.

$$(\quad)\quad(\quad)x\quad(\quad)x$$

9. Generally, these small pastries are pretty good, and you will
    want to eat more than just one of them. When you want to tell
    the cook just how good they are, how are you going to put the
    word into the plural?

Verify: $(\quad)x\quad(\quad)x$

10. Now, here are the above four items again. This time look at
    them as you are saying them.

hotel	( )x	hotéis	( )x
papel	( )x	papéis	( )x
anel	( )x	anéis	( )x
pastel	( )x	pastéis	( )x

11. Notice that the open E appears in the stressed syllable of
    these words. Notice, too, that this open E is retained in
    the plural where it is part of the stressed diphthong -Ei-.

21.15

hotéis	(	)x	(	)x
papéis	(	)x	(	)x
anéis	(	)x	(	)x
pastéis	(	)x	(	)x

12. Here are a few additional, less commonly heard words that
    follow the above pattern. Follow along visually below, and
    repeat these items as they are given to you.

    A. First, just the singular forms.
       (1) pincel   ( )x ( )x   'paint brush'
       (2) quartel   ( )x ( )x   'barracks'
       (3) coronel   ( )x ( )x   'colonel'
       (4) cascavel   ( )x ( )x   'rattlesnake'
       (5) carrossel   ( )x ( )x   'carrousel'

    B. Now, the singular forms followed by the plural forms.
       (1) pincel   ( )x pincéis   ( )x ( )x
       (2) quartel   ( )x quartéis   ( )x ( )x
       (3) coronel   ( )x coronéis   ( )x ( )x
       (4) cascavel   ( )x cascavéis ( )x ( )x
       (5) carrossel   ( )x carrosséis( )x ( )x

13. Words ending in stressed -ol (open O) also have a diphthong
    in their plural endings. The only word that you have had
    thus far that ends in stressed -ol is the word for 'Spanish',
    which can be both adjective and noun.

                    espanhol   ( )x ( )x

14. Espanhol is just the masculine form (the feminine is espanhola).
    Here is the masculine plural form, with the diphthong.

                 ( ) ( )x ( )x ( )x

15. This is what it looks like:

   <u>espanhóis</u>   ( )x   ( )x

16. Thus, if you want to say 'They are Spanish', you will say:

   <u>Eles são espanhóis</u>   ( )x   ( )x

17. And, if you want to say 'Spanish restaurants', you will say:

   <u>restaurantes espanhóis</u> ( )x   ( )x

18. How would you say 'Spanish accents'?

(sotaques espanhóis)

   Verify: ( )x   ( )x

19. How about 'Spanish friends (masc.)?'

(amigos espanhóis)

   Verify: ( )x   ( )x

20. Other words that end in stressed -<u>ol</u> occur with somewhat
    less frequency in the language. Among them are the following
    two:

   a. anzol   ( )x   ( )x   'fishing rod'
   b. farol   ( )x   ( )x   'headlight'

21. Now, repeat the plural forms along with the singular.

   a. anzol   ( )x   ( )x   anzóis   ( )x   ( )x
   b. farol   ( )x   ( )x   faróis   ( )x   ( )x

22. So far we have taken care of the plural forms of words ending
    in stressed -<u>al</u>, -<u>el</u> and -<u>ol</u>. Is there a similar pattern
    for words ending in stressed -<u>ul</u> and stressed -<u>il</u>? For -<u>ul</u>,
    yes, there is. But the examples are few. The only one
    worth mentioning at this point is the adjective 'blue'.
    Here is the singular form.

   <u>azul</u>   ( )   ( )x   ( )x   ( )x

23. And here is the plural form.

   <u>azuis</u>   ( )   ( )x   ( )x   ( )x

24. Thus, is you want to say 'blue car', you will say it like
    this.

    <u>carro</u> <u>azul</u>   (   )x   (   )x

25. And if you want to say the plural form, 'blue cars', you
    will say it like this.

    <u>carros</u> <u>azuis</u>   (   )x   (   )x

26. How would you say the singular, 'blue book'?
(livro azul)

    Verify: (   )x   (   )x

27. How about the plural, 'blue books'?
(livros azuis)

    Verify: (   )x   (   )x

28. How would you say 'blue mountains'?
(montanhas azuis)

    Verify: (   )x   (   )x

29. This is the way you say 'the mountain is blue'.

    <u>A</u> <u>montanha</u> <u>é</u> <u>azul</u>   (   )x   (   )x

30. How do you say 'The mountains are blue'?
(As montanhas são azuis)

    Verify: (   )x   (   )x

31. Do words that end in stressed –<u>il</u> follow the same pattern and
    have a diphthong in their plural forms? No, they do not.
    They simply change the <u>l</u> to <u>s</u>. Here are a few such words,
    first in their singular forms.

    <u>barril</u>   (   )x   (   )x   'barrel'
    <u>civil</u>   (   )x   (   )x   'civil'
    <u>gentil</u>   (   )x   (   )x   'kind', 'polite'

32. This time repeat the singular and plural forms together.

<u>barril</u> ( )X ( )X   <u>barris</u> ( )X ( )X
<u>civil</u> ( )X ( )X   <u>civis</u> ( )X ( )X
<u>gentil</u> ( )X ( )X   <u>gentis</u> ( )X ( )X

33. This is the way you say 'He is very kind (polite)'.

<u>Ele é muito gentil</u> ( )X ( )X

34. How would you say 'They are very kind'?
(Eles são muito gentis)

Verify: ( )X ( )X

35. This is the phrase 'one barrel'.

<u>um barril</u> ( )X ( )X

36. How do you say 'three barrels'?
(três barris)

Verify: ( )X ( )X

Review Practice
    Repeat these singular and plural items as they are given to you on the tape.

1.	pastel	( )X	pastéis	( )X
2.	anel	( )X	anéis	( )X
3.	formal	( )X	formais	( )X
4.	capital	( )X	capitais	( )X
5.	quartel	( )X	quartéis	( )X
6.	espanhol	( )X	espanhóis	( )X
7.	farol	( )X	faróis	( )X
8.	azul	( )X	azuis	( )X
9.	legal	( )X	legais	( )X
10.	civil	( )X	civis	( )X
11.	gentil	( )X	gentis	( )X
12.	hotel	( )X	hotéis	( )X

DIALOG - Part I

Yara

Onde você mora?   Where do you live?

Jack

Eu moro em Alexandria.   I live in Alexandria.

Yara

    antes   before, previously

Onde você morava antes?   Where did you (use to) live
                                    before?

Jack

Eu morava em Filadélfia.   I used to live in Philadelphia.

Yara

    nascer   to be born

Você nasceu lá?   Were you born there?

Jack

    nasci   (I) was born
    a capital   the capital

Não, eu nasci em Harrisburg,   No. I was born in Harrisburg,
a capital.   the capital.

Part II

Yara

Onde é que você trabalhava, Frank?	Where did you use to work, Frank?

Frank

Londres	London
seção	section
política	political
Eu trabalhava em Londres, na seção política.	I worked (use to work) in London, in the political section.

Yara

viajar	to travel
Você viajava?	Did you (customarily) travel?

Frank

aliás	actually, as a matter of fact
a Inglaterra	England
Viajava. Aliás, eu viajava muito, na Inglaterra mesmo.	I did. As a matter of fact, I travelled a lot, in England itself.

End of Tape 10A

Tape 10B

Part III

Yara

Ana	Anna
Chinês	Chinese
Você sabe, Ana, que o Jorge falava Chinês muito bem?	Do you know, Anna, that George used to speak Chinese real well?

Jorge

Eu? Que Chinês? Eu não falava Chinês.	Me? What (do you mean) Chinese? I didn't use to speak Chinese.
inventar	to invent
cada	each
Você inventa cada uma!	You invent the darnedest things! (Literally, You invent each one!)

Expansion Exercise 1. (Recorded)

    This is additional practice with the verb <u>viajar</u>. Repeat these
items as they are given to you on the tape.

Present

1. Você viaja muito?
2. Vocês viajam amanhã?
3. Nós não viajamos hoje, viajamos amanhã.
4. Quem viaja mais, você ou ele?
5. Eu não viajo nada.
6. Quando é que a senhora viaja? No sábado?

Past

7. Eles viajaram para o Brasil ontem.
8. Eu já viajei pela Pan American. Gostei muito.
9. Você viajou pela Varig?
10. Nós já viajamos três vezes ao Rio. Que cidade!
11. Quem viajou com vocês?

Neutral form

12. Quem quer viajar com ele?
13. Nós só vamos viajar segunda-feira.
14. Eu não vou viajar de carro. É longe.
15. Eles também pretendem viajar domingo?

Expansion Exercise 2. (Recorded)

    Note well these instances of the use of <u>aliás</u>. Repeat first
the part of the utterance that precedes the word <u>aliás</u>, then
repeat the part that begins with the word.

1. Eu me levanto cedo; aliás, eu me levanto às seis e meia.
2. Eu não quero comer estes sanduíches; aliás, eu não estou
    com fome.
3. Acho que ele sai amanhã; aliás, eu tenho certeza.
4. Ele vai viajar pela Braniff; aliás, ele já reservou as
    passagens.

5. O professor Ferreira dá muitas provas; aliás, ele vai dar uma hoje.
6. O sanduíche é bom, viu? Aliás, é ótimo.
7. Você tem razão; aliás, você _sempre_ tem razão.

Expansion Exercise 3.

Note well these examples of the exclamation _Que_ used in the approximate sense of _what_ _do_ _you_ _mean?_ In each instance it should be easy to imagine that the speaker is disputing something that has just been said.

(with a noun)
1. Que Chinês! Eu não falo Chinês.
2. Que festa! Eu não vou dar uma festa.
3. Que sanduíches! Eu não vou levar sanduíches, viu?
4. Que Coca-cola! Aqui a gente não bebe Coca-cola.
5. Que feriado! Amanhã não é feriado.
6. Que notícias dele! Eu não recebi notícias dele.
7. Que filha! Ele não tem filha, viu?

(with an adjective)
8. Que espanhol! Ele é brasileiro.
9. Que velha! Ela não é velha!
10. Que solteira! Ela é casada.

(with a verb)
11. Que parar na Flórida! Eu não vou parar na Flórida.
12. Que fazer um passeio! Eu quero descansar, viu?
13. Que levar sanduíches! Nós vamos comer num restaurante.
14. Que preparar o diálogo! Hoje é sábado, viu?
15. Que passou bem a noite! Eu não dormi nada.
16. Que mandar um cartão! Eu vou escrever uma carta.
17. Que viajar pela Braniff! Eu vou viajar pela VARIG, viu?
18. Que moramos em Washington! Nós moramos em Maryland.
19. Que nasceu na Virginia! Eu nasci na Pennsylvania.
20. Que trabalhava em Londres! Ela trabalhava em Bonn.
21. Que está resfriado! Eu estou cansado só.
22. Que caiu no sono! Eu estou acordado, viu? Você inventa cada uma!

Translations

Be prepared to participate in these brief interchanges either with your teacher or a follow student.

1. A. Você falava espanhol?
   B. Falava. Eu morava em Caracas.

2. A. Os senhores moravam na África?
   B. Morávamos. Nós trabalhávamos na embaixada em Cairo.

3. A. Eu nasci em Harrisburg.
   B. Mesmo? A minha esposa nasceu perto de lá.

4. A. Eu sou de Albany. Eu nasci lá.
   B. Mesmo? Eu trabalhava lá.

5. A. A Yara falava francês (French) bem, mas ela já esqueceu muito.
   B. Eu também falava. Mas agora falo bem pouco.

6. A. Eu passava muitos fins de semana em Chicago. Eu trabalhava em Gary.
   B. Mesmo? Eu conheço bem a cidade. Eu sou de lá.

7. A. Quando nós morávamos em Londres, nós jantavamos tarde.
   B. E agora?
   A. Agora nós jantamos cedo, lá pelas seis.

8. A. Quando eu morava em Nova Iorque eu levantava cedo.
   B. E agora?
   A. Agora eu levanto tarde, lá pelas oito.

9. A. Você trabalhava muito, não é?
   B. Trabalhava. Eu ficava na Embaixada até às sete e só chegava em casa às oito.

21.24

10. A. A que horas os senhores começavam o dia?
    B. Nós começávamos às oito e quarenta e cinco, mais ou menos.

11. A. Das nove até às dez você sempre estudava?
    B. Não. Eu descansava. Eu não gostava de estudar a essa hora.

12. A. Não dava para ir às montanhas?
    B. Não dava. Nós sempre ficávamos na cidade.

13. A. Você falava espanhol bem?
    B. Não. O francês sempre atrapalhava.

14. A. Você levava sanduíches?
    B. Levava. Eu não gostava da comida do restaurante.

15. A. Eu voltava da praia cedo.
    B. E eu ficava até bem tarde. Eu gostava tanto!

16. A. Eu praticava francês com ela.
    B. Ela falava bem?
    A. Falava. Ela nasceu em Paris, viu?

UNIT 22

In the last unit we dealt with the concepts of 'used to'
and/or 'would' in -ar type verbs. In this unit we will deal
with these concepts in -er and -ir type verbs.

1. Listen to these verb forms.
    a. (   )   (   )
    b. (   )   (   )
    c. (   )   (   )
    d. (   )   (   )

2. You may recognize the stems of these verbs but you
    probably do not recognize their ending. Here is the
    ending. Listen and repeat.

    (   )   (   )x   (   )x   (   )x

3. Now let's attach this ending to the stems of four verbs,
    as we did in frame 1, above. This time you should repeat.

    a. (   )x   (   )x
    b. (   )x   (   )x
    c. (   )x   (   )x
    d. (   )x   (   )x

4. Now let's attach the ending to four more verbs. Listen
    and repeat.
    a. (   )   (   )x   (   )x
    b. (   )   (   )x   (   )x
    c. (   )   (   )x   (   )x
    d. (   )   (   )x   (   )x

5. The ending that we have been dealing with looks like this
    in print: -ia.

    (   )x   (   )x   (   )x

6. It can be attached to the stem of -er type verbs.
    a. (   )x   (   )x
    b. (   )x   (   )x
    c. (   )x   (   )x
    d. (   )x   (   )x

22.1

7. It can also be attached to the stem of -ir type verbs.
   a. ( )x ( )x
   b. ( )x ( )x
   c. ( )x ( )x
   d. ( )x ( )x

8. This is what the four -er type verbs in frame 6 look
   like with this ending attached.
   a. Stem beb- plus ending -ia = bebia
   b. Stem com- plus ending -ia = comia
   c. Stem escrev- plus ending -ia = escrevia
   d. Stem receb- plus ending -ia = recebia

9. Now, repeat again.
   a. bebia ( )x ( )x
   b. comia ( )x ( )x
   c. escrevia ( )x ( )x
   d. recebia ( )x ( )x

10. This is what the four -ir type verbs in frame 7 look
    like with this ending attached.
    a. Stem dorm- plus ending -ia = dormia
    b. Stem repet- plus ending -ia = repetia
    c. Stem dirig- plus ending -ia = dirigia
    d. Stem abr- plus ending -ia = abria

11. Now, repeat again.
    a. dormia ( )x ( )x
    b. repetia ( )x ( )x
    c. dirigia ( )x ( )x
    d. abria ( )x ( )x

12. The -ia ending signifies 'used to' or 'would' for -er
    and -ir type verbs, just as -ava does for -ar type verbs.
    Thus the form comia can be translated as 'used to eat'
    or 'would eat' and the form dormia can be translated
    as 'used to sleep' or 'would sleep'.

22.2

13. How would you translate this form?   Listen.

( ) ( )

(used to/would eat)

14. How would you translate this form?

( ) ( )

(used to/would write)

15. How about this form?

( ) ( )

(used to/would open)

16. And this form?

( ) ( )

(used to/would repeat)

17. And this one?

( ) ( )

(used to/would drive)

18. And this one?

( ) ( )

(used to/would receive)

19. Here are the neutral forms of many of the -er and -ir type verbs that you have learned so far. Run through this list aloud, with the tape, to refresh your memory and also to prepare yourself for the frames that follow.

comer	( )x	dormir	( )x
beber	( )x	repetir	( )x
escrever	( )x	dirigir	( )x
esquecer	( )x	abrir	( )x
chover	( )x	preferir	( )x
saber	( )x	sentir	( )x
receber	( )x	sair	( )x
fazer	( )x	cair	( )x
conhecer	( )x	ir	( )x
acontecer	( )x		
ler	( )x		

22.3

20. Now, we will take just the -er type verbs from the
    above list and we will practice them in their 'used to/
    would' forms.
    a. comia   (   )x   (   )x
    b. bebia   (   )x   (   )x
    c. escrevia (   )x   (   )x
    d. esquecia (   )x   (   )x
    e. chovia   (   )x   (   )x
    f. sabia   (   )x   (   )x
    g. recebia (   )x   (   )x
    h. fazia   (   )x   (   )x
    i. conhecia (   )x   (   )x
    j. acontecia (   )x   (   )x

21. The 'used to/would' form for ler ('read') may seem
    strange to you since it is so short.
        lia (   )x   (   )x

22. However, this form follows the same pattern as the
    others: the stem l- is followed by the ending -ia.
        lia (   )x   (   )x

23. Now we will take the -ir type verbs from the above list
    and we will practice saying their 'used to/would' forms.
    a. dormia   (   )x   (   )x
    b. repetia (   )x   (   )x
    c. dirigia (   )x   (   )x
    d. abria   (   )x   (   )x
    e. preferia (   )x   (   )x
    f. sentia   (   )x   (   )x
    g. saía   (   )x   (   )x
    h. caía   (   )x   (   )x
    i. ia   (   )x   (   )x

24. If items (g) and (h) seem a bit strange to you it is only
    because of their stems. Their stems are relatively short,
    and they end in a vowel. The stems are sa- and ca-.
        sa-ía (   )x   (   )x
        ca-ía (   )x   (   )x

22.4

25. Item (i) may seem to lack a stem, and perhaps it does, but the form is complete. It is the 'used to/would' form for the verb ir. (When you remove the ir portion to look for a stem, you realize immediately that there is nothing left. No stem to attach ia to. So the ending ia becomes the whole form.)

ia (   )x (   )x

26. The forms that we have been practicing are both I-forms and he-forms. The form dormia, for example, is the form that is called for when you want to say 'I used to/ would sleep' and it is also the form that is called for when you want to say 'He' or 'You' or 'Maria' or 'the Ambassador used to/would sleep'.

Practice I (Recorded)

Learn how to say these short, paired sentences.

1. I used to eat a lot. (Eu comia muito.)
2. I would eat everything. (Eu comia tudo.)

3. I used to leave early. (Eu saía cedo.)
4. I would leave at six. (Eu saía às seis.)

5. He used to sleep a lot. (Ele dormia muito.)
6. He would sleep 10 hours. (Ele dormia dez horas.)

7. He used to fall asleep early. (Ele dormia cedo.)
8. He would fall asleep at nine. (Ele dormia às nove.)

9. She used to read a lot. (Ela lia muito.)
10. She would read until midnight. (Ela lia até a meia-noite.)

11. It used to rain a lot there. (Chovia muito lá.)
12. It would rain every day. (Chovia todos os dias.)

13. He used to drive a lot. (Ele dirigia muito.)
14. He would drive every day. (Ele dirigia todos os dias.)

15. He used to go to the movies a lot. (Ele ia muito ao cinema.)
16. He'd go everyday. (Ele ia todos os dias.)

22.5

Practice II   (Recorded)

Now, be sure you can say these pairs of sentences.

1. John wouldn't go to   (João não ia à praia.)
   the beach.

   He'd go to the   (Ele ia às montanhas.)
   mountains.

2. I wouldn't drink coke.   (Eu não bebia Coca-cola.)

   I'd drink other soft   (Eu bebia outros
   drinks.   refrigerantes.)

3. I wouldn't read 'The   (Eu não lia 'The News'.)
   News'.

   But I would always   (Mas eu sempre lia 'The Post.')
   read 'The Post'.

4. Jorge wouldn't go out   (Jorge não saía com a Yara.)
   with Yara.

   But he would always go   (Mas ele sempre saía com a Sandra,
   out with Sandra, yes,   claro!)
   indeed!

5. Yara wouldn't go through   (A Yara não ia por Brasília.)
   (por) Brasilia.

   She'd go directly to   (Ela ia diretamente ao Rio.)
   Rio.

6. He wouldn't forget   (Ele não esquecia só o livro.)
   just his book.

   He'd forget everything.   (Ele esquecia tudo.)

7. The holiday wouldn't   (O feriado não caía na segunda.)
   fall on Monday.

   It would fall on the   (Caía no fim de semana.)
   weekend.

Practice III   (Recorded)

Now make sure you can say these. Notice how easily the words
'always' and 'never' fit into these situations.

1. I always used to leave   (Eu sempre saía cedo.)
   early.

   My wife would never   (Minha esposa nunca saía cedo.)
   leave early.

22.6

2. I used to always sleep   (Eu sempre dormia até tarde.)
   late.

   My son would never   (O meu filho nunca dormia até
   sleep late.   tarde.)

3. I would always forget.   (Eu sempre esquecia.)

   Yara would never for-   (A Yara nunca esquecia.)
   get.

4. I would always drink   (Eu sempre bebia Coca-cola.)
   Coke.

   Yara would never drink   (A Yara nunca bebia Coca-cola.)
   Coke.

5. I always used to receive   (Eu sempre recebia uma carta.)
   a letter.

   Yara would never   (A Yara nunca recebia carta.)
   receive a letter.

6. I would always go   (Eu sempre ia ao centro.)
   downtown.

   Yara would never go   (A Yara nunca ia ao centro.)
   downtown.

7. I always used to do   (Eu sempre fazia isso.)
   that.

   Yara never used to do   (A Yara nunca fazia isso.)
   that.

Practice IV   (Recorded)

Do this question and answer practice either with your teacher
or with a fellow student. This type of practice is designed for
you to take the English of one column and put it into Portuguese
while your partner does the same thing with the other column. Each
of you can easily check the translation of the other by referring
to your own column. When finished, trade columns with your partner.

                A   B

1. Did you use to eat a lot?   (Você comia muito?)
   (Comia, sim.)   Yes, I did.

                            22.7

2. Did you use to go out with   (Você saía com Yara?)
   Yara?
   (Saía, sim.)   Yes, I did.

3. Did you use to know Sandra?   (Você conhecia a Sandra?)
   (Conhecia, sim.)   Yes, I did.

4. Would you sleep till noon?   (Você dormia até o meio-dia?)
   (Dormia, sim.)   Yes, I would.

5. Would you read till midnight?   (Você lia até a meia-noite?)
   (Lia, sim.)   Yes, I would.

6. Would you take a drive?   (Você fazia um passeio?)
   (Fazia, sim.)   Yes, I would.

7. Would John forget?   (O João esquecia?)
   (Esquecia, sim.)   Yes, he would.

8. Would Barbara go on Varig?   (A Bárbara ia pela Varig?)
   (Ia, sim.)   Yes, she would.

9. Would Sonia drink coffee?   (A Sônia bebia café?)
   (Bebia, sim.)   Yes, she would.

10. Would it rain a lot?   (Chovia muito?)
    (Chovia, sim.)   Yes, it would.

    27. Now let's examine the we-form. Here is the ending
        for the we-form.
              ( )   ( )x   ( )x

    28. Here are several examples of the we-form.
        a. ( )   ( )x   ( )x
        b. ( )   ( )x   ( )x
        c. ( )   ( )x   ( )x
        d. ( )   ( )x   ( )x

    29. Here are the same examples in print. Repeat again.
        a. dormíamos   ( )x   ( )x
        b. repetíamos   ( )x   ( )x
        c. comíamos   ( )x   ( )x
        d. bebíamos   ( )x   ( )x

                            22.8

30. So, how would you say 'we used to eat'?
(comíamos)

Verify: (   )x

31. How would you say 'we used to repeat'?
(repetíamos)

Verify: (   )x

32. How would you say 'we used to receive'?
(recebíamos)

Verify: (   )x

33. How about 'we used to know? (<u>conhecer</u>)
(conhecíamos)

Verify: (   )x

34. And how about 'we used to leave'? (<u>sa-ir</u>).
(saíamos)

Verify: (   )x

35. How would you say 'we used to read'? (<u>l-er</u>)
(líamos)

Verify: (   )x

36. Now let's look at the they-form. Here is just the ending for the they-form. Do not repeat yet.

(   ) (   )

37. Here are several examples of the they-form. Do not repeat yet.

a. (   ) (   )
b. (   ) (   )
c. (   ) (   )
d. (   ) (   )

38. The ending for these forms is composed of the stressed vowel <u>i</u> plus the unstressed diphthong <u>ão</u>. Standard spelling doesn't show us everything that we would like it to show us, so with a view towards good pronunciation let us temporarily visualize this ending as follows:

<u>í</u> + <u>ão</u> = <u>íão</u>

39. Repeat this sequence from the tape.
> (í)x   (í)x
> (ão)x   (ão)x
>
> Slowly: (í ão)x   (í ão)x
> Normal: (íão)x   (íão)x

40. This is what the ending looks like in standard spelling.
Repeat as you just did.
> iam   (   )x   (   )x   (   )x

41. Now repeat the following they-forms from the tape.
> a. (   )x   (   )x
> b. (   )x   (   )x
> c. (   )x   (   )x
> d. (   )x   (   )x

42. Here are the same four forms in print. Repeat again.
> a. dormiam   (   )x   (   )x
> b. repetiam   (   )x   (   )x
> c. comiam   (   )x   (   )x
> d. bebiam   (   )x   (   )x

43. What is the form for 'they used to/would sleep'?
(dormiam)
> Verify: (   )x

44. What is the form for 'they used to/would eat'?
(comiam)
> Verify: (   )x

45. What is the form for 'they used to/would open'?
(abriam)
> Verify: (   )x

46. How about the form for 'they used to know'?
(Neutral form = saber)
(sabiam)
> Verify: (   )x

47. How about the form for 'they used to do, or make'?
        (Neutral form = <u>fazer</u>)
(faziam)

             Verify: (   )x

48. How about 'they would write'?
        (Neutral form = <u>escrever</u>)
(escreviam)

             Verify: (   )x

49. And, finally, what is the form for 'they would leave'?
        (Neutral form = <u>sair</u>)
(saíam)

             Verify: (   )x

Practice V   (Recorded)

    Learn how to say the following short sentences.

1. They used to sleep   (Eles dormiam muito.)
    a lot.
    They would sleep until   (Eles dormiam até o meio-dia.)
    noon.

2. They used to eat a lot.   (Eles comiam muito.)
    They would eat all day.   (Eles comiam o dia todo.)

3. They used to go out a   (Eles saíam muito.)
    lot.
    They would go out   (Eles saíam juntos.)
    together.

4. We used to go to the   (Nós íamos à praia.)
    beach.
    We would go there   (Nós íamos lá todos os dias.)
    every day.

5. We used to get lots   (Nós recebíamos muitas notícias
    of news about him.   dele.)
    We would get news   (Nós recebíamos notícias todos
    every day.   os dias.)

6. We used to drink lots   (Nós bebíamos muito café.)
    of coffee.
    We would drink [it]   (Nós bebíamos todos os dias.)
    every day.

Practice VI   (Recorded)

Now learn how to say these sentences which utilize negatives
and 'always' and 'never'.

1. We used to go directly to   (Nós íamos diretamente a
    New York.   Nova York.)

    We wouldn't go through   (Nós não íamos por Filadélfia.)
    (por) Philadelphia.

2. We used to always read   (Nós sempre líamos 'O Jornal'.)
    'O Jornal'.

    We would never read 'The   (Nós nunca líamos 'The Post'.)
    Post'.

3. They would always go to   (Eles sempre iam às
    the mountains.   montanhas.)

    They would never go to the   (Eles nunca iam à praia.)
    beach.

4. They would always open   (Eles sempre abriam tarde.)
    late.

    They would never open   (Eles nunca abriam antes das dez.)
    before ten.

5. They would always drink   (Eles sempre bebiam café.)
    coffee.

    They would not drink Coke.   (Eles não bebiam Coca-cola.)

6. We always used to leave   (Nós sempre saíamos ao meio-dia.)
    at noon.

    We would never leave earlier.   (Nós nunca saíamos mais cedo.)

7. They would always eat at   (Eles sempre comiam em casa.)
    home.

    They would never eat in a   (Eles nunca comiam no
    restaurant.   restaurante.)

22.12

Practice VII   (Recorded)

Practice these questions and answers so that you can do them
in class without reference to the printed Portuguese.   In this
practice 'you' = os senhores.

1. Did you use to sleep late?   (Os senhores dormiam até tarde?)
    - - - Yes, we did.   (Dormíamos, sim.)

2. Did you use to go out a lot?   (Os senhores saíam muito?)
    - - - No, we didn't.   (Não, não saíamos.)

3. Would you eat in the   (Os senhores comiam no
    restaurant across the   restaurante em frente?)
    street?
    - - - Yes, we would.   (Comíamos, sim.)

4. Would you go on Pan Am?   (Os senhores iam pela Pan Am?)
    - - - No, we wouldn't.   (Não, não íamos.)

5. Did you (use to) know   (Os senhores conheciam a
    his daughter?   filha dele?)
    - - - Yes, we did.   (Conhecíamos, sim.)

6. Would you go to the movies?   (Os senhores iam ao cinema?)
    - - - No, we wouldn't.   (Não, não íamos.)

7. Did you (use to) write   (Os senhores escreviam muitas
    lots of letters?   cartas?)
    - - - Yes, we did.   (Escrevíamos, sim.)

DIALOG

In this unit we are presenting not <u>one</u> <u>dialog</u> but rather a series of two line exchanges, all of which start out pretty much the same way. You are to work them all in the usual way then pick any that may be applicable to you and make them a part of you. We hope that by this time you feel free to check with your instructor or perhaps a dictionary for limited, additional vocabulary that you need in order to adapt the materials we give you to your own personal circumstances.

<u>Exchange No. 1</u>
Professor

fazia	used to do
Eduardo	Edward
<u>O que é que você fazia antes, Eduardo</u>?	<u>What did you use to do, Eduardo</u>?

Eduardo

a empresa	company, firm
particular	private
<u>Eu trabalhava para uma empresa particular</u>.	<u>I used to work for a private company</u>.
vendia (neutral form = <u>vender</u>)	used to sell
os seguros	insurance
<u>Eu vendia seguros</u>.	<u>I sold (used to sell) insurance</u>.

22.14

Exchange No. 2

Professor

O que é que você fazia lá em Buffalo, Marcos?	What did you use to do there in Buffalo, Mark?

Marcos

local	local
Eu escrevia para um jornal local.	I used to write for a local newspaper.

Exchange No. 3

Professor

O que é que a senhora fazia em Minnesota, dona Lúcia?	What did you use to do in Minnesota, Miss Barnes?

Dona Lúcia

era[1]	was, used to be
ensinava (neutral form = ensinar)	used to teach
a história	history
Eu era professora. Eu ensinava história.	I used to be a teacher. I taught history.

Exchange No. 4

Professor

Ricardo	Richard
a Alemanha	Germany
O que é que você fazia na Alemanha, Ricardo?	What did you use to do in Germany, Dick?

---

[1]Era is the 'used to/would' form for ser. Its shape is irregular. Often the most convenient English equivalent is simply 'was'.

Ricardo

o funcionário	officer
consular	consular
Eu era funcionário da Seção Consular.	I was an officer in the Consular Section.

Exchange No. 5

Professor

o departamento	department

O que é que você fazia no Departamento de Estado, Ângela?	What did you do (used to do) in the State Department, Angela?

Ângela

a secretária	secretary
batia (neutral form = bater)	used to beat (type)
a máquina	machine (typewriter)
Eu era secretária. Eu batia cartas à máquina o dia todo.	I was a secretary. I'd type letters all day long.

Exchange No. 6

Professor

O que é que vocês faziam nos fins de semana, Inês?	What would you do on weekends, Inez?

Inês

às vezes	at times
fora	out (side)
Nós íamos à praia e às vezes comíamos fora.	We would go to the beach and at times we'd eat out.

End of Tape 10B

EXPANSION EXERCISES

Common Names

First, review the following common names, all of which have already appeared in this book. Repeat aloud as you follow along with the tape.

Male	Female
Paulo	Yara
José	Maria
Roberto	Sandra
João	Sônia
Jorge	Bárbara
Geraldo	Luísa
Eduardo	Lúcia
Marcos	Ângela
Ricardo	Inês
Luís	Glória
Carlos	Ana

Expansion Exercise 1 (Recorded)

Here are several more common names that you will run across sooner or later. Since these are new, they are recorded twice each. Repeat aloud.

Male	Female
Sérgio	Tânia
Antônio	Vânia
Gustavo	Carmen
Cláudio	Lourdes
Henrique	Margarida
Alberto	Regina
Emílio	Cláudia
Mário	Beatriz
Fernando	Raquel, Rachel
Sebastião	Denise

Francisco	Alice
Jaime	Marli
Ernesto	Rosa
Júlio	Vera
Leonardo	Cristina
Afonso	Helena

Expansion Exercise 2 (Recorded)

Many times given names appear in pairs. Repeat the following common combinations.

Female	Male
Ana Maria	Luís Sérgio
Maria Lúcia	Afonso Henrique
Ana Helena	João Carlos
Regina Lúcia	Francisco José
Vera Maria	Carlos Fernando
Teresa Cristina	Luís Antônio
Maria Helena	José Luís
Maria Luísa	Antônio Jorge
Maria Teresa	José Carlos

Expansion Exercise 3 (Recorded)

Here are some opportunities to use some additional forms of the verb <u>vender</u>. Practice saying these short sentences until you can translate them easily from the English.

I.   A.   O senhor vai vender o seu carro?   Are you going to sell your car?

      B.   Eu já vendi.   I already sold it.

      A.   Quando o senhor vendeu?   When did you sell it?

      B.   Vendi ontem.   I sold it yesterday.

II.   A.   Nós já vendemos a casa.   We already sold our house.

      B.   Quando é que os senhores venderam?   When did you sell it?

      A.   Vendemos segunda-feira.   We sold it Monday.

III. A. Luís vendia seguros.   Luís used to sell insurance.
      B. Júlio vendia carros.   Júlio used to sell cars.
      C. E eu, quando era   And I, when I was a lad, used
          menino, vendia jornais.   to sell newspapers.

Translations

Be prepared to do this practice with another student or with
your teacher. Each of you should take a column for your own and
work within that column. As you transpose the English of your
column into Portuguese you can also be checking the Portuguese
responses being given by your partner.

1. What did you [use to] do   (O que é que o senhor fazia
    in London?   em Londres?)

    (Eu era funcionário da   I was an officer in the
    Seção Consular.)   Consular Section.

2. (O que é que o senhor   What did you [use to] do in
    fazia na Embaixada?)   the Embassy?

    I worked in the Political   (Eu trabalhava na Seção
    Section.   Política.)

3. What did you [use to] do   (O que é que a senhora fazia
    in Florida?   na Flórida?)

    (Eu ia à praia todos os   I'd go to the beach everyday.
    dias.)

4. (O que é que a senhora   What did you [use to] do in
    fazia em Buffalo?)   Buffalo?

    I was a teacher. I taught.   (Eu era professora. Eu
                                    ensinava.)

5. What did you [use to] do   (O que é que o senhor
    in the office?   fazia no escritório?)

    (Eu fazia de tudo.   I would do everything.   I'd
     Trabalhava o dia todo.)   work all day.

6. (O que é que o senhor   What did you [use to] do on
    fazia nos fins de semana?)   weekends?

    I wouldn't do anything.   (Eu não fazia nada.   Eu
    I'd rest.   descansava.)

7. Mario was an Embassy   (O Mário era funcionário da
    official.   Embaixada.)

    (O que é que ele fazia?)   What did he do?

    He worked [used to] in the   (Trabalhava na Seção Política.)
    Political Section.

8. (O senhor Watson era   Mr. Watson used to be a
    professor.)   teacher.

    Where did he [use to]   (Onde ele ensinava?)
    teach?

    (Ensinava em Cornell.)   He taught at Cornell.

9. Marcos was a teacher.   (O Marcos era professor.)

    (O que é que ele ensinava?)   What did he [use to] teach?
    He taught history.   (Ele ensinava história.)

10. Alice was a secretary.   (Alice era secretária.)
    (O que é que ela fazia?)   What did she do?
    She'd type all day.   (Ela batia à máquina o dia todo.)

11. (Raquel era secretária.   Raquel was a secretary. She
    Ela trabalhava na Seção   used to work in the Consular
    Consular.)   Section.

    Did she [customarily]   (Ela falava espanhol?)
    speak Spanish?

    (Falava, sim.)   Yes, she did.

12. Tania used to be a   (Tânia era secretária também.
    secretary too. She worked   Ela trabalhava no Brasil.)
    in Brazil.

    (Ela gostava?)   Did she [use to] like it?

    Yes, she did.   (Gostava, sim.)

13. (Eu era professor. Eu   I used to be a teacher.
    ensinava em Denver.)   I taught in Denver.

    Did you like it?   (Você gostava?)

    (Não, não gostava.)   No, I didn't.

14. I used to work for a   (Eu trabalhava para uma empresa
    private company.   particular.)

    (O que é que você fazia?)   What did you [use to] do?

    I was the president.   (Eu era o presidente.)

15. He used to be good.   (Ele era bom.)
    (E ele ainda é, viu?)   And he still is!

16. (Ele era solteiro.)   He was a bachelor.
    And he still is!   (E ele ainda é, viu?)

17. His English used to be   (O inglês dele era péssimo.)
    terrible.

    (E ainda é, viu?)   And it still is!

18. (O português dela era   Her Portuguese was great.
     ótimo.)

     And it still is!   (E ainda é, viu?)

19. Sergio was a sleepyhead.   (Sérgio era dorminhoco.)

     (E ele ainda é, viu?)   And he still is!

20. (Alberto era casado.)   Albert was married.
     And he still is!   (E ainda é, viu?)

UNIT 23

1. In the last unit where we were continuing our presentation
   of the 'used to/would forms, you learned the irregular
   form <u>era</u>. We noted at that time that this form is
   commonly translated as 'was'. Repeat these examples.

<u>Ele era americano</u>.	( )x	( )x
<u>Eu era solteiro</u>.	( )x	( )x
<u>Ela era casada</u>.	( )x	( )x

2. The form <u>era</u> is both the I-form and the he-form.

<u>Eu era professor</u>.	( )x	( )x
<u>Ele era funcionário</u>.	( )x	( )x

3. Here is the we-form. (Translation: 'used to be', or
   'were')

   <u>éramos</u>   ( )x   ( )x

4. Here it is preceded by the pronoun <u>nós</u>.

   <u>nós éramos</u>   ( )x   ( )x

5. So, this is the way you would say 'We were single'.

   <u>Nós éramos solteiros</u>.   ( )x   ( )x

6. And this is the way you would say 'We were officers'.

   <u>Nós éramos funcionários</u>. ( )x   ( )x

7. How would you say 'We were secretaries'?
(Nós éramos secretárias)

   Verify: ( )x   ( )x

8. And how would you say 'We were Americans'?
(Nós éramos americanos)

   Verify: ( )x   ( )x

23.1

9. Now, here is the they-form. (Translation: 'used to be',
   or 'were')
   <u>eram</u>   (   )x   (   )x

10. Here it is preceded by several appropriate pronouns.
    <u>eles</u> <u>eram</u>   (   )x   (   )x
    <u>elas</u> <u>eram</u>   (   )x   (   )x
    <u>vocês</u> <u>eram</u>   (   )x   (   )x
    <u>os</u> <u>senhores</u> <u>eram</u>   (   )x   (   )x

11. So, this is the way you might say 'They were single'.
    <u>Eles</u> <u>eram</u> <u>solteiros</u>. (   )x   (   )x

12. And this is the way you might say 'They were great'.
    <u>Eles</u> <u>eram</u> <u>ótimos</u>.   (   )x   (   )x

13. How would you say 'They were Americans'?
(Eles eram americanos)
              Verify: (   )x   (   )x

14. How would you say 'They were Brazilians'?
(Eles eram brasileiros)
              Verify: (   )x   (   )x

15. And how would you say 'They were from Rio'?
(Eles eram do Rio)
              Verify: (   )x   (   )x

16. This is a good time to introduce another irregular form,
    the form which corresponds to 'used to have', or 'would
    have'. (The neutral form is <u>ter</u>.)
    <u>tinha</u> (   )x   (   )x   (   )x

23.2

17. This form is both the I-form and the he-form. Repeat.
     <u>eu</u> <u>tinha</u>   ( )x   ( )x
     <u>ele</u> <u>tinha</u>   ( )x   ( )x
     <u>você</u> <u>tinha</u>   ( )x   ( )x
     <u>José</u> <u>tinha</u>   ( )x   ( )x

18. Notice the contrast between the present tense form,
    'I have', and this new form, 'I used to have'.
    a. <u>eu</u> <u>tenho</u>   ( )x   ( )x
    b. <u>eu</u> <u>tinha</u>   ( )x   ( )x

19. This is the way you would say 'I used to have
    *[a] Chevrolet'.
         <u>Eu</u> <u>tinha</u> <u>Chevrolet</u>.   ( )x   ( )x

20. And this is the way you would say 'She used to have
    *[a] Ford'.
         <u>Ela</u> <u>tinha</u> <u>Ford.</u>   ( )x   ( )x

21. How would you say 'She used to have [a] house'?
(Ela tinha casa)
         Verify: (   )x   (   )x

22. How would you say 'You used to have [an] accent'?
(Você tinha sotaque)
         Verify: (   )x   (   )x

23. How would you say 'I used to have two cars'?
(Eu tinha dois carros)
         Verify: (   )x   (   )x

24. Now, what do you suppose is the we-form of this verb?
    Venture a guess, then check the tape to see if you are
    right.
                        ( )x   ( )x   ( )x
    You were right, right?
*Under some circumstances it is normal to use the indefinite article
and say <u>Eu</u> <u>tinha</u> <u>um</u> <u>Chevrolet</u> (<u>Ford</u>). Do not be concerned right
now about the presence or absence of the article.

25. Here is the we-form preceded by the pronoun nós.

  nós tínhamos   (   )x   (   )x   (   )x

26. So, then, this is the way you will say 'We used to have two cars'.

  Nós tínhamos dois carros. (   )x   (   )x

27. And here is the way you will say 'We used to have a good view'.

  Nós tínhamos uma vista boa. (   )x   (   )x

28. How would you say 'We used to have a marvelous view'?
(Nós tínhamos uma vista maravilhosa)

  Verify: (   )x   (   )x

29. Remember that the Portuguese equivalent of 'to be right' is 'to have reason'. So, how would you say 'We were always right', i.e. 'We always had reason'?
(Nós sempre tínhamos razão)

  Verify: (   )x   (   )x

30. How would you say 'We were always sure'? Literally, 'We always had certainty.'
(Nós sempre tínhamos certeza)

  Verify: (   )x   (   )x

31. What do you suppose is the they-form? Venture a guess, then check the tape for verification.

  (   )x   (   )x   (   )x
  You were right again, weren't you?

32. Here is the they-form preceded by two pronouns.

  eles tinham   (   )x   (   )x
  elas tinham   (   )x   (   )x

23.4

33. So, this is the way you will say 'They used to have
[a] Ford'.
      <u>Eles</u> <u>tinham</u> <u>Ford</u>.   (   )x   (   )x

34. And this is the way you will say 'They always used
to be right.' (be right = <u>have</u> reason)
      <u>Eles</u> <u>sempre</u> <u>tinham</u> <u>razão</u>. (   )x   (   )x

35. How would you say 'They always used to be sure'?
(be sure = <u>have</u> certainty)
(Eles sempre tinham certeza)
      Verify: (   )x   (   )x

36. And how would you say 'They used to have two houses'?
(Eles tinham duas casas)
      Verify: (   )x   (   )x

37. Now let's go back several units to look at one of the
forms that is regular in its shape, the form <u>estava</u>.
Do you remember it in this phrase?
      <u>Eu</u> <u>estava</u> <u>com</u> <u>tanta</u> <u>pressa</u>   'I was in such a
                                  hurry'

38. Repeat:
      <u>Eu</u> <u>estava</u> <u>com</u> <u>tanta</u> <u>pressa</u> (   )x   (   )x

39. The form <u>estava</u> is from the infinitive <u>estar</u> 'to be'.
Like <u>era</u>, which comes from the infinitive <u>ser</u>, <u>estava</u>
also translates as 'used to be', or, frequently, 'was'.

40. Repeat the following phrases from the tape.
      1. I was hungry. (   )x   (   )x
      2. I was sleepy. (   )x   (   )x
      3. I was tired. (   )x   (   )x

41. <u>Estava</u> is also the he-form. Repeat these phrases
    from the tape.
    1. He was hungry. (   )x   (   )x
    2. He was sleepy. (   )x   (   )x
    3. He was tired.   (   )x   (   )x

42. Can you guess what the 'we-form' is? Try it, then
    check the tape for confirmation.
    (   )   (   )x   (   )x

43. This is what it looks like: <u>estávamos</u>. Be sure to
    stress it on the right syllable.
    (   )x   (   )x

44. Now repeat these phrases.
    1. We were hungry. (   )x   (   )x
    2. We were sleepy. (   )x   (   )x
    3. We were tired.   (   )x   (   )x

45. You should be able to guess what the they-form is.
    Try it, then verify with the tape.

    (   )   (   )x   (   )x

46. This is what it looks like: <u>estavam</u>. Repeat these
    phrases.
    1. They were hungry. (   )x   (   )x
    2. They were sleepy. (   )x   (   )x
    3. They were tired.   (   )x   (   )x

<u>Comment</u>

We must point out that in all of the above examples
involving 'hungry', 'tired', and 'sleepy' we are not necessarily
dealing with <u>recurring</u> situations. We might simply be describing
how somebody felt <u>yesterday</u>, for example, or <u>at the concert last</u>

23.6

night, or <u>when</u> <u>he</u> <u>got</u> <u>up</u> <u>this</u> <u>morning</u>, with no thought whatsoever
as to whether or not such feelings were of a recurrent nature.
Hence in these cases we are not forced to think in terms of 'used
to' or 'would' as we have had to do heretofore with most verbs in
their <u>ava</u> (and <u>ia</u>) forms. Instead we can think in terms of 'past
description', i.e. the description of conditions and circumstances
that existed at some time in the past.

The concept of 'past description' offers another useful
approach to all the verb forms we have been working with in the
last several units. The term suggests another way of looking at
and interpreting the range of meaning that these forms encompass.
With some verbs, because of their very nature, it is quite easy
to think of 'past description'. This is particularly true of
<u>ser</u>, <u>estar</u> and <u>ter</u>, as we have just seen. With other verbs the
association may not always be quite so easy to make.

<u>Practice 1.</u> (Recorded)
Thinking in terms of 'past description', how would you say
these brief thoughts in Portuguese? Practice these until you
can say them easily.

Group I
    1. I was awake.
    2. I was tired.
    3. I was sleepy.
    4. He was in a hurry.
    5. He was hungry.
    6. I had a cold. (<u>estava</u> <u>resfriado</u>)
    7. The traffic was terrible.

Group II
    1. I had [an] English accent.
    2. She had [a] Portuguese accent.
    3. I had [a] Ford.
    4. She had [a] Chevrolet.

5. We were sure (had certainty).
6. They were right (had reason).
7. We had two.
8. They had three.

Group III   (Omit items in brackets.)
1. I was [an] officer.
2. She was [a] teacher.
3. We were Americans.
4. They were Brazilians.
5. She was [a] secretary.
6. She was single.
7. He was the president.
8. He was married.
9. They were from New York.
10. We were from Pennsylvania.

Comment

The instances of 'past description' just given involve states of being or identification of some sort; the verbs are not verbs of action. The concept of 'past description' can also be applied to action verbs. Many of the action verbs of the past two units that we have translated as 'would/used to' offer past description. When we say, for example, that 'Roberto would/used to get up late' we are describing one aspect of Roberto's life in the past. Pay attention to how this operates in the next several practices.

Practice 2. (Recorded)

Learn to give this 'past description' of Bill. Do not translate items in brackets.
1. Bill was [an] American.
2. He was an officer in the State Department.
3. He spoke Portuguese well.
4. He had a lot of chance to practice.
5. Why? Because he lived and worked in Rio.

23.8

Practice 3. (Recorded)
    Now learn to give this 'past description' of Yara.
    1. Yara was [a] Brazilian.
    2. She was from São Paulo.
    3. She spoke English well.
    4. She spoke [it] without [an] accent.
    5. She worked in Rio.
    6. She travelled (would travel) a lot.
    7. She spent (would spend) weekends at home.
    8. She went (would go) to the beach.
    9. She liked her work (work ▪ o trabalho).

(We continue now with our programming.)

    47. This is the way you say 'I am planning to return'.
             Eu pretendo voltar   (   )x   (   )x

    48. If you wish to say 'I was planning to return', thus
         describing your thoughts and desires at some time in
         the past ('past description'), you would use the form
         pretendia.
             Eu pretendia voltar   (   )x   (   )x

    49. How would you say 'I was planning to sleep'?
(Eu pretendia dormir)
             Verify: (   )x   (   )x

    50. How would you say 'He was planning to read'?
(Ele pretendia ler)
             Verify: (   )x   (   )x

    51. How would you say 'She was planning to send'?
(Ela pretendia mandar)
             Verify: (   )x   (   )x

52. What is the form for 'We were planning'?
(Nós pretendíamos)
Verify: ( )x ( )x

53. And what is the form for 'They were planning'?
(Eles pretendiam)
Verify: ( )x ( )x

54. So, how would you say 'They were planning to stay'?
(Eles pretendiam ficar)
Verify: ( )x ( )x

55. And how do you say 'We were planning to leave'?
(Nós pretendíamos sair)
Verify: ( )x ( )x

56. We can perform similar operations with forms of the
verb 'want'. We can begin with the sentence 'I want
to take'.
Eu quero levar ( )x ( )x

57. Let's change the ending in order to say 'I wanted to
take', which is, you will agree, a kind of description
of my thoughts and desires at some time in the past.
Eu queria levar ( )x ( )x

58. How would you say 'I wanted to spend a week'?
(Eu queria passar uma semana)
Verify: ( )x ( )x

59. Following the same pattern, say the following:
a. I wanted to work. ( )x
b. I wanted to stop. ( )x
c. He wanted to drive. ( )x
d. He wanted to rest. ( )x
e. She wanted to change the subject. ( )x

23.10

60. What are the we-form and the they-form of 'wanted'?
(nós queríamos)
(eles queriam)
             Verify: (   )x   (   )x
             Verify: (   )x   (   )x

61. So, this is the way you would say 'We wanted to stay'.
             Nós queríamos ficar. (   )x   (   )x

62. And this is the way you would say 'They wanted to leave'.
             Eles queriam sair. (   )x   (   )x

63. Continuing in the same vein, say the following:
        a. They wanted to begin.   (   )x
        b. We wanted to begin.   (   )x
        c. We wanted to buy.   (   )x
        d. We wanted to sell.   (   )x
        e. They wanted to eat lunch. (   )x
        f. They wanted to forget.   (   )x

64. We can perform similar operations with forms of the
verb 'go'. We can begin with 'I am going to study'.
             Eu vou estudar.   (   )x   (   )x

65. Let's put that sentence in the past and say 'I was
going to study'. You already know the form ia.
             Eu ia estudar. (   )x   (   )x

66. How would you say 'I was going to send'?
(Eu ia mandar)
             Verify: (   )x   (   )x

67. How would you say 'He was going to send'?
(Ele ia mandar)
             Verify: (   )x   (   )x

68. Do you recall the appropriate we-form?
(íamos)
             Verify: (   )x   (   )x

69. So how would you say 'We were going to stay'? Use <u>nós</u>.
(Nós íamos ficar)

        Verify: (   )x (   )x

70. What is the corresponding they-form?
(iam)

        Verify: (   )x (   )x

71. How do you say 'They were going to stay'? Use <u>eles</u>.
(Eles iam ficar)

        Verify: (   )x (   )x

72. Continuing, say the following in Portuguese.
        a. They were going to sell.
        b. They were going to rest.
        c. We were going to rest.
        d. We were going to eat.
        e. I was going to write.
        f. He was going to prepare.
        g. I was going to drive.
        h. She was going to begin.

73. We can perform similar operations with the verb 'have'.
Remember the present tense construction 'I have to
study': <u>Eu</u> <u>tenho</u> <u>que</u> <u>estudar</u>. This kind of construction obviously describes <u>present</u> circumstances; it
describes what I feel obligated to do <u>now</u>.

        <u>Eu</u> <u>tenho</u> <u>que</u> <u>estudar</u> (   )x (   )x

74. If I wish to describe what I felt obligated to do at
some time in the <u>past</u>, I will use the form <u>tinha</u> 'I had'.
This is past description: it describes a certain set
of circumstances (i.e. my feelings of obligation) that
existed for me at some time in the past. Thus if I
want to say 'I had to study', I will say it like this.

        <u>Eu</u> <u>tinha</u> <u>que</u> <u>estudar</u> (   )x (   )x

75. How would you say 'I had to work'?
(Eu tinha que trabalhar)
     Verify: ( )x ( )x

76. How about '<u>He</u> had to work'?
(Ele tinha que trabalhar)
     Verify: ( )x ( )x

77. Continuing, how would you say the following?
  a. He had to practice. ( )x
  b. He had to write. ( )x
  c. We had to speak. ( )x
  d. We had to sell. ( )x
  e. They had to read. ( )x
  f. They had to prepare. ( )x

78. Another verb that is frequently used in the context
  of past description is <u>sabia</u> 'knew'.
   <u>sabia</u> ( )x ( )x

79. If I say <u>Eu</u> <u>sabia</u> <u>a</u> <u>lição</u> 'I knew the lesson'
  I am describing a certain state of affairs that
  existed in the past.
  <u>Eu</u> <u>sabia</u> <u>a</u> <u>lição</u>. ( )x ( )x

80. What is the we-form?
(sabíamos)
     Verify: ( )x ( )x

81. Using the pronoun <u>nós</u>, how would you say 'We knew the
  lesson'?
(Nós sabíamos a lição)
     Verify: ( )x ( )x

82. Using the pronoun <u>eles</u>, how would you say 'They knew
  the lesson'?
(Eles sabiam a lição)
     Verify: ( )x ( )x

83. It is very common to find <u>sabia</u> followed by <u>que</u> plus
    another verb which also gives past description. For
    example: 'I knew that José was Brazilian'.
    <u>Eu</u> <u>sabia</u> <u>que</u> <u>o</u> <u>José</u> <u>era</u> <u>brasileiro</u>. (   )x (   )x

84. Another example: 'I knew that José spoke Portuguese.'
    <u>Eu</u> <u>sabia</u> <u>que</u> <u>o</u> <u>José</u> <u>falava</u> <u>português</u>. (   )x (   )x

85. A further comment about José: 'I knew that José
    sold insurance'.
    <u>Eu</u> <u>sabia</u> <u>que</u> <u>o</u> <u>José</u> <u>vendia</u> <u>seguros</u>. (   )x (   )x

86. And a final comment about the activities of our friend,
    Joe: 'I didn't know that José slept so much'.
    <u>Eu</u> <u>não</u> <u>sabia</u> <u>que</u> <u>o</u> <u>José</u> <u>dormia</u> <u>tanto</u>. (   )x (   )x

87. Poor Joe! Still the sleepyhead! So......on to the
    dialog.

23.14

Dialogs/Exchanges

Exchange No. 1

o sapato	shoe
reparou	(you) noticed

A. Você reparou o sapato que ele usava?

A. Did you notice the shoes he was wearing?

B. Reparei, sim.

B. Yes, I did.

Exchange No. 2

o terno	suit

A. Por que é que o senhor não comprou o terno?

A. Why didn't you buy the suit?

custava	(it) cost
suficiente	enough
o dinheiro	money

B. Custava muito caro. Eu não tinha dinheiro suficiente.

B. It cost a lot. I didn't have enough money.

Exchange No. 3

procurou	(he) looked for
o emprego	job

A. Por que é que ele procurou outro emprego?

A. Why did he look for another job?

B. Porque ele não gostava do que tinha.

B. Because he didn't like the one he had.

Exchange No. 4

se perdeu	(he) got lost

A. Por que é que ele se perdeu?

A. Why did he get lost?

B. Porque ele não conhecia bem a cidade.

B. Because he didn't know the city well.

verdade	true (truth)

A. É verdade? Que pena!

A. Is that right? What a shame!

23.15

Expansion Exercises (Recorded)

I. The verb <u>reparar</u> 'to notice'
   Practice these sentences aloud. Be sure you know what they
   mean.
   1. O senhor reparou o sapato?
   2. O senhor reparou o sotaque dela?
   3. O senhor reparou que ele estava cansado?
   4. O senhor reparou que ele não sabia?
   5. O senhor reparou que ele não queria?
   -
   6. Eu não reparei.
   7. Eu não reparei isso.
   8. Eu não reparei a Alice.
   9. Eu não reparei que ela estava cansada.
  10. Eu não reparei que você queria falar comigo.

II. The verb <u>procurar</u> 'to look for'
   Practice these sentences with the tape. Be sure you know
   what they mean.
   1. Eu vou procurar outro emprego.
   2. Eu vou procurar mais dinheiro.
   3. Eu já procurei outro carro.
   4. Ela já procurou casa.
   5. Ele já procurou outra secretária.
   6. Sérgio vai procurar a dona Regina.
   7. Antônio procurava a dona Vera.
   8. Eles procuravam outro presidente.
   9. Nós estamos procurando a Seção Consular.
  10. Eles estão procurando a Embaixada Francesa.
  11. Ele está procurando outro sapato.
  12. Eu estou procurando a minha secretária.

23.16

III. The verb perder-se 'to get lost'
      Likewise, practice these with the tape and be sure you
      know what they mean.
      1. Eu me perdi.
      2. Ele se perdeu também.
      3. Você se perdeu também?
      4. Como é que você se perdeu?
      5. Ela nunca se perde.

IV.   A. Remember the verb dá? Notice how nicely it fits with
          dinheiro in these sentences. Follow along with the
          tape. If you need to, check the English in B below.
          1. O dinheiro dá?
          2. O dinheiro dá para comprar dois?
          3. O dinheiro dá para ir à praia?
          4. O dinheiro dá para todos?
          5. O dinheiro dá para comer num restaurante?
          6. O dinheiro dá para ficar mais um dia?
          7. O dinheiro dá para ir e voltar?

      B. Now, try putting these back into Portuguese.
          1. Is there enough money?
          2. Is there enough money to buy two?
          3. Is there enough money to go to the beach?
          4. Is there enough money for all?
          5. Is there enough money to eat in a restaurant?
          6. Is there enough money to stay one more day?
          7. Is there enough money to go and return?
                              (make a round trip)

      C. Practice repeating both roles in these exchanges.
          1. O dinheiro dá?
               Dá. Não custa nada.
          2. O dinheiro dá?
               Dá, sim. Custa muito pouco.

                              23.17

3. O dinheiro dá?

    Dá, sim. Custa um dólar só.

4. O dinheiro dá?

    Não, não dá. Custa muito caro.

    Que pena!

5. O dinheiro dá?

    Eu acho que dá.

End of Tape 11A

Tape 11B

V. More practice with _ava_ and _ia_ forms. (Recorded)

Note well the _ia_ and _ava_ forms in these sentences. Practice along with the tape.

1. O senhor sabia que ele era solteiro?
2. O senhor sabia que ele estava em Washington?
3. O senhor sabia que ele ia ao cinema?
4. O senhor sabia que ele ficava até tarde?
5. O senhor sabia que ele falava Chinês?
6. O senhor sabia que ele comia tanto?
7. O senhor sabia que ele não se sentia bem?
8. O senhor sabia que ele morava no Leme?
9. O senhor sabia que ele trabalhava na seção política?
10. O senhor sabia que ele não conhecia a cidade?
11. Eu não sabia que você tinha tanto dinheiro.
12. Eu não sabia que você era secretária.
13. Eu não sabia que você estava com pressa.
14. Eu não sabia que você estudava tanto!
15. Eu não sabia que você pretendia ficar.
16. Eu não sabia que você pretendia acordar cedo.
17. Eu não sabia que você ia almoçar aqui.
18. Eu não sabia que você ia morar em Copacabana.
19. Eu não sabia que você tinha que fazer isso.
20. Eu não sabia que você tinha que trabalhar amanhã.
21. Eu não sabia que você queria ler.
22. Eu não sabia que você queria ir comigo.
23. Eu não sabia que você queria levar sanduíches.
24. Eu não sabia que você falava francês.
25. Eu não sabia que você podia sair cedo.

23.18

VI. <u>More Names</u> (Recorded)

A. <u>First Names</u>

Practice these familiar looking first names which seem to be borrowed from English.

Mílton   Édson   Gíbson

Nélson   Wílson

B. <u>Family Names</u>

Here are just a few of the more common family names. We are limiting ourselves to one-syllable and two-syllable names. The longer ones will appear in the next unit.

1. <u>Two-syllable names</u>

Practice these with the tape.

Santos	Lopes	Silva	Prado
Campos	Gomes	Lima	Mello
Bastos	Fontes	Gama	Castro
Barros	Mendes	Costa	Lobo
Ramos	Neves	Rocha	
Mattos	Alves	Prata	
	Chaves	Cunha	
	Nunes	Braga	
	Marques	Fraga	
	Borges		

<u>With Diphthongs</u>

Moura	Leite
Souto	Freire
Sousa*	Freitas
	Eiras
	Queirós

---

*This is the same name as that of the American bandmaster and composer John Philip Sousa, whose father was Portuguese. If you didn't recognize the name when you first heard it, it's because you are used to hearing it pronounced differently in English.

With Nasal Diphthongs

Galvão

Leitão

Simão

Simões

2. **One-syllable names**

There are not many of these. Practice them with the tape.

Cruz

Reis (diphthong)

Vaz

Translations (Recorded)

I. Practice both roles in these exchanges. There is space on the tape for repetition after each sentence. The English equivalents appear in II below.

1. Por que é que você não comeu mais?
   Eu não estava com fome.

2. Por que é que você não deitou cedo?
   Eu não estava com sono.

3. Por que é que você não estudou ontem à noite?
   Eu não tinha o livro.

4. Por que é que você não foi lá ontem?
   Eu estava sem carro.

5. Por que é que você não foi ao cinema?
   Porque eu estava sem dinheiro.

6. Por que é que você não procurou outro emprego?
   Eu gostava do que eu tinha.

7. Por que é que você não falou com Dona Tânia?
   Porque eu estava atrasado. ('late')

8. Por que é que você não foi ao Rio?
   Ficava caro.

9. Por que é que você não estudou a outra lição também?
   Era difícil.

II. Now, practice putting these back into Portuguese. Check
     the tape or I above for confirmation.
     1. Why didn't you eat more?
         I wasn't hungry.
     2. Why didn't you go to bed early?
         I wasn't sleepy.
     3. Why didn't you study last night?
         I didn't have my (the) book.
     4. Why didn't you go there yesterday?
         I didn't have my car. (Use estar sem)
     5. Why didn't you go to the movies?
         Because I didn't have the money. (Use estar sem)
     6. Why didn't you look for another job?
         I liked the one I had.
     7. Why didn't you talk to dona Tânia?
         Because I was late.
     8. Why didn't you go to Rio?
         It was expensive. (Use ficar.)
     9. Why didn't you study the other lesson too?
         It was difficult.

III. Practice both roles in these exchanges.
      1. Ele procurou outro emprego?
          Procurou. Ele não gostava do que tinha.
      2. Ele chegou atrasado?
          Chegou. Antes tarde do que nunca, não é?*
      3. Você reparou o terno dele?
          Reparei. Era bonito, não era?
      4. Você ficou em casa?
          Fiquei. Eu estava cansado.
      5. Você comprou o Chevrolet?
          Não, não comprei. Custava muito caro.
      6. Você comprou o livro?
          Não, não comprei. Eu já tinha.

*Better late than never.

23.21

7. Você reparou como a Vera estava bonita?

Reparei, sim.

8. Você se perdeu?

Me perdi. Eu não conhecia a cidade.

9. Você chegou atrasado?

Cheguei. Eu não sabia que horas eram.

IV. Now, put these back into Portuguese. Check with III in case of doubt.

1. Did he look for another job?

He did. He didn't like the one he had.

2. Did he get here late?

He did. Better late than never, right?

3. Did you notice his suit?

I did. It looked nice, didn't it?

4. Did you stay home?

I did. I was tired.

5. Did you buy the Chevrolet?

No, I didn't. It cost too much.

6. Did you buy the book?

No, I didn't. I already had [it].

7. Did you notice how pretty Vera was?

Yes, I did.

8. Did you get lost?

Yes, I did. I didn't know the city.

9. Did you get here late?

Yes, I did. I didn't know what time it was.

V. Practice these very brief 'give and takes' with your teacher. The more expressive you are with these, the more fun they are.

1. É verdade?

Claro.

Nossa!

2. É verdade?
   Não, não é.
   Que bom!

3. É verdade?
   É, sim.
   Que pena!

4. É verdade?
   É, sim.
   Ah, é?

5. É verdade?
   É, sim.
   Não pode ser!
   Mas é!
   Nossa!

6. É verdade?
   É mesmo!
   Opa!*

*Another one of those untranslatable Brazilian gems. This one
shows surprise.

23.23

Unit 24

Part I

1. In past units you have practiced a number of words whose
    singular forms end in stressed -el (open E).

    a. papel   (   )x   (   )x
    b. pastel   (   )x   (   )x
    c. hotel   (   )x   (   )x

2. In this unit you will practice several words in which the
    -el ending is unstressed. You already know one of these
    words.

    horrível   (   )x   (   )x

3. Notice that you hear the stress on the i, not the final -el.
    According to the conventions of spelling the stress is indeed
    written over the i.

    horrível   (   )x   (   )x

4. The e of el is unstressed and closed. Repeat again.

    horrível   (   )x   (   )x

5. Here is a new word. Can you guess what it means?

            (   )   (   )
    (possible)

6. Here it is again. This time repeat.

    possível   (   )x   (   )x

7. How would you say 'It is possible'?
    (É possível)

            Verify: (   )x   (   )x

24.1

8. He1e is another new word. You should be able to guess its
    meaning too.

          (   )   (   )

    (impossible)

9. Now repeat.
          impossível   (   )x   (   )x   (   )x

10. So, how would you say 'It is impossible'?

    (É impossível)

          Verify: (   )x   (   )x

11. Here is another word which you can also probably guess at.

          (   )   (   )

    (probable)

12. Now, listen again and repeat.

          provável   (   )x   (   )x

13. Be sure to get the stress on the right syllable, that is,
    on the middle one.

          (   )x   (   )x   (   )x

14. So how would you say 'It's probable'?

    (É provável)
          Verify: (   )x   (   )x

15. And how would you say 'It's not probable'?

    (Não é provável)
          Verify: (   )x   (   )x

16. Can you guess what this word means?
            (   )   (   )
(improbable)

17. Now, listen again and repeat.
            improvável   (   )x   (   )x

18. How do you say 'It's improbable'?
(É improvável)
            Verify: (   )x   (   )x

19. You know the verb evitar which means 'avoid'. Therefore
     you should be able to guess what this word means.
            (   )   (   )
(avoidable)

20. Now, listen again and repeat.
            evitável   (   )x   (   )x   (   )x

21. What does this one mean?
                    (   )   (   )
(Unavoidable, inevitable)

22. Listen again and repeat.
     inevitável   (   )x   (   )x   (   )x

23. So how would you say 'It's inevitable'?
(É inevitável)
            Verify: (   )x   (   )x

24. The verb aceitar means 'accept'. Repeat.
            (   )x   (   )x

24.3

25. What, then, does this word mean?

( ) ( )

(acceptable)

26. Listen again and repeat.

aceitável ( )x ( )x ( )x

27. How do you say 'It's acceptable'?
(É aceitável)

Verify: ( )x ( )x

28. What do you suppose this word means?

( ) ( )

(unacceptable)

29. Listen again and repeat.

inaceitável ( )x ( )x ( )x

30. Finally, then, how do you say 'It's unacceptable'?
(É inaceitável)

Verify: ( )x ( )x

31. The above items are all adjectives and they are in their
singular forms. When they are used with plural nouns they
will appear in their plural forms. Here, for example, is
the plural form of 'horrible'.

( )x ( )x ( )x

32. Here it is again. The -eis diphthong has the closed e.

horríveis ( )x ( )x

33. Try the singular and the plural together. Be sure the stress
    is on the right syllable, that is, the middle one.

    <u>horrível</u>   (   )x   (   )x
    <u>horríveis</u> (   )x   (   )x

34. This is the way you say 'horrible party'.

    (   )x   (   )x

35. And this is the way you say the plural, 'horrible parties'.

    (   )x   (   )x

36. How would you say 'horrible cities'?
(cidades horríveis)
        Verify: (   )x   (   )x

37. How would you say 'horrible machines'?
(máquinas horríveis)
        Verify: (   )x   (   )x

38. How about 'horrible dialogs'?
(diálogos horríveis)
        Verify: (   )x   (   )x

39. If the plural of <u>horrível</u> is <u>horríveis</u>, you should be able
    to guess at the plural of <u>possível</u>. What is it?
(possíveis)
    Right! Now, verify just to be sure. (   )x   (   )x

40. Likewise, what is the plural form of <u>provável</u>?
(prováveis)
        Verify: (   )x   (   )x

41. What is the plural of <u>inevitável</u>?

(inevitáveis)
Verify: (   )x   (   )x

42. And what is the plural of <u>aceitável</u>?
(aceitáveis)
Verify: (   )x   (   )x

43. Practice saying the following:
    a. São possíveis   (   )x   (   )x
    b. São prováveis   (   )x   (   )x
    c. São aceitáveis   (   )x   (   )x
    d. São inevitáveis   (   )x   (   )x
    e. São impossíveis   (   )x   (   )x
    f. São inaceitáveis   (   )x   (   )x

44. All of the above items are adjectives. There are, however,
     some nouns that follow the same pattern. One of them is the
     word 'tunnel', which you probably remember.
        (Sing.) <u>túnel</u>   (   )x   (   )x
        (Pl.)   <u>túneis</u> (   )x   (   )x

45. Another is 'automobile'.
        (Sing.) <u>automóvel</u>   (   )x   (   )x   (   )x
        (Pl.)   <u>automóveis</u> (   )x   (   )x   (   )x

46. So, if you wanted to, you could construct the sentence:
     'The two automobiles have to pass through the tunnels'.
     <u>Os</u> <u>dois</u> <u>automóveis</u> <u>tem</u> <u>que</u> <u>passar</u> <u>pelos</u> <u>túneis</u>.

        (   )   (   )x   (   )x   (   )x

47. Now let us move to a related subject. You will recall that
     you have practiced saying several words that end in <u>stressed</u>
     <u>-il</u>.
        a. <u>civil</u>   (   )x   (   )x
        b. <u>gentil</u>   (   )x   (   )x

48. In this unit you will practice saying several words that end
    in unstressed -il. One of them is already familiar to you.

    difícil   (   )x   (   )x

49. Perhaps you have already run across the word which means
    just the opposite of difícil; i.e. the word for 'easy'.
    They make a logical pair.

    fácil   (   )x   (   )x

50. Be sure that you get the stress on the next-to-the-last
    syllable of both words.

    difícil   (   )x   (   )x
    fácil   (   )x   (   )x

51. Here is another common word which is often cited along with
    fácil and difícil as another example of the same sort. It
    is certainly a useful item.

    útil   (   )x   (   )x

52. Can you guess what this useful item means? Have we given
    you enough clues?
(useful)

53. Even if we hadn't given you the clues, you might have guessed
    that útil means useful by association with the English word
    'utilitarian'. Always give cognates a try! Now, repeat again.
    Notice that the first syllable is ú, not you.

    1. ú   (   )x   (   )x
    2. til   (   )x   (   )x
    3. útil (   )x   (   )x

54. Practice saying these short utterances, all of which begin
     with 'It is...'.
         1. É fácil   (   )x   (   )x
         2. É difícil   (   )x   (   )x
         3. É útil   (   )x   (   )x

55. The above words end in unstressed eis in their plural forms.

     fáceis   (   )x   (   )x
     difíceis (   )x   (   )x
     úteis   (   )x   (   )x

56. Now practice saying the following:
         a. São fáceis   (   )x   (   )x
         b. São difíceis   (   )x   (   )x
         c. São úteis   (   )x   (   )x

57. This is the way you say 'difficult dialogs'.
     diálogos difíceis   (   )x   (   )x

58. How would you say 'easy dialogs'?
(diálogos fáceis)
         Verify: (   )x   (   )x

59. How would you say 'useful dialogs'?
(diálogos úteis)
         Verify: (   )x   (   )x

60. How would you say 'useful books'?
(livros úteis)
         Verify: (   )x   (   )x

61. How about 'easy books'?
(livros fáceis)
         Verify: (   )x   (   )x

62. And 'difficult books'?
(livros difíceis)
           Verify: (   )x   (   )x

Note: The practices that follow will give you additional
       experience using some of the above adjectives in their
       singular forms.

Practice 1.   (Recorded)

Practice saying these sentences.
1. É fácil trabalhar com ele.
2. É fácil bater à máquina.
    - - - - - - - - - - - -
3. É difícil falar português.
4. É difícil conhecer o Jorge.
    - - - - - - - - - - - -
5. É possível sair cedo.
6. Não é possível fazer isso.
    - - - - - - - - - - - -
7. É impossível saber a verdade.
8. Não é impossível voltar hoje.
    - - - - - - - - - - - -
9. É útil saber isso.
10. Não é muito útil falar inglês.
    - - - - - - - - - - - -
11. É horrível morar lá!
12. É horrível viajar com ele.

Practice 2.

You can form various interesting combinations by putting the
items on the left together with the items on the right. Experi-
ment a bit. All combinations are possible and most are likely.
Just a few of them have been recorded for you.

24.9

1. É fácil	a. trabalhar com ele
2. É difícil	b. vender o carro
3. É possível	c. bater à máquina
4. É impossível	d. morar em Recife
	e. ensinar história
	f. ser bom funcionário
	g. comprar as passagens aqui
	h. falar com Alice
	i. fazer isso
	j. voltar cedo
	k. levar sanduíches
	l. falar português

Practice 3. (Recorded)

Combinations of the sort practiced above can also be cast into
the past. Repeat these short phrases.
1. Foi fácil sair cedo.
2. Foi difícil preparar o diálogo.
3. Foi possível fazer tudo.
4. Foi impossível voltar ontem.
5. Foi útil falar com ela.
6. Foi horrível trabalhar para essa empresa.
7. Foi fácil escrever essa carta.
8. Foi muito difícil acordar cedo.

Practice 4. (Recorded)

Such combinations are also commonly cast into the future mold,
i.e. in terms of 'It's going to be.......' Repeat the following
sentences.
1. Vai ser impossível falar com ele.
2. Vai ser fácil sair cedo.
3. Vai ser muito difícil esquecer isso.
4. Vai ser útil conhecer o Presidente.
5. Vai ser horrível ficar em casa hoje.

6. Vai ser possível sair cedo amanhã.
7. Não vai ser fácil levantar às cinco.
8. Não vai ser possível começar hoje.

Practice 5. (Recorded)

Practice participating in these very brief exchanges.
1. É difícil?
   Não, é muito fácil.
2. É difícil?
   É, sim. Muito difícil.
3. É fácil?
   Não, não é. É difícil.
4. É difícil?
   É, sim. Mas é possível.
5. É possível?
   É, sim. Mas é difícil.
6. É impossível?
   Não, não é. Mas é muito difícil.
7. É fácil?
   Não, não é. Mas é possível.
- - - - - - - - - - -
8. Foi fácil?
   Foi, mesmo. Muito fácil!
9. Foi difícil?
   Foi, mesmo. Difícil demais!
10. Foi possível?
    Não, não foi. Foi impossível!

Part II

1. Recall this item from a previous dialog.
   <u>vistas</u> <u>maravilhosas</u>   ( )x   ( )x

2. Notice the open <u>o</u> in <u>maravilhosas</u>.
   <u>maravilhọsas</u>   ( )x   ( )x

24.11

3. Now look at the singular form: 'marvelous view'.
    <u>vista</u> <u>maravilhosa</u>   (   )x   (   )x

4. Again, notice the open <u>o</u> in <u>maravilhosa</u>.
    <u>maravilhOsa</u>   (   )x   (   )x

5. Now, examine the item 'marvelous state'. Remember, 'state'
    is masculine.
    <u>estado</u> <u>maravilhoso</u>   (   )x   (   )x

6. Did you notice that the first <u>o</u> of -<u>oso</u> is the closed <u>o</u>,
    and not the open <u>O</u>? Listen again, and repeat.
    <u>estado</u> <u>maravilhoso</u>   (   )X   (   )X

7. Compare the open <u>O</u> with the closed <u>o</u>.
    <u>maravilhOsa</u>   (   )X   (   )X
    <u>maravilhoso</u>   (   )X   (   )X

8. A number of adjectives that have the open <u>O</u> in their feminine
    forms will have the closed <u>o</u> in their masculine forms. Here
    is the adjective 'famous' used with a feminine noun.
    <u>senhora</u> <u>famosa</u>   (   )X   (   )X

9. Notice the open <u>O</u> in <u>famosa</u>.
    <u>senhora</u> <u>famOsa</u>   (   )X   (   )X

10. Now, here is 'famous' used to describe 'book', a masculine
    noun.
    <u>livro</u> <u>famoso</u>   (   )X   (   )X

11. Notice the closed <u>o</u> in <u>famoso</u>.
    <u>livro</u> <u>famoso</u>   (   )X   (   )X

12. You will hear another new adjective in this item: 'tasty
    (or 'delicious') food'.
    comida gostosa   ( )x   ( )x

13. Listen to the open O in gostosa.
    gostOsa   ( )x   ( )x

14. In 'tasty sandwich' the o is closed since sandwich is
    masculine.
    sanduíche gostoso   ( )x   ( )x

15. You have had the adjective 'new' in the phrase novo
    professor.*
    novo professor   ( )x   ( )x

16. Notice the closed o.
    novo professor   ( )x   ( )x

17. Listen to what happens when you say 'new (lady) teacher'.
    nova professora   ( )x   ( )x

18. Did you notice the open O of nova? Here it is again.
    nOva professora   ( )x   ( )x

19. Now, listen to and repeat these contrasting forms again.
    a. novo   ( )x   nOva   ( )x
    b. famoso   ( )x   famOsa   ( )x
    c. gostoso   ( )x   gostOsa   ( )x
    d. maravilhoso ( )x   maravilhOsa ( )x

---

* 'New' is one of those adjectives that sometimes comes before
the noun.

24.13

Practice 1.   (Recorded)

Repeat the following items several times until you feel comfortable with them.

1. americano famoso
2. livro famoso
3. jornal famoso

----

4. americana famosa
5. praia famosa
6. casa famosa

----

7. livro maravilhoso
8. sanduíche maravilhoso
9. feriado maravilhoso

----

10. cidade maravilhosa (otherwise known as Rio de Janeiro)
11. praia maravilhosa
12. máquina maravilhosa

----

13. dia gostoso*
14. café gostoso
15. passeio gostoso

----

16. comida gostosa
17. praia gostosa
18. vista gostosa

----

19. novo presidente.
20. novo funcionário
21. novo consulado

----

22. nova idéia
23. nova amiga
24. nova professora

----

* gostoso/a can also mean 'pleasant, agreeable'.

24.14

(We return now to our programmed format.)

20. How would you say 'famous restaurant'?
(restaurante famoso)
        Verify: (   )x   (   )x

21. How would you say 'famous avenue'?
(avenida famosa)
        Verify: (   )x   (   )x

22. How would you say 'marvelous party'?
(festa maravilhosa)
        Verify: (   )x   (   )x

23. How about 'marvelous Portuguese'?
(português maravilhoso)
        Verify: (   )x   (   )x

24. How would you say 'delicious soft-drink'?
(refrigerante gostoso)
        Verify: (   )x   (   )x

25. And how about 'delicious meal'?
(comida gostosa)
        Verify: (   )x   (   )x

26. Here is 'delicious sandwich', with the stressed o̲ closed.
    sanduíche gostoso   (   )x   (   )x

27. Listen to what happens if we make it plural. Do not
    repeat yet.
    sanduíches gostosos   (   )   (   )

28. The stressed o̲ of gostosos is OPEN! Listen and repeat.
    gostos̲os   (   )x   (   )x

29. Now, again, listen and repeat.
         sanduíches gost_O_sos   (   )X   (   )X

30. Here is the way you say 'famous books'.
         livros fam_O_sos   (   )X   (   )X

31. And here is 'marvelous restaurants'.
         restaurantes maravilh_O_sos   (   )X   (   )X

32. What we are showing you here is that adjectives of this
    type have the open _O_ in the masculine <u>plural</u> forms, even
    though they have the closed _o_ in the masculine <u>singular.</u>
    Compare the following. ˙
         1. livro famoso   (   )X
         2. livros fam_O_sos   (   )X
             ----
         3. americano famoso   (   )X
         4. americanos fam_O_sos   (   )X
             ----
         5. refrigerante gostoso
         6. refrigerantes gost_O_sos (   )X
             ----
         7. novo professor   (   )X
         8. n_O_vos professores   (   )X

33. It may be easier to look at it this way: adjectives of the
    above sort have the open _O_ except in the masculine singular
    form.   Compare.
         1. praia fam_O_sa   (   )X
         2. praias fam_O_sas   (   )X
         3. livros fam_O_sos   (   )X
                 (but)
         4. livro famoso   (   )X

34. Examine this series.
    1. festa maravilh<u>o</u>sa   (   )x
    2. festas maravilh<u>o</u>sas   (   )x
    3. feriados maravilh<u>o</u>sos (   )x
           (but)
    4. feriado maravilhoso   (   )x

35. Now, examine this series.
    1. comida gost<u>o</u>sa   (   )x
    2. comidas gost<u>o</u>sas   (   )x
    3. dias gost<u>o</u>sos   (   )x
           (but)
    4. dia gostoso   (   )x

36. Finally, examine this series.
    1. n<u>o</u>va casa   (   )x
    2. n<u>o</u>vas casas   (   )x
    3. n<u>o</u>vos livros   (   )x
           (but)
    4. novo livro   (   )x

37. On to the dialog!

DIALOG

Aluno A

O senhor vai para Porto Alegre,
não é?

You're going to Porto
Alegre, aren't you?

Aluno B

Não. Eu ia, mas agora eu
vou para o Rio.

No. I was going, but
now I'm going to Rio.

Aluno A

Por quê? O que é que
aconteceu?

Why? What happened?

Aluno B

chefe   boss
telefonou   telephoned
(neutral form = telefonar)

Bom, o meu chefe me telefonou
ontem à noite.

Well, my boss phoned me
last night.

Aluno A

aí   there
E daí?   And so? (And from there?)*

Aluno B

precisam   they need
   (neutral form = precisar)
alguém   someone
comercial   commercial

Eles precisam de alguém na
seção comercial de lá!

They need someone in the
Commercial Section there.

---

* de + aí = contraction daí.

                              24.18

Aluno A

vai ver	maybe
acabar	to end (up), to finish
indo (neutral form = <u>ir</u>)	going

<u>Vai ver que EU vou acabar indo</u>
<u>para Porto Alegre</u>!

<u>Maybe I'll end up going to</u>
<u>Porto Alegre.</u>

Aluno B

pois	so, then

<u>Pois é.</u>

<u>That's right.</u>

Expansion Exercises   (Recorded)

I.   The verb acabar + -ndo form

   1. Eu vou acabar estudando mais.

   2. Eu vou acabar praticando menos.

   3. Eu vou acabar comprando outro.

   4. Eu vou acabar esquecendo tudo.

   ----

   5. Ele vai acabar morando no Rio.

   6. Ele vai acabar almoçando em casa.

   7. Ele vai acabar bebendo só água ('water').

   8. Ele vai acabar trabalhando para uma empresa particular.

II. The verb precisar

   1. Eles precisam de uma secretária.

   2. Eles precisam de outro carro.

   ----

   3. Eu precisava de outro livro.

   4. Eu precisava dum refrigerante.

   ----

   5. Ela vai precisar dum emprego.

   6. Ela vai precisar de outra passagem.

   ----

   7. Nós precisamos de outro presidente.

   8. Nós precisamos de mais dinheiro.

End of Tape 11B

III. <u>Last</u> <u>Names</u>

A.   Practice saying these 3-syllable last names.   All
but the last two are stressed on the next-to-the-last
syllable.

Andrade	Fernandes
Aranha	Fonseca
Barbosa	Gonçalves
Botelho	Tavares
Cardoso	Amaral (last syllable stressed)
Carvalho	Avelar (last syllable stressed)
Castelo	
Coelho	

B.   These also have three syllables but we have
grouped them together because they all have the <u>ei</u>
diphthong.

Almeida	Carneiro
Silveira	Monteiro
Moreira	Ribeiro
Ferreira	Pinheiro
Pereira	Medeiros
Siqueira	Peixoto
Nogueira	
Teixeira	
Caldeira	
Bandeira	
Correia	
Vieira	

C.   These have the stressed nasal diphthong ãe.
Magalhães
Guimarães

24.21

D.   Now practice these 4-syllable last names.

Albuquerque

Alvarenga

Azevedo

Cavalcante

Oliv<u>ei</u>ra   (<u>ei</u> diphthong again)

Figu<u>ei</u>redo   (<u>ei</u> diphthong again)

Vasconcelos

D'Alcântara (stressed on third-from-last syllable)

Brief Exchanges

I. A. Practice these exchanges with the tape. Check B on the
next page for the English.

1. Você acha que ele vai trabalhar na Seção Comercial?
Bom, é bem possível.

2. Vocês vão jantar no restaurante em frente?
É bem provável.

3. Vocês vão chegar lá às sete horas?
É impossível. É cedo demais.

4. O vocabulário* desta** lição é bom, não é?
É. É muito útil.

5. Ela gosta de estudar francês?
Gosta, sim. Mas é difícil.

6. O senhor sabe chegar na nossa casa?
Sei, sim. É fácil.

---

* A new word, but a cognate!
** Another contraction: de + esta = desta.

24.23

7. O senhor leu os livros?
   Li, sim. São muito úteis.

B. Now put these into Portuguese.

1. Do you think he's going to work in the Commercial
   Section?
   Well, it's quite possible.

2. Are you (all) going to have dinner in the restaurant
   across the street?
   It's very probable.

3. Are you (all) going to get there at seven?
   It's impossible. It's too early.

4. The vocabulary of this lesson is good, isn't it?
   Yes. It's very useful.

5. Does she like to study French?
   Yes, she does. But it's difficult.

6. Do you know how to get to our house?
   Yes, I do. It's easy.

7. Did you read the books?
   Yes. They're very useful.

II. A. Practice these with the tapes. The English is in B. below.

1. Você acha que ele já está aqui?
   Não, eu não acho possível.

2. Você acha que ele já saiu?
   Eu acho muito possível, sim.

24.24

3. Você acha que eu vou gostar?
   Eu acho muito provável, sim.

4. Você acha que a gente pode?
   Bom....eu acho muito difícil.

5. Você acha que a gente tem que viajar <u>hoje</u>?
   Eu acho inevitável.

6. Você acha que o dinheiro dá?
   Não, não acho. É impossível.

B. 1. Do you think he's already here?
      No, I don't think [it's] possible.

   2. Do you think he has left already?
      I think [it's] very possible, yes.

   3. Do you think I'm going to like [it]?
      I think you probably will, yes.

   4. Do you think we can?
      Well....I think it's very difficult.

   5. Do you think we'll have to travel <u>today</u>?
      I think it's inevitable.

   6. Do you think there's enough money?
      No, I don't. It's impossible.

III. A. Now try these. Numbers 4-10 deal with the construction
não + verb + mais. This translates as 'any more', 'any
longer' or 'not now', depending on the sentence. See
B. below for the English.

1. Eu achava que ela ia para o Rio.
   Ela ia, mas agora ela vai para São Paulo.

2. Eu achava que a gente ia a Baltimore.
   A gente ia, mas o pneu furou.

3. Eu achava que a gente ia à praia.
   Ia, mas agora parece que vai chover.

4. Eu achava que ela ia à festa.
   Ela ia, mas não vai mais. Ela vai ficar em casa.

5. Eu achava que você ia estudar.
   Ia, mas não vou mais. Eu vou ao cinema.

6. Nós achávamos que a senhora morava no Leblon.
   Eu morava, sim. Mas não moro mais.

7. A gente achava que o senhor trabalhava na seção
   comercial.
   Trabalhava. Mas eu não trabalho mais.

8. Eu achava que a festa ia ser na sua casa.
   Ia, sim. Mas não vai ser mais.

9. Eu achava que ela era solteira.
   Era. Mas não é mais. Ela é casada.

10. Eu achava que vocês tinham uma casa na praia.
    Tínhamos, sim. Mas não temos mais. Nós vendemos.

24.26

B. 1. I thought she was going to Rio.
        She was, but now she's going to São Paulo.

    2. I thought we were going to Baltimore.
        We were, but the tire blew out.

    3. I thought we were going to the beach.
        We were, but now it looks like it's going to rain.

    4. I thought that she was going to the party.
        She was, but she isn't any longer. She is going
        to stay home.

    5. I thought that you were going to study.
        I was going to, but not now. I'm going to the movies.

    6. We thought you lived in Leblon.
        I did, but I don't live there any more.

    7. We thought you worked in the Commercial Section.
        I did, but I don't work there any more.

    8. I thought the party was going to be at your place.
        It was, yes, but not now.

    9. I thought she was single.
        She used to be, but she's not any more. She's married.

   10. I thought you had a house on the beach.
        We used to, but we don't have [it] any longer.
        We sold [it].

I V.   These will give you some more insight into the use of
       '<u>e daí</u>?', meaning 'and so?'.

    1.   Vai chover amanhã.
       E daí?
       A gente não vai poder ir à praia.

    2.   Ele só vai me dar o dinheiro sexta-feira.
       E daí?
       Eu preciso do dinheiro hoje.

    3.   Nós só vamos ao Rio.
       E daí?
       Nós queríamos ir a São Paulo também.

    4.   O pneu furou.
       E daí?
       A gente não vai.

    5.   Eu tenho só cinco cruzeiros.
       E daí?
       A gente não come hoje.

    6.   Eu não gosto de levantar cedo nos fins de semana.
       E daí?
       Eu tenho que levantar muito cedo amanhã.

Unit 25

REVIEW

This review has been divided into three sections.

Section I.   Nouns, Contractions, Adjectives

Section II.   Verbs

Section III.   The verbs <u>Ser</u>, <u>Estar</u>, <u>Ir</u>, <u>Ter</u>

25.1

Section I

Nouns, Contractions, Adjectives

Nouns

Practice 1. The definite articles

Be sure you know the gender of the following items. Translate these aloud.
1.   the newspaper
2.   the examination
3.   the beach
4.   the book
5.   the ticket
6.   the door
7.   the daughter
8.   the soft drink
9.   the mountain
10. the officer
11. the company
12. the section
13. the sandwich
14. the night
15. the hour
16. the opportunity
17. the weekend
18. the post card
19. the holiday
20   the heat

Practice 2. The indefinite articles

Be sure you know the gender of these. Translate aloud.

1. a party
2. a park
3. a tunnel
4. an avenue
5. a week
6. a city
7. an idea
8. a restaurant
9. a sleepyhead
10. a bridge
11. a letter
12. a lady
13. a gentleman
14. a secretary
15. a house
16. a school
17. a suit
18. a day

Practice 3. 'Some'

Go through the above list of words (those in Practice 2) and make them plural, i.e. be sure you can say 'some parties, some parks, some tunnels', etc. Do them aloud.

Practice 4. 'This' and 'that'; 'these' and 'those'

Now try these. Do them aloud.

1. this lesson
2. this view
3. this car
4. this state
5. this office
6. this embassy

25.3

7. that word
8. that idea
9. that accent
10. that coffee
11. that letter
12. that girl
----
13. these mountains
14. these beaches
15. these days
16. these matters
17. these houses
18. these lessons
----
19. those gentlemen
20. those books
21. those sandwiches
22. those machines
23. those words
24. those tunnels

Practice 5. Possessives: 'my', 'your', 'our'

Do these aloud too.
1. my house
2. my book
3. my mother
4. my money
5. my accent
6. my son
7. my shoes (singular)
----
8. your English
9. your coffee
10. your wife

25.4

11. your tire
12. your grammar
13. your office
14. your friend
----
15. our son
16. our daughter
17. our embassy
18. our money
19. our door
20. our teacher (masc.)
21. our teacher (fem.)
22. our school
23. our car
24. our hour!

The following all deal with plural items.

25. my ideas
26. my windows
27. my friends (masc.)
28. my parents
29. my books
30. my daughters
31. my sons
----
32. your parties
33. your letters
34. your parents
35. your newspapers
36. your opportunities
37. your words
38. your teachers (masc.)
----
39. our tickets
40. our machines
41. our sandwiches

25.5

42. our tables
43. our friends
44. our cities
45. our weekends

Practice 7. Possessives: 'his', 'her'

Remember that you can say 'his car' by rephrasing it as 'the car of him' — o carro dele. The dele is a contraction of de + ele. Likewise, 'her car' is phrased as 'the car of her' — o carro dela. The dela is a contraction of de + ela. With this in mind, try the following.

1. His money
2. His accent
3. His wife
4. His daughter
5. His son
6. His shoes (singular)
7. His Chevrolet
----
8. Her party
9. Her typewriter (machine)
10. Her coffee
11. Her breaktime
12. Her letter
13. Her job
14. Her Ford

The following are plural, so you will begin each one either with os for masculine items or as for feminine items.

15. His cars
16. His sandwiches
17. His daughters
18. His parents
19. His sons
20. His words

25.6

21. Her cars
22. Her sandwiches
23. Her daughters
24. Her parents
25. Her words

Practice 8. Possessives with names

Remember that you can say 'Paul's car' by rephrasing it as 'the car of Paul' = <u>o carro do Paulo</u>. Likewise, 'Mary's car' = <u>o carro da Maria</u>. With this in mind, do the following.

1. Paul's book
2. Paul's accent
3. Paul's secretary
4. Paul's ticket
----
5. Luís's wife
6. Luís's money
7. Luís's house
8. Luís's shoes (singular)
----
9. Sonia's son
10. Sonia's idea
11. Sonia's English
12. Sonia's letter
----
13. Inês's coffee
14. Inês's ticket
15. Inês's food
16. Inês's Chevrolet

The following are plural.
Example: <u>os carros do Bill</u> = Bill's cars
Example: <u>as crianças do Bill</u> = Bill's children

25.7

17. Antônio's books
18. Antônio's friends
19. Antônio's tickets
20. Antônio's sons
----
21. Angela's children
22. Angela's letters
23. Angela's parents
24. Angela's friends (fem.)

Contractions: ao and à

Practice 9. (Warm-up)

Practice saying these items containing the contractions
ao and à.

ao Rio
ao parque
ao centro
ao restaurante
ao escritório
ao Consulado
ao funcionário
ao departamento
ao meio-dia

à secretária
à empresa
à cidade
à Embaixada
à Seção Consular
à professora
à Alemanha
à Dona Lúcia

25.8

Practice 10.

Now, translate these.

1. I'm going to Rio.
2. I'm going downtown.
3. I'm going to the office.
4. I'm going to the Embassy.
5. I'm going to the Political Section.
6. I'm going at noon.

----

7. Let's go to the restaurant.
8. Let's go to the park.
9. Let's go to the city.
10. Let's go to the Consulate.
11. Let's go to England.
12. Let's go to Joe's house.

----

13. We sent [him] to the Consulate.
14. We sent [him] to the Embassy.
15. We sent [him] downtown.
16. We sent [him] to Germany.
17. We sent [him] to Rio.
18. We sent [him] to Brazil.
19. We sent [him] to her house.

----

20. I went to bed at 11:00.   (deitar)
21. I fell asleep at midnight.   (cair no sono)
22. I awoke at 6:30.   (acordar)
23. I got up at 7:00.   (levantar)
24. I left at 8:00.   (sair)
25. I arrived at 8:30.   (chegar)
26. I began at 9:00.   (começar)
27. I ate lunch at noon.   (almoçar)

Contractions: plural <u>aos</u> and <u>às</u>

Practice 11. (Warm-up)
    Repeat these examples.

    aos pais
    aos filhos
    aos funcionários
    aos escritórios
    aos brasileiros
    aos americanos
    aos senhores

    às cidades
    às senhoras
    às festas
    às sete
    às oito
    às professoras
    às montanhas

Practice 12.
    Now, translate these sentences.

    1.   I am going to the mountains.
    2.   He is going to the cities.
    3.   We are going to the parties.
    4.   She is going at seven.
    5.   We went to the parks.
    6.   He went to the offices downtown.
    7.   They are going to the restaurants.
    8.   I went at ten.
    9.   She went yesterday at three.
    10. They went to the schools.

Contractions: <u>do</u>, <u>da</u>, <u>dos</u>, <u>das</u>

<u>Practice 13</u>. (Warm-up)

First, warm up with these examples.

do senhor
do funcionário
do jornal
do fim de semana
do sanduíche
do José
----
dos senhores
dos funcionários
dos jornais
dos fins de semana
dos sanduíches
dos meninos
----
da senhora
da secretária
da Seção Política
da máquina
da professora
da Vera
----
das senhoras
das secretárias
das seções
das máquinas
das professoras
das crianças

25.11

Practice 14.

Now, practice saying these sentences as you hear them on the tape. Pay attention to the contractions.

1. Eu gosto do Brasil.
2. Eu não gosto da cidade.

3. Eu gosto do Senhor Campos.
4. Eu não gosto da Dona Vânia.

5. Eu gosto muito do Senhor Gomes.
6. Eu não gosto da secretária dele.

7. Nós falamos muito dos professores
8. Eles falam muito dos alunos.

9. Ela falou bem da empresa.
10. Ele falou bem da secretária.

11. O que é que o senhor acha da Seção Consular?
12. O que é que o senhor acha do Departamento de Estado?

13. O que é que o senhor falou da Dona Regina?
14. O que é que o senhor falou do Senhor Lopes?

15. O que é que ele achou das crianças?
16. O que é que ele achou dos pais?

17. Ela é da Inglaterra.
18. Ele é da Alemanha.

19. O senhor precisa da máquina?
20. A senhora precisa do carro?

25.12

21.   Este sapato é do Luís.

22.   E este terno, é do Marcos?

23.   A senhora é do Brasil?

24.   Sou. Sou do Rio.

Contractions: <u>no</u>, <u>na</u>, <u>nos</u>, <u>nas</u>

<u>Practice 15</u>.   (Warm-up)

    Repeat these examples after the voice on the tape.

no departamento

no carro

no feriado

no fim de semana

no Rio

no sanduíche

no jornal

----

na máquina

na terça-feira

na Seção Consular

na empresa

na montanha

na ponte

na praia

----

nos jornais

nos departamentos

nos carros

nos feriados

nos fins de semana

nos escritórios

nos passeios

----

nas notícias
nas máquinas
nas montanhas
nas praias
nas pontes
nas embaixadas
nas cidades

Practice 16.

Now, participate in these exchanges as you hear them on the tape.

1. Onde é que ele está?
2. Está no escritório.

3. Ele estava na praia?
4. Não, estava nas montanhas.

5. Onde o senhor trabalhava antes?
6. Trabalhava na Embaixada Americana.

7. Onde o senhor leu isso?
8. Li nos jornais.

9. Onde a gente fala mais?
10. Na Seção Política.

11. A gente vai segunda-feira?
12. Não, o feriado cai na terça.

13. Onde está a minha carta?
14. Ainda está na máquina.

15. Onde é que ele ficou?
16. Ficou no centro.

25.14

Adjectives

Practice 17. (Warm-up)

Repeat these adjectives in their masculine and feminine forms.

bom	boa
bonito	bonita
casado	casada
solteiro	solteira
muito	muita
atrasado	atrasada
cansado	cansada
resfriado	resfriada
acordado	acordada
ótimo	ótima
péssimo	péssima
caro	cara
brasileiro	brasileira
americano	americana
português	portuguesa
gostoso	gostosa
famoso	famosa
maravilhoso	maravilhosa

Now repeat these that do not change their forms for gender.

fácil
difícil
útil
horrível
possível
impossível
provável
azul

25.15

particular
local
legal
formal
comercial

Practice 18.

Now, taking the first sentence in each group as a model,
translate the following sentences.

A. 1. O carro dele é bonito.
   2. "   "   "   " (expensive).
   3. "   "   "   " (blue).
   4. "   "   "   " (useful).
   5. "   "   "   " (horrible).
   6. "   "   "   " (famous).

B. 1. Tânia é brasileira.
   2. "   " (pretty).
   3. "   " (single).
   ----
   4. Vânia é portuguesa.
   5. "   " (married).
   6. "   " (old).

C. 1. O senhor Mattos trabalha numa empresa particular.
   2. "   "   "   "   "   " (American).
   3. "   "   "   "   "   " (Brazilian).
   4. "   "   "   "   "   " (old).
   5. "   "   "   "   "   " (local).
   6. "   "   "   "   "   " (famous).
   7. "   "   "   "   "   " (commercial).

25.16

D. 1. O trabalho dele é fácil.
2. "   "   "   " (difficult).
3. "   "   "   " (good).
4. "   "   "   " (useful).
5. "   "   "   " (terrible).
6. "   "   "   " (political).

E. 1. Marli tem uma vista maravilhosa.
2. "   "   "   " (good).
3. "   "   "   " (horrible).
4. "   "   "   " (pretty).
5. "   "   "   " (great). Use <u>ótima</u>.

F. 1. Cláudia comprou um sapato brasileiro.
2. "   "   "   " (pretty).
3. "   "   "   " (blue).
4. "   "   "   " (expensive).
5. "   "   "   " (American).
6. "   "   "   " (good).

G. 1. Vai ser um dia difícil.
2. "   "   "   " (pretty).
3. "   "   "   " (easy).
4. "   "   "   " (wonderful).
5. "   "   "   " (useful).
6. "   "   "   " (terrible).
7. "   "   "   " (great).
8. "   "   "   " (pleasant). Use <u>gostoso</u>.

<u>End of Tape 12A</u>

25.17

Section II

Verbs

Practice 1.

Take each verb form given below, repeat it, then give the corresponding form in the past (the <u>did</u> form). For example, in Number 1, after saying <u>eu</u> <u>compro</u> 'I buy', you should say <u>eu</u> <u>comprei</u> 'I bought'. Follow along and verify your responses with the tape. Be careful! You will find -<u>ar</u>, -<u>er</u> and -<u>ir</u> type verbs, all three.

1. eu compro
2. eu trabalho
3. eu dirijo
4. eu mando
5. eu escrevo
6. eu saio
7. eu acho
8. eu vendo
9. eu durmo   ('sleep')
10. eu gosto
11. eu almoço
12. eu leio
13. eu fico
14. eu aceito
15. eu vou
    ----
16. ele estuda
17. ele pratica
18. ele bebe
19. ele sai
20. ele muda
21. ele lê
22. ele deita

25.18

23. ele começa
24. ele acorda
25. ele prepara
26. ele recebe
27. ele lembra
28. ele dirige
29. ele deixa
30. ele vai
----
31. nós gostamos
32. nós moramos
33. nós recebemos
34. nós compramos
35. nós dormimos
36. nós descansamos
37. nós batemos
38. nós ensinamos
39. nós voltamos
40. nós procuramos
41. nós perdemos
42. nós reparamos
43. nós viajamos
44. nós comemos
45. nós vamos
----
46. eles saem
47. eles viajam
48. eles dormem
49. eles gostam
50. eles chegam
51. eles falam
52. eles lêem
53. eles praticam
54. os senhores vendem

55. os senhores ensinam
56. os senhores esquecem
57. os senhores dirigem
58. os senhores almoçam
59. os senhores vão

Practice 2.

Now, practice these brief exchanges with your teacher or a
fellow student.   Each time the response is 'I already did'.

1. Eu vou estudar.
    Eu já estudei.

2. Eu vou almoçar.
    Eu já almocei.

3. Eu pretendo ler.
    Eu já li.

4. Eu pretendo ir.
    Eu já fui.

5. Eu quero esquecer.
    Eu já esqueci.

6. Vamos jantar.
    Eu já jantei.

7. Vamos comer.
    Eu já comi.

8. Vamos tomar café.
    Eu já tomei.

25.20

9. Vamos mandar a carta.
   Eu já mandei.

10. Vamos comprar o livro.
    Eu já comprei.

11. Vamos vender o sapato.
    Eu já vendi.

12. Vamos lá agora.
    Eu já fui.

Practice 3.

Answer (and ask) these questions.

1. O senhor jantou?
   Jantei, sim.

2. O senhor tomou?
   Tomei, sim.

3. O senhor leu?
   Li, sim.

4. O senhor comeu?
   Comi, sim.

5. O senhor preparou?
   Preparei, sim.

6. O senhor notou?
   Notei, sim.

7. O senhor saiu?
   Saí, sim.

25.21

8. O senhor comprou?
   Comprei, sim.

9. O senhor recebeu?
   Recebi, sim.

10. O senhor começou?
    Comecei, sim.

----

11. Os senhores jantaram?
    Não, não jantamos.

12. Os senhores já receberam as notícias?
    Não, ainda não recebemos.

13. Os senhores já começaram?
    Não, ainda não começamos.

14. Os senhores já leram o jornal?
    Não, ainda não lemos.

15. Os senhores dormiram?
    Não, não dormimos.

16. Os senhores já saíram?
    Não, ainda não saímos.

17. Os senhores já foram?
    Não, ainda não fomos.

18. Os senhores descansaram?
    Não, não descansamos.

19. Os senhores repetiram?
    Não, não repetimos.

20. Os senhores esqueceram?
    Não, não esquecemos.

Practice 4.

Go through this sequence with your tape and/or your teacher.
You should be able to add several more of your own.

1. Ele ainda não comeu. Vai comer às sete.
2. Ele ainda não chegou. Vai chegar às oito.
3. Ele ainda não começou. Vai começar às nove.
4. Ele ainda não saiu. Vai sair às dez.
5. Ele ainda não jantou. Vai jantar mais tarde.
6. Ele ainda não almoçou. Vai almoçar ao meio-dia.
7. Ele ainda não deitou. Vai deitar à meia-noite.
8. Ele ainda não levantou. Vai levantar agora!

Practice 5.

Practice saying these sentences which illustrate the 'used
to/would' forms of verbs.

1. João saía muito porque ele tinha carro.
2. Alberto comia muito porque ele sempre estava com fome.
3. Ana não jantava no centro porque era caro demais.
4. Jorge ia muito ao cinema porque gostava.
5. Tom falava espanhol porque ele não sabia português.
6. Júlio deitava cedo porque levantava às seis.
7. Nélson sempre estava cansado porque trabalhava demais.
8. Édson nunca estudava porque não gostava.
9. Yara levantava cedo porque trabalhava longe.
10. Marcos não lia 'The Post' porque ele achava que o inglês
    era muito difícil.
11. Luís não viajava muito porque não tinha muita oportunidade.
12. Wilson voltava cedo porque trabalhava perto.

25.23

13. Vânia escrevia bem à máquina porque era secretária.
14. Sandra viajava muito porque trabalhava para a Varig.
15. Beatriz sempre chegava atrasada porque nunca sabia que horas eram.
16. Eduardo almoçava no escritório porque morava longe.
17. Sebastião trabalhava aos domingos porque precisava do dinheiro.

----

18. Sam morava perto mas ele sempre chegava atrasado.
19. Lúcia sempre estava cansada mas ela nunca deitava cedo.
20. Ângela trabalhava longe mas ela sempre saía tarde.
21. Geraldo precisava de dinheiro mas ele não trabalhava muito.
22. Marli sempre queria comprar mais mas o dinheiro nunca dava.
23. Antônio era português mas ele falava inglês sem sotaque.
24. Cristina morava em Copacabana mas nunca ia à praia.

----

25. Eu sempre saía cedo e voltava tarde.
26. Eu sempre almoçava no centro e jantava em casa.
27. Yara sempre deitava tarde e levantava cedo.
28. Inês lia inglês bem e falava sem sotaque.
29. Roberto conhecia a cidade e não se perdia.
30. João era casado e passava os fins de semana em casa.
31. Bill era americano e gostava da comida americana.
32. Marcos era de Fortaleza e ia muito a Fortaleza.
33. Paulo era o chefe e fazia tudo.
34. Fazia calor e chovia muito no Panamá.

Practice 6.   (More on 'used to/would')

Following the models given, have some fun putting these into Portuguese.

1. Nossa! Eu achava que ele era solteiro.
2. (Gosh! I thought he had money.)
3. (Gosh! I thought you knew that.)
4. (Gosh! I thought Marcos was going too.)
5. (Gosh! I thought Yara was at home.)

25.24

6. Desculpe. Eu achava que o senhor se sentia bem.
7. (Excuse me. I thought you knew Paul.
8. (Excuse me. I thought you spoke English.)
9. (Excuse me. I thought you lived in Leme.)
10. (Excuse me. I thought you worked here.)

11. Sinto muito. Eu achava que você saía agora.
12. (I'm sorry. I thought we (a gente) were going to the beach.
13. (I'm sorry. I thought the party was today.)
14. (I'm sorry. I thought it was a good idea.)
15. (I'm sorry. I thought it was ten o'clock.)
16. (I'm sorry. I thought you were taking the soft drinks.)

17. Hoje? Eu não sabia que você ia hoje.
18. (Today? I didn't know you were practicing today.)
19. (Tomorrow? I didn't know you were leaving tomorrow.)
20. (Now? I didn't know you were planning to go now.)
21. (At 5? I didn't know the party was at five.)
22. (Tonight? I didn't know you had to work tonight.)

23. Ah, é? Eu não sabia que ele era o chefe.
24. (Oh, really?! I didn't know she was Portuguese.)
25. (Oh, really?! I didn't know Recife was (ficava) so far.)
26. (Oh, really?! I didn't know Júlio had so much money.)
27. (Oh, really?! I didn't know Maria got home so late.)

28. Já?! Eu não sabia que ele estava com tanta fome.
29. (Already?! I didn't know he was in such a hurry.)
30. (Already?! I didn't know he knew so much.)
31. (Already?! I didn't know what time it was.)
32. (Already?! I didn't know it was time to stop.)

25.25

Section III

A. The verb <u>ser</u> 'to be'

<u>Practice 1</u>. (Warm-up)
   Repeat these examples of the <u>é</u> form of <u>ser</u>.

<u>Identification</u> and <u>Classification</u>

1. Jack é americano.
2. Luís é espanhol.
3. Afonso é brasileiro.
4. Tom é inglês.
5. Gustavo é português.
6. Alberto é francês.
7. Roberto é funcionário.
8. Sérgio é presidente.
9. Júlio é professor.
10. Jaime é aluno.
11. Leonardo é chefe.
12. Ernesto é amigo.
13. Francisco é solteiro.
14. Alberto é bonito. (good-looking)
15. Emílio é casado.
16. Cláudio é dorminhoco.
17. Mário é famoso.

----

18. Luísa é espanhola.
19. Inês é brasileira.
20. Margarida é portuguesa.
21. Sandra é americana.
22. Rosa é professora.
23. Cristina é aluna.
24. Bárbara é secretária.
25. Helena é solteira.
26. Lúcia é casada.

27. Regina é bonita.
28. Glória é famosa.
29. Denise é chata.
30. Beatriz é impossível!

----

31. Paris é uma capital famosa.
32. Londres é uma cidade velha.
33. Alaska é um estado novo.
34. Braniff é uma empresa particular.
35. Recife é uma cidade brasileira.
36. Copacabana é uma praia bonita.

Origin

37. Marcos é do Rio.
38. Ângela é de São Paulo.
39. Antônio é do Brasil.
40. Ricardo é de Portugal.
41. A carta é do Rio.
42. O cartão é de São Paulo.

Possession

43. O Chevrolet é do Luís.
44. O Ford é da Ângela.

45. Este terno é do Luís Sérgio.
46. Este sapato é da Maria Lúcia.

47. Este sanduíche é dele.
48. Este refrigerante é meu.

Permanent, fixed location

49. A Embaixada é em Brasília.
50. A Seção Consular é na Embaixada.
51. O Leme é no Rio.

52. A empresa é na cidade.
53. A casa é na praia.
54. O Departamento de Estado é em Washington.
55. Buffalo é em Nova Iorque.
56. O túnel é muito perto.
57. A praia é muito longe.

Time

58. É meia-noite.
59. É meio-dia.
60. É uma hora.

Practice 2.

Participate in this quick question and answer session with various forms of ser. Warning: the tenses are mixed.

Person A	Person B
1. O senhor é americano?	Sou, sim.
2. O senhor era funcionário?	Era, sim.
3. Ela era secretária?	Não, não era.
4. Ele é professor?	Não, não é.
5. Eles eram brasileiros?	Não, não eram.
6. Eles eram solteiros?	Eram, sim.
7. Ela é casada?	Não, não é.
8. Elas são portuguesas?	São, sim.
9. Ela é a Dona Bárbara?	É, sim.
10. Ela é bonita?	Não, não é.
11. A carta é da Dona Ana?	É, sim.
12. Este carro é do Sérgio?	É, sim.
13. Este sanduíche é o meu?	É, sim.
14. Estes livros são meus?	São, sim.
15. É uma hora?	É, sim.
16. Afonso era o chefe?	Não, não era.
17. É uma empresa particular?	Não, não é.

18. O João é o presidente?   É, sim.
19. A escola é longe?   Não, não é.
20. É perto?   É, sim.
21. O restaurante é em frente?   É.

B. The verb <u>estar</u> 'to be'

<u>Practice 1</u>. (Warm-up)

Repeat these examples of the <u>está</u> form of <u>estar</u>.

<u>Non-fixed</u> <u>location</u>

1. Eduardo está em casa.
2. A Yara está na Embaixada.
3. A Cláudia está no Consulado.
4. O Luís está no Brasil.
5. Vera está na escola.
6. Antônio está comigo.
7. Ângela está com a mãe dela.
8. O carro está no centro.
9. A comida está em cima da mesa.
10. O dinheiro não está aqui.

<u>Non-permanent</u> <u>state</u> <u>or</u> <u>condition</u>

11. Vera está resfriada
12. Sônia está cansada.
13. Paulo está atrasado.
14. A Regina está com fome.
15. O Henrique está com pressa.
16. Sebastião está acordado.
17. Glória está com sono.

25.29

With the -ndo form of verbs

18. Raquel está trabalhando.
19. Carmem está dormindo.
20. Lourdes está lendo.
21. Fernando está praticando.
22. Júlio está almoçando.
23. João está lembrando.
24. Ana está saindo.
25. Luísa está procurando.
26. Margarida está falando.
27. Francisco está levantando.
28. Tânia está comendo.
29. Vânia está esquecendo.
30. Édson está começando.
31. Gibson está viajando.
32. Nélson está estudando.
33. Está chovendo.
34. Está fazendo calor.
35. Quem está preparando e escrevendo tanto?

Practice 2.

Participate in this quick question and answer session with estar.

Person A	Person B
1. Você está com sono?	Estou, sim.
2. Você está com fome?	Estou, sim.
3. Você estava cansado?	Estava, sim.
4. Você estava com pressa?	Estava, sim.
5. Ele estava aqui?	Estava, sim.
6. Ele está no Consulado?	Está, sim.
7. Ela estava resfriada?	Estava, sim.
8. Eles estão acordados?	Estão, sim.
9. Vocês estão no restaurante?	Estamos, sim.
10. Os senhores estão em casa?	Estamos, sim.

11.	Yara está na escola?	Está, sim.
12.	Marcos estava lá?	Estava, sim.
13.	Wilson está na praia?	Está, sim.
14.	Eles estão no escritório?	Estão, sim.
15.	Eu estou com fome?	Não, não está!

16.	Já estamos chegando?	Estamos, sim.
17.	Você está lembrando?	Não, não estou.
18.	Jorge está dirigindo?	Está.
19.	Maria está jantando?	Não, não está.
20.	O senhor está gostando?	Estou, sim.
21.	As moças estão gostando?	Estão.
22.	Está chovendo?	Está, sim.
23.	Você está se sentindo bem?	Estou.
24.	Ele está caindo!?	Não, não está!
25.	Estamos voltando?	Estamos.
26.	Os meninos estão descansando?	Estão, sim.
27.	O senhor Lopes está morando no Rio?	Está, sim.
28.	O espanhol está atrapalhando?	Está!
29.	Milton está procurando outro emprego?	Não, não está.
30.	O senhor está acabando?	Estou! (Finalmente!)

C. The verbs <u>ser</u> and <u>estar</u> mixed.

   Translate these items. Take them in order and they make up a brief narrative. Omit items in brackets.

   1. Gloria is [an] American; she's from Duluth.
   2. She's [a] secretary.
   3. She's pretty, and [she] is married.
   4. She's not at the office today.
   5. She's at home.
   6. Her home is in Copacabana.
   7. She has a cold.
   8. She's not hungry.
   9. She's not in a hurry now.
   10. She's resting.

----

11. George is Brazilian.
12. He is from Bahia.
13. He's single, and he's good-looking.
14. He's [a] teacher.
15. George is my friend, and he's [a] sleepyhead!
16. It's nine o'clock, and he's here in the Consulate.
17. But he's not awake yet.
18. He's still sleepy.
19. He's hungry too.
20. He's drinking coffee and eating a sandwich.
21. At times he's impossible!

D. The verb ir 'to go'

Practice 1. (Warm-up)
     Run over these brief couplets designed for rapid review of
the forms of ir.
     1. Eu vou agora.
         Ela vai amanhã.

     2. Nós vamos às cinco.
         Eles vão às oito.

     3. Você vai ao Rio?
         Eu vou a São Paulo.

     4. Eu ia ao parque.
         Mas eles iam ao centro.

     5. Eu fui ontem.
         E o Paulo foi hoje.

     6. Roberto vai começar.
         E Marli vai acabar.

7. Nós vamos sair.
    Mas eles vão ficar.

8. Você vai esquecer, claro!
    Mas eu vou lembrar.

9. Yara ia estudar.
    E as outras iam descansar.

10. As meninas iam às montanhas.
    Nós íamos à praia.

Practice 2.

Participate in this quick question and answer session
dealing with the verb ir. Warning: The tenses are mixed. You
should be able to respond to these without referring to the
printed page.

Person A	Person B
1. Ele vai?	Vai, sim.
2. Você foi?	Fui, sim.
3. Nós vamos?	Vamos.
4. Eles foram?	Foram, sim.
5. Eles vão hoje?	Não, não vão.
6. Eu vou também?	Não, não vai.
7. Nós vamos?	Não, não vão.
8. Ela foi ontem?	Foi.
9. O senhor ia?	Ia, sim.
10. Vocês iam?	Íamos, sim.

E.   The verb <u>ter</u> 'to have'

<u>Practice 1</u>.   (Warm-up)

Run through these brief couplets designed for rapid review of the forms of <u>ter</u>.

1.   Eu tenho um.
     Ele tem dois.

2.   Nós temos muitos.
     Eles têm poucos.

3.   Yara tem Chevrolet.
     Eu tenho Volkswagen.

4.   Jorge tem mais.
     Os meninos têm menos.

5.   Nós temos muito trabalho.   .
     Os senhores têm que sair agora?

6.   Luís tem tudo.
     Eu não tenho nada.

7.   Maria tem que sair.
     Yara tem que ficar.

8.   Roberto tem que trabalhar.
     Eu tenho que descansar.
----
9.   Nós tínhamos cinco.
     Quantos os senhores tinham?

10. Eu tinha um Ford.
     O que é que você tinha?   <u>End of Tape 12B</u>

FOREIGN PHRASE BOOKS Series

Barron's new series gives travelers instant access to the most common idiomatic expressions used during a trip—the kind one needs to know instantly, like "Where can I find a taxi?" and "How much does this cost?"

Organized by situation (arrival, customs, hotel, health, etc.) and containing additional information about pronunciation, grammar, shopping plus special facts about the country, these convenient, pocket-size reference books will be the tourist's most helpful guides.

Special features include a bilingual dictionary section with over 2000 key words, maps of each country and major cities, and helpful phonetic spellings throughout.

Each book paperback, 256 pp., 3 ³/4" x 6"

ARABIC AT A GLANCE, Wise (0-8120-2979-8) $6.95, Can. $8.95
CHINESE AT A GLANCE, Seligman & Chen (0-8120-2851-1) $7.95, Can. $10.75
FRENCH AT A GLANCE, 2nd, Stein & Wald (0-8120-1394-8) $6.95, Can. $8.95
GERMAN AT A GLANCE, 2nd, Strutz (0-8120-1395-6) $6.95, Can. $8.95
ITALIAN AT A GLANCE, 2nd, Costantino (0-8120-1396-4) $6.95, Can. $8.95
JAPANESE AT A GLANCE, 3rd, Akiyama (0-7641-0320-2) $8.95, Can. $11.95
KOREAN AT A GLANCE, Holt (0-8120-3998-X) $8.95, Can. $11.95
RUSSIAN AT A GLANCE, Beyer (0-8120-4299-9) $6.95, Can. $8.95
SPANISH AT A GLANCE, 2nd, Wald (0-8120-1398-0) $6.95, Can. $8.95

Barron's Educational Series, Inc.
250 Wireless Blvd., Hauppauge, NY 11788
Call toll-free: 1-800-645-3476
In Canada: Georgetown Book Warehouse, 34 Armstrong Ave.
Georgetown, Ont. L7G 4R9, Call toll-free: 1-800-247-7160
Visit our website at: www.barronseduc.com

Books may be purchased at your bookstore, or by mail from Barron's. Enclose check or money order for total amount plus sales tax where applicable and 15% for postage and handling (minimum charge $4.95). Prices subject to change without notice.
Can. $ = Canadian dollars

(#25) R 1/99